THE THREE SECTOR SOLUTION

Delivering public policy in collaboration
with not-for-profits and business

THE THREE SECTOR SOLUTION

Delivering public policy in collaboration
with not-for-profits and business

EDITED BY JOHN R. BUTCHER
AND DAVID J. GILCHRIST

Australian
National
University

PRESS

ANU PRESS

the Australia and New Zealand
School of Government

Published by ANU Press
The Australian National University
Acton ACT 2601, Australia
Email: anupress@anu.edu.au
This title is also available online at press.anu.edu.au

National Library of Australia Cataloguing-in-Publication entry

Title: The three sector solution : delivering public policy in
              collaboration with not-for-profits and
              business / David Gilchrist (editor) ;
              John Butcher (editor).

ISBN: 9781760460389 (paperback) 9781760460396 (ebook)

Series: ANZSOG series.

Subjects: Nonprofit organizations--Political aspects.
              Nonprofit organizations--Government policy.
              Public-private sector cooperation--Government policy.
              Public administration.

Other Creators/Contributors:
              Gilchrist, David, editor.
              Butcher, John, editor.
              Australia and New Zealand School of Government.

Dewey Number: 361.763

Cover design and layout by ANU Press.

Contents

Figures vii

Tables ix

Abbreviations xi

Acknowledgements xv

Contributors xvii

Foreword xxvii

Contextualising the Imperative of Cross-Sector Working

1.   Introduction 3
     David J. Gilchrist and John R. Butcher

2.   Three Sectors, One Public Purpose 23
     Peter Shergold

Part 1. Cross-Sector Working: The rhetoric and the reality

Overview 35
Meredith Edwards

3.   From New Public Management to New Public Governance:
     The implications for a 'new public service' 41
     Helen Dickinson

4.   Partnerships between Government and the Third Sector at a
     Subnational Level: The experience of an Australian subnational
     government 61
     David J. Gilchrist

5.   The Contribution of Not-for-Profits to Democratic Process 79
     Tessa Boyd-Caine

Part 2. Three Sectors: Three change agendas

Overview 107
Penny Knight

6.   Policy Impediments to Social Investments by Australian
     Businesses 113
     Leeora D. Black

7. Navigating Reform in Contested Spaces: Reflections on
    not-for-profit sector regulatory reform in Australia, 2010–2013 131
    Krystian Seibert

8. Shining a Light on the Black Box of Collaboration:
    Mapping the prerequisites for cross-sector working 157
    Robyn Keast

Part 3. Great Expectations: Outcomes and social impact

Overview 181
Nina Terrey

9. Does Outcomes-Based Reporting Contribute to or Contradict
    the Realisation of Social Outcomes? 185
    Emma Tomkinson

10. Not-for-Profit Accountability: Addressing potential barriers 215
    Dale Tweedie

11. Results, Targets and Measures to Drive Collaboration:
    Lessons from the New Zealand Better Public Services reforms . . .235
    Rodney Scott and Ross Boyd

Part 4. New Tools for Policymakers and Practitioners

Overview 261
Ursula Stephens

12. Redesigning Procurement Strategies for Complex Policy Spaces. . .265
    Ann Nevile

13. Alliance Contracting: How to progress in a world of uncertainty . . .285
    Cassandra Wilkinson

14. Expanding the Role of Cooperative and Mutual Enterprises
    in Delivering Public Services: Disrupting the status quo 301
    Melina Morrison and Cliff Mills

15. The Boundaries of Budgets: Why should individuals make
    spending choices about their health and social care? 319
    Catherine Needham

Cross-Sector Working: Meeting the challenge of change

16. The Challenge of Change. 337
    Paul Ronalds

17. Conclusion. 353
    John R. Butcher and David J. Gilchrist

Figures

Figure 8.1: Continuum of interorganisational relationships:
The five Cs 159

Figure 9.1: The changing role of government 187

Figure 9.2: Changing expectations of government 189

Figure 9.3: Red tape issues for NGOs 193

Figure 9.4: The impact analysis cycle 204

Figure 11.1: Stylised representation of performance management
in the New Zealand Government 237

Tables

Table 3.1: Elements of new public governance, in contrast with
        public administration and new public management 44

Table 4.1: Year-on-year response rates 68

Table 7.1: Chronology of the ACNC reform process 141

Table 8.1: Summary of the key presenting processes used 164

Table A8.1: Summary of collaboration exemplars 178

Table 9.1: Job Services Australia star rating and star percentages . . 200

Table 11.1: Results, targets and measures 239

Abbreviations

ABS	Australian Bureau of Statistics
ACAG	Australasian Council of Auditors-General
ACNC	Australian Charities and Not-for-profits Commission
ACOSS	Australian Council of Social Service
ACT	Australian Capital Territory
ACTU	Australian Council of Trade Unions
ANAO	Australian National Audit Office
ANDI	Australian National Development Index
ANZSOG	Australia and New Zealand School of Government
APS	Australian Public Service
ARC	Australian Research Council
ASX	Australian Securities Exchange
ATO	Australian Taxation Office
ATSI	Aboriginal and Torres Strait Islander
BCCM	Business Council of Co-operatives and Mutuals
BPS	Better Public Services (NZ)
C4C	Communities for Children
CAD	computer-aided design
CBA	cost–benefit analysis
CDC	consumer-directed care
CEO	chief executive officer
COAG	Council of Australian Governments
CPSU	Community and Public Sector Union
CRN	Collaborative Research Network
CSCI	Commission for Social Care Inspection (UK)

CSD	Community Services Directorate (ACT)
CSI	corporate social investment
CSR	corporate social responsibility
DCSP	Delivering Community Services in Partnership
DES	disability employment services
DGR	deductible gift recipient
EHRC	Equality and Human Rights Commission (UK)
ESA	employment service area
FYN	Family and Youth Network
GDP	gross domestic product
GST	Goods and Services Tax
IBSEN	Individual Budgets Evaluation Network
ICA	International Co-operative Alliance
IYC	United Nations International Year of Cooperatives
KPI	key performance indicator
LHA	Local Housing Allowance (UK)
LNP	Liberal National Party
ML	Medicare Local
MOU	memorandum of understanding
NAB	National Australia Bank
NCEA	National Certificate of Educational Achievement
NCSMC	National Council for Single Mothers and their Children
NDIS	National Disability Insurance Scheme
NFP	not-for-profit
NGO	non-governmental organisation
NHS	National Health Service (UK)
NPC	New Philanthropy Capital
NPG	new public governance
NPM	new public management
NSW	New South Wales
NZQF	New Zealand Qualifications Framework
OECD	Organisation for Economic Co-operation and Development
PAF	private ancillary fund

PHN	Primary Health Network
PSP	preferred service provider
R&D	research and development
SA	South Australia
SBB	social benefit bond
SHS	Specialist Homelessness Services
SIP	Services Integration Project
UBIT	unrelated business income tax
UK	United Kingdom
WA	Western Australia
YWCA	Young Women's Christian Association

Acknowledgements

The editors would like to thank the Dean of the Australia and New Zealand School of Government (ANZSOG), Professor Gary Banks AO, for his support and encouragement. The editors are grateful, too, for the generous financial support provided by Professor John Wanna, Sir John Bunting Chair of Public Administration at The Australian National University, and the Curtin Not-for-Profit Initiative, Curtin University.

We also wish to thank the ACT Government's Community Service Directorate for generously meeting the costs of recording the workshop, and cameraman Martin Helmreich for his capable videorecording and post-production work. With regard to the organisation of the workshop, the editors are indebted to Professor Wanna's executive assistant, Claire Dixon; Jamie Kidson and the multimedia team at The Australian National University; and to Jacqui Burkitt, Nicole Mallick and Susie Bate from ANZSOG's marketing team for their invaluable practical assistance.

Thanks go also to Isi Unikowski for pitching in to help at the workshop, as well as to Sam Vincent for shepherding the manuscript through the prepublication process, Jan Borrie for her usual astute and meticulous copyediting and the team at ANU Press.

Of course, neither the workshop nor this book would have been possible without the generous and enthusiastic commitment of the authors and presenters, the discussants and the session chairs. The last deserve special mention as they are not named elsewhere: Professor Andrew Podger, The Australian National University; Dr Alison Procter, ACT Community Services Directorate; and David Casey, Department of the Prime Minister and Cabinet.

Special thanks go to Natalie Howson, former director-general of the ACT Community Services Directorate, and Simon Rosenberg, CEO of Northside Community Service, for setting the scene in their remarks to the pre-workshop dinner. And, of course, the editors are grateful for the enthusiasm shown by the workshop audience, who remained vitally engaged in the conversation throughout a packed and intellectually demanding day.

Contributors

Dr Leeora Black

Dr Leeora Black is Director of the Australian Centre for Corporate Social Responsibility and a leading authority on corporate social responsibility (CSR). Her work focuses on building competitive advantage and stakeholder wealth through CSR, integrating social responsibility into business operations and strategies and solving complex CSR issues and problems. Leeora works with listed companies, government businesses and social sector organisations providing services such as framework and strategy development, stakeholder research and engagement, reporting and executive learning programs. Her doctoral thesis on corporate social responsiveness pioneered a framework and methodology for developing and assessing management capabilities in the area of CSR.

Ross Boyd

Ross Boyd (BA Hons, NZTC, MEdAdmin) is a principal analyst in the State Sector Performance Hub, based in the State Services Commission, Wellington, New Zealand. Ross leads the Better Public Services (BPS) Results work stream. He has taken the BPS Results work from policy design in 2011 through implementation during 2012 and now monitors and reports on progress. He is currently leading a refreshment of the program so that it aligns with current and emerging policy initiatives, particularly the investment approach to social policy. Ross has spent the past nine years working in central agencies, starting with the Department of the Prime Minister and Cabinet's Policy Advisory Group; moving to the State Services Commission, where he was the manager responsible for introducing New Zealand's Performance Improvement Framework; then joining central agency teams responsible for the policy and implementation of State sector reform. Before his central agency work, Ross held several operational and policy management roles at the Ministry of Education.

Dr Tessa Boyd-Caine

At the time of writing her chapter, Tessa was Deputy CEO at the Australian Council of Social Service. She is now CEO of the National Centre for Health Justice Partnership. Tessa was recipient of the inaugural 2013 Fulbright Professional Scholarship in Non-Profit Leadership, through which she examined how American philanthropic and charitable organisations develop transparency and accountability. In the United States, she worked with the Foundation Center in New York City and the Urban Institute in Washington, DC, and visited not-for-profit charitable and philanthropic organisations across the country. Tessa has participated extensively in policy processes with government, the community sector and the business community. She has also worked in the areas of human rights, mental health law and criminal justice, in Australia and internationally. Tessa's PhD from the London School of Economics examined the role of executive discretion and the public protection agenda in decisions about the release of mentally disordered offenders. Her book *Protecting the Public? Detention and release of mentally disordered offenders* was published by Routledge in 2010.

Dr John Butcher

Dr John Butcher earned his PhD at The Australian National University in 2014. He also has an MA and BA from the University of British Columbia. John has a long-standing interest in the impact of government policy on the not-for-profit sector and has worked at the front line of policy reform for two levels of government. Currently an adjunct researcher at The Australian National University, he is co-author of *Policy in Action* (UNSW Press) and has published widely on not-for-profit policy.

Associate Professor Helen Dickinson

Associate Professor Helen Dickinson was educated at the universities of Manchester and Birmingham in the United Kingdom. Helen joined the University of Melbourne in 2013 as Associate Professor in Public Governance. She has published widely on topics such as governance, leadership, organisational behaviour and rationing in journals such as *Public Administration*, *Public Management Review*, *Social Science and Medicine* and *Evidence and Policy*. Helen has authored, co-authored or edited 16 books on topics such as governance, leadership and the reform of health care. She is also a co-editor of the *Australian Journal of Public Administration*.

Professor Meredith Edwards

Professor Meredith Edwards AM is Emeritus Professor at the Institute for Governance and Policy Analysis at the University of Canberra. She was deputy vice-chancellor from 1997 at that university and director of its National Institute for Governance until 2004. Before joining the University of Canberra, Meredith was a senior policy adviser in the Australian Public Service involved in a range of major social policy reforms across several departments from 1983 to 1993, and deputy secretary in the Department of the Prime Minister and Cabinet until 1997. An economist, a Fellow of the Institute of Public Administration Australia, ANZSOG Fellow, and Fellow of the Academy of Social Science in Australia (ASSA), in 2001 Meredith published a book on policy development processes, *Social Policy, Public Policy: From problem to practice*. In 2012 she co-authored *Public Sector Governance in Australia* and in 2015 co-authored *Not Yet 50/50: The barriers to the progress of senior women in the APS*. Meredith is a member of the United Nations Committee of Experts on Public Administration.

Professor David J. Gilchrist

Professor David J. Gilchrist has held a number of senior roles in the not-for-profit, public and commercial sectors. Most recently, he was Assistant Auditor General Standards and Quality in Western Australia, and prior to that, Associate Dean of Business at the University of Notre Dame Australia. He is currently Director of Curtin's School of Accounting Not-for-profit Initiative, a research group focusing on developing industry-ready research outcomes for the not-for-profit and charitable sector. He currently holds a number of industry roles including as chairman of Nulsen Disability Services, chairman of the Kimberley Individual and Family Support Association and is a member of Chartered Accountants Australia and New Zealand's National Not-for-profit Advisory Committee. David is also a member of the Australian Charities and Not-for-profits Commission Advisory Board, the Australian Accounting Standards Board Academic Advisory Panel and is a joint principal author of a number of key national reports, including the seminal report *Australian Charities 2013* and the *Australian National Costing and Pricing Framework* issued jointly with National Disability Services. He has published widely as an academic and journalist.

Professor Robyn Keast

Professor Robyn Keast is a research professor in the School of Business and Tourism at Southern Cross University and Chair of the Collaborative Research Network: Policy and Planning for Regional Sustainability. Her research is focused on networked arrangements and collaborative practices within and across sectors. A current research focus is on the management and impact of collaborative research networks and the development of sociocultural approaches to client-centred networked service systems. She recently co-authored three books *Negotiating the Business Environment: Theory and practice for all governance styles*, *Network Theory in the Public Sector: Building new theoretical frameworks,* and *Social Procurement in New Public Governance* (Routledge) and has developed several network tools for service practitioners, including 15 fact sheets on collaborative practice and a collaboration decision support tool. Robyn also has an extensive background as a practitioner, policy officer and senior manager within the Queensland public sector. This work experience has also extended to the non-governmental sector in Queensland, New Zealand and Canada. She also established and directed a prominent departmental research unit that provided evaluation and analysis of service interventions and emergent issues as well as the external review of critical incidents within related departments and across the sector.

Penny Knight

Penny Knight is a Senior Research Fellow with the Curtin Business School and Research Director for the Curtin Not-for-profit Initiative. She has worked for Western Australia's Department of Treasury undertaking sector and program evaluations and leading the evaluation and improvement of the government's outcomes-based management structure; she has co-founded and run an internet business; and has worked as a consultant for PriceWaterhouseCoopers and KPMG on diverse projects including whole-of-government reform, improving service delivery and efficiency, developing a customer service culture and change management.

Cliff Mills

Cliff Mills is a solicitor in the United Kingdom and a leading expert in the law and governance of cooperative, mutual and member-based organisations, with more than 20 years' experience writing constitutions and advising on mergers and governance. Since the late 1990s, he has been extensively involved in public sector reform, designing new mutual ownership and governance structures as a means of establishing a directly accountable, citizen-based approach to modern public ownership. Based on a multi-constituency approach involving users, employees and citizens, he has established new mutual organisations in health care (including National Health Service Foundation Trusts), social housing, leisure services and youth services. Cliff has been much involved in the development of cooperative and community benefit society law in the United Kingdom since 2000, working with Members of Parliament on private members' bills and supporting government-sponsored legislation. He has written extensively about cooperative and mutual ideas and concepts through the mutual consultancy Mutuo, and is one of the joint authors of the *Blueprint for a Cooperative Decade*.

Melina Morrison

Melina Morrison is the inaugural CEO of Australia's first peak body for co-operatives and mutuals, the Business Council of Co-operatives and Mutuals. She is an advocate for all forms of mutually owned enterprise, regularly contributing commentary and appearing as a spokesperson for the sector. Melina has commissioned, edited and co-written the sector's first national mapping reports. Melina's former roles in the co-operative sector include five years as editor of *ICA Digest*, the flagship publication for the global peak body, the International Co-operative Alliance (ICA). Melina wrote the message platform for the ICA's global strategy, *Blueprint for a Co-operative Decade*. Her advocacy work for the sector resulted in Australia minting a coin commemorating the International Year of Co-operatives in 2012.

Melina was also successful in lobbying for a Senate inquiry into the co-operative and mutual business sector, which handed down its report on the 17 March 2016.

Dr Ann Nevile

Dr Ann Nevile is a social policy researcher at The Australian National University. A major focus of Ann's research is the impact of funding and performance frameworks on third-sector service delivery agencies and their clients, most recently in the area of disability employment, where she has been lead chief investigator and sole chief investigator in two Australian Research Council-funded Linkage projects. A second strand of Ann's research is focused on values—in particular, identifying differences and similarities in the values held by service providers and policy elites and what those with experience of poverty value. Her research on values led to an edited book on human rights and social policy that explored the links between international and European Union human rights frameworks and service delivery on the ground.

Dr Catherine Needham

Dr Catherine Needham is a Reader in Public Policy and Public Management at the Health Services Management Centre, University of Birmingham. Her areas of special interest include reform of public services through coproduction and personalisation, social care services, individualised budgets within public services and public sector workforce reform. She has published a wide range of articles, chapters and books for academic and practitioner audiences, many of them focused on social care and individualised funding schemes. Her most recent book, *Debates in Personalisation*, was published by the Policy Press in 2014. Her current projects include an evaluation of microenterprises in social care and a knowledge exchange project on the twenty-first-century public servant in partnership with Birmingham City Council. She tweets as *@DrCNeedham*.

Paul Ronalds

Paul Ronalds is the CEO of Save the Children Australia. Before joining Save the Children, Paul held senior executive roles in government, domestic and international non-profits and the private sector. In particular, Paul had responsibility for implementing the Gillard Government's not-for-profit reform and social inclusion agendas and led the establishment of the first national-level Office for the Not-for-Profit Sector in Australia. In the non-profit sector, Paul worked for World Vision Australia as deputy CEO and director of strategy, and as chief operating officer of Urban Seed, an innovative and dynamic non-profit that provides a range of services to marginalised people in inner-city Melbourne. Paul holds degrees in economics and law (with honours) from Monash University and a master's degree in International Relations from Deakin University. He is the author of *The Change Imperative: Creating a next generation international non-government organisation.*

Dr Rodney Scott

Dr Rodney Scott is the Principal Analyst and Principal Research Fellow for the State Services Commission of New Zealand. He is also an Adjunct Senior Lecturer at the University of New South Wales (School of Business), an Adjunct Research Fellow of the Australia and New Zealand School of Government and serves on the editorial board for the journal *Evidence Base*. Rodney was awarded a PhD on 'System dynamics in public management' from the University of Queensland. His thesis, 'Group model building and mental model change', won the 2015 Best Doctoral Dissertation Award from the Australia and New Zealand Academy of Management. Rodney has published extensively in leading international journals on topics including system dynamics, governance and decision-making. Rodney has previously been a principal adviser to several government departments and has held executive management positions in the private and not-for-profit sectors.

Krystian Seibert

Krystian Seibert is the Policy and Research Manager at Philanthropy Australia, Australia's national peak body for philanthropy. He has broad experience in public policy development and an in-depth awareness of government, legislative and political processes, with particular expertise in not-for-profit sector policy and regulatory reform. Krystian previously served as an adviser to former Australian Assistant Treasurer David Bradbury. In this role, he oversaw the delivery of major not-for-profit sector reforms including the passage of Australia's first comprehensive statutory definition of charity, the *Charities Act 2013*, and the establishment of Australia's first independent charities regulator, the Australian Charities and Not-for-profits Commission. Krystian holds a master's degree focusing on regulatory policy from the London School of Economics and Political Science, and a Bachelor of Laws and a Bachelor of Commerce (Economics) from Deakin University.

Professor Peter Shergold

Professor Peter Shergold AC began his term as Chancellor of Western Sydney University in January 2011. Peter's academic credentials include a BA Hons (First Class) in Politics and American Studies from the University of Hull, an MA in History from the University of Illinois at Chicago Circle and a PhD in Economics from the London School of Economics. After a distinguished academic career, Peter served in the Australian Public Service for two decades, latterly as secretary of the Department of the Prime Minister and Cabinet from 2003 to February 2008. From 2008 to 2012, Peter was the founding chief executive of the Centre for Social Impact. In 2011, Peter assisted the Western Australia Government in the development of the Delivering Community Services in Partnership Policy; in 2013 he completed the report *Service Sector Reform: A roadmap for community and human services reform* for the Victorian Government; and in 2016 his report to the Commonwealth Government was released as *Learning from Failure: Why large government policy initiatives have gone so badly wrong in the past and how the chances of success in the future can be improved*.

Dr Ursula Stephens

Dr Ursula Stephens is a former Labor Senator for New South Wales in the Australian Parliament. First elected to the Senate in 2001, Ursula was appointed Parliamentary Secretary for Social Inclusion and the Voluntary Sector (2007–10) and Parliamentary Secretary Assisting the Prime Minister for Social Inclusion (2007–09). Ursula was instrumental in mapping out the Rudd Labor Government's strategic framework for not-for-profit sector reform. After her term as a Senator ended in 2014, Ursula turned her attention to supporting community organisations and enterprises. She is an Adjunct Professor at the University of Technology Queensland and a Director of the Australian Centre for Philanthropy and Non-Profit Studies. She also serves on the board of the School for Social Entrepreneurs Australia and contributes as a member of the Advisory Board for the Human Security Centre, an international think tank on human rights.

Dr Nina Terrey

Dr Nina Terrey is Partner and Director of ThinkPlace, a leading firm in applying strategic design methods to public problems. Nina is also an Adjunct Associate Professor at the Institute for Governance and Policy Analysis at the University of Canberra. A business graduate by training, Nina has evolved her career to span from private sector marketing to public sector design. Her 2012 PhD dissertation, 'Managing by design', explored the adoption and embedding of design as a management practice in the Australian Taxation Office. As one of ThinkPlace's global executive team, Nina works with senior leaders and clients who are seeking advice and leadership in co-design and innovation to drive change and transform experiences for an organisation's staff and clients.

Emma Tomkinson

Emma Tomkinson is a social impact analyst living and working in Perth. She is particularly interested in addressing barriers to evidence-based policy, with a focus on measurement of outcomes. She is the founder of Community Insight Australia, a software social enterprise that is improving access to data about Australians in need. Emma created the Social Impact Bond Knowledge Box for the Centre for Social Impact Bonds at the Cabinet Office in the United Kingdom and also developed the social impact bond concept for application in New South Wales. Emma has a MSc in Operational Research from the London School of Economics and a Master of Special Education in psychometrics from the University of Western Australia.

Dr Dale Tweedie

Dr Dale Tweedie is a Senior Research Fellow at the International Governance and Performance (IGAP) Research Centre at Macquarie University. His research focuses on contemporary issues in workplace organisation, governance and corporate social responsibility. Before joining the IGAP Research Centre, he was a research associate on an Australian Research Council-funded investigation of workplace organisation in Australia. Dale has published research on work, ethics and accountability in leading international journals.

Cassandra Wilkinson

Cassandra Wilkinson has a diverse background covering the not-for-profit sector, politics and the media. She has held executive roles in the state and federal public sectors and has undertaken external affairs roles in business and the education sector. She has expertise in infrastructure, transport, public policy, public sector management, Australian contemporary arts and innovation. Her publications include chapters in six books on topics from leadership and inequality to happiness economics. She has two books of her own on politics and parenting, *The Kids are Alright: 10 good reasons to let kids be kids* and *Don't Panic: Nearly everything is better than you think*. Cassandra has been a speaker at the Sydney Writers' Festival, Festival of Dangerous Ideas, Davos Forum, Battle of Ideas (UK) and the ABC's Big Ideas.

Foreword

It is an honour to introduce this collection of articles about collaboration across sector boundaries.

This is a subject of great relevance to our work at the ACT Government Community Services Directorate (CSD). Our collaboration with the community sector is currently in the spotlight as we work to develop and implement reforms to respond to unsustainable levels of demand for services, to change service delivery and regulation models and to examine funding mechanisms. Throughout this work, we have also identified the need to support the sector through the changes it is experiencing.

One of seven directorates in the Australian Capital Territory, CSD is responsible for a wide range of human services functions, the largest of which include children, youth and family support services and public and community housing. We also have responsibility for services and policies relating to Aboriginal and Torres Strait Islander affairs, multicultural affairs, older people, women, community services and community disaster recovery.

We work closely with the community sector to achieve our vision of *better lives for everyone with better services*.

The community sector is a critical part of the ACT human services system. There are nearly 4,000 employees working in the community sector in the Australian Capital Territory, employed by about 160 community sector organisations, and many more in care services for children and older people.

The non-governmental sector in the Australian Capital Territory is particularly active and is marked by a large number of organisations, with about 50 per cent more organisations per head of population than in New South Wales.

In 2015–16, the ACT Government provided $389 million to support vulnerable Canberrans across areas including young people, families, seniors, domestic violence, public housing, and disability and therapy.

Philanthropic giving also contributes to the sector, with research in 2007 finding there was great interest in philanthropy within the Australian Capital Territory and that the majority of the territory's community organisations either have received or are receiving philanthropic giving. The relationship between the ACT Government and the community sector is strong and is guided by the *Social Compact* that outlines principles of good communication and partnership for the benefit of all people and communities in the Australian Capital Territory.

Canberra is known as one of the world's most liveable cities, with the highest national proportions of people of working age, average income, level of post-school qualifications, work participation rates, self-assessed health status and levels of participation in sport, recreation and culture.

Yet ACT Government calculations have estimated that more than 40,000 Canberrans experience high levels of disadvantage. Because so many of the city's residents are relatively advantaged, disadvantage and marginalisation can be hidden. Disadvantage in Canberra is generally 'salt and peppered' across the territory. Some Canberra suburbs—for example, Red Hill and Reid—have high numbers of both the most and the least disadvantaged individuals.

Despite the increased investment in services highlighted above, disadvantage and associated demand for services are continuing to grow. We are seeing sustained growth in demand across areas including disability services, out-of-home care, homelessness and housing services, and family violence crisis services.

There is a clear need in this environment to ensure public investment is achieving the desired social impacts and that human services are both effective and sustainable.

In late 2013, the community sector joined the ACT Government to co-design major reforms aimed at achieving this. The result was the 2014 *Human Services Blueprint*, a multiyear framework for health, education, justice and community services to work together as one human services system, driving person-centred, outcomes-focused responses. The blueprint aims to make services sustainable by providing quality and value-for-money services, and by responding early to reduce future demand for higher-cost services.

The blueprint's innovative and genuine co-design process has attracted interest from other jurisdictions, including Singapore and Victoria.

The Human Services Taskforce was established, comprising community sector and government leaders with a co-chair arrangement, and advice was prepared for the taskforce by a core design team of community sector and government membership. Maintaining a healthy relationship with the sector in this way was conducive to fostering innovation. Strong sector partnerships are crucial to government's delivery of appropriate services to the community.

Three 'proof of concept' initiatives are currently running to test the blueprint's aim of a cohesive human services system: the West Belconnen Local Services Network, the Strengthening Families program for families with multiple and complex needs and the One Human Services Gateway.

In recent years, government has been relying increasingly on the service delivery expertise of the sector, shifting to place choice and control in the hands of the consumer. This has meant exiting from direct service delivery.

Perhaps the most compelling example of this in our portfolio is the National Disability Insurance Scheme (NDIS), which is seeing CSD gradually withdraw from the provision of specialist disability and therapy services over a three-year period. The aim is to increase the range of non-governmental organisations working in this area. Service providers are being given tailored assistance to ensure that people with a disability in the Australian Capital Territory have a sufficient pool of providers from which to purchase their support and services. The Australian Capital Territory remains the only jurisdiction where the whole disability sector is moving into the NDIS, and I expect other states and territories will be watching our progression closely.

The ACT Government has also recently released A Step Up for Our Kids, the five-year strategy to reform out-of-home care services for children and young people who cannot safely live with their parents.

This represents another significant shift of delivery from government to non-governmental service providers. Currently, Child and Youth Protection Services within CSD is the largest provider of out-of-home care services, with 53 per cent of children and young people in care residing with kinship carers supervised by Child and Youth Protection Services.

When A Step Up for Our Kids is fully implemented, all parental responsibility and case management of children on long-term orders, support for kinship carers of children on long-term orders and support for care leavers where agencies have exercised case management and parental responsibility for the young person will be transferred to the non-governmental sector.

Transferring service delivery to the non-governmental sector has required us to consider our duty of care and ongoing regulation responsibilities. For example, when the territory removes a child from their parents' care, it must actively exercise its duty of care to ensure that the child or young person is cared for in a safe environment and receives a better standard of care than she or he would have received at home.

The Human Services Registrar within CSD has been established to provide risk-responsive regulation of these care and protection non-governmental organisations along with other service providers in community housing, disability, mental health, home and community care, and disability educational and early intervention services.

Person-centred funding, as seen through the NDIS, is another transformational change that is likely to begin to have an impact on other areas of service delivery. Different funding models are also now being considered, such as commissioning for outcomes, rather than simply purchasing outputs.

In the Australian Capital Territory, the Community Sector Reform Program is supporting the sector to respond to the changes it is experiencing, as well as mobilising its capability to do things differently. It includes a capacity-building program that has delivered support for chief executive officers (CEOs) and board members in governance, financial management, tendering and procurement, working with government, collaboration and strategic risk management. It also includes red tape reduction, such as rethinking the purchasing of community services—something that requires considerable cultural change and maturation of capabilities in government and the community sector.

It is an exciting time to be working in government, requiring us to think differently, work together and trial new approaches to ensure our investment is achieving the desired social impacts for the benefit of our community, particularly those who need it most. I thank all the contributors to this book: your work will help inform how public policy professionals can better support some of the most vulnerable members of our community.

Sue Chapman
Director-General (Acting)
Community Services Directorate
December 2015

Contextualising the Imperative of Cross-Sector Working

1

Introduction

David J. Gilchrist and John R. Butcher

There is a long history of Australian governments and the not-for-profit (NFP) sector working together to address social problems. The relationship between government and the NFP sector is important: for government, owing to its increasing reliance on NFP providers of publicly funded social services; for NFP organisations reliant on government for funding and subject to government regulation; and for those communities, families and individuals whose well-being depends on government and NFP organisations working towards shared public purposes.

For the most part, the relationship between governments—federal, state/territory and local—and the NFP sector is both productive and mutually beneficial. It is, however, also a complex relationship—a complexity exacerbated by the various roles governments undertake as regulator, commissioner and purchaser of services delivered by NFP sector organisations.

First, the NFP sector is highly heterogeneous: it is segmented by industry and policy domains, as well as by size, mission, values, legal structure and operating norms (Lyons 2001; Salamon 1995). Second, it is economically significant and accounts for a growing share of gross domestic product (GDP) (estimated at 3.8 per cent in 2012–13) and a growing share of the Australian workforce (Knight and Gilchrist 2014; McGregor-Lowndes 2014). Third, Australia's NFP sector is subject to continuous change in terms of its regulatory and operating environment—particularly so in recent years as government investment in the sector has become more strategic and narrowly instrumental. Fourth, to the extent that governments and NFP organisations work together to achieve agreed public purposes, the relationships this engenders are complex because the sometimes 'wicked' problems they seek to resolve are themselves highly complex.

This relationship is also complicated by changing community expectations of the type, quantity and quality of services provided or enabled by government as well as the need to coordinate responses to multiple and complex needs across portfolio, clinical and sectoral boundaries. Nowhere is this more evident than in the contemporary policy drive towards person-centred care and individualised funding models. These expectations affect the NFP sector in a number of important ways. For instance, in an environment of resource scarcity and in which the configuration of service interventions is very much shaped by agency and programmatic 'silos', NFP organisations can be constrained in their ability to provide services that are at once highly responsive to the needs of users and provided to a high standard. The challenge is also felt by government agencies confronted by the need to develop new skills, new ways of thinking and new ways of governing the relationship—challenges that are often very difficult for government agencies to accommodate within their existing accountability frameworks.

The history of this relationship plays a role in the current challenges. The sector has traditionally been seen as mendicant to the various government agencies that have provided funding for service delivery and which have—again, traditionally—set the parameters of service delivery and expenditure as well as of quality and assurance. This history has ensured that both the government agencies themselves and the NFPs they fund have a shared experience and have developed capacity framed by past operating methods.

Broad paradigmatic shifts in governance and policy in the past half-century have shaped the shifting frontier of government/NFP sector relations in Australia and abroad (Lewis 1999; Lyons 2001). Whereas at the beginning of the twentieth century charities founded on a mix of faith and social purposes were dominant in the provision of education, health care and social support, by the beginning of the twenty-first century, large parts of the NFP sector had been effectively co-opted as instruments—indeed agents—of government policy. The introduction in the mid 1990s of market-style mechanisms (for example, the establishment of quasi-markets to support the procurement of services via competitive tendering processes) and, more recently, the shift towards policies promoting individualised funding and person-centred care have been built on claims that such mechanisms will result in more efficient and appropriate service delivery. Equally important as a driver of the externalisation of service delivery are the fiscal pressures on government arising from increasing expectations (and genuine needs) in the face of stagnating public revenue.

This book is not intended to be a broad critique of market-focused approaches to government investment in the NFP sector; nevertheless, it is essential that we acknowledge the importance of this debate as a backdrop to the ideas presented here. In many respects, the relationship between governments and the NFP sector is a 'work in progress'; rapid recalibrations of policy in response to emerging fiscal and social contingencies have meant that the policy landscape is constantly shifting. New policy settings and policy frameworks enjoy a limited shelf life. Thus, many of the authors contributing to this volume focus on emerging policy conundrums such as the entrance of commercial organisations into areas of service traditionally served by NFP organisations; the development of often quite complex alternatives to traditional funding models; and the changing nature of government administration itself, which, as a matter of course, impacts on the NFP sector.

The capacity of governments and the NFP sector to work together to address complex social policy problems is the core concern of this volume. Indeed, a presumption of cross-sector cooperation has become embedded in the national policy discourse and in formal policy rhetoric. A second and related concern is the extent to which this discourse is in fact shaping policy and whether that policy is achieving the intended outcomes. This element, which we refer to as 'rhetoric versus reality', permeates the following chapters and frames the overall purpose of this book: to examine how we move from rhetorical hypothesising to a reality that sees the promise of the discourse realised.

Of course, it is not an unusual situation to have political rhetoric at variance with policy reality (Salamon 1995). Governments and the NFP sector are well-versed in policy 'catch phrases'—such as joined-up government, collaboration, mission-centricity, market solutions, choice, government/NFP partnership and outcomes versus outputs—just as they are often painfully aware of the gaps between the rhetoric and the facts on the ground.

For the contributors to this volume, the extent to which the rhetoric has been implemented and has borne the expected fruit is a key question. Indeed, this question provided the catalyst for a workshop entitled 'Cross-Sector Working for Complex Problems: Beyond the rhetoric', co-convened by the Australia and New Zealand School of Government (ANZSOG) and the Curtin University Not-for-profit Initiative, and held at The Australian National University in Canberra in August 2015. The workshop included 90 participants drawn from academia, government and the NFP sector, and 15 speakers with recognised expertise in boundary-spanning collaboration and public administration. This book brings together the presentations and ideas shared at the workshop.

Developments in the not-for-profit policy space

It has long been recognised that the regulatory environment in which NFPs operate—nationally and subnationally—needs to be modernised (Lyons 2003). Although the Rudd and Gillard Labor governments implemented important structural reforms (Butcher 2012), key reforms such as the creation of a national charity regulator and a statutory definition of charity did not enjoy the support of the Abbott Coalition Government elected in 2013 (Murray 2014). At the national level, Australia once again lapsed into a kind of policy stand-off—between a government bent on reversing hard-won policy reform and the majority of charities and NFPs seeking to preserve the momentum for reform.

Initially, the election of a Coalition Government also effectively stalled efforts at regulatory harmonisation in the NFP policy space and impaired the national regulator's influence (Gilchrist 2015a, 2015b). However, very recently the change in leadership has seen a rethinking within the government that has resulted in the confirmation of the Australian Charities and Not-for-profits Commission (ACNC) as the national charities regulator and this has breathed new life as well as new optimism into the national conversation.

Government commissioners and their NFP 'partners' will, however, continue to be obliged to navigate a complex and sometimes dysfunctional regulatory and policy terrain. The history and complexity of social outcomes sought ensure that the default practices of governments remain, effectively, 'regulation by contract' and regulation by administrative edict, notwithstanding the rhetoric of partnership, mission focus and choice.

The legacies of contractualism: An ongoing challenge

Over the past 15 years all Australian jurisdictions have outsourced significant shares of human services delivery to NFP organisations— usually via competitive contracting and tendering or, more recently, via experimental instruments such as social benefit bonds (Butcher and Dalton 2014; KPMG 2014; Gilchrist and Wilkins 2016). Along the way, each jurisdiction has wrestled with the tensions inherent in managing a diverse portfolio of NFP service providers with diverse values, organisational cultures, operating environments and capabilities (Butcher 2015).

In addition, the operational policies and contracting practices of commissioning agencies have imposed significant financial and operational burdens on NFP providers and on the agencies themselves (OAG WA 2000; PAEC 2002; QAO 2007; Productivity Commission 2010; VAGO 2010; Knight and Gilchrist 2015). In some cases, it has been observed that the practices of commissioning agencies have contributed to the adoption by NFP providers of behaviours and practices that are maladaptive and/or inimical to the stated policy aims of government (Minkoff and Powell 2006; Gazely and Brudney 2007; Van Slyke 2007; Heinrich et al. 2010; Verbruggen et al. 2011; Verschuere and De Corte 2014).

If, as Peter Shergold observed in his recent report to the Victorian state government, public servants need to become facilitators of 'cross-sectoral collaboration in the design, delivery and evaluation of outcomes-based services', they will need to be better equipped to take on this role (Shergold 2013). Accordingly, Shergold recommended that:

> [Victorian] Departments, individually or in partnership, should work with international and national organisations, such as the Institute of Public Administration Australia (Victoria) or the Australian and New Zealand School of Government (ANZSOG), to develop training programs that will enhance the ability of senior public servants to facilitate cross-sectoral collaboration and system stewardship of government services. (Shergold 2013: 32)

Similarly, the staff of NFP organisations with responsibility for managing and maintaining relationships with government funding agencies and commissioners need to better understand the statutory, political and institutional constraints under which public servants are obliged to act, and become more effective and impactful advocates for systemic change.

Organisation of this volume

Each of the authors contributing to this volume addresses the connections between policy rhetoric and observed policy impacts— both intended and unintended. Intended impacts include desired changes in the circumstances of target populations or desired changes in institutions or organisations. Unintended impacts might include the implementation of administrative measures that impair the capacity of NFP organisations to deliver services effectively and sustainably. Each of the authors points to the importance of framing policy on the basis of *evidence* (as opposed to ideology) as well as the importance of post-implementation assessment and evaluation.

Readers should bear in mind that this discussion does not attempt to range over the entire interface between government and the NFP sector. Rather, the authors focus on the delivery of human services (for example, community-based social services, youth and family services, disability services, mental health services, child protection services and so on) and, while it is not explicitly introduced, the

NFP sector described here largely constitutes the charities subsector. The editors and authors well understand that the NFP sector intersects with government policy across a wide range of policy domains, including sport and recreation, the environment, justice, consumer affairs and the arts. It is also recognised that each of these policy domains has its own history of institutional relationships, organisational cultures and foundation myths. It is, however, in the human services domain that governments have vigorously pursued policy innovations aimed at enlisting NFP organisations as quasi-agents of mandated service delivery—owing largely to the size of government expenditures in this area (Butcher and Dalton 2014; Davidson 2011).

Like the workshop itself, this book is framed according to four organising themes to emphasise the areas of focus and to bracket the contributions of the authors. Naturally, to address the complex issues identified above, the format, focus and prioritisation of topics discussed in this volume involve a level of arbitrariness and subjectivity. Of course, in a volume of this nature one cannot hope to canvas every important issue. However, it is our hope that the organisation of the book reflects a logical flow of ideas and observations from the theoretical to the practical.

Contextualising the imperative of cross-sector working

The text of Peter Shergold's opening address to the workshop provides the prologue for this book. Shergold's address offers a poignant, impassioned and, at times, very frank examination of the issues from the perspective of someone with considerable practical and policy experience. Shergold titled his address 'Three Sectors, One Public Purpose', a framing that neatly encapsulates a positive vision for a form of future governance that enables the public, NFP and business sectors to work collaboratively in the pursuit of agreed social aims. Shergold reflects—sometimes self-critically—on his experience as a public sector administrator, and he challenges conventional thinking about the 'norms' relating to the relationship between the three sectors. Shergold argues in favour of an authorising environment that is adaptive: one that embraces experimentation and accepts the inevitability—and benefits—of risk-taking. He argues that 'the considerable frontline experience that business and not-for-profit organisations possess needs to be incorporated into the design of government programs' and concludes by emphasising the importance of a 'clear and persuasive narrative of purpose' around the theme of 'adaptive government'.

Part 1: Cross-sector working—The rhetoric and the reality

Joined-up government, crosscutting solutions, networked governance, collaboration and cross-sector working—language such as this has been employed since the end of the previous century to accentuate the importance of engaging societal actors across organisational, institutional, domain and sectoral boundaries to address complex policy problems. But how far beyond the rhetoric have we moved and what is working and what is not? In this part, authors explore the key drivers of, and policy/political conundrums affecting, progress towards effective multisector collaboration.

Meredith Edwards provides an overview for Part 1. This part sets the scene by examining the philosophy associated with the changing relationship between government and the NFP sector and the reality evinced by experience. In Chapter 3, Helen Dickinson examines the impact of new public management (NPM) on the thinking of policymakers and on the government/NFP sector relationship. Dickinson interrogates claims in the academic literature of 'purported shifts' away from transactional governance (NPM) to relational governance ('new public governance', NPG), in which 'multiple different actors contribute to the delivery of public services and the policymaking system'.

As a counterpoint to Dickinson's theoretical and historical analysis, David Gilchrist presents in Chapter 4 his empirical research focusing on a major policy initiative in Western Australia. Gilchrist examines the evidence arising from the third annual evaluation of the 'funded sector' in that state and describes the challenges being faced by the NFP sector as a result of the implementation of new funding policies.

In Chapter 5, Tessa Boyd-Caine points out that NFP organisations engaged in the community services sector often seek to address problems of democratic deficit by enabling democratic participation by those experiencing social exclusion. Boyd-Caine explores the contributions to democratic process made by NFP organisations, arguing 'that a strong and independent civil society balances out the power and control that can otherwise be centralised in democratic governance and decision-making'. She draws on comparative examples from the United States, based on work undertaken during a Fulbright Professional Scholarship in Nonprofit Leadership in 2014, and considers alternative ways in which the Australian NFP sector could engage with democratic processes.

Part 2: Three sectors—Three change agendas

In the contemporary environment, cross-sector working requires the formation of what former director-general of the World Trade Organization Pascal Lamy calls 'creative coalitions' between government, civil society organisations and businesses. These three broad 'industry' sectors are not only distinct from one another (in terms of the normative parameters of their operations, rules, incentives and behaviours); each also represents enormous internal diversity. In this part, the authors reflect on the adaptive changes required to bridge the gaps in understanding and disconnects in expectations and practice that impede effective cross-sector working and collaboration and to consider where the boundaries might be.

Part 2, introduced by Penny Knight, drills down into the critical policy areas of funding, regulation and collaboration—areas frequently cloaked in formal policy rhetoric. In these policy spaces the aspirational terms such as 'value', 'impact', 'accountability', 'partnership' and 'collaboration' tend to dominate. These terms are often invoked—by leaders in government, the NFP sector and business—to signal the desired direction of change, as opposed to accurately describing the existing state of affairs. Beyond the rhetoric, however, one sometimes finds that structural and systemic barriers and gaps act to impede the realisation of these aspirational aims.

In Chapter 6, Leeora Black takes stock of important initiatives in government, and in the business sector itself, to create pathways for the investment of private capital in social purposes. She identifies a number of policy and structural obstacles to private social investment and suggests a number of opportunities available to government to promote such investment. According to Black, government can: mandate investment through better regulation; facilitate investment, for example, by establishing financial intermediary organisations; partner better with institutional investors; and endorse private investment by establishing mechanisms for the accreditation and recognition of firms that invest in social impact.

In Chapter 7, Krystian Seibert offers a retrospective analysis of the Rudd and Gillard Labor governments' NFP reform agenda. Seibert emphasises the complexity of the reform task facing the government and the achievements made—almost against the odds. Seibert draws on his own experience as a policy actor involved in the establishment of the ACNC to cast light on the practical and political difficulties that needed to be overcome to bring the national regulator into being. He reflects on the fortunes of the ACNC following the change of government in 2013 and speculates about those aspects of the government's engagement with stakeholders in the NFP sector that might have been handled differently. Seibert concludes by arguing that the creation of the ACNC offers a number of valuable practical lessons for policymakers.

In Chapter 8, Robyn Keast rounds out the discussion by closely examining the various markers of successful (and unsuccessful) collaboration between government agencies and NFP organisations. Keast points out that while 'authentic' collaboration is unfamiliar territory to many, far from being a 'black box', there is ample knowledge on which we might draw to deliver successful collaborations. The prime ingredients, according to Keast, include: interpersonal relationships based on trust, reciprocity and reputation; a recognition of interdependency and mutuality; acceptance of the need to share power and knowledge; and joint ownership and governance systems that allow the parties to create and claim shared value. That said, Keast observes that collaboration is full of ambiguities, nuances and unexpected turns; effective and constructive collaboration requires a 'fit-for-purpose' approach adapted to the policy and programmatic context, the range of actors involved and the nature of the problem being addressed. Collaboration also requires active sponsors and champions—as well as reflective practice—to make it work well.

Part 3: Great expectations—Outcomes and social impact

A focus on outcomes has for some time been the Holy Grail of policy implementation. Growing demands on governments coupled with static or declining revenues have led public sector commissioners to sharpen their focus on demonstrating the impact of social investment. So, too, the value proposition for social investment needs to be well argued if governments are to convince the business sector to co-invest in social programs. In this part, authors address the importance of, and difficulties inherent in, delivering sustainable outcomes based on evidence and supported by appropriate reporting.

Part 3, introduced by Nina Terrey, leads us deep into the territory of outcomes and social impact. In Chapter 9, Emma Tomkinson considers the implications of the reporting burden placed by governments on NFP providers of outsourced services. In particular, she observes that our perception of what it means to spend money 'well' has changed over recent years and points to a change in emphasis from 'what was money spent on' and 'how much activity occurred' to 'what outcomes resulted'. Drawing on international experience, Tomkinson examines the value of reporting *for* NFPs and their government funders and looks at ways in which this value can be increased. She concludes that if funders are to truly focus on outcomes, the design of their reporting requirements, and the publication and use of reported information, must be altered to further the outcomes they pursue.

In Chapter 10, Dale Tweedie highlights three potential 'disconnects' that can compromise NFP organisations' capacity to be accountable in practice for the quality or impact of their services, and explores potential responses to overcome these disconnects. Drawing on in-depth interviews with staff, directors and regulators in the NFP sector in Australia, Tweedie identifies three potential disconnects: 1) between reporting to funders and service quality; 2) between directors and NFP members; and 3) between reducing red tape and maintaining minimum service standards. Tweedie's findings suggest that reporting to funders can become 'detached' from service quality when measured outputs are weakly linked to service outcomes. He also argues the need for greater member oversight or evaluation of boards, and suggests that regulatory reforms undertaken in an increasingly cost-sensitive funding environment might inadvertently threaten standards that are critical to maintaining service quality.

In Chapter 11, Rodney Scott and Ross Boyd offer a detailed account of the design, implementation and performance of the 'results approach' operating across the New Zealand state sector. In New Zealand, government has taken the bold step of nominating 10 'results' that would improve the lives of New Zealanders. The results approach relies on the collective accountability of multiple departments for achieving targets and social impacts selected, according to Scott and Boyd, 'because they were important and long-standing problems that had proven resistant to previous attempts at change, and because making meaningful progress would require collaboration between multiple organisations'. The authors conclude that the results approach has helped to 'make progress in 10 previously intractable problems, where numerous previous attempts have failed'. Although their focus is on the New Zealand state sector, they suggest that by 'understanding the benefits and potential pitfalls in public sector targets, other sectors can help design successful impact measures for use in cross-sectoral collaboration'. Scott and Boyd also go on to suggest that 'even the most pure mission-driven organisation should … be thinking about the management accountability functions of targets'.

Part 4: New tools for policymakers and practitioners

Cross-sector working is predicated on a mix of institutions and actors engaging across institutional, domain and sectoral boundaries to address complex problems. Even so, it is essential to be clear-eyed about the nature of the incentives that motivate policy actors from the public, NFP and business sectors, recognising points of convergence and accounting for points of divergence. Furthermore, it is necessary to accept the need to develop and trial a mix of approaches—some of them experimental in nature. This requires an appetite for risk and a willingness to risk failure. In this part, authors canvass the necessary policy preconditions for exploring alternative approaches to addressing social need.

Part 4 is introduced by Ursula Stephens. In Chapter 12, Ann Nevile argues that, despite commitments to reduce the administrative burden placed on disability employment service providers, the current contracting regime acts to constrain providers' capacity to deliver flexible, individualised services. Nevile presents evidence for the assertion that introducing a person-centred approach will lead to better employment outcomes, before going on to consider the policy prerequisites for the introduction of a voucher system to support the delivery of flexible, individualised services and the realisation of improved employment outcomes.

In Chapter 13, Cassandra Wilkinson explores the potential of alliance contracting as an instrument through which service delivery can be better shaped to the aspirations and preferences of end users. Highlighting the significant opportunity costs associated with unsuccessful service delivery, Wilkinson proposes a model intended to operationalise evidence-based approaches to service delivery within a shared risk framework. Wilkinson argues that existing systems for social procurement are too opaque to drive the transition from volume-based contracting to value-based contracting and commissioning. The establishment of choice-based markets and/or social-purpose capital markets, Wilkinson argues, requires active collaboration between policymakers, providers and their clients.

In Chapter 14, Melina Morrison and Cliff Mills mount a case for Australian mutual and cooperative organisations to play a more substantial role as pillars of public service delivery. The authors argue that there is a window of opportunity for Australian mutual and cooperative organisations to take on the mantle of 'providers of choice', especially as market-based solutions and state-based command-and-control approaches seem to be increasingly problematic. Although Morrison and Mills concede that mutuality 'lost traction' midway through the past century (having been the pre-eminent force in social provision from the late nineteenth century), interest in mutuality has revived in step with growing interest in a values-based economy. The authors take the long view of mutualism as a movement based on the principle of 'collective self-help', and step us through its mid-century decline and its relatively recent revival in a somewhat corrupted form in the United Kingdom. Nevertheless, Morrison and Mills are able to point to positive examples of mutuals and cooperatives from the United Kingdom, especially in the areas of social housing and community health, offering hope that a new, modernised form of mutuality can emerge.

In Chapter 15, Catherine Needham interrogates the rationale for, and the claims made in support of, individualised or person-centred funding. Her analysis is supported by evidence from the United Kingdom, where personal budgets for care have been a feature of the policy mix since the 1980s and are given legal force through the 1996 *Community Care (Direct Payments) Act*. Needham tells us that in the United Kingdom personal budgets are held by more than 50 per cent of older people and people with a disability although the take-up of direct payments is much lower. While Needham says that personal budgets 'have been a hugely positive intervention for some people using social care services', she goes on to suggest that the 'claim that controlling money is a valuable educative process is harder to sustain' and the 'argument that budgets themselves will fix systemic problems in care provision is also unconvincing'. A 'highly commodified sector', she asserts, 'has delivered a poor quality of care to those with and without their own purchasing power'. Consequently, Needham cautions that as Australia's National Disability Insurance Scheme gathers momentum, 'it is vital that good-quality information and advocacy are in place so that people with budgets can build relationships and communities and not just pick care items off a shopping list'.

Cross-sector working: Meeting the challenge of change

Paul Ronalds' closing address to the workshop provides the postscript for this collection by revisiting the challenge of change in the context of his personal experience in the senior ranks of the Commonwealth bureaucracy and as a senior executive in the NFP sector. Ronalds observes that a tendency for risk-averse behaviour and an obsessive focus on compliance impede the ability of public servants to exercise initiative and innovation. Ronalds also speaks about the various sources of 'systems failure' and pays particular attention to the perverse incentive structures operating in the public, NFP and business sectors that lead to suboptimal social outcomes. Although he emphasises the importance of evidence to increase transparency about costs and results, and to thereby elicit more thoughtful responses on the part of governments, he also offers the following words of caution:

> Too often we have sought to use rational policy arguments, evidence and moral suasion to argue for improved ways of working. When these

fail, we double our efforts, futilely believing that by simply arguing harder, conducting further pilots or gathering more evidence things will change.

They won't.

It's not that these things aren't important. It's just that they won't be sufficient. We need to change the system's incentives. This is the challenge of change to making progress with complex problems.

Ronalds also acknowledges the realpolitik of change by pointing to the need to better celebrate successful policy and service delivery innovations, which will, in his words, 'give politicians more cover to implement reforms'.

Conclusion

In Chapter 17, John R. Butcher and David J. Gilchrist reflect on the foregoing papers in an attempt to hone in on and amplify a set of crossover issues relevant to the core question about how to work better across sectoral boundaries. The authors observe that each of the contributors has—either overtly or by implication—drawn attention to the critical nature of gaps and disconnects as determinants of success (or rather failure). Rather than simply summarise and restate the observations made and conclusions drawn by the contributors, Butcher and Gilchrist attempt to identify potential avenues for further research. Although Australia has a large NFP sector—larger per capita than the NFP sector in comparable countries—its non-profit research community is comparatively small, institutionally siloed and geographically dispersed.

There is broad agreement among the contributors to this volume about the value of working better across institutional, sectoral and domain boundaries in the pursuit of public purposes. Similarly, the ambition, breadth and diversity of policy thinking and scholarship evidenced in the work herein presented argue powerfully for greater research collaboration across institutional and sectoral boundaries. There *is* a surfeit of rhetoric in the NFP policy space. Fortunately, there are scholars and thinkers of high calibre capable of meeting the urgent need for enhanced analysis and discussion based on evidence.

The potential of the collective impact of that policy thinking could be even greater if better coordinated and supported. It is our hope that this book constitutes an important start in that direction.

References

Alford, J. L. and J. O'Flynn. 2012. *Rethinking Public Service Delivery: Managing with external providers.* Basingstoke, UK: Palgrave Macmillan.

Butcher, J. 2012. 'The National Compact: Civilising the relationship between government and the not-for-profit sector in Australia.' In *Government–Nonprofit Relations in Times of Recession*, ed. R. Laforest, 165–88. Toronto: McGill-Queen's University Press.

Butcher, J. 2015. 'Australian sub-national compacts with the not-for-profit sector: Pathways to cross-sector cooperation.' In *New Accountabilities, New Challenges*, ed. J. Wanna, 297–341. Canberra: ANU Press, with ANZSOG.

Butcher, J. and B. Dalton. 2014. 'Cross-sector partnership and human services in Australian States and Territories: Reflections on a mutable relationship.' *Policy and Society* 33(2): 141–53.

Davidson, B. 2011. 'Contestability in human services markets.' *Journal of Australian Political Economy* 68: 213–39.

Gazely, B. and J. L. Brudney. 2007. 'The purpose (and perils) of government–nonprofit partnership.' *Nonprofit and Voluntary Sector Quarterly* 36: 389–415.

Gilchrist, D. J. 2014. Partnerships between government and the third sector at a sub-national level: Experience of an Australian sub-national government. Paper presented at the Maximising the Benefits of Decentralisations: 2014 Greater China–Australia Dialogue on Public Administration, Hangzhou, China, 20–22 October.

Gilchrist, D. J. 2015a. 'Dumping Markets Advisory Board is another independent voice lost.' *The Conversation*, 21 April.

Gilchrist, D. J. 2015b. 'Charities responding to ACNC.' *WA Business News*, 25 May.

Gilchrist, D. J. and P. Wilkins. 2016. 'Social impact bonds: The role of evaluation.' In *Doing Public Good? Private actors, evaluation and public value*, eds R. Pablo Guerrero O. and P. Wilkins, 147–58. New Brunswick, NJ: Transaction Publishing.

Heinrich, C., L. E. Lynn Jr, and H. B. Milward. 2010. 'A state of agents? Sharpening the debate and evidence over the extent and impact of the transformation of governance.' *Journal of Public Administration Research and Theory* 20(SI): i3–i19.

Knight, P. and D. J. Gilchrist. 2014. *Australian charities 2013: The first report on charities registered with the Australian Charities and Not-for-profits Commission*. Report for the Australian Charities and Not-for-profits Commission. Melbourne: ACNC.

Knight, P. and D. J. Gilchrist. 2015. *2014 Evaluation of the Sustainable Funding and Contracting with the Not-for-profit Sector Initiatives and Associated Procurement Reforms*. Perth: Government of Western Australia.

KPMG. 2014. *Evaluation of the Joint Development Phase of the NSW Social Benefit Bonds Trial*. Sydney: KPMG Government Advisory Services. Available from: www.dpc.nsw.gov.au/__data/assets/pdf_file/0006/168333/Evaluation_of_the_Joint_Development_Phase.pdf (accessed 22 June 2016).

Lewis, J. 1999. 'Reviewing the relationship between the voluntary sector and the state in Britain in the 1990s.' *Voluntas: International Journal of Voluntary and Nonprofit Organizations* JO(3).

Lyons, M. 2001. *Third Sector: The contribution of non-profit and cooperative enterprises in Australia*. Sydney: Allen & Unwin.

Lyons, M. 2003. 'The legal and regulatory environment of the third sector.' *The Asian Journal of Public Administration* 25(1): 87–106.

McGregor-Lowndes, M. 2014. *The not for profit sector in Australia: Fact sheet*. ACPNS Current Issues Information Sheet 2014/4, August. Australian Centre for Philanthropy and Nonprofit Studies, QUT Business School, Brisbane. Available from: eprints.qut.edu.au/75397/4/75397(updated).pdf (accessed 21 April 2016).

McGregor-Lowndes, M. and C. Ryan. 2009. 'Reducing the compliance burden of non-profit organisations: Cutting red tape.' *Australian Journal of Public Administration* 68(1): 21–38.

Minkoff, D. C. and W. W. Powell. 2006. 'Nonprofit mission: Constancy, responsiveness or deflection?' In *The Non-Profit Sector: A research handbook*, eds W. W. Powell and R. Steinberg, 157–63. 2nd edn. New Haven, Conn., and London: Yale University Press.

Murray, I. 2014. 'Not-for-profit reform: Back to the future?' *Third Sector Review* 20(1): 109–39.

NSW Government. 2012. *Red Tape Reduction Plan for NGOs*. Sydney: Department of Family and Community Services. Available from: adhc.nsw.gov.au/__data/assets/file/0009/255690/Red_Tape_Reduction_Plan.pdf (accessed 1 August 2012).

Office of the Auditor-General, Western Australia (OAG WA). 2000. *A Means to an End: Contracting not-for-profit organisations for the delivery of community services*. Perth: Office of the Auditor-General, Western Australia. Available from: audit.wa.gov.au/reports/pdfreports/report2000_03.pdf (accessed 24 February 2010).

Public Accounts and Estimates Committee (PAEC). 2002. *Report on the Department of Human Services: Service agreements for community, health and welfare services*. Melbourne: Public Accounts and Estimates Committee, Parliament of Victoria. Available from: parliament.vic.gov.au/images/stories/committees/paec/reports/47th_report_-_DHSServiceAgreements_2002.pdf (accessed 3 August 2012).

Productivity Commission. 2010. *Contribution of the Not-for-Profit Sector*. Canberra: Productivity Commission. Available from: pc.gov.au/projects/study/not-for-profit/report (accessed 24 February 2012).

Queensland Audit Office (QAO). 2007. *Results of Performance Management Systems Audit of Management of Funding to Non-Government Organisations*. Brisbane: Queensland Audit Office. Available from: qao.qld.gov.au/files/file/Reports/2007%20Report%20No.%202.pdf (accessed 21 April 2016).

Salamon, L. M. 1995. *Partners in Public Service*. Baltimore: The Johns Hopkins University Press.

Saunders, P. 2009. 'Supping with the devil: Government contracts and the non-profit sector.' In *Supping with the Devil: Government contracts and the non-profit sector*, eds P. Saunders and M. Stewart-Weeks, 1–15. Sydney: Centre for Independent Studies.

Shergold, P. 2008. Contracting out government: Collaboration or control? Neil Walker Memorial Lecture. Centre for Social Impact, University of New South Wales, Sydney. Available from: www.uws.edu.au/__data/assets/pdf_file/0009/1098207/contracting_out_government_collaboration_or_control.pdf (accessed 29 June 2016).

Shergold, P. 2013. *Service sector reform: A roadmap for community and human services reform. Final report.* Melbourne: Department of Human Services. Available from: vcoss.org.au/documents/2013/11/FINAL-Report-Service-Sector-Reform.pdf (accessed 22 June 2016).

Victorian Auditor-General's Office (VAGO). 2010. *Partnering with the Community Sector in Human Services and Health.* Melbourne: Victorian Auditor-General's Office. Available from: audit.vic.gov.au/reports__publications/reports_by_year/2009-10/20102605_comm_sector_partner.aspx (accessed 3 August 2012).

Van Slyke, D. M. 2007. 'Agents or stewards: Using theory to understand the government–nonprofit social service contracting relationship.' *Journal of Public Administration Research and Theory* 17(2): 157–87.

Verbruggen, S., J. Christiaens and K. Milis. 2011. 'Can resource dependence and coercive isomorphism explain nonprofit organizations' compliance with reporting standards?' *Nonprofit and Voluntary Sector Quarterly* 40(1): 5–32.

Verschuere, B. and J. De Corte. 2014. 'The impact of public resource dependence on the autonomy of NPOs in their strategic decision making.' *Nonprofit and Voluntary Sector Quarterly* 43: 293–313.

2

Three Sectors,
One Public Purpose

Peter Shergold

The conveners of the workshop from which the chapters in this volume are drawn invited Professor Peter Shergold AC, Chancellor of Western Sydney University, to give an opening address contextualising the importance of learning to work across sectoral boundaries towards solutions to pressing social problems. This he did with characteristic verve and deep insight. The chapter that follows is from the approved text of Professor Shergold's address. This can also be viewed on the ANZSOG YouTube channel at: youtube.com/watch?v=bUskU0X4_To.

I am delighted to have been afforded the opportunity to speak at this workshop on cross-sector working. I speak to you as an enthusiast, albeit a person chastened by the experience of how difficult it can be to turn the easy rhetoric of reciprocated trust and mutual respect into substantive reality. My passion is largely undimmed by cautious realism. The institutions of the public service can work—and on occasions do work—in full partnership with the private and community sectors to design and deliver the goals of democratic government. More often, however, the potential to collaborate for public purpose has been sold short. My address is a heartfelt plea for greater ambition and more courage.

In writing on this subject, I have learned to utilise the language of public management. I have spoken of the advantages of network governance. That term should not be limited to the commissioning of third-party agents to deliver services to citizens (predominantly, although not exclusively, by contracting not-for-profit organisations to implement government programs in areas such as aged, disability, health and community care, and training or employment services). There is great value in the mechanism of public–private partnerships, although the contractual conditions that are agreed in particular cases need careful attention. There are benefits—too often constrained by the bureaucratic processes of outsourcing—to creating a contestable market in which citizens can be given greater choice, flexibility and control, including through consumer-directed care (CDC). These developments foreshadow the potential creation of a public economy stretching far beyond the institutions of the public service.

There is much more significant advantage if public administrators can engage commercial and social enterprises in the co-design and co-production of the programs that make manifest the policy objectives of government. Performance-based outcomes can allow business and community organisations to have a greater chance to be rewarded for results rather than paid for process. There is a need for tenders that encourage providers to pursue agreed outcomes in their own way.

I emphasise that my belief in cross-sectoral working is not the consequence of a sudden late-age epiphany. Rather, my views reflect a long personal journey. It began before I joined the Australian Public Service (APS) in the mid 1980s, when, as an academic, I undertook with Dr Loucas Nicolaou a report for the Department of Immigration. It was based on detailed focus group discussions with ethnic communities. Its title, taken from the pithy comment of a participant, became our unsubtle message: *Why Don't They Ask Us? We're not dumb.* We argued that refugee and migrant groups should be given the chance to contribute to the arrangement of the settlement services they received. Ironically, the things that most organisations wanted (a typewriter, a Gestetner printing machine, a community meeting room or access to a trained interpreter) were mostly modest.

I kept that faith in community wisdom and individual capacity through my two decades as a public servant, from the year I established the Office of Multicultural Affairs in 1987 (for Prime Minister Bob Hawke) to the time I spent as Secretary of the Department of the Prime Minister and Cabinet from 2002 to 2007 (for Prime Minister John Howard). The collaborative impulse inspired me when I had responsibility, as head of the Department of Education, Employment and Workplace Relations in 1997, for the oversight of that bold Commonwealth experiment in cross-sectoral working, the Job Network (from 2009, also known as Job Services Australia; and from 2015, jobactive). In that capacity, I learned the language of market testing and benchmarking. I am relieved that I eschewed dim-witted references to the so-called 'yellow pages' test (if the private sector could be shown to offer a service then the public service should vacate the space). Unfortunately, the end result of outsourcing labour market programs has been at most a revolution half-fulfilled: jobseekers are still given too little real choice and providers afforded too little real freedom to innovate.

But my faith remains strong. I said in my valedictory speech on departure from the public service in 2007 that public and not-for-profit organisations needed to work together to deliver government policy. Almost eight years on and that perspective still informs the report I have recently handed to the Commonwealth Government on the lessons to be learned from the manifold mistakes that characterised the execution of the Home Insulation Program (Shergold 2016). In that instance, the benefits of cross-sector working were sacrificed on the altar of implementation speed, with tragic consequences. I am persuaded that serving the public purpose needs to be a shared endeavour: 'Whilst I love the making of public policy, and I believe that the APS contributes mightily to that effort in extraordinarily beneficial ways, I am increasingly persuaded that it is far too important to be left to governments and public services' (Shergold 2012: 63).

So why has the path to effective cross-sectoral collaboration been so slow, circuitous and erratic? Partly because working together calls for considerable emotional intelligence. It is often hard to imagine the world from the perspective of other parties. Most successes bear testimony to the leadership of particular committed individuals who have exhibited the capacity to stand in the shoes of their counterparts and see challenges through their eyes.

Partly it is because the rhetoric of partnership has actually been too modest. Cross-sectoral working in the public interest has the potential not just to improve cost-effectiveness and 'customer' service, but also to widen and reinvigorate the participatory nature of democratic governance. It offers the potential for adaptive government. The concept refers to those circumstances in which collaboration— driven by trials and subject to errors—allows public administration to become more agile and experimental.

In general, cross-sector working has been marked by failures of implementation, nerve and imagination. That is not a cause for despair. It is feasible to learn the lessons from both grievous mistakes and modest successes and to re-envision collaborative endeavour. At least that's the real-world experience that I'm trying to benefit from … and I have the advantage of being able to draw my insights from a bulging volume of personal errors.

So let me, *Star Trek* fashion, split my infinitives 'to boldly go where no man has gone before' (or, after *Star Trek VI*, in a bow to gender-neutral language, to go where no one has gone before). Here, I suggest, is what democratic governance may look like in the immediate years ahead; these 'are its voyages and its adventures'.

In the future, elected governments, as today, will set the public interest and answer to the electorate at the ballot box for the decisions they make in pursuit of their agenda. They will continue to establish policy goals and budgetary parameters. Subject to Parliamentary support and judicial interpretation, governments will determine the services and regulatory environment that give effect to their choices. Public services, for their part, will still be expected to serve faithfully successive governments, providing robust advice on the complex and wicked problems of public policy and overseeing the implementation of the programs that give the policy effect. So far, same old, same old Westminster.

What changes in the new world is that public service agencies will no longer aspire to wield monopoly control over the advice that governments receive. Nor will they seek to use their situational authority to command and control the manner in which contracted organisations deliver programs. Rather, public servants will judge their leadership by the extent to which they have acted as stewards of public resources and facilitators of cross-sectoral collaboration. They will actively involve and commission others to help design government policies and to plan the legislative and administrative architecture that frames their implementation.

Commissioned organisations will be viewed not merely as agents *of* government but also as partners *in* government, working collaboratively with public service departments to create and maintain a public economy. Providers will have far greater control over how services are delivered. They will be able to tailor programs to place and community. They will be encouraged to empower citizens as consumers to exercise greater control over which services they require and which providers (public or private) they prefer to deliver them. The ethos of impact investment will be embraced, allowing non-governmental partners (such as community organisations) to raise funds in the private market, and to pay a return to those who offer debt or equity—but only if they can successfully deliver the public outcomes that have been agreed. The introduction of social benefit bonds in New South Wales, and soon in South Australia and New Zealand, provides a good example of how public, private and community organisations can work together not just to design but also to fund government programs. I set out the broad parameters of cross-sectoral collaboration in my 2013 report for the Victorian Minister for Community Services: 'The collaborative relationship between the public service agencies and non-government organisations that together deliver government programs should be founded on appreciation of the constraints under which all sides operate, mutual respect, reciprocated trust, authentic consultation, and a shared recognition of common purpose' (Shergold 2013: 17).

In short, the driving ethos of public servants who apolitically serve the government of the day will be to expedite greater levels of participation in the processes of democratic governance. They will encourage private and community providers as well as citizen users to have greater influence on decision-making. Some of these developments are already occurring on the exciting peripheries of public administration. The question is: what do government agencies need to do to transform the core of their institutional being? I suggest four things.

First, public services must look outwards. By being more open to experience beyond the public sector, they can significantly improve the creativity and productivity of public administration. This is not intended to deprecate in any measure the considerable vocational skills required of senior public servants working in a world of contested and ambiguous political power. They must continue to shoulder the necessary burden of public scrutiny, responsibility, answerability and accountability.

In this most fundamental sense, public servants must remain public servants. But they also need to recognise that the world of market contest (whether directed to sustaining shareholder profit or to winning the philanthropic dollar) drives competitive impulses in a manner that can enhance public benefits. Public services are not the only institutional reflections of officialdom. Many large corporate and charitable ventures have bureaucratic structures of vertical hierarchy and horizontal demarcation that match the organisational rigidity of any department of state. The difference is that big businesses and big charities face constant pressure from disruptive innovation in the form of new products, new services, new distribution channels, new competitors and the evolving expectations of their customers or donors.

For that reason, they tend to set far higher store on assessing and managing risk appetite and project implementation. Even the largest and most traditional of private or community organisations exhibits a form of structured entrepreneurship rarely seen in public sector agencies. Their market experience can teach the public sector to be more adaptive: operationalising new ideas early, piloting and evaluating new approaches and, on that basis, failing quickly, adapting progressively or scaling up methodically.

Second, public services must embrace partnership. There are at least two aspects to this entreaty. Public services need to recognise the value that can be added to policy development and program design by universities, think tanks, research institutes and consultancy companies. Too often public servants direct their research capabilities to identifying policy-based evidence to justify a political outcome that has already been decided. That is clever but unsatisfactory. There is far greater merit in actively working with collaborators in pursuit of evidence-based policy with which to influence political decisions. Of course, public servants must continue to apply their conceptual and analytical skills, not just to articulate the research in a manner that is relevant to government priorities, but also to translate academic findings into the sort of practical knowledge that governments can properly comprehend and apply.

At the same time, the considerable frontline experience that businesses and not-for-profit organisations possess needs to be incorporated into the design of government programs. I have sought to walk my talk.

In Western Australia, I set up and chaired the Partnership Forum that brings together the state's directors-general and community sector chief executive officers (CEOs). As Coordinator-General for Refugee Resettlement in New South Wales, I have established a Joint Working Group of senior public servants and community leaders to work together in identifying policy gaps and how they can best be addressed. These experiences persuade me that contracted organisations can add significant value to consideration of the structures by which government payments and services are delivered. Of course, both sides have to be aware of and carefully manage the probity issues involving conflicts of pecuniary interest around government tendering. Incidentally, providers are not the only ones who can contribute to collaborative design. Program managers too often underappreciate the first-hand experience of those more junior public servants who are actively engaged with the public. As a consequence, the considerable creativity of frontline staff is spent finding work-arounds to highly prescriptive administrative guidelines that reduce the common-sense autonomy they can exercise to improve customer service. There is a need for policy to be designed from the bottom up and power devolved from the top down.

Third, public services must empower citizens. It is apparent, to choose the most egregious example, that too much of the assistance directed to citizens in need (payments, concessions, subsidies, programs and services) is provided in ways that can perpetuate their sense of social exclusion and dependence. A safety net to catch people when they fall can be very difficult for them to climb out of. If public servants treat people as recipients or cases to be managed, many, not surprisingly, will learn helplessness.

That is the significance of the recent government emphasis on consumer-directed care, particularly in the delivery of services to those with a disability or in the provision of assistance to senior citizens living at home. Cross-sectoral working should be driven as much as possible by the preferences of those receiving public support. The fact that both government agencies and contracted community providers may find it financially more secure and administratively more convenient to agree on an inflexible block grant approach to service delivery does not mean it is in the best interests of the recipient. Collaboration between the public contractor and the private/community provider should not become an excuse for mutual self-interest. The driving principles must be choice and contestability. Citizens need to be encouraged and assisted to make decisions for themselves. The danger is that public servants will oversight too careful a rendition of CDC, in which choices for citizens are carefully limited; it will be far better to widen ambitions and put citizens firmly in control of the choices that they wish to make for themselves: 'The future of assertive citizenship lies in finding collaborative approaches to engage individuals in building a new form of public economy ... They can be encouraged to become state actors in a more networked form of governance' (Shergold 2014: 70).

Fourth, public servants must continue to extol public purpose. The concept of public service, if not its institutional manifestation, remains profoundly persuasive. As a nation, we face intimidating challenges. Too few Australians trust politicians (thankfully, public servants poll rather better). Too few young Australians set high store by the value of democracy as a form of government.

Yet the picture is not unremittingly bleak. Many Australians, given half a chance, will willingly volunteer their time to the pursuit of public purpose: think, as instances, of the thousands of readers who voluntarily correct digitised newspaper text for the National Library of Australia as part of its Trove project; or of the hundreds of people eager to attend the annual GovHack events and design new apps for the benefit of the public. This goodwill and enthusiasm can be harnessed. As the new Digital Transformation Office recognises, there are increasing opportunities to use deliberative techniques of online democracy to engage the public in policy discussions. The importance that the new Prime Minister, Malcolm Turnbull, places on this potential may perhaps be gauged by the fact that the office has now become part of the Prime Minister's portfolio.

So what do these four pillars of cross-sector working mean for the structure of public administration? They require senior public servants to embrace new forms of leadership. The demands of public administration have increased and have become more complex and the exercise of authority needs to be more sensitive and subtle. It will require the leadership of facilitation. Success will be judged by the extent to which cross-sector working can be fully exploited for public benefit. The old-style modes of behaviour were based on controlling, contracting, consulting and communicating. In the new world, the dominant form of authority will be collaborating, co-designing, coproducing ... and communicating: 'Genuine collaboration ...

requires public servants who, with eyes wide open, can exert the qualities of leadership necessary to forsake the simplicity of control for the complexity of influence' (Shergold 2008: 21).

Success will depend on public servants being appropriately trained in the skills of negotiation, discussion, empathetic listening and openness. It will require them actively to encourage innovative forms of cross-sectoral partnership, founded on citizen engagement and driven by the challenge of applying scarce public resources most effectively to the achievement of public good.

I do not underestimate how difficult it will be to create this new form of governance. It will almost certainly require greater levels of political authority than have been exhibited until now. Australian political leaders, often with good reason, do not naturally embrace sweeping new approaches such as the 'third way' or 'big society'. Fortunately, for sound pragmatic reasons, the future of public administration is already taking shape. Both Commonwealth and state governments, to varying extents, are introducing customer service improvements, performance-based commissioning, consumer-directed care, place-based funding and public impact investing. At the heart of these diverse activities lies cross-sector working. Unfortunately, the new approaches are largely hidden from public view. Perhaps we just need to be able to tell the story of public innovation clearly? For public servants, just as much as for politicians, a clear and persuasive narrative of purpose is important. 'Adaptive government' might serve as a title.

I very much hope that this important workshop can contribute to that task.

References

Shergold, P. 2008. 'Governing through collaboration.' In *Collaborative Governance: A new era of public policy in Australia?*, eds J. O'Flynn and J. Wanna, 13–22. Canberra: ANU E Press.

Shergold, P. 2012. 'In the national interest.' In *With the Benefit of Hindsight: Valedictory reflections from departmental secretaries 2004–11*, eds J. Wanna, S. Vincent and A. Podger, 53–64. Canberra: ANU E Press.

Shergold, P. 2013. *Service sector reform: A roadmap for community and human services reform.* Report for the Victorian Minister for Community Services. Victorian Government, Melbourne.

Shergold, P. 2014. 'Assertive citizenship.' In *Connected Government Compendium*, ed. J. Dan, 66–75. Sydney: Telstra.

Shergold, P. 2016. *Learning from failure: Why large government policy initiatives have gone so badly wrong in the past and how the chances of success in the future can be improved.* Report, 5 February. Australian Public Service Commission, Canberra. Available from: www.apsc. gov.au/publications-and-media/current-publications/learning-from-failure (accessed 5 April 2016).

Part 1. Cross-Sector Working: The rhetoric and the reality

.

Overview

Meredith Edwards

I had two immediate thoughts when I read the chapters in this section. The first was how disparate they were—at least on the surface. Helen Dickinson provides the bigger picture on where public governance has come from and how we arrived at the hybrid forms we have today. The second paper, by David J. Gilchrist, presents an only too rare evaluation of processes around new contractual arrangements from the perspective of not-for-profits (NFPs) in Western Australia. The third chapter, by Tessa Boyd-Caine, presents some key themes to govern the relationship between the public and NFP sectors and civil society. So you could well ask—as I did—what these three chapters have in common.

As I see it, the common thread across the three chapters is the respective roles of the public and NFP sectors into the future at a time when no one sector can solve complex problems on its own and when considerable uncertainty and change are compounding the complexity of sectoral relationships.

The second thought I had is that what is being discussed in these chapters is hardly new. By way of example, more than a decade ago a forum was held by the University of Canberra with Canadian and Australian presenters on the topic 'New Players, Partners and Processes: A public sector without boundaries?' (Edwards and Langford 2002). Our broad goal was to ask critical questions about the nature of governance in an era when boundaries are blurring across the public, private and NFP sectors. As a Canadian participant at the forum remarked: 'Despite the rhetoric there have not been enough examples of genuine collaborative partnerships between government and the third sector to begin to adequately measure the effectiveness of this mode of boundary spanning' (Edwards and Langford 2002: 9).

Sadly, the same could be said today despite the excellent Australian Government publication *Connecting Government* in 2004, with its assessment, case studies and practical suggestions for more collaborative arrangements (APSC 2004). Indeed, the Organisation for Economic Co-operation and Development (OECD) has regularly bemoaned the fact that '[m]ost OECD countries are still at [the] early stages of public engagement' (2015: 33).

First to Dickinson's chapter, which is an eminently sensible overview based on a solid evidence base of interviews with public sector players. A main conclusion is the mismatch between the rhetoric relating to more horizontal relationships and the reality, which is much more mixed, suggesting that now and into the future there will be layers of different reform processes rather than more wholesale shifts in organisational arrangements, behaviours or cultures.

My pessimistic comment here is that, unfortunately, there is evidence in the public sector of some backward moves that need to be built into any mixed-modes framework. There is evidence that some agencies have become more and not less hierarchical with stronger executive control, and public servants have become more and not less risk-averse, with middle management becoming less and not more empowered (for example, Behm 2015: 135–36; APSC 2014: 41). Unless considerable change beyond the incremental takes place into the future (as is indicated below) then it follows that the reality will be a widening gap or mismatch between the problems to be solved on the one hand and, on the other, public institutions and behaviours. There is a need to adapt the organisations to fit the problem wherever the problems do not fit the boundaries, rather than expect the problems to change to fit organisational structures.

The WA Government is to be commended for the transparency it is showing in its evaluation of the Delivering Community Services in Partnership (DCSP) program, as reflected in Gilchrist's chapter. The government is working in partnership with the NFP sector on changes to contracting arrangements with a focus on individuals and their outcomes. Gilchrist points out, among other things, the inconsistency across agencies in dealing with NFPs that suggests that crossing boundaries is an internal public sector challenge at least as important as the challenge of external relationships. Gilchrist also suggests a difference in perceptions of the state government and

NFP sector organisations of the impact of the change; this could lead to government rhetoric on collaborative partnering arrangements differing from the reality, at least as far as the NFP sector experiences it.

Gilchrist's chapter raises questions about the role of government in the context of a greater focus on outcomes rather than outputs—for example, is there a greater role for government to facilitate learning across sectors about what works and what does not? Relatedly, the chapter raises several questions about the broader framework of principles on which the relationship between the two sectors is based—in particular, there are issues around who becomes involved and when in the process of learning as policies are developed and implemented as well as what working across sectors means for accountability of the partners—issues to which I will return.

Boyd-Caine's chapter has two parts to it—both seem to take a well-considered position on how to gain better sharing of power and collaborative arrangements between the public and NFP sectors and with civil society more broadly. Importantly, she emphasises the value of collaboration across sectors and with citizens in policy design and the development of policy as well as the delivery end; whenever this does not occur, I call it a 'decision-making deficit' (Edwards 2012).

The first part of the chapter, with its five themes, is the starting point for some principles about the relationship across sectors; the second part focuses on the particular advantages to both sectors of working with shared data. The availability now of large-scale digital systems and platforms has the potential to transform many aspects of the way in which governments work. A key responsibility of governments into the future is to ensure that this information and related analyses are shared with others—an important mechanism for improving power relationships across sectors.

This forum is about cross-sector workings for complex problems: climate change, Indigenous quality of life, homelessness, child abuse and domestic violence, to name just a few. In the light of such important and complex issues dominating the policy and political agendas, I want to turn to two issues I think were not well enough covered in the chapters before us.

The first issue deals with the learning that can come from close relationships across the sectors as the players together explore and experiment with what works. This is not the place to acquaint you with the experimentalist governance framework as espoused by Sabel and others (for example, Sabel and Simon 2011; de Burca et al. 2014); suffice to say, this framework emphasises several elements including participatory and deliberative as well as local processes of setting broad goals. The practice of learning is reflected in the monitoring of implementation and continuous improvement processes as well as the process of adaptive problem solving. The cooperation of civil society actors is indispensable to the success of experimentalist regimes. Although accountability is built into the framework, it is about cross-sectoral and peer learning from failures as well as successes.

The second and related issue that has not had sufficient attention to date I call the 'accountability deficit' (Edwards 2012). When sectors work together to achieve shared outcomes, it follows that attention needs to be given to shared accountabilities and how those are handled. The Australian National Audit Office (ANAO), in its recent *Public Sector Governance* better practice guide, recognises this, calling for, among other things, 'visible lines of accountability for managing multiple accountabilities' (2014: 61). A key success factor it sees for cross-entity arrangements is management of shared risks and shared accountabilities—in terms of both shared outcomes and managing collaborative efforts (for further explanation, see Edwards 2013).

Let me leave you with a big-picture idea that I would like to see gaining traction. It is a picture painted by Geoff Mulgan (2012: 20), who argues: 'in the next few years, governments should not only address trust indirectly through outputs and outcomes, but also directly, through their relationships with citizens, as well as citizens' relationships with each other.'

This would commonly entail a transformative change in government relationships, organised around relationships and acting with others rather than doing things to or for them. The general idea here is that of a 'relational state' and, hence, the concept of 'relational trust' (Mulgan 2012). This would mean governments giving more feedback, co-designing services and experimenting and innovating in the context of collaboration.

References

Australian National Audit Office (ANAO). 2014. *Public Sector Governance: Strengthening performance through good governance.* Better Practice Guide, June. Canberra: Australian National Audit Office.

Australian Public Service Commission (APSC). 2004. *Connecting Government: Whole of government responses to Australia's priority challenges.* Canberra: Australian Public Service Commission Management Advisory Committee.

Australian Public Service Commission (APSC). 2014. *State of the Service Report 2013–2014.* Canberra: Australian Government.

Behm, A. 2015. *No, Minister.* Melbourne: Melbourne University Press.

de Burca, G., R. Keohanne and C. Sabel. 2014. *Global experimentalist governance.* School of Law Working Paper 14-44, September. New York University, New York.

Edwards, M. 2012. Decision-making and accountability deficits in public governance. Presentation to United Nations Committee of Experts on Public Administration, 11th meeting, New York, April.

Edwards, M. 2013. '"Shared accountability" in service delivery: Concepts, principles and the Australian experience.' In *A UN/ INTOSAI Joint Project: Collection of Important Literature on Strengthening Capacities of Supreme Audit Institutions on the Fight against Corruption*, 317–46. New York: United Nations.

Edwards, M. and J. Langford. 2002. *New Players, Partners and Processes: A public sector without boundaries.* Canberra: National Institute for Governance, University of Canberra.

Mulgan, G. 2012. 'Government with the People: The outlines of a relational state.' In *The Relational State: How recognising the importance of human relationships could revolutionise the role of the state*, eds G. Cooke and R. Muir, 20–34. London: Institute for Public Policy Research. Available from: ippr.org/files/images/ media/files/publication/2012/11/relational-state_Nov2012_9888. pdf?noredirect=1 (accessed 22 April 2016).

Organisation for Economic Co-operation and Development (OECD). 2015. *Government at a Glance*. Paris: Organisation for Economic Cooperation and Development.

Sabel, C. and W. H. Simon. 2011. 'Minimalism and experimentalism in the administrative state.' *Georgetown Law Journal* 100: 53.

3

From New Public Management to New Public Governance: The implications for a 'new public service'

Helen Dickinson

Introduction

Rarely a day goes by without the performance of government and public services providing a topic of discussion and debate within the media. Whether this is in relation to child protection services, the quality of built infrastructure, the operation of border controls or rising healthcare costs, what is clear is that there is extensive public scrutiny of governments and the services they deliver and to a degree we have not previously seen. This greater focus on the activities of governments takes place against a background of transition. The reasons for this have been well rehearsed and relate to factors such as shifting demographic structures and disease burden, rising citizen expectations, rapid advances in technology and a host of other related challenges, all of which mean that governments are under pressure to be more efficient and effective. Reform has become a common refrain within many governments around the world in their search for new ways in which to deliver services that are less expensive and more appropriate to the wants and needs of individuals and communities.

Within this context, the reform of governance has received significant attention. Governance can, and has been, defined in any number of ways (for example, Kjaer 2004; Pierre and Peters 2000). For the purposes of this chapter, governance can be understood as the coordination of institutions and agency in a given policy area towards collective objectives. It therefore describes the division of control and patterns of interaction among key (types of) actors in that policy area. Over the past 30 years it has been argued that governance reform has been a necessary action—first, in response to the perceived failings of 'big government' and, subsequently, in response to the unanticipated consequences of the market mechanisms that were intended corrections to unwieldy government arrangements. In more recent years, the concept of new public governance (NPG) has come to the fore to describe the plural nature of the contemporary state, where multiple different actors contribute to the delivery of public services and the policymaking system. This chapter explores the purported shifts in governance forms and the degree to which these have resulted in significant changes to the practice of public services. Rhetorically speaking, it would seem that governments have gone through a period of profound governance reform; however, in practice, the impacts of this reform process are less palpable. The reality is that hybrid forms of governance prevail, with a complex overlay of different governance arrangements. This observation has significant implications for the way we organise public services and the kinds of skills and values we require of public servants. The chapter considers these implications in terms of how we might research hybrid forms, and sets out three lessons concerning the management of these arrangements in practice.

The rise of new public governance

The period from the late 1940s until the 1970s is often characterised in governance terms as being a time of hierarchy and the era of public administration (Peck and Dickinson 2008). Over time this mode was critiqued for being inefficient, consuming too much of a nation's resources and serving the interests of public service professionals rather than those of citizens. It was often perceived that tight-knit networks dominated the centre of governments, and that these were difficult to penetrate and served only the interests of a few (Dickinson 2014b). The solution to these challenges in many liberal economies was to make governments more 'businesslike' by the introduction of markets into some areas of the public sector and, in the process, 'hollowing out' government (Peters 1993). In many countries the paradigm of new public management was felt strongly as governments sought to shift governance forms away from hierarchies and towards markets (Ferlie et al. 1996). As public services started to be delivered, not just by the public sector, but also by commercial and community organisations on the basis of contracts, government started to become more fragmented. The process also resulted in the reduction of the discretion and influence of public service professionals, in turn also 'hollowing out' their role (Skelcher 2000).

Fragmentation emerged from the turn to the market, meaning that a range of organisations needed to cooperate with one another to deliver public services. In effect, the marketisation process essentially served to *multiply* the networks it was intended to replace. As Bevir and Rhodes (2011: 205) explain:

> Fragmentation created new networks but also ... increased the membership of existing networks, incorporating both the private and [the] voluntary sectors ... government swapped direct for indirect control, so that central departments are no longer either necessarily or invariably the fulcrum of a network. The government can set the limits to network actions: after all, it still funds the services. But it has also increased its dependence on multifarious networks.

A primary implication of the introduction of market forms was that there were now ever more complex processes of interactions between a range of different partners and these often had a great deal of autonomy from the state. This gave rise to a new form of governance but one 'without government' (Rhodes 1996). As Rhodes (1997: 15) explains, governance became understood as 'self-organizing [sic], inter-organisational networks' that are typically interdependent while enjoying significant autonomy from the state. Networks started to receive attention as they were viewed as a way to 'overcome the limitations of anarchic market exchange and top-down planning in an increasingly complex and global world' (Jessop 2003: 101–02). This latest shift towards networked forms of governance is largely equated with the move towards what Osborne (2006) refers to as new public governance, which has a strong focus on collaboration and horizontal ties between individuals and agencies. Table 3.1 sets out an overview of Osborne's three-stage model, characterising public administration, new public management and new public governance.

Table 3.1: Elements of new public governance, in contrast with public administration and new public management

Paradigm/key elements	Theoretical roots	Nature of the state	Focus	Emphasis	Relationship to external (non-public) organisational partners	Governance mechanism	Value base
Public administration	Political science and public policy	Unitary	How policy is made	Policy implementation	Potential elements of the policy system	Hierarchy	Public sector ethos
New public management	Economics (particularly rational/ public choice theory) and management studies	Disaggregated	Intra-organisational management	Service inputs and outputs	Independent contractors in market place	Market through traditional contracts	Competition in market context
New public governance	Organisational sociology and network theory	Plural and pluralist	Inter-organisational governance	Service processes and outcomes	Preferred suppliers and interdependent agents within ongoing relationships	Trust or relational contracts	Neo-corporatist

Source: After Osborne (2006: 383).

The account set out here is necessarily brief and has been rehearsed in a number of other settings in much detail (for example, Dickinson 2014b). To summarise the key points, the academic literature suggests what we have seen is the transformation of the state in terms of the ways in which it governs society, away from a strongly centralised executive and a controlling unified state to a fragmented and decentralised entity (Rhodes 2007).

> The predominant focus is on the increasing significance of governance through networks as an alternative to markets and hierarchy … The state, it is argued, can no longer assume a monopoly of expertise or resources necessary to govern, and must look to a plurality or interdependent institutions drawn from the public, private and voluntary sectors. (Newman 2004: 71)

In the next section, we examine the degree to which the shift from hierarchical through market to network forms of governance has been realised in practice.

A new public service?

Whether these shifts in governance forms have created a new public service is difficult to answer given that public services are continually evolving and, as Brunsson (2009) reminds us, reform is not necessarily always driven by the goal of making specific changes, but may instead be largely symbolic in nature:

> [R]eform can be regarded as part of organizational stability rather than of organizational change. Reforms are often presented as dramatic one-off changes, and they may sometimes lead to changes. But reform in itself is more often a standard repetitive activity. Reforms are routines rather than breaks in organizational life. (Brunsson 2009: 44)

Having noted this, indications seem to suggest we have not seen an expansive shift in governance forms or indeed the creation of 'new' public services (Bell and Hindmoor 2009). While there has been extensive rhetoric concerning governance shifts, the reality is that rather than seeing wholesale shifts we are faced instead with overlapping layers of different reform processes. Rather than there being a clear dominant mode of governance, we are faced with hybrid arrangements (Crouch 2005). As Brandsen et al. (2005: 750) explain, 'empirically speaking, it appears far easier to find arrangements that are hybrid or "fuzzy arrangements"'.

Jessop (2004: 66) explains that 'whilst the state may have become less hierarchical and less centralised, that trend does not necessarily exclude a continuing and central political role for nation states'. Indeed, some commentators suggest these changes could, in fact, increase the state's control over society. As Marinetto (2003: 606) argues, 'these characteristics of modern government should not be equated with the permanent paralysis of the state. Although government has been subject to restructuring, these reforms have tended to reinforce the ability of the central core to exert control.' Indeed, with fewer 'hard' levers of power, 'softer' policy instruments have become more appropriate (Pierre and Peters 2000). These are more indirect instruments of control, but arguably they are just as effective in contemporary society (see, for example, debates over notions of the role of governments in 'nudging' citizens into action: Thaler and Sunstein 2008). Although governments may no longer be directly in charge of individuals and departments, as they would be in a hierarchical arrangement, governments may still set 'the rules of the game' so that all interactions take place in the 'shadow of hierarchy' (Scharpf 1997; Jessop 2000, 2003). The state may also maintain a steering role through the use of its considerable resources (Skelcher 2000; Holliday 2000).

The analogy of a palimpsest is helpful in understanding the impact of successive governance reform processes. Originating in ancient Roman times, a palimpsest is a page that has text scraped or washed off so that it can be used for another document. In employing such an approach, the majority of text might be removed, but it is often possible to still view aspects of the previous content. Within the discipline of geography, this analogy has been used to understand landscapes. In a region where the landforms that make up the landscape are not of the same age, each successive episode of landscape change is considered to be a different 'layer', which is laid like a blanket across the surface of the landscape (Bailey 2007). This analogy is used to show that successive landscape-changing episodes may have different manifestations in time and space and can also create unequal signatures—that is, some landscapes are very sensitive to external forces, while others have changed very little over significant periods. If we extend this analogy to governance reform and public services, we find similar patterns. In some policy areas the reforms associated with public administration have stuck more firmly, while others have been more significantly impacted by NPM or NPG-type reforms. The result of this are governance landscapes that bear the markers of these successive reform efforts, presenting as different forms of hybrid arrangements that involve 'combinations of modes of governance that are temporally and contextually unique' (Skelcher et al. 2013: 2).

This section has sought to demonstrate that the reform of governance is rarely as simple or straightforward as is suggested and that layers of previous governance regimes often endure, interacting in a range of different ways. Miller et al. (2008: 944) write that 'despite the comforting demarcation of domains accomplished by words such as economy, society, technology and politics, "impurity" is the rule and hybrids are the norm'. Crouch (2005) concurs, arguing that hybrids are no longer the exception, but the norm, in advanced capitalist economies. Yet conceptually most scholars remain wedded to ideal governance forms (van der Heijden 2015), and in practice public service delivery debates fixate on long-held dualisms such as public/private, market/hierarchy and consumer/bureaucrat. This can be problematic for those acting in a hybrid world, and the next section seeks to explore ways to navigate complex contexts.

Operating in a hybrid world

To date research has not considered the unique challenges that hybridity creates in a comprehensive way, nor the demands it places on the skills and capabilities of managers and leaders (van der Heijden 2015). While there is an extensive literature that examines the skills and capabilities needed for collaboration (Sullivan et al. 2011) and boundary spanning (Williams 2012) and the various competencies needed for different forms of relationships with service providers (Alford and O'Flynn 2012), there is no coherent theoretical model that brings these together, nor guidance on what this means for the management of complex service delivery systems in practice. This section considers first how we might better understand hybrid forms through a model of decentred governance and then sets out three areas that are helpful to consider in thinking about navigating hybridity: changing relationships; value and values; and workforce capacities and capabilities.

Decentred governance

In the governance literature, Bevir and Rhodes (for example, 2003, 2006, 2011) have argued that what is needed is a decentred account of the state. They concur with the view that governance processes are not clear-cut, are more complex than the mainstream literature would suggest and, 'if governance is constructed differently, contingently and continuously, we cannot have a tool kit for managing it' (Rhodes 2007: 1257). They argue that, to date, governance theories have attempted to identify essential properties and then imply that these must be general and characteristic of all cases of governance. Yet such a perspective makes sense only if we consider that government has some sort of essence that exists in a real, ontological sense. A decentred position moves away from this perspective, arguing that essentialist structures are not what is important, but rather the understandings and meanings that individuals attach to actions, practices and institutions (Rhodes 2007).

Practically, what these arguments mean for the everyday operation of public services is that we need to move from thinking about reform and change being driven primarily through structural factors and focus more on the personal agency of actors. As Newman (2001: 20) explains, 'theories of governance that focus on self-steering capacities of networks and partnerships tend to marginalise issues of agency and individual, institutional and state power'. Within the decentred account of governance, agency and micro-institutional factors are viewed with far more importance than simply macro-level structures. As such, we cannot treat individuals as unitary subjects or culture as undifferentiated. A decentred analysis instead:

> Places agency and meaning at the heart of network governance. It focuses on the diverse practices of governance, practices that are themselves composed of multiple individuals acting on changing webs of beliefs rooted in overlapping traditions. Patterns of governance arise as the contingent products of diverse actions and political struggles informed by the beliefs of agents as they arise in the context of traditions. This approach focuses on beliefs and ideas, on the games people play, and on the role of both in explaining how the practices of network governance change. (Rhodes 2007: 1252)

While a decentred approach acknowledges there have been changes in terms of the dominant modes of governance, it does not characterise this as a unilateral change that has been experienced in the same way by all people. Patterns of rule are understood to emerge from a range of diverse actions and political struggles. Agents confront dilemmas that are brought about in the course of everyday life when beliefs are encountered that contrast with their own. These dilemmas push people into reconsidering their own beliefs, which gives rise to rival positions and the reformation of governance.

A decentred approach focuses on the importance of narratives and stories, rather than simply macro-structures of governance (Bevir and Rhodes 2006). Rhodes (2007) goes as far as to suggest that we should give up the search for management techniques and strategies for practice and instead tell and listen to stories: 'a decentred approach focuses on the social construction of patterns of rule through the ability of individuals to create meanings in action' (Bevir and Rhodes 2011: 209). Such a change involves moving attention away from institutions, structures and social logics and replacing 'aggregate concepts that refer to objectified social laws with narratives that explain actions by relating them to the beliefs and desires that produce them' (Bevir and Rhodes 2011: 210). The focus of research therefore moves away from the state and instead focuses on 'a diverse range of agencies, apparatuses and practices producing varied mechanisms of control and varied forms of knowledge that make areas or aspects of social life available for governmental action' (Finlayson and Martin 2006: 167).

Changing relationships

The above discussion offers some sense of how we might go about researching governance forms, but offers little for individuals and organisations managing complex hybrid governance forms in practice. A first lesson to consider in managing hybrid governance arrangements is that the days of certainty and stability are long gone. What singular macro-governance structures give are a sense of stability and the rules of the game at any one time. Operating in a hybrid context means there may be multiple and conflicting systems interacting with one another at any time. Before reflecting on this further, it is important to acknowledge that uncertainty is not a new thing and it is highly unlikely there was ever such a thing as a time of certainty for all.

There is often a tendency to romanticise the past and remember aspects of context that were never really true of particular periods and then to bemoan the loss of particular aspects that never were. Relationships between individuals and/or groups are rarely static and the kinds of mechanisms that are used to govern these links will invariably change over time. What may be the issue in this case is the magnitude of changes to relationships.

At present there is significant debate concerning the relationship between the state, civil society and community organisations. Community organisations are facing increased pressure to demonstrate their value as governments move away from grant-based systems of funding towards contracting for particular services. This is not a new phenomenon by any degree, but arguably has become more pressing in recent months with the rise of the commissioning agenda (Dickinson 2014c) and initiatives such as the National Disability Insurance Scheme (Dickinson et al. 2015). Some in the community sector have argued that these changes are fundamentally detrimental to the nature and existence of the sector. As an example of this, in a speech, the Chief Executive of the Brotherhood of St Laurence, Tony Nicholson (2014), argued that 'in the next year or two decisions will be made about' the community welfare sector 'that in all likelihood will be irrevocable. I fear if the wrong decisions are taken, they will inevitably lead to the erosion of what our voluntary organisations have stood for [for] over a century.' The idea that we can know what might constitute 'right' and 'wrong' decisions in this context is a difficult one given that the community sector has always comprised a range of different individuals, groups, interests, values and world views, making it difficult for the sector to hold one consistent and comprehensive perspective on any range of issues (Alcock 2010).

The idea that the relationship between the community sector and the state has been static for the previous 30 years seems to be at odds with the lived experience of most. As Rob Macmillan (2013) argues, the relationship between different actors and agencies is always in flux and is highly contingent on the kinds of changes and events taking place in broader society. Relationships are not fixed, but are constantly in a process of negotiation and renegotiation at a micro level, with structural and macro-governance forces explaining only some of the shifts in the parameters of these relationships. At some times this change is more noticeable than the general day-to-day change, and Macmillan refers to these times as a period of great unsettlement, when there is a more rapid wholesale change across a sector. The analogy of an earthquake is helpful in thinking about this. The Earth's shell is divided into a number of tectonic plates that glide over the mantel (the rocky inner layer just above the core). Most of the time, these plates move past one another without us noticing, but the stress that builds up over time eventually leads to an earthquake, which can unleash significant damage. Similarly, the boundaries between the various sectors are often in flux, but we may not always recognise this until there is a significant shift. Those on the boundaries may feel this more intensely than those who are further away from the epicentre and will often live with foreshocks or aftershocks from this boundary shift.

Building on the earthquake analogy, we might suggest that relationships between government and the community sector in Victoria are either in the wake of this sort of earthquake event or just on the cusp. Similar sorts of debates and tensions are also taking place in other jurisdictions, and these periods of great upheaval have also existed historically (Macmillan and Buckingham 2013). No doubt this is a difficult time for many in the community welfare sector, but not all community organisations will react in the same way to these changes, and nor should they. This is a diverse sector and we should celebrate this, even if this does make it somewhat difficult to 'steer' at times. In times of change there are always opportunities for agency, no matter how small. Earthquakes, of course, are rarely good things for those in affected areas in the short term, although some positives have been drawn from recent experiences in New Zealand and also Haiti. It is often a time of rebuilding, and community cohesion emerges in overcoming adversity. Where earthquakes are minor, it can remind people of the importance of making sure that structures are able to withstand possible further shocks. Just because there has been an earthquake it does not mean the tectonic plates stop moving, and the relationship between sectors will always be in a process of negotiation in a similar way. We should not take stability for granted and should therefore always be prepared for potential change.

Value and values

If we do not have consistency in terms of governance and relationships between sectors, the issue of value and values becomes incredibly important in navigating hybridity. Value typically refers to the worth or the impact of a particular activity or initiative (Dickinson 2008). Values refer to the subjectively held norms or principles of individuals or groups (Bozeman 2007).

Many argue that community sector organisations are values based and this influences how they conduct activities and make decisions (Westall 2009). Being clear about the kinds of values that underpin different sorts of activities and the ways different groups add value to processes may help us navigate hybridity in practice. Of course, this is easy to say and sometimes more challenging to do, and the current focus on commissioning and associated contracting processes is forcing community organisations to think about the value they produce and to be mindful of straying too far from their initial values. In practice, values and value creation may be connected. When we focus on the types of value produced, we need to be cognisant that, if values are part of that creation process, the ways in which community sector organisations and government interact do not undermine this. For example, it has been argued that delivering services under contract with government has led to 'mission drift', where organisations have moved away from activity that has previously been their core concern (Greer and Horst 2014), thus presenting a challenge to their values. Where community organisations can be clear about their values and strengths, they are able to challenge issues that are not appropriate and advocate on behalf of their communities. Community organisations need not be 'policy victims', but for this to be achieved there needs to be constructive dialogue on all sides and not just finger pointing (Dickinson 2014a).

There are various forms of value that are created by the community sector, but comparing forms of value is challenging as we often lack the metrics or techniques for comparison. Deciding the most important forms on which to focus requires negotiation and discussion to reach some form of resolution (Trainor 2006). It is important to note that specific forms of value are not an innate trait of a particular organisational form or sector. While there is lots of attention given to the notion that community sector organisations create particular forms of value, or that they hold unique sets of value, this is not necessarily the case. This means that neither specific organisational forms nor specific sectors hold a natural advantage in creating specific forms of value. Recent research from social care services in the United Kingdom suggests that rather than the sector within which an organisation resides being the most important factor in driving performance, the size of the organisation makes an important contribution, with micro-providers offering the potential to provide more personalised support than larger providers (Needham et al. 2015).

While formal governance processes are clearly important in terms of influencing the ways in which organisations behave, they also signal to individuals and groups what is to be valued within that setting. It has been shown repeatedly that organisations respond to stimuli in their environment and that, in commissioning processes and service design processes, government must be cognisant of how incentives influence action. It cannot be assumed that community sector organisations will always create particular forms of value; the environment within which they operate matters and shapes roles, behaviour and characteristics. For example, if more market-based models are used, and incentives geared towards satisfying self-interest are embedded, it is no surprise that community sector organisations may begin to behave more like what we would expect from private sector organisations (Alford and O'Flynn 2012). It is also the case that the lines of demarcation between government, business and the community sector are blurring under a new order 'where the private sector practises social responsibility and states seek to be more entrepreneurial, while community organisations become more and more business-like' (Smyth 2014: 2). What this means for commissioning processes is being explicit about the particular sorts of value we seek to reach the desired community outcomes. It is also critical for government to be clear about the forms of value it seeks when undertaking service delivery design processes, to ensure it does not create incentives that will focus providers away from the value that is needed to produce outcomes.

Workforce competency and capacity

The final lesson in navigating hybridity relates to the competencies and capacities of workforces. In terms of the skill sets and capabilities of public servants, Alford and O'Flynn (2012) argue that the effective management of different relational forms draws on sets of competencies that are very different to those that are traditionally thought to be central to public services. This was clearly illustrated in recent research by Dickinson and Sullivan (2014), drawing on research into Australian public services, but is also reflected in the broader literature (Needham et al. 2014) and UK-based research (Needham and Mangan 2014). These various investigations suggest that public services typically recruit for quite traditional sets of skills and capabilities—often related to professional roles. Yet, in navigating complex hybrid systems, there is a series of 'softer' and more relational skills required of the workforce, such as the ability to communicate narratives effectively, collaborate, critically analyse multiple forms of evidence, coproduction skills and international literacies. While elements of these are present in the existing system, this is often despite recruitment and development processes, rather than because of them.

What this means in practice is that public and community organisations alike need to pay close attention to the skills and capabilities of their workforce in a strategic sense. Typically, workforces have been built up over time by recruiting to particular programs and services without thinking about the workforce's capacity and capability in a broader way. A number of different commentators have argued for a return to more traditional values of government, albeit with a new emphasis.

Geoff Mulgan (2012: 21) speaks of the relational state, which 'connects back to the longstanding concern of governments of all kinds to retain and grow public trust. But in other respects it is new, a product of specific 21st-century circumstances that are forcing governments to attend much more systematically to the quality of their relationships with citizens.' Rod Rhodes (2014) similarly argues for the importance of human facets of managing and that public administrators need to rediscover the 'craft' of this endeavour. Most commentators agree that now and in the future it will not be sufficient for governments and third-party providers of government services to focus on measures of efficiency and effectiveness, and careful consideration will need to be given to the relational aspects of service delivery (Dickinson 2014b). Moreover, evidence from the United Kingdom suggests that successful commissioning lies not simply in contracting abilities, but also in market stewardship (Livingstone and Macmillan 2015), working collaboratively with providers (Miller and Rees 2014) and developing legitimacy in the eyes of a range of different constituencies (Dickinson et al. 2010). Taken together, these tasks suggest that we may need to think about recruitment, management and development of workforces in both public and private sectors in rather different ways if we are to enable individuals to develop and use these kinds of skills.

Conclusions

The academic literature on the reform of governance offers a compelling narrative of government and public services, suggesting that traditional hierarchical arrangements have, over time, been replaced with more effective and efficient mechanisms of governance. The rather simplistic argument suggests that market forces were introduced to overcome the inherent limitations of hierarchies. When the inevitable limitations of markets eventuated, a discourse of networks and NPG emerged ostensibly to counter these challenges. This chapter has explored the experience of this transition in governance arrangements to examine whether the reality of this transition has kept pace with the rhetoric. It finds that the transition between governance arrangements is rarely as clear-cut and straightforward as the academic literature typically presents it to be. Rather than a wholesale shift to new governance regimes, what happens in practice is that a rather more complex picture emerges of hybrid arrangements comprising features of different forms of governance systems at the same time. Yet, despite hybridity being a relatively well-established concept in the literature, we still lack effective theorisation of this and detail concerning how to navigate the complexities that this produces or the implications for the kinds of skills and abilities that public servants require to operate within this context. There are, however, lessons that we might take from the literature such as moving away from certainties, understanding the importance of values and paying close attention to the skills and capabilities of the workforce. While there are no easy answers when it comes to issues of managing hybridity, paying attention to these factors ultimately affords greater agency and a sense of humanity to the delivery of public services.

References

Alcock, P. 2010. *Partnership and mainstreaming: Voluntary action under New Labour*. Working Paper 32. Third Sector Research Centre, Birmingham, UK.

Alford, J. and J. O'Flynn. 2012. *Rethinking Public Services: Managing with external providers*. Basingstoke, UK: Palgrave Macmillan.

Bailey, G. 2007. 'Time perspectives, palimpsests and the archaeology of time.' *Journal of Anthropological Archaeology* 26: 198–223.

Bell, S. and A. Hindmoor. 2009. *Rethinking Governance: The centrality of the state in modern society*. Cambridge: Cambridge University Press.

Bevir, M. and R. A. W. Rhodes. 2003. *Interpreting British Governance*. London: Routledge.

Bevir, M. and R. A. W. Rhodes. 2006. *Governance Stories*. London: Routledge.

Bevir, M. and R. A. W. Rhodes. 2011. 'The stateless state.' In *The SAGE Handbook of Governance*, ed. M. Bevir, 203–17. London: Sage.

Bozeman, B. 2007. *Public Values and Public Interest: Counterbalancing economic individualism*. Washington, DC: Georgetown University Press.

Brandsen, T., W. van de Donk and K. Putters. 2005. 'Griffins or chameleons? Hybridity as a permanent and inevitable characteristic of the third sector.' *International Journal of Public Administration* 28: 749–65.

Brunsson, N. 2009. *Reform as Routine: Organizational change and stability in the modern world*. Oxford: Oxford University Press.

Crouch, C. 2005. *Capitalist Diversity and Change: Recombinant governance and institutional entrepreneurs*. Oxford: Oxford University Press.

Dickinson, H. 2008. *Evaluating Outcomes in Health and Social Care*. Bristol: Policy Press.

Dickinson, H. 2014a. Blog. powertopersuade.org.au.

Dickinson, H. 2014b. *Performing Governance: Partnerships, culture and New Labour*. Basingstoke, UK: Palgrave Macmillan.

Dickinson, H. 2014c. 'Public service commissioning: What can be learned from the UK experience?' *Australian Journal of Public Administration* 73(1): 14.

Dickinson, H. and H. Sullivan. 2014. *Imagining the 21st Century Public Service Workforce*. Melbourne: School of Government, University of Melbourne.

Dickinson, H., E. Peck, J. Durose and E. Wade. 2010. 'The role of cultural performance in health care commissioning.' In *Culture and Climate in Health Care Organizations*, eds J. Braithwaite, P. Hyde and C. Pope, 196–207. Basingstoke, UK: Palgrave Macmillan.

Dickinson, H., H. Sullivan and C. Needham. 2015. 'Self-directed care funding: What are the implications for accountability?' *Australian Journal of Public Administration* 73(4): 417–25.

Ferlie, E., L. Ashburner, L. Fitzgerald and A. Pettrigrew. 1996. *The New Public Management in Action*. Oxford: Oxford University Press.

Finlayson, A. and J. Martin. 2006. 'Post-structuralism.' In *The State: Theory and issues*, eds C. Hay, M. Lister and D. Marsh, 155–71. Basingstoke, UK: Palgrave Macmillan.

Greer, P. and C. Horst. 2014. *Mission Drift: The unspoken crisis facing leaders, charities and churches*. Ada, Mich.: Bethany House Publishers.

Holliday, I. 2000. 'Is the British state hollowing out?' *Political Quarterly* 71: 167–76.

Jessop, B. 2000. 'Governance failure.' In *The New Politics of British Local Governance*, ed. G. Stoker, 11–32. Basingstoke, UK: Macmillan.

Jessop, B. 2003. 'Governance and meta-governance: On reflexivity, requisite variety and requisite irony.' In *Governance as Social and Political Communication*, ed. H. Bang, 101–16. Manchester: Manchester University Press.

Jessop, B. 2004. 'Multi-level governance and multi-level metagovernance: Changes in the European Union as integral moments in transformation and reorientation of contemporary statehood.' In *Multi-Level Governance*, eds I. Bache and M. Flinders, 49–74. Oxford: Oxford University Press.

Kjaer, A. M. 2004. *Governance*. Cambridge: Polity Press.

Livingstone, I. and R. Macmillan. 2015. 'More than a provider: The voluntary sector, commissioning and stewardship for a diverse market in criminal justice.' *Voluntary Sector Review* 6(2): 221–30.

Macmillan, R. 2013. 'De-coupling the state and the third sector? The "big society" as a spontaneous order.' *Voluntary Sector Review* 4(2): 185–203.

Macmillan, R. and H. Buckingham. 2013. 'A strategic lead for the third sector? Some may lead, but not all will ever follow.' In *Third sector futures dialogues*. Big Picture Paper 5. Third Sector Research Centre, Birmingham, UK.

Marinetto, M. 2003. 'Governing beyond the centre: A critique of the Anglo-governance school.' *Political Studies* 51(3): 592–608.

Miller, P., L. Kurunmäki and T. O'Leary. 2008. 'Accounting, hybrids and the management of risk.' *Accounting, Organizations and Society* 33: 942–67.

Miller, R. and J. Rees. 2014. 'Mental health commissioning: Master or subject of change?' *Mental Health Review* 19(3): 145–55.

Mulgan, G. 2012. 'Government with the people: The outlines of a relational state.' In *The Relational State*, eds G. Cooke and R. Muir, 20–34. London: Institute for Public Policy Research.

Needham, C. and C. Mangan. 2014. *The 21st Century Public Servant*. Birmingham, UK: University of Birmingham.

Needham, C., K. Allen, K. Hall, S. McKay, J. Glasby, S. Carr, R. Littlechild and D. Tanner. 2015. *Micro-enterprises: Small enough to care?* Birmingham, UK: University of Birmingham.

Needham, C., C. Mangan and H. Dickinson. 2014. *The 21st Century Public Service Workforce: Eight lessons from the literature.* Birmingham, UK: University of Birmingham.

Newman, J. 2001. *Modernising Governance: New Labour, policy and society.* London: Sage.

Newman, J. 2004. 'Modernizing the state: A new form of governance?' In *Remaking Governance: Peoples, politics and the public sphere,* ed. J. Newman, 119–38. Bristol: The Policy Press.

Nicholson, T. 2014. The future of the community welfare sector. Speech, 27 May 2014. Available from: library.bsl.org.au/jspui/handle/1/5804 (accessed 18 August 2015).

Osborne, S. P. 2006. 'The new public governance?' *Public Management Review* 8(3): 377–87.

Peck, E. and H. Dickinson. 2008. *Managing and Leading in Inter-Agency Settings.* Bristol: Policy Press.

Peters, B. G. 1993. 'Managing the hollow state.' In *Managing Public Organizations: Lessons from contemporary European experience,* eds K. A. Eliassen and J. Kooiman. London: Sage.

Pierre, J. and B. G. Peters. 2000. *Governance, Politics and the State.* Basingstoke, UK: Macmillan.

Rhodes, R. A. W. 1996. 'The new governance: Governing without government.' *Political Studies* 44(4): 652–67.

Rhodes, R. A. W. 1997. *Understanding Governance: Policy networks, governance, reflexivity and accountability.* Buckingham, UK: Open University Press.

Rhodes, R. A. W. 2007. 'Understanding governance: Ten years on.' *Organization Studies* 28: 1243–64.

Rhodes, R. A. W. 2014. Recovering the 'craft' of public administration in network governance. Plenary Address to the International Political Science Association World Congress, Montreal, 19–24 July. Available from: raw-rhodes.co.uk/wp-content/uploads/2014/07/Rhodes-2014-IPSA-Craft-Governance-final.pdf (accessed 22 August 2014).

Scharpf, F. W. 1997. *Games Real Actors Play. Actor-centred institutionalism in policy research*. Boulder, Colo.: Westview Press.

Skelcher, C. 2000. 'Changing images of the state: Overloaded, hollowed-out, congested.' *Public Policy and Administration* 15(3): 3–19.

Skelcher, C., H. Sullivan and S. Jeffares. 2013. *Hybrid Governance in European Cities: Neighbourhood, migration and democracy*. Basingstoke, UK: Palgrave Macmillan.

Smyth, P. 2014. The Lady Vanishes: Australia's disappearing voluntary sector. Seminar given at the Brotherhood of St Laurence, Melbourne, 14 August. Available from: library.bsl.org.au/jspui/bitstream/1/6511/1/Smyth_The_lady_vanishes_Australias_disappearing_voluntary_sector_paper_14Aug2014.pdf (accessed 6 October 2014).

Sullivan, H., P. Williams and S. Jeffares. 2011. 'Leadership for collaboration: Situated agency in practice.' *Public Management Review* 14(1): 41–66.

Thaler, R. H. and C. R. Sunstein. 2008. *Nudge: Improving decisions about health, wealth and happiness*. London: Yale University Press.

Trainor, S. F. 2006. 'Realms of value: Conflicting natural resource values and incommensurability.' *Environmental Values* 15(1): 3–29.

van der Heijden, J. 2015. 'Interacting state and non-state actors in hybrid settings of public service delivery.' *Administration & Society* 47(2): 99–121.

Westall, A. 2009. *Value and the third sector: Working paper on ideas for future research*. Working Paper 25. Third Sector Research Centre, Birmingham, UK.

Williams, P. 2012. *Collaboration in Public Policy and Practice: Perspectives on boundary spanners*. Bristol: Policy Press.

4

Partnerships between Government and the Third Sector at a Subnational Level: The experience of an Australian subnational government

David J. Gilchrist

Introduction

Since World War II and the establishment of the Welfare State in countries influenced by the United Kingdom, including Australia, government has used not-for-profits (NFPs) or the NFP sector to deliver services associated with much of its social policy. While the extent of this phenomenon has waxed and waned in accordance with the political philosophy of each successive party in government, the delivery of services via this sector has been increasing, particularly since the 1980s, and is a source of considerable political angst (Mendes 2008; Productivity Commission 2010).

Primarily, this angst arises because governments wish to continue to provide services via the NFP sector but also reduce expenditure, control service delivery and retain the political capital derived from such activities. On the other hand, NFPs struggle constantly with poor resourcing, increasing pressure from governments to perform more with less, the provision of services in accordance with their mission, mission creep caused by funder priorities and, sometimes, religious and other drivers (Salamon 1995; Frumkin 2002; Barraket 2008). Overall, Young (2006), in discussing the US experience, identifies that NFPs can have several relationships with government at once, neatly identifying them as adversarial, complementary or supplementary. This complexity ensures there is constant tension between governments and NFPs.

The Australian experience is somewhat similar and there has been a constant drive to find an arrangement for improving the government–NFP relationship in the interests of achieving better outcomes for communities. Reverting to received wisdoms as they might be from time to time, at the highest level, concepts such as government–NFP partnerships, market-based economic solutions and private sector financing options have all been considered (Garton 2009; McGregor-Lowndes 2008; Roth 2011; Center for Law and Social Policy 2014). Emphasising the importance of the NFP–government relationship, these ideas have been implemented and examined at the highest levels, including formal parliamentary examinations (see, for example, OAG WA 1998, 2000, 2003, 2012, 2013a, 2013b; PAC WA 2000; VAGO 2013).

This debate has most recently seen the manifestation of the Delivering Community Services in Partnership (DCSP) Policy in Western Australia, a small state by population if not by geographic size in the Australian federation. It is this policy, and the author's longitudinal evaluation of the outcomes achieved to date under the policy, that is the central focus of this chapter. Further, the research itself uniquely evaluates both the government side of the DCSP Policy and the NFP sector side so a more holistic view of the impact of the DCSP can be understood. While comments are made here relating to the government side, it is in fact the NFP side that is primarily evaluated in this chapter due to space constraints—the government side being evaluated in future outputs.

This chapter is divided into five sections. In section two, I review the DCSP Policy and identify its major elements. In section three, I provide an overview of the review methodology, and in section four, I discuss the findings. Section five consists of concluding remarks.

The DCSP Policy

In Western Australia, in 2011, the state government issued the DCSP (WA Government 2011). This policy was arrived at after the incoming Barnett Government (elected in 2008) implemented an audit of all government activity and expenditure. The resulting audit report identified a number of recommendations pertaining to the NFP sector and its relationship with government (Economic Audit Committee 2009).

Of the Economic Audit Committee's major findings, those most important to the NFP sector included (paraphrased and condensed):

1. That the NFP sector is best placed to provide services to the community.
2. As such, government should pass more services over to the sector.
3. Such services should be purchased via the identification of a supplier-sustainable price.
4. Services should be funded by individually recognising resources allocated to recipients (individualised funding).
5. Recipients should have control over purchase decisions and the services they receive (person-centred care).
6. The administrative burden created by contracting processes should be minimised.
7. The evaluation of programs and funding should be undertaken via the examination of outcomes rather than outputs.

The DCSP Policy was developed such that it encapsulated the principles above. It was implemented after the establishment of the Partnership Forum comprising NFP representatives and senior public sector personnel. This forum continues to meet regularly and subgroups of its members have been created to review certain aspects of the implementation of the policy, including identification of outcomes.

The government instructed all of its agencies involved in the provision of funding to, or service procurement from, NFPs for service delivery to implement the requirements of the policy. It also established a unit within the Department of Finance with responsibility for oversight of the transition, to provide training and resources to both the public and the NFP sectors to support implementation, and to provide ad hoc advice. The Forum established a subgroup focused on the evaluation of the implementation of the DCSP Policy.

Commensurate with the audit committee's findings and the DCSP Policy's prescription of maintaining a supplier-sustainable price for service purchases, the WA Government provided top-up funding to meet systemic underfunding identified via the Partnership Forum. It made provision in the 2010–11 and 2011–12 state budgets for $600 million in additional funding in two tranches, Component I and Component II (Gilchrist and Knight 2013b). Component I was paid during the 2011–12 and 2012–13 financial years. Component II was paid during the 2013–14 financial year.

Critically, the Parliament required the government to undertake an evaluation of the DCSP Policy annually for five years, and this chapter reports the first three years of evaluation findings—relative principally to the NFP side—of that evaluation carried out by the author.

Review methodology and response rates

As described above, the DCSP Policy is to be reviewed annually for five years beginning in 2012. To date, the author has completed three reviews, one each for 2012, 2013 and 2014 (Gilchrist 2013; Gilchrist and Knight 2013b; Knight and Gilchrist 2015). Each review is undertaken and a report created that is, initially, provided to the Partnership Forum and then published. Typically, these reports have been published quite late in the year of evaluation or early the next year. The results of the 2014 evaluation are the ones explored in this chapter as these encapsulate the 2012 and 2013 results, compare the three years and provide a longitudinal view.

The evaluation consisted of two main tasks. NFPs that had service agreements based on the new policy and which received Component I funding were surveyed. We also surveyed and interviewed state government agencies that administer contracts for community services provided by the NFP sector. In other words, the research focused on both the commissioners and the service providers in an attempt to assess the full implementation effects. All research activities were undertaken after meeting Curtin University's ethics policies and processes, and after achieving an ethics clearance.

Overall, the adoption of the DCSP Policy was intended to increase the sustainability of the NFP sector, reduce the administrative burden and build capacity for increased work to be transferred from the government sector to the NFP sector. As such, the evaluation process was aimed at assessing, on an annual basis, the extent to which the above had been achieved. Therefore, in undertaking the review of the DCSP Policy, focus was placed on outcomes achieved in relation to the following areas, which were also the central focus of the policy itself:

1. sustainability;
2. DCSP Policy implementation (principally in relation to the establishment of outcomes-based contracts and increased service delivery); and
3. the impact of the DCSP Policy on NFPs and government agencies.

State government agency interviews and surveys

A unique aspect of this research program was the fact that the examination considered both NFPs commissioned by government agencies and the commissioning agencies themselves. While it is reiterated that this chapter focuses on the NFP side of the research program, this section very briefly describes the research methodology employed in examining the commissioning government agencies applying the DCSP Policy, to place the results of the research pertaining to the NFP sector in context, and to better explain and demonstrate the findings associated with the NFP sector.

The methodology employed in 2012 in evaluating the government agencies was different to that employed in 2013 and 2014. In 2012 a questionnaire/data-collection tool was sent to each agency to establish a baseline in terms of contract numbers, NFP numbers and identity, values of contracts, service types and so on. Once these data were collected and analysed, a semistructured interview was undertaken with the seven government agencies that commissioned the majority of contracts involving NFP human service delivery. Indeed, the seven agencies making up this group accounted for 94 per cent of the value of commissioned contracts with the NFP sector and 87 per cent of the number of contracts. These interviews examined topics associated with the DCSP Policy such as the extent to which the policy had been implemented, the issues raised on the government side as a result and the extent to which outcomes could be identified, and contracts developed based on them.

NFP survey

After the initial identification of relevant NFPs as a result of the first year's research involving government agencies, each year from 2012 key state government agencies were requested by Treasury to provide a current list of email addresses for the chief executive or key contact within each funded NFP organisation commissioned to provide services on behalf of the state government, and which had also received Component I of increased funding. These lists were de-duplicated by the research team and, in 2012, resulted in a list of 486 individual NFP organisations together with the name and contact details of their representative. For longitudinal consistency and research efficacy, these 486 NFPs became the survey population for each of the following evaluation years. It must be acknowledged at the outset, however, that it proved difficult to maintain total consistency in the population set due, primarily, to immature data collection and contract management systems within government. The substantive population group was, however, maintained.

For the first evaluation, a questionnaire was developed and approved by the Partnership Forum working group subgroup. In relation to that first evaluation, the Partnership Forum subgroup also approved a covering email to be sent to respondents describing the purpose of the survey and containing a link to the questionnaire. The questionnaire was uploaded into Qualtrics survey software and tested with a small number of representatives of NFP organisations to check structure, terminology, flow and technical aspects. Subsequent questionnaires were simply sent to the original survey population via an email from Treasury but always after being tested.

Essentially, this process was carried out each subsequent year, although the Partnership Forum and the Partnership Forum subgroup were not engaged in the survey confirmation process or communications with the NFPs after the first year. The survey questions were retained for the 2013 and 2014 iterations, though the original survey had questions added focusing on growth and confidence in 2013 and these were also retained in 2014. These questions allowed for a deeper analysis to be undertaken and returned important data focused on the trajectory of likely change in the structure of the NFP sector.

In each of the evaluation years 2012 and 2013, the population of 486 NFPs which had contracts for human service delivery with the state government and which received Component I were forwarded an email incorporating a link to a Qualtrics survey, which included an ethics statement and confirmation of willingness to participate.

In October 2014, a similar covering email was distributed to the population of 437 NFPs remaining of the original 486. The fall-off in numbers resulted from organisations discontinuing the provision of services commissioned by the state government. Similarly to the previous two years, in 2014 the email contained an individualised link to the survey. This approach ensured that only one response was received per organisation and only those organisations in the sample would be included in the results. The senior most person in the targeted NFP was asked to respond.

As the NFP respondents have an important, long-term relationship with government through the agencies that purchase services from them, and because the subject of the survey was considered highly topical, it was expected that all or nearly all NFP organisations would respond. A full response is also important in supporting our ability to understand the overall demographics of the sector, and as the basis for monitoring the impact of the reforms on all NFPs over time.

In each year, however, the response rate was less than expected. The final rate achieved in 2014 for total responses was 34.55 per cent—down from 48.56 per cent in 2012 and a high of 48.97 per cent in 2013. In 2014, of the 437 emails distributed, 151 NFPs responded: 138 or 91.39 per cent completed the survey in full; another 13 or 8.61 per cent submitted a partial response. The final sample included in the survey and summarised in the report was therefore variable, with a minimum sample size of 167. The year-on-year response rates are provided in Table 4.1.

Table 4.1: Year-on-year response rates

Evaluation	2012	2013	2014
Survey date	November 2012	September 2013	October 2014
Population	486	486	437
Survey respondents	236	238	151
Percentage of population responded	48.56%	48.97%	34.55%
Completed responses	181	167	138
Percentage completed responses	76.69%	70.17%	91.39%
Partial responses	55	71	13
Percentage partial completions	23.31%	29.83%	8.61%

Source: Author's compilation.

While the response rates were not as high as expected, they are sufficient for a reliable interpretation of the results. Completed survey responses declined from 236 in 2012 to 151 in 2014, while the population was reduced by 10.1 per cent due to the fact that 49 NFPs were no longer being commissioned. As the government did not want to make responses mandatory, the survey relied on the goodwill of the sector to respond. Likely causes of the declining response rate between 2012 and 2014 include that the sector has been the target of considerable research in recent history and 'respondent exhaustion' is likely to have ensured smaller response and completion rates. Further, it may be the case that the initial burst of enthusiasm accompanying the launch of the DCSP Policy had faded by 2014 and the sector may have had insufficient interest in the policy such that responding to the survey was lower in the priorities of senior managers.

Further, there was a rise in response rates and completion rates in 2013. This can be explained by the fact that, in 2012, relatively few contracts were established under the DCSP Policy (Gilchrist 2013: 23), while in 2013 agencies reported that 367 of the 1,373 contracts with NFPs were established under the policy and both agencies and NFPs were reporting that administration impacts were considerable, as was the complexity of contracting under the DCSP Policy, primarily due to the requirement to contract for outcomes rather than outputs (Gilchrist and Knight 2014: 41–42, 45). It is likely that the DCSP Policy was impacting on NFPs in a practical way in 2014, and the challenges that had incentivised NFPs to respond to the survey previously to ensure their frustrations were recorded were less of a dominating factor by the end of 2014.

Limitations on the interpretation of findings

There were no data on the total population of contracting NFP organisations regarding turnover, employment, sector of operation or location. As such, it is not possible to determine whether the 2012, 2013 or 2014 surveys fully reflected the state government-funded sector in its entirety. The organisations that responded to the survey in each year have similar profiles in terms of turnover and location of service delivery, but differ in total employment and sector of operation. For instance, 64 organisations were identified as having responded to both the 2012 and the 2013 surveys. The differences in the survey samples were taken into consideration in the analysis. The government agencies responding to the survey are considered to be reflective of the impact of the DCSP Policy on government agencies primarily because they undertake the majority of such activity.

Findings

In considering the findings, I have presented the survey results for each sector below in consecutive subsections and then provided concluding remarks in the next section. Suffice to say, the results reported here constitute the most significant findings and a number of minor or lesser results have been left out due to space limitations. The primary results reported are those for 2014, with comparatives for previous years considered where useful to the reader in understanding the trajectory of change or the results reported. I begin with some high-level results pertaining to the government side to place the following NFP results in context.

DCSP Policy implementation: A brief comment on the government side

In 2014, 13 state government agencies were invited to participate in the evaluation (seven in 2012; 13 in 2013) and 12 responded (seven in 2012; 11 in 2013). The 2014 respondents accounted for 99 per cent of the

$1.428 billion in 2014–15 estimated contract value and for 98 per cent of relevant contracts. Agencies reported that there were approximately 200 full-time equivalent positions working in procurement—up from 164.5 in 2012.[1] The procurement and contract management databases used by agencies varied in their capacity to provide information. The total number of service agreements was reported as 1,443, but this was not consistent with other data provided and is unlikely to be comparable with the 2012 total reported of 994.[2] The use of preferred service provider (PSP) status (requiring less ongoing administrative activity) varied from zero to 100 per cent depending on the agency. Based on the information provided in 2014, 65 per cent of service agreements were established on a PSP basis. Further, 963 contracts were reported as being compliant with the DCSP Policy compared with 367 in 2013.

In implementing a more balanced contracting framework, the DCSP Policy also requires agencies to establish longer-term contracts to give NFPs confidence and longevity of funding and to reduce administrative burden. The survey results identified that nearly all service agreements were for periods of three years or longer. The 2014 survey identified that the intention of agencies was, by and large, to extend these contract periods to reduce the administrative burden attendant on recontracting processes. Some 43 per cent of contracts were three to five years in length, while 11 per cent were reported as extending beyond five years.

Results: NFP sustainability

In assessing sustainability, the DCSP Policy was evaluated in terms of employment numbers, investment capacity and investment, and new employment intention. Given that part of the purpose of the DCSP Policy is to maintain and enhance sustainability via the provision of a sustainable price, the evaluation of employment numbers, investment capacity and confidence, as represented by intention to invest, are all indicators of longitudinal improvement or decline in organisations' perspectives of their sustainability.

---

1   This excludes staff not attached to central procurement offices or working only occasionally in procurement as part of their other duties.
2   For instance, Treasury reported 1,546 relevant agreements.

Employment numbers and employment intention are indications of sustainability and confidence. The 2014 survey identified that staff vacancies had fallen since 2013, with 69 per cent of respondents reporting that they had no unfilled positions, compared with 56 per cent in 2012, representing a vacancy rate of about 3 per cent. Given that 73 per cent of the Component I increased funding was used to supplement salaries (Gilchrist 2013), respondents reported higher staff morale and responded positively to the impact of the policy in this regard. However, it must also be remembered that the WA economy had a concurrent easing of growth as the minerals boom declined, so these employment results are not necessarily reflective of the impact of the DCSP Policy. The overall impact of the declining economic conditions probably also had an impact on the decline in the reported time taken to fill vacancies since 2012. Respondents reported that 58 per cent of vacancies were filled within four weeks, while a further quarter of vacancies were filled within the five to eight-week period. Compared with 2012 and 2013, this change signalled a positive shift in the time taken to fill vacancies.

Further, 38 per cent of respondents reported that they had more staff than in 2013, while only 9 per cent reported that they had fewer staff. This finding needs to be considered in terms of the size of the respondent organisation, where 70 per cent of organisations with a turnover of more than $10 million reported that they had more staff, while only 23 per cent of organisations with turnover of $2 million or less reported having more staff and 12 per cent of those small organisations reported having fewer staff.

In terms of confidence, 85 per cent of respondents reported that their organisation was in a stronger position than in 2013, continuing the consistent reporting of positive opinions relating to NFPs' capacity. However, the same dichotomy seems to have manifested in this context as in the employment section above. Smaller organisations reported less confidence in their capacity compared with larger organisations. Specifically, 73 per cent of organisations turning over $5 million or more reported that they were stronger than at the same time in 2014 compared with only 59 per cent of organisations with a turnover of less than $2 million.

When considering aspects of financial sustainability and investment intent, respondents reported that they had confidence in being able to meet their debts as and when they fell due, with 97 per cent reporting that they had at least adequate capacity to pay debts. This result is an improvement on that reported in 2012, as 73 per cent of respondents reported that their organisation was very strong in being able to meet its debts compared with 67 per cent responding in the same way in 2012. This improvement is very likely associated with the payment of Component I increased funding.

This optimism in financial outcomes was replicated when prospective investment in the replacement of existing assets or the purchase of new assets was considered. Some 78 per cent of respondents reported that they believed their organisation had at least adequate capacity to replace assets in 2012 and, again in 2014, a marginal improvement was reported as 47 per cent of those reporting positively in 2014 considered that they were strong in this area compared with 42 per cent in 2012. Having said this, there appears to be a consistent group of organisations at the other end of the scale reporting that they believe they are weak in this area (22 per cent in 2012 and 2014).

In terms of investing in new assets, respondents were marginally less optimistic, with 33 per cent reporting that they were strong in the area in 2012 compared with 27 per cent in 2013. This picture is reinforced when data are disaggregated by organisational turnover. For instance, in 2014, 87 per cent of organisations with a turnover of more than $10 million reported that they were in a strong or very strong position with respect to paying debts when they fell due compared with 62 per cent of those with a turnover of less than $500,000 and 65 per cent of those with a turnover of between $500,000 and $1 million. Interestingly, the organisations reporting as most able to invest in assets to improve the quantity or quality of their services were those turning over $2 million to $45 million (67 per cent compared with 59 per cent in the turnover category of more than $10 million).

In terms of organisational capacity to pursue the mission, there remained a strong dichotomy in results when large organisations were compared with smaller organisations. Overall, in 2014, 81 per cent of respondents stated that they believed their capacity to meet their mission was strong or stronger compared with 73 per cent in 2012.

However, when size is considered, smaller NFPs were less optimistic than larger NFPs. Some 87 per cent of larger NFPs (turning over $10 million or more) reported that they expected to be stronger or much stronger in terms of capacity to meet mission in the future compared with 76 per cent of those organisations turning over $1 million to $2 million, or 78 per cent of those turning over between $500,000 and $1 million. Overall, 87 per cent of organisations turning over $10 million or more reported that they expected to be stronger—10 per cent more than the average of all of the smaller organisations.

The impact of the DCSP Policy on NFPs

While evaluating perceptions of sustainability is critical, this section reports on questions raised in the survey pertaining to the DCSP Policy itself and the impact it has had on NFPs contracting with government. In making this assessment, each annual survey asked questions pertaining to capacity for implementation, outcomes development and management, data collection and reporting, and perceptions of administrative burden.

An important aspect of the implementation of the DCSP Policy is the level of knowledge apparently held by NFPs in relation to the policy. Between 2012 and 2013, NFPs reported a significant increase in their rating of knowledge pertaining to the DCSP Policy. Indeed, in 2012, 46 per cent of respondents reported that they had a 'good' or 'very good' level of knowledge pertaining to the policy and, by 2013, this had risen to 76 per cent. However, the 2014 results indicate that the respondents are less confident in their knowledge of the policy. Indeed, only 55 per cent of respondents reported that they believed they had 'good' or 'very good' knowledge. It is likely this latest response gives a more realistic view of understanding, as these organisations would, over this time, have developed a greater appreciation of the complexity that the DCSP Policy represents in terms of administration, outcomes identification and reporting—an appreciation that would likely come of lived experience.

Axiomatically, the implementation of a policy such as the DCSP will result in administrative increases as individualised funding and person-centred care lead to a dramatic increase in numbers of contracts to be administered, and outcomes identification and reporting result in greater complexity of recording and reporting data. While in 2013 respondents reported that they felt the time taken to establish and manage a new contract had increased since 2012 (30 per cent reported an increase in elapsed time to final arrangements in 2012, compared with 40 per cent in 2013 and 26 per cent in 2014; 24 per cent reported an increase in time taken to manage contracts in 2012, compared with 50 per cent in 2013 and 37 per cent in 2014), overall, there were improvements in reported administrative time taken between 2013 and 2014.

NFP respondents' comments on the implementation of the DCSP Policy were mostly mixed (Knight and Gilchrist 2015: 41). There was frustration with inconsistent approaches being used across agencies and a perception of increased administrative burden. This is an interesting finding given that the focus of the policy is on individual recipient satisfaction with expected concomitant reductions in administrative burden. However, it is to be expected that increased administrative burden will flow out of the process of policy adoption as, for instance, block-funding contracts will be replaced with individual contracts focused on individual recipients.

Concluding remarks

The above review of the DCSP Policy evaluation undertaken in 2012, 2013 and 2014 is necessarily limited in its capacity to communicate the full findings of the study undertaken due to space constraints. The major findings relate to the impact of administrative burden, and much of that arose out of the change from the contractual focus on outputs to outcomes and from block-funding arrangements to individualised funding and person-centred services. Reported increases in time taken to agree on contractual arrangements and to devise suitable outcomes indicators capable of being metricised and reported were substantial. These increases in difficulty and administrative burden are likely to have arisen out of the complexity associated particularly with the identification of outcomes in the context of the human services subsector. This is the sector where most of the WA Government funding is allocated.

It is still too early to assess the aspects of the DCSP Policy associated with individualised funding and person-centred care from the recipient's perspective. These two aspects of the policy relate to the person-focused improvements anticipated in the policy, which were identified by the original audit committee. Other research undertaken by me has identified that it is highly likely that additional difficulties will arise with respect to administrative burden and increased clinical risk. This burden is somewhat denied by a commentariat and policy community that desire a reduction in red tape while increasing the administrative burden associated with individualised contracting arrangements. Indeed, some administrative burden is absolutely necessary but it does cost money. A lack of funding made available to support the change management process represents a challenge for both agencies and the NFP sector, and this lack will likely have an impact on the ongoing move towards person-centred care and individualised funding in future years (see, for instance, Gilchrist and Knight 2014).

Finally, there is also a need for ongoing and increased partnership between government and the NFP sector to achieve the outcomes sought in the DCSP Policy itself. Funding for training and change management resources will be required over the next few years. Analysis of the survey results associated with each category of organisation indicated that there is still a sense of the respective camps standing off from each other. The key question that only experience will answer is whether or not the DCSP Policy will result in real partnership between government and the NFP sector.

Future research will focus on the impact on government and the extent to which outcomes management is likely to be achieved within the context of the DCSP Policy. Further, as the DCSP Policy impacts on the structure of the NFP sector, further research is being undertaken in the areas of change management and supported structural reform. Additionally, it is expected that some variation will occur in the application of the policy, as some human services are particularly suited to outcomes reporting within a framework of individualised funding and person-centred care. However, other services are not and it is expected that block and other forms of funding will be continued in relation to these areas.

References

Barraket, J., ed. 2008. *Strategic Issues for the Not-for-Profit Sector.* Sydney: UNSW Press.

Center for Law and Social Policy. 2014. *Social Impact Bonds: Overview and considerations.* Washington, DC: Center for Law and Social Policy. Available from: clasp.org/resources-and-publications/publication-1/CLASP-Social-Impact-Bonds-SIBs-March-2014.pdf (accessed 22 April 2016).

Economic Audit Committee. 2009. *Putting the public first: Partnering with the community and business to deliver outcomes.* Report to the WA Government, Perth.

Frumkin, P. 2002. *On Being Nonprofit: A conceptual and policy primer.* London: Harvard University Press.

Garton, J. 2009. *The Regulation of Organised Civil Society.* Oxford: Hart Publishing.

Gilchrist, D. J. 2013. *2012 Evaluation of the Sustainable Funding and Contracting with the Not-for-Profit Sector Initiatives and Associated Procurement Reforms.* Perth: WA Government.

Gilchrist, D. J. and P. A. Knight. 2013a. *Annual funded sector report.* Report prepared for the Disability Services Commission, Perth.

Gilchrist, D. J. and P. A. Knight. 2013b. *2013 Evaluation of the Sustainable Funding and Contracting with the Not-for-Profit Sector Initiatives and Associated Procurement Reforms.* Perth: WA Government.

Gilchrist, D. J. and P. A. Knight. 2014. *Community employers, person centred care and individualised funding: Final report.* Joint report undertaken with Community Employers WA, Perth.

Knight, P. A. and D. J. Gilchrist. 2015. *2014 Evaluation of the Sustainable Funding and Contracting with the Not-for-Profit Sector Initiatives and Associated Procurement Reforms.* Perth: WA Government.

McGregor-Lowndes, M. 2008. 'Is there something better than partnership?' In *Strategic Issues for the Not-for-Profit Sector*, ed. J. Barraket, 45–73. Sydney: UNSW Press.

Mendes, P. 2008. *Australia's Welfare Wars Revisited: The players, the politics and the ideologies*. Sydney: UNSW Press.

National Audit Office (NAO). 2005. *Working with the Third Sector*. London: National Audit Office. Available from: nao.org.uk/wp-content/uploads/2005/06/050675.pdf (accessed 14 August 2013).

Office of the Auditor-General, Western Australia (OAG WA). 1998. *Accommodation and Support Services to Young People Unable to Live at Home*. Perth: Office of the Auditor-General. Available from: audit.wa.gov.au/wp-content/uploads/2013/05/report98_11.pdf (accessed 8 August 2013).

Office of the Auditor-General, Western Australia (OAG WA). 2000. *A Means to an End: Contracting Not-for-Profit Organisations for the Delivery of Community services*. Perth: Office of the Auditor-General. Available from: audit.wa.gov.au/wp-content/uploads/2013/05/report2000_03.pdf (accessed 8 August 2013).

Office of the Auditor-General, Western Australia (OAG WA). 2003. *Contracting Not-for-Profit Organisations for Delivery of Health Services*. Perth: Office of the Auditor-General. Available from: audit.wa.gov.au/wp-content/uploads/2013/05/report2003_02.pdf (accessed 12 August 2013).

Office of the Auditor-General, Western Australia (OAG WA). 2012. *Working Together: Management of partnerships with volunteers*. Perth: Office of the Auditor-General. Available from: audit.wa.gov.au/wp-content/uploads/2013/05/report2012_01.pdf (accessed 12 August 2013).

Office of the Auditor-General, Western Australia (OAG WA). 2013a. *Delivering Western Australia's Ambulance Services*. Perth: Office of the Auditor-General. Available from: audit.wa.gov.au/wp-content/uploads/2013/06/report2013_05.pdf (accessed 12 August 2013).

Office of the Auditor-General, Western Australia (OAG WA). 2013b. *Sustainable Funding and Contracting with the Not-For-Profit Sector – Component I*. Perth: Office of the Auditor-General. Available from: audit.wa.gov.au/wp-content/uploads/2013/09/report2013_13-Component-1-Funding.pdf (accessed 19 September 2013).

Productivity Commission. 2010. *Contribution of the Australian not-for-profit sector*. Research Report. Productivity Commission, Canberra.

Public Accounts Committee, Western Australia (PAC WA). 2000. *Accountability and not-for-profit organisations*. Report No. 49. Public Accounts Committee, Perth. Available from: parliament. wa.gov.au/parliament/homepage.nsf (accessed 14 August 2013).

Roth, L. 2011. *Social impact bonds*. e-Brief. New South Wales Parliamentary Library Research Service, Sydney. Available from: www.parliament.nsw.gov.au/researchpapers/Documents/social-impact-bonds/e-briefsocial%20impact%20bonds.pdf (accessed 19 May 2016).

Salamon, L. M. 1995. *Partners in Public Service: Government–nonprofit relations in the modern welfare state*. Baltimore: The Johns Hopkins University Press.

Victorian Auditor-General's Office (VAGO). 2013. *Implementation of the Strengthening Community Organisations Action Plan*. Melbourne: Victorian Auditor-General's Office. Available from: audit.vic.gov. au/publications/20131016-Community-Action-Plan/20131016-Community-Action-Plan.pdf (accessed 19 October 2013).

WA Government. 2011. *Delivering Community Services in Partnership: A policy to achieve better outcomes for Western Australians through the funding and contracting of community services*. Perth: WA Government.

Young, D. R. 2006. 'Complimentary, supplementary or adversarial: Nonprofit–government relations.' In *Nonprofits & Government: Collaboration and conflict*, eds E. T. Boris and C. E. Streuerle, 37–80. 2nd edn. Washington, DC: The Urban Institute Press.

5

The Contribution of Not-for-Profits to Democratic Process

Tessa Boyd-Caine

Introduction

Community organisations are often identified first and foremost with social services such as those for people experiencing homelessness or those needing emergency relief or financial counselling. Yet not-for-profit (NFP) organisations play a critical role within civil society more broadly, enabling democratic participation in myriad ways. These roles are not necessarily divergent, but they are reflective of the range of relationships and processes by which NFPs contribute to society. This chapter explores some of these relationships and processes and the contribution to civil society that NFP organisations make through them. It argues that a strong and independent civil society balances out the power and control that can otherwise be centralised in democratic governance and decision-making, enabling the participation of people and communities in the decisions made about them and facilitating leadership from and participation by communities, including people affected by poverty, inequality and injustice.

Beyond the ever evolving understanding of who and what civil society is, it is important to understand the relationship between civil society broadly and its component parts, such as non-governmental, non-profit organisations, as well as the actors with whom civil society engages, such as governments and the private sector. At its heart, the value offered by NFPs to democratic process is in these organisations' contribution to civil society and through it to public life, including through policy ideas, leadership and social change.

This chapter takes as its central framework five themes developed by the Australian Council of Social Service (ACOSS) to understand the contribution of NFPs to democratic process.[1] Drawing on examples taken from ACOSS in recent years, these themes are contextualised within current policy and public debate to show how NFPs can contribute to democratic process and where that contribution can be constrained or ineffectual. It also draws on comparative examples from the United States, based on work undertaken during a Fulbright Professional Scholarship in Nonprofit Leadership in 2014, to consider alternative ways in which the NFP sector could engage with such processes.

Sharing power and control: Our role in governance and decision-making

Understanding and challenging the distribution of power in society, including its consequences for people's sense of control and agency, are core components of the contribution made by a strong and independent civil society. Key elements of this contribution include the capacity to reflect on the concentration of power in Australian society, and developing a range of strategies to shift and share power. We need to know and name where power is concentrated, to claim the right to share power in processes that impact on people less powerful and to challenge the status quo, proposing big new ideas and expressing our dissent. Some recent examples of the NFP sector's efforts in sharing power with Australian governments are set out below, to consider how effective those efforts have been.

Collaboration between agents with differing degrees of power is a key process through which civil society often works to share power and control. In 2015, for example, in articulating the social and economic challenges of our time, community and business interests were repeatedly framed as divergent. Whether in tax reform,

---

1   These themes were developed by ACOSS from its Civil Society Forum, held on 25 February 2014 in Sydney.

industrial relations and employment or climate change, the dominant narrative setting out the case for reform in these areas routinely (and respectively) pits business interests (such as support for tax cuts) as oppositional to community interests (such as increased revenue to support adequate provision of community services). The assumption that business interests in enhanced industrial competitiveness conflict with workers' interests in decent wages presents a similar oppositional view, as does the portrayal of economic growth as a choice over environmental sustainability, health and well-being.

Each of these issues was identified by the National Reform Summit in 2015, which was an effort in collaboration across community, business, industry and union organisations. The summit was an explicit attempt to challenge this repeated framing of dichotomous interests as a barrier to achieving reform in a deliberately non-political process to identify common ground on the social and economic policy challenges facing Australia. The collaboration among sectoral interests—hitherto regarded as opposing—was an achievement in itself; consensus over the reform agenda produced by the summit was an even more important achievement. It was a collaboration that challenged an age-old narrative of conflict rather than coherence in policy proposals from non-governmental actors—a framing that had perpetuated competitive assumptions that one interest must win out over others and that certain interests had more power than others.

Community interests were represented at the summit through ACOSS as the peak body for charities and a voice for people experiencing poverty and inequality, the Australian Youth Affairs Coalition, the Council on the Ageing and National Seniors. This representation ensured that the summit's focus on productivity and participation as economic drivers of growth was grounded in the lived experience of people seeking to access (in the case of young people) or remain involved (in the case of older people) in the labour market.

Given that the perspectives of people locked out of the labour market are often excluded from economic debate, the National Reform Summit demonstrated how collaboration can shift concentrations of power in policy debates. But it was not unique in using collaboration to bring new voices to established debates. Before the Summit, many of the same organisations had come together in the articulation of a set of principles to guide policy on climate change in the interests of economic, as well as environmental, sustainability (Australian

Climate Roundtable 2015). Separately, ACOSS had also been working in partnership for several years with its peak body counterparts the Business Council of Australia and the Australian Council of Trade Unions (ACTU) on an agenda for 'collaborative action' focused on 'providing employment opportunities for Australians who are disadvantaged in the labour market; and giving employers access to workers who meet their skills needs' (ACOSS et al. 2012a). Beyond the policy gains made in each of these individual efforts, such collaboration speaks to a broader objective to build policy consensus through decision-making processes that better reflect the wide and shared interests of all parts of our society and our economy, in a way that partisan politics finds very hard to do. For ACOSS, ensuring the voice of people experiencing poverty and inequality in Australia is reflected in national policy debates and decision-making alongside the voices of business, industry or organised labour is a core objective of working collaboratively in this way.

Reflecting the voice of people or communities affected by policy debates is a vital role played by the NFP sector as it seeks to ensure that the governance and decision-making of the nation take account of community interests broadly. Several recent examples indicate the persistent need for this contribution to democratic process from civil society. For instance, in 2015, the Coalition Government announced that the board of the National Disability Insurance Agency, which administers the National Disability Insurance Scheme (NDIS), was going to be spilled to make way for greater representation from companies listed on the Australian Securities Exchange (ASX). Representation of the lived experience of people with disabilities, their families, carers and communities was absent from the government's announcement, despite the fact that this was a reform to the governance of one of the most significant social policies of the period, the specific objective of which was to support people with disabilities. In theory, lived experience of disability could be sourced from ASX-listed companies, but Australia's poor performance in employment participation for people with disabilities makes this unlikely (People with Disability Australia 2015). The failure to acknowledge the explicit and important relationship between the NDIS and the people it is intended to support was a clear indictment of institutional power structures that consolidate governance and decision-making away from those most affected by the decisions being made.

The experience of people who rely on income-support payments has been similarly marginalised by the policymaking processes of successive governments, aided by a willing media. Rhetoric such as 'welfare cheats' and 'lifters versus leaners' is designed particularly to justify harsh welfare measures and budget savings that target people who rely on income support (see, for example, ABC 2015; AFR 2014). This narrative pits the interests of governments who collect tax revenue, or notional 'taxpayers', against people in receipt of working-age payments. This strategy was evident when the same government's 2014 Federal Budget introduced a raft of measures aimed at people relying on income support, such as a six-month waiting period for young people seeking the (working-age payment) Newstart Allowance.[2] Then treasurer Joe Hockey argued explicitly: 'We must always remember that when one person receives an entitlement from the government, it comes out of the pocket of another Australian' (AFR 2014). Implicit in the government's justification of this measure was a view that young people were too lazy to look for paid work and that working-age payments were largesse the government could not afford. This narrative undermined the legitimate voice of young people in the policy debate. It also ignored the structural challenge of obtaining paid work within a labour market where there was one job available for every five jobseekers (Cox 2014).

The rhetoric of 'encouraging participation' in the workforce has similarly been employed against sole parents, such as when the previous (Labor) government reduced the value of income-support payments to sole parents with children over eight years of age. Efforts to justify budgetary savings measures targeting those on the lowest incomes were framed paternalistically as 'tough love' (Karvelas 2013). In addition to the likelihood of increasing poverty for many sole parents affected, such framing alienated sole parents themselves from the debate, directly undermining their capacity to play an active role in the decision-making about them. These examples show just how easily power can be concentrated to the exclusion of people directly affected by the decisions governments make.

2   The (ultimately unsuccessful) youth measure would have cost young people $255 per week for those aged 22–29 years, saving the Federal Budget $1.253 billion over four years (ACOSS 2014b).

The role of NFP community organisations advocating for shared power in such decision-making is a key contribution to democratic process. Yet, if we reflect closely on our own practices, we need to acknowledge that the NFP sector does not always model full sharing of power in governance and decision-making itself. In 2012, ACOSS partnered with the Young Women's Christian Association (YWCA) and Women on Boards to run the first survey of gender diversity in leadership positions within Australia's NFP and community sector. In a sector in which almost 80 per cent of the workforce is female (Workplace Gender Equality Agency 2015a), the survey found 60 per cent women to 40 per cent men in the composition of senior management teams (ACOSS et al. 2012b). At one level this compared favourably with relevant benchmarks, such as Australian Bureau of Statistics (ABS) data that showed women held 34.9 per cent of management roles. Yet the healthcare and social assistance sector, which includes the community sector, has consistently shown the largest gender pay gap in Australian industries, of about 30 per cent (Workplace Gender Equality Agency 2015b). While women were doing well in community sector senior management in comparison with other sectors, they were working in a sector that underpaid them. Moreover, 60 per cent representation in senior positions was far from parity in a workforce in which women made up 80 per cent (ACOSS et al. 2012b). Such persistent gender disparity in the leadership of the NFP sector is a sobering reminder of the need to be ever vigilant about how we challenge power and control within our own structures, even as we reflect on the role of the NFP sector in challenging dominant power structures and sharing control in other areas.

Developing a clear shared agenda: Our clarity of purpose

Harnessing collective power through developing a shared agenda for action is critical to civil society's effectiveness overall. While acknowledging the diversity of perspectives within civil society, there are a number of areas of common interest around which a shared agenda might be constructed. They include:

- the pursuit of equity and justice
- promoting a flourishing democracy
- economic, social and environmental sustainability

- creating the conditions for living a truly decent human life, with the time and space necessary to make meaningful human connections and contributions within our communities and society.

Identifying common interests is an important start; but the value of a shared agenda requires not just clarity of purpose but also agreement about how we assess our effectiveness in meeting that purpose. We need to measure progress and understand success. Equally importantly, we need to be able to recognise failure and commit to addressing it.

One of the great challenges for NFP organisations in contributing to the project of a shared agenda is the lack of clarity about, and duplication of, decision-making and coordinating mechanisms. The architecture of three layers of government alone creates inconsistency, across federal, state or territory and local government areas; and areas by electorate simply duplicate that inconsistency for the purpose of addressing complex problems. When different bureaucracies at different levels of government use different geographical and spatial areas for efforts to support coordination at the local level, it simply creates barriers for community organisations to try to usefully engage, even where they wish to. For example, the previous federal government's Medicare Locals (MLs) reform did not align with the structure of area health services in New South Wales, and the current federal government's Primary Health Networks (PHNs) have not resolved that lack of alignment. Yet the stated intention of both reforms was precisely to connect federal funding with health policy towards improving primary care through the local provision of health and medical services: the tagline of MLs was 'connecting health to meet local needs' (See, for example, Metro North Brisbane Medicare Local, 2016, mnbml.com.au), while the PHNs are intended to 'increase the efficiency and effectiveness of medical services for patients, particularly those at risk of poor health outcomes … improving coordination of care to ensure patients receive the right care in the right place at the right time' (Department of Health 2015b).

As civil society continually works to find new ways to come together over shared agendas, Australian governments will come under increasing pressure to agree to the core architecture for local community coordination and planning across their own local, state and territory and federal forms. The lack of such a coordinated approach is a key barrier to the identification of shared agendas to address complex problems, our ability to work collaboratively in the interests of those agendas and our capacity to assess our own effectiveness in meeting them.

Giving real meaning to collaboration and partnership: The way we work with others

Complex problems require complex solutions that engage the capacity of both social and economic actors. While no one actor (be they in government, civil society, business or industry) can solve complex problems alone, improved collaboration is essential to maximise the capacity and effectiveness of all sectors working together. At the same time, the disparity in resources available to these different actors is itself a barrier to better collaboration. This is particularly evident within the funding processes for community organisations. Government funding is virtually absent for dedicated, stable community development-related activities such as research, collaboration, design and innovation, policy, advocacy and evaluation. Even as Australia looks to expand philanthropic funding for community organisations, the lessons of the United States—a country with a strong and developed philanthropic culture and sector—tell us that these core capacities are always difficult to fund privately. The sector's funders—both government and non-governmental—need to recognise that the true value of community organisations in all the ways outlined above needs to be resourced; their effectiveness depends on capacity. Community and economic development-related activities need to be seen as central, not tangential, to the objectives funders are seeking to support when they provide resources to NFPs.

Strikingly, one of the ways we have been best able to understand the importance of the NFP sector's capacity to collaborate, and the value of that collaboration, has been through the application of economic analysis to the work and contribution of the sector. The Productivity Commission's (2010) study of the contribution of Australia's NFP sector was a landmark report in this respect, bringing an economic analysis to the social contribution of the sector. It found that the sector contributed 5 per cent of gross domestic product (GDP) and 8 per cent of employment nationally. The commission found that government funding for services often covered only 70 per cent of the cost of delivering those services, yet this was never explicitly identified by either government or sectoral organisations. Equally significantly, the Productivity Commission demonstrated that the sector's capacity to produce 'spillover' effects beyond the services for which it was specifically funded, such as long-term investment in the communities to which it delivered services, constituted a significant part of its value to government and to the community broadly. Even the voices calling for increased competition in community services, such as the Coalition Government-commissioned National Competition Review in 2014, reaffirmed the value provided by community organisations over and above the delivery of specific funded services as a key benefit for government and communities alike that needed to be taken into account in government funding and procurement models (National Competition Review 2014).

A key function provided by Australia's NFP sector is the delivery of social services, and the sector attracts significant levels of government funding to do so. Consequently, the design and delivery of funded programs can be critical to the effectiveness of community services and outcomes for the people being supported. At the Commonwealth level, there are a number of examples of programs that have approached these spillover benefits of community organisations as being central to their value for government funding. The Partners in Recovery program provides coordinated support and flexible funding for 'people with severe and persistent mental illness with complex needs and their carers and families, by getting multiple sectors, services and supports they may come into contact with (and could benefit from) to work in a more collaborative, coordinated and integrated way' (Department of Health 2015a). While evaluation of the program is currently under way, it is a model that reflects one of the core tenets advocated for by the community-based mental health sector: financial incentives to support collaboration and partnership in mental health services (Mental Health Council of Australia 2014).

The Communities for Children (C4C) program is a comparable model, providing prevention and early intervention services to families with children up to the age of twelve. Funded by the Department of Social Services (DSS 2014), the C4C program includes funding for partner programs that 'develop and facilitate a whole of community approach to support and strengthen local service networks that contribute to child safety'. Specifically, the partner programs provide one organisation with the capacity to fund other organisations as part of the integration and coordination of services by community organisations for the communities they support. C4C also funds services that 'provide activities directly to individual services to deliver early intervention and prevention family support, tailored to the needs of the local community' (DSS 2014). As an evaluation of the program has found, 'the C4C model—offering services on a universal basis, an emphasis on partnership and collaboration, flexibility, and an NGO [non-governmental organisation] playing the role of facilitator and coordinator of local services—could have much wider application in the delivery of community services' (Benevolent Society 2009).

Notwithstanding these examples, it is ironic that even as the government-commissioned evidence of the sector's economic contribution *through* its community value has mounted, government funding processes have undermined that value. In particular, the impact of competitive tendering processes and the rise of the contract state are weakening the very processes of building trust in communities and the collaborative relationships between community organisations through which their spillover value is provided. This is particularly evident within government-funded community services, as organisations compete both for resources and for 'air space' for their particular social purpose. Government-designed open competitive tendering and short procurement processes have driven out capacity for engagement from the local to the national as well as for stable, longer-term community development such as through local planning, delivery and evaluation. Each of these elements works together to address community needs, yet each is also essential to securing durable and effective community leadership and collaboration. While NFP community services seek to work in partnership with governments to achieve these aims, their efforts to do so are frequently frustrated (see further discussion of this in Bletsas 2015).

From 2012 to 2014, the federal government stripped $1.6 billion in funding from community services across the portfolios of health, social services and attorney-general's and funding for Aboriginal and Torres Strait Islander (ATSI) communities within the Department of the Prime Minister and Cabinet. In the face of these cuts, restructures to funding policy and programs and new competitive tendering processes sought to distribute what funding was left on the basis of priority areas of need. For many in the sector, the results have been disastrous, with a loss of funding without any capacity to plan for transitioning to new funding models. At the same time, under the guise of 'probity', organisations were being told they could not share information about their own funding, and organisations which lost funding were refused information from their funders about who, or whether anyone, had picked up funding for the services, areas or populations in which they worked. These conditions fractured, undermined and in some cases destroyed entirely the collaborative relationships community organisations had developed over years—with one another and with the communities in which they worked. Even more significant than the impact of organisations and staff facing closure and job losses, these processes impacted directly on the communities intended to benefit from community service funding.

Case study: Coordinated and integrated services

AccordWest had been delivering essential support services to some of the most at-risk families, couples and individuals in the south-west of Western Australia for more than 30 years. In 2013–14 they supported more than 18,000 people. After the $270 million cut to funding for the Commonwealth DSS, the uncertainty about what if any funding would be delivered meant they lost key staff who were uncertain about their future employment. They were unable to reassure vulnerable clients about the continuity of services they relied on, and their capacity to secure the infrastructure needed to deliver effective services well in the community was reduced (ACOSS 2014a).

The impact of the DSS funding cut included the destruction of community relationships vital to the effectiveness of services for people who depended on them. Equally destructive was the stifling of information about the funding process after this cut—an issue highlighted by a Senate inquiry into the process (Senate Standing Committees on Community Affairs 2015). Analysis of gaps in service provision that guided funding decisions was not released. Departmental policies required confidentiality by organisations including over what funding they had been offered, if any; and in the interests of privacy, the DSS refused to publish information about which organisations had been offered funding and which had not. This stifling of information left community organisations unable to understand the evidence on which funding decisions had been made and with no capacity to advise their clients or communities on what, if any, alternative services would be provided—sometimes for months at a time. An alternative approach—for instance, enabling community organisations to determine for themselves what information they would like to share, either with sector colleagues directly or in the public domain—would have significantly reduced the negative impact of the decision to cut funding in the first place.

Undoubtedly, opportunities for effective collaboration between civil society, governments and the market exist and must be strengthened if we are to make gains on the most 'wicked' and entrenched social and economic problems, from lack of affordable housing to long-term unemployment and the social determinants of chronic disease. Improving collaborative processes requires preparedness to accommodate tension and disagreement, but, if achieved, will provide the foundation on which to develop a shared agenda that has the power to effect both vertical and horizontal changes.

In the end, while resourcing for capacity is critical, there are also important questions of principle and design that need to be addressed to ensure strong and effective collaboration. What principles should underpin our collaborative work? Can we collectively push for greater sharing of decision-making and design in our policy, advocacy and service delivery efforts? What would we need to change about ourselves to achieve more collaborative approaches, more effective services and greater local participation in the decisions that affect our communities?

Enabling leadership and participation by those affected by poverty, inequality and injustice: The way we work with those we support

Recognising that organisations and formal structures represent only one expression of civil society, there is great value in a broad conception of civil society founded on informal relationships, networks, voluntary associations and participation at all levels of the community. Facilitating the exercise of power and agency by the people we serve is crucial to success. Yet there are fears that the marketisation of civil society—that is, as 'consumers' or 'customers'—has led to a weakening of the connection between civil society's institutions and the needs and lived experiences of the individuals and communities we claim to serve. Other fears include the risk that a focus on civil society, or even on related notions such as philanthropy, can dilute the critical importance of government providing a social safety net, both in human services (universal in health and education, social services) and in income support. The directions of the 'big society' shift in the United Kingdom and the lack of a social welfare state in the United States both speak to the legitimacy of such concerns.

There are a number of ways civil society can support such leadership and participation:

- By engaging in local, community-focused conversations that connect structural issues with local concerns—for example, as demonstrated by justice reinvestment approaches in Australia and the United States, including in the regional NSW town of Bourke (Just Reinvest NSW 2015) and the US state of Texas (CSG Justice Center 2015).

- By being the change we want to see through our own organisations, including through structuring institutional and governance processes to support the leadership and participation of people directly affected—for example, in disabled people's organisations controlled by a majority of people with disability (51 per cent) at the board and membership levels, such as People with Disability Australia.

- By challenging institutional models of local connection and representation, such as through the 'Voices for Indi' movement that ultimately saw an independent elected to a Victorian seat that had been held by the same major party since 1977 (Cassidy 2013).

- By building local advocacy capacity and creating platforms for people affected by the issues to mobilise for change, such as through the 'Places You Love' alliance supporting local community engagement in national policymaking about nature conservation (placesyoulove.org).

To give effect to such aims, we have to relinquish our own power and control and facilitate the leadership and participation of the people with whom we work. But it is important to see these directions as enhancing the effectiveness of democratic decision-making, incorporating as a central component the role of government, particularly in the social safety net. For community organisations particularly, we can drive change in our organisations and our communities through our governance, employment and service practices, as well as in our research, policy development and advocacy. In these processes, government is an important, but not the only, object of our efforts.

Two examples of recent work by ACOSS speak to efforts by community NFPs to practise the principles we wish to see demonstrated by others. The first is the leadership of sole parents acting against the cuts to the sole parenting payment introduced by the federal Labor Government in 2012. Sole parents experience some of the most significant poverty and inequality in Australia today. They are highly represented among the more than two million people living in poverty, and their caring responsibilities place them at a significant disadvantage in the labour market. Notwithstanding this vulnerability, the government determined to cut the value of the income-support payments many sole parents relied on by $56 per week, as a savings measure worth $156 million over four years in the 2011 Federal Budget (ACOSS 2011).

ACOSS opposed this measure and advocated publicly against it, based on detailed analysis of evidence showing it was unlikely to be effective in supporting sole parents into paid work and more likely to increase their experience of poverty. It was, however, the mobilisation of sole parents themselves—a majority of whom are women— that was a critical element of the strong opposition to the measure. Through representative structures such as the National Council for Single Mothers and their Children (NCSMC) and a range of grassroots organisations comprising people affected by the change, sole parents were a strong voice outlining the impact of this cut and how much it would harm them and their families. ACOSS worked in partnership with its member organisation NCSMC to develop a media and political engagement strategy that combined technical analysis of the policy and its implications with the expertise of lived experience from sole parents, many of whom undertook multiple part-time or casual low-paid jobs and struggled to meet their family expenses. This partnership was critical in ensuring that the voice of people directly affected by federal government policy was heard in the advocacy against that policy. It also seeded other opportunities to maintain the strength of that voice, such as through the '10 Stories' project (10storiesofsinglemothers.org.au/). While the policy was ultimately introduced, the Labor Government subsequently apologised for the measure (Karvelas 2014), recognising it had unfairly and disproportionately impacted on people who could least withstand it.

Another partnership, between ACOSS and Aboriginal community organisations, has seen the development of a set of principles between Aboriginal and Torres Strait Islander organisations and non-Aboriginal community services aimed at supporting Aboriginal community control over the funding and delivery of social services and support in Aboriginal communities (ACOSS 2013). Over successive decades, the level of funding for ATSI people and communities has risen, yet the number of Aboriginal community-controlled organisations has declined in the same period. Non-Aboriginal community services have accepted funding to deliver services to Aboriginal people and in Aboriginal communities, without ensuring Aboriginal control within those services or investing adequately in the capacity of Aboriginal communities to identify their own needs and be resourced to meet them. These Partnership Principles seek a commitment from non-Aboriginal organisations to work in collaborative partnership, not in competition, with ATSI communities and community organisations. Informed by an initial process in the Northern Territory, the development of the national principles was undertaken by the peak organisations for ATSI legal, healthcare, childcare and women's and family violence services and ACOSS. Once the principles were drafted, the lead organisations worked with non-Aboriginal community organisations and NFPs to build commitment to them, and with government in the hopes of affecting decision-making about government funding for Aboriginal communities and services. While there is a long way to go in achieving self-determination by Aboriginal people and communities, the Partnership Principles were an important effort at a sector-led agenda to reverse years of practice by community organisations that had undermined the capacity of Aboriginal people and communities to support themselves strongly and effectively.

Being clear about the roles and responsibilities of civil society, government, the market and business: Creating the solid foundations for our work together

The role of the market is raising new and important questions about democratic process and the contribution of civil society. These include how the market interacts with NFP organisations and the communities they support, and what role, if any, it can usefully play in solving complex social and economic problems. There is strong support in some quarters for market-based financing models that can leverage private funds to achieve positive social outcomes—for instance, through social impact bonds and impact investment. On the other hand, there are legitimate concerns about the long-term impact of such models on the fabric of civil society. We have already seen how the marketisation of human services through competitive tendering can undermine the core value and contribution of community services, particularly where it undermines or fractures the relationships on which that value is based.

Related concerns have also been expressed about the construction of people who rely on human services primarily as 'consumers', particularly people experiencing poverty and inequality, and the natural tendency of market-based mechanisms to cherry-pick profitable services over those that are not, irrespective of need (ACOSS 2014c). As consumer advocate Choice (2015) points out, 'consistent quality and access for Australians should be the priority, and pursuing competition as an end in itself can actually do more harm than good'.

The NDIS is a useful example to think through some of these issues.[3] The issues paper released as part of the National Competition Review made the following assertions about the NDIS:

> Under the National Disability Insurance Scheme (NDIS), Australians with significant and permanent disability will have an individualised plan which sets out their care and support needs and their goals. Providers will be engaged by each individual NDIS participant to deliver support in accordance with the person's plan. Organisations and individuals can apply to be a registered provider and then enter into a written agreement that clearly sets out the support they will provide to an individual. In effect, much of what has been provided by state and territory governments could in future be provided by individuals, non-for-profit organisations and the private sector. (Competition Review 2014: 26 at 4.11)

One of the concerns expressed by civil society is that this competition-based assessment misrepresents both the policy intent of the NDIS and the practices that are already evident in its implementation. The

---

3   The following discussion is taken from ACOSS (2014c: 9).

NDIS does not, nor has it ever been intended to, provide for the sum total of the needs of people living with disability. Income support is one example of a necessary support never intended to be provided through the NDIS. Yet it is a key social support that remains necessary given Australia's continuing failure to include people with disability in the labour market (OECD 2010), which is further evidence that market-based mechanisms cannot meet every need. While it is a significant public policy achievement, it does not, in itself, signal the end of a need for government activity directly, nor for government-funded services for people living with disability in Australia.

Case study: ACT Government and the NDIS

In the Australian Capital Territory, the launch of the NDIS has led to government withdrawing from the provision of services in some areas (specifically early childhood intervention and residential homes). But the ACT Government has now recognised it cannot do that without first developing the markets intended but not yet in existence. It has also recognised a need to continue to provide block funding for tier-two services that are not commensurate with the individualised funding model and to ensure that those people who are not eligible for the NDIS are still able to access services they need.

By giving participants market-based power as consumers, the policy intention of individualised funding is central to the effort to attract markets into delivering services under the NDIS. But the majority of people living with disability will not be in receipt of individualised funding packages, thereby undermining their ability to access and define the services they want, and creating tensions around resources for service development and delivery. The creation of markets will not solve these tensions and the role of governments as funders will need to continue.

One of the core assumptions of the NDIS is that other human services such as health and education will provide access and support when people within the NDIS use them. Even early in the NDIS trial phase, community organisations have begun reporting that this is not occurring, so some people within its scope are already missing out. Meanwhile, a number of groups, such as people with chronic health needs, are not in scope for the NDIS, yet are unable to access adequate, affordable services within the health system. Thus, while the NDIS is an effort to establish a market-based mechanism for vital human services, both its design and its implementation demonstrate some of the pitfalls of assuming market-based mechanisms can meet the full and complex needs of people and communities, particularly those experiencing poverty and inequality.

Conclusion

Civil society plays a central role in challenging and shifting power and control. Power comes in many forms. The examples discussed cover representative power, decision-making power and reputational power. Another key area of power is knowledge: the power of data to demonstrate particular problems such as unemployment or homelessness; and the power of evidence to support particular solutions for redress such as through improved health and well-being. Governments routinely collect and analyse swathes of data about the people and communities they govern—data that become key tools in decision-making about those communities. Yet communities and the organisations that support them rarely have access to such knowledge or information. This further alienates communities from the decisions that affect them, such as those made by governments.

Governments can and should open up access to data on community and economic well-being—for example, in education, employment, health, housing and social services. Many governments, however, have been reticent to do so. This is despite the clear evidence of the role and value of data as the major driver of technological innovation worldwide, with its multiple uses underpinning everything from scientific research breakthroughs to evolving models of democratic participation and sharing economies. Government reticence to follow suit also shirks a key accountability to the people and communities they serve, which would benefit from the publication of data such as whether and how government policies and services funded by tax revenue are providing adequate and effective support—for instance, in the management of chronic disease or the prevention of poverty.

Domestically, efforts to establish social progress indicators are one example of the role civil society has played in advancing a research agenda that would support greater sharing of power and knowledge. The Australian National Development Index (ANDI) is one such example, where academic and other researchers have come together with community and social justice organisations to identify a gap in Australia's evidence base: that while we measure GDP and can demonstrate business confidence, we are poorly equipped when it comes to routine, reliable indicators of social progress or well-being (andi.org.au/what-is-progress). Yet if we are serious about ensuring that our economic progress and growth are inclusive, we need measures of social impact to balance out those of economic impact. The ANDI project is one strategy for filling this void.

In the digital age, the combination of more data being available than ever before and increasingly innovative technological platforms through which those data can be manipulated is significantly changing public expectations of those who hold data and the possibilities of what they do with it. Beyond influencing the public narrative about social progress and well-being, civil society's pursuit of reliable measures to track social progress also opens the way for advocacy to governments and others who collect and hold data about how transparent they are in the data they hold and their willingness to share it. In the United States, the open data debate has focused on the quantity of data collected by agencies across the government, non-governmental and private sectors, and has developed an agenda within which those sectors are expected to make available their data in the interests of transparency and accountability. In Australia, this discussion is still in its infancy, with attention paid mostly to the protection of data in the interests of individual confidentiality. But the driver of transparency and accountability is likely to bring increasing pressure to bear on any and all who hold data, and on how they can produce and disseminate those data for public benefit.

American NFPs have seized the opportunity that access to data provides, as they have steered an agenda towards strong accountability and transparency across their own sector. For NFP and particularly charitable organisations, transparency and accountability are critical to sustaining the support they need to do their work—from funders, donors, volunteers, workers and the beneficiaries of that work.

If we are going to extend the incentives to other organisational forms that ostensibly serve the public good, we should also be sure they are subject to mandatory reporting requirements that will contribute to transparency. Otherwise, we will be left with anecdote, marketing, self-reported data and the occasional survey to assess the extent to which they are serving the public good in exchange for the public incentive they receive (Smith 2014).

For some in the sector, transparency and accountability are ends in themselves. The global project of the Open Society Foundations (2015) reflects this, working 'to build vibrant and tolerant democracies whose governments are accountable to their citizens'. Beyond this focus, the emergence of a range of NFP organisations has provided various platforms from which to analyse charitable data and develop knowledge about the sector as a whole. Transparency and accountability are explicit in the purpose of these organisations, forming the backbone of the research agenda on American NFPs. They also effectively constitute the sector's own research arm, driving and supporting a sector-led agenda of transparency and accountability on which public understanding and support of charities are based.

Through a combination of research organisations and ratings agencies, the US NFP sector has developed a research landscape through which it turns the baseline data collected by charity regulators into a wealth of information and knowledge about itself, and whose role includes the publication and dissemination of this information for public, as well as sectoral, interest.

This spectrum of research organisations enables the sector to set its own agenda of transparency and accountability. Basic information covers the core dimensions of the sector, such as the size and breadth of activity undertaken by US charities, philanthropists and NFPs. There is more detailed information available at both national and local levels, such as how many organisations provide early intervention to children or what kinds of arts organisations are active in any part of the country. The US NFP sector has built highly sophisticated mechanisms to track its activities, from the sources of funding, where they flow and the activities they fund to the dimensions of its workforce and the pay scales of its leadership.

The accountability charities have to the people with whom they work and support may be the most important of all in terms of purpose and impact. Yet it is also the accountability least likely to have structured requirements—and sometimes not even well-defined relationships. Sometimes referred to as a relationship of benefit—as in the 'beneficiary' of charity—this is regarded by critics as a paternalistic notion reflective of more traditional approaches to charity or philanthropy as an act of giving by those with wealth to those without. Other notions such as capacity building, community development or collective impact seek to shift the power in the relationship away from charitable organisations and towards the people and communities they support. For others still, the language of 'constituencies' is an effort to reflect this more strengths-based approach (see, for example, Smith 2010; ACOSS 2014d).

It matters less how charities and NFPs, or governments, structure their transparency and accountability than that they recognise how central transparency and accountability are to the communities within which they work. As we have seen, sharing power and control not only requires civil society to challenge government practices (or those of business or industry). It also requires courage and preparedness to reflect on the practices of institutions and how they relate to people and communities, to understand the power relationships within Australian society. It requires reflection on our own responsibility for sharing power, and advocacy for the partnerships and other processes through which power can be shared across and beyond governments, business and even NFPs. Civil society organisations can and must play a role in including people who are directly affected by the decisions we make and the services we provide in our decision-making structures, our service design and delivery, the use of information to inform our work and our policy advocacy. In doing so, we can strengthen our effectiveness in shifting power towards the interests of people less powerful in Australian society, both in our external engagement and within our own networks and services.

References

Australian Broadcasting Corporation (ABC). 2015. 'Senior police officer to lead welfare fraud taskforce to be established by Government.' *ABC News*, 24 May. Available from: abc.net.au/news/2015-05-24/senior-police-officer-to-lead-welfare-fraud-taskforce/6492804 (accessed 1 October 2015).

Australian Climate Roundtable. 2015. *Joint Principles.* 29 June. Australian Climate Roundtable. Available from: australian climateroundtable.org.au/ (accessed 1 October 2015).

Australian Council of Social Service (ACOSS). 2011. *Federal Budget 2011–2012: Initial ACOSS Analysis.* Sydney: ACOSS. Available from: acoss.org.au/wp-content/uploads/2015/06/2011-12_Initial_ Budget_Analysis_final.pdf (accessed 1 October 2015).

Australian Council of Social Service (ACOSS). 2013. *Principles for a Partnership-centred approach for NGOs Working with Aboriginal and Torres Strait Islander Organisations and Communities.* Sydney: ACOSS. Available from: acoss.org.au/principles-for-a-partnership-centred-approach/ (accessed 1 October 2015).

Australian Council of Social Service (ACOSS). 2014a. *$1 billion in federal cuts to community services.* Briefing Paper. Sydney: ACOSS. Available from: acoss.org.au/images/uploads/ACOSS%20Sector%20 Funding%20cuts%20Briefing.pdf (accessed 1 October 2015).

Australian Council of Social Service (ACOSS). 2014b. *A Budget that Divides a Nation: ACOSS 2014–15 budget analysis.* Sydney: ACOSS. Available from: acoss.org.au/federal-budget-2014-15/ (accessed 1 October 2015).

Australian Council of Social Service (ACOSS). 2014c. *Joint COSS Network Submission to Competition Policy Review.* Sydney: ACOSS. Available from: acoss.org.au/images/uploads/COSS_Competition_ Review_submission_november_2014.pdf (accessed 1 October 2015).

Australian Council of Social Service (ACOSS). 2014d. *Tax Reform for the Common Good.* Sydney: ACOSS. Available from: www.acoss. org.au/tax_reform_for_the_common_good/ (accessed 9 February 2015).

Australian Council of Social Service (ACOSS), Australian Council of Trade Unions (ACTU) and Business Council of Australia (BCA). 2012a. *Opportunity for all.* Joint statement on ACOSS, ACTU and BCA Cooperation. Sydney: ACOSS. Available from: acoss.org. au/media_release/joint_statement_on_acoss_actu_and_bca_ cooperation/ (accessed 1 October 2015).

Australian Council of Social Service (ACOSS), YWCA Australia and Women on Boards. 2012b. *Reflecting Gender Diversity: An analysis of gender diversity in the leadership of the community sector*. Sydney: ACOSS. Available from: acoss.org.au/wp-content/uploads/2015/06/NFP_Boards_and_Gender_Diversity_2012_final.pdf (accessed 1 October 2015).

Australian Financial Review (AFR). 2014. 'Joe Hockey: We are a nation of lifters, not leaners.' *Australian Financial Review*, 14 May. Available from: afr.com/news/policy/tax/joe-hockey-we-are-a-nation-of-lifters-not-leaners-20140513-ituma#ixzz3np2KVzxv (accessed 1 October 2015).

Bletsas, A. 2015. *Independence in the not-for-profit sector*. A report by ACT Council of Social Services and SA Council of Social Services. ACTCOSS, Canberra. Available from: www.sacoss.org.au/independence-not-profit-sector (accessed 7 July 2016).

Benevolent Society. 2009. *Evaluation of The Benevolent Society's Communities for Children Programs*. Sydney: Benevolent Society. Available from: benevolent.org.au/~/media/2B01AA851B0A8EA2CCE9F9DC0E08EF81.ashx (accessed 1 October 2015).

Cassidy, B. 2013. 'The story of how Cathy McGowan stormed Indi.' *ABC News*, 13 September. Available from: abc.net.au/news/2013-09-13/cassidy-indi/4955258 (accessed 1 October 2015).

Choice. 2015. 'Competition Policy Review delivers consumer reforms.' *Choice*, 2 April. Available from: choice.com.au/shopping/consumer-rights-and-advice/your-rights/articles/harper-competition-policy-review-020415 (accessed 1 October 2015).

Competition Review. 2014. *Issues Paper*. Canberra: Australian Government. Available from: competitionpolicyreview.gov.au/ (accessed 1 October 2015).

Council of State Governments Justice Center (CSG Justice Center). 2015. *Collaborative Approaches to Public Safety*. Washington, DC: CSG Justice Center. Available from: csgjusticecenter.org/jr/tx/ (accessed 1 October 2015).

Cox, E. 2014. 'When job seekers outnumber jobs 5 to 1, punitive policy is harmful.' *The Conversation*, 9 July. Available from: theconversation.com/when-job-seekers-outnumber-jobs-5-to-1-punitive-policy-is-harmful-28839 (accessed 1 October 2015).

Department of Health. 2015a. *Partners in Recovery*. Canberra: Australian Government. Available from: health.gov.au/internet/main/publishing.nsf/content/mental-pir (accessed 1 October 2015).

Department of Health. 2015b. *Primary Health Networks*. Website. Australian Government, Canberra. Available from: health.gov.au/internet/main/publishing.nsf/content/primary_health_networks (accessed 5 August 2015).

Department of Social Services (DSS). 2014. *Communities for Children*. Canberra: Australian Government. Available from: dss.gov.au/our-responsibilities/families-and-children/programs-services/family-support-program/family-and-children-s-services (accessed 1 October 2015).

Just Reinvest NSW. 2015. *JR in Bourke*. Sydney: Just Reinvest NSW. Available from: justreinvest.org.au/projects/jr-in-bourke/ (accessed 1 October 2015).

Karvelas, P. 2013. 'Labor's tough love puts 4000 single mothers into work.' *The Australian*, 10 April. Available from: theaustralian.com.au/national-affairs/industrial-relations/labors-tough-love-puts-4000-single-mothers-into-work/story-fn59noo3-1226616636246 (accessed 1 October 2015).

Karvelas, P. 2014. 'Gillard government "got it wrong" on single parent payments, says Jenny Macklin.' *The Australian*, 26 March. Available from: theaustralian.com.au/national-affairs/gillard-government-got-it-wrong-on-single-parent-payments-says-jenny-macklin/story-fn59niix-1226864738080 (accessed 1 October 2015).

Mental Health Council of Australia. 2014. *Submission to the National Mental Health Commission's Review of Existing Mental Health Programs and Services*. Canberra: Mental Health Council of Australia. Available from: mhaustralia.org/sites/default/files/docs/mhca_submission_to_the_nmhcs_review_of_existing_mental_health_programs_and_services_june_2014.pdf (accessed 1 October 2015).

National Competition Review. 2014. *Final Report*. Canberra: Australian Government. Available from: competitionpolicyreview.gov.au/ (accessed 1 October 2015).

Open Society Foundations. 2015. Website. Open Society Foundations, New York. Available from: opensocietyfoundations.org/about (accessed 8 July 2015).

Organisation for Economic Co-operation and Development (OECD). 2010. *Sickness, Disability and Work: Improving social and labour-market integration of people with disability*. Paris: OECD. Available from: oecd.org/els/soc/46488022.pdf (accessed 1 October 2015).

People with Disability Australia. 2015. *Get Real on Jobs*. Sydney: People with Disability Australia. Available from: pwd.org.au/pwda-publications/get-real-on-jobs2.html (accessed 1 October 2015).

Productivity Commission. 2010. *Contribution of the Non-Profit Sector*. Canberra: Productivity Commission. Available from: pc.gov.au/ inquiries/completed/not-for-profit/report (accessed 1 October 2015).

Senate Standing Committees on Community Affairs. 2015. *Impact on Service Quality, Efficiency and Sustainability of Recent Commonwealth Community Service Tendering Processes by the Department of Social Services*. 16 September. Canberra: Australian Government. Available from: aph.gov.au/Parliamentary_Business/Committees/ Senate/Community_Affairs/Grants/Final_Report (accessed 1 October 2015).

Smith, B. 2010. 'Foundations need to be more transparent.' *Philantopic*, 29 January. Available from: pndblog.typepad.com/ pndblog/2010/01/foundations-need-to-be-more-transparent.html (accessed 20 August 2014).

Smith, B. 2014. Comment by Foundation Center President, Brad Smith, on Lucy Bernholz's blog 'A practical and existential challenge to nonprofits'. *Philanthropy 2173: The future of good*, 7 May. Available from: philanthropy.blogspot.com/2014/05/a-practical-and-existential-challenge.html (accessed 20 August 2014).

Workplace Gender Equality Agency. 2015a. *Gender Composition of the Workforce: By industry*. Sydney: Workplace Gender Equality Agency. Available from: wgea.gov.au/sites/default/files/Gender-composition-of-the-workforce-by-industry.pdf (accessed 1 October 2015).

Workplace Gender Equality Agency. 2015b. *Gender Pay Gap Statistics*. Sydney: Workplace Gender Equality Agency. Available from: wgea.gov.au/sites/default/files/Gender_Pay_Gap_Factsheet.pdf (accessed 1 October 2015).

Part 2. Three Sectors: Three change agendas

Overview

Penny Knight

In a world in which many major problems cannot be resolved by a single person, organisation or solution, it is essential for leaders of transformational change to build high-level skills in collaboration. These skills include the ability to identify and gather a coalition of people with influence and access to resources, including funding, to communicate a compelling need and to create structures and processes that keep people on task and accountable. The chapters presented by Dr Leeora Black, Krystian Seibert and Robyn Keast present different perspectives on both the theory and the reality of leading collaborative work, provide examples of success and systemic constraints and challenge us to consider our own roles in leading and supporting change.

Dr Black's chapter addresses the key issue of funding social services and the opportunity to access more resources by collaborating with the private sector. It also addresses the role government can play in supporting (or inhibiting) private investment.

Black uses Big Society Capital's definition of social investment, which is 'the use of repayable finance to achieve social as well as financial returns', thereby clearly differentiating it from the donation of capital, whether in full or partially through an acceptance of a lower than market return. She provides examples of the opportunities for direct and indirect investment and highlights the important role of financial intermediaries, such as banks and superannuation funds, in channelling investor funds into social initiatives rather than into the more traditional financial products. She also comments on investors' growing interest in ethical and impact investing and that achievement of financial returns and social returns does not necessarily require a trade-off in that regard.

In examining the different roles that financial intermediaries play, Black observes that funding is not fungible and each of these providers will be looking for different forms of collaboration and return. For example, investors in social impact bonds compare these instruments with other forms of investment, including other social investments, and seek the highest return for the lowest risk. Each investor may value the social impact differently. They may also aim to create portfolios of investments with particular risk and impact profiles. In contrast, philanthropists and governments will weigh up the outcome that can be achieved by each social investment opportunity and compare it with a wide range of funding priorities, seeking to identify which will achieve the biggest impact.

Governments have a range of mechanisms through which they can support (or hinder) increased private investment in social services, and Black identifies five in particular that are relevant in the Australian context—being the opportunity to: create new business structures; build a greater awareness of the benefits of shared valued; establish a specific intermediary organisation to facilitate investment; provide a range of tax concessions for social investment; and provide clarification of the 'sole-purpose test' in regard to the duties of superannuation fund trustees and allow them to take social impact into account when making investment decisions.

She concludes by stating that investment in social outcomes will be increased when they can be shown to achieve both a financial and a social return, when there is a greater understanding of shared value and when the financial service sector and governments each play their part in channelling private funds into social investments.

Krystian Seibert's reflection on the establishment of the Australian Charities and Not-for-profits Commission (ACNC) provides deep insight into a specific and recent example of cross-sector collaboration. The establishment of the ACNC was, in effect, a single large-scale collaborative reform project with a beginning, middle and end. As such, it required different leadership and coworking skills to those needed to build and maintain collaborations between governments, funders and service providers to achieve the kind of social outcomes that Black introduces.

Seibert's case study also highlights the fact that some collaborative projects are not always universally supported. The establishment and first years of the ACNC were met with heavy resistance from some quarters and required leaders from across government agencies, the not-for-profit sector, academia and others to come together, 'hold the line' and continue the push for change. Further, it shows how difficult it can be to gain support for a new, unknown future state, particularly when many do not see harm in maintaining the status quo. Given these circumstances, the establishment and survival of the ACNC is an excellent example of effective cross-sector working and the skilled application of change techniques, including those of understanding stakeholders, maintaining clarity and focus, co-production, establishing a supportive culture and adjusting the speed and approach as required. Seibert concludes that collaborations succeed best when the processes and relationships are managed as carefully as the outcomes.

In the final chapter of this section, Keast summarises recent academic research and provides a strong scaffold for framing further discussion of best practice in cross-sector working. She places collaboration clearly on a spectrum ranging from competition to consolidation and highlights the characteristics that separate collaboration from other forms of coworking. Collaboration is not simply sharing information or aligning existing operations, but aiming to meet a shared goal through achieving something new or different by implementing initiatives that would not be possible for individual organisations.

Importantly, she forcefully challenges the received wisdom that 'effective collaboration is a black box'—that is, good in theory, but doing it well is a mystery or a matter of luck. Instead, she sets out some pragmatic advice regarding the factors critical to success. Arguably, the most important of these is recognising that the skills required for collaboration are unique and that it is important not to assume leaders or others know how to do it. (Given that more than half of all collaborations fail to meet their objectives, clearly many do not.) She also highlights research showing that providing training in collaborative working and recognising and rewarding collaborative work improve outcomes.

To do this, Keast examines a number of case studies of collaborative initiatives and identifies a range of collaborative processes, supplementary processes and 'micro-processes' used by those who have achieved success. She emphasises the need for leaders to undertake a stocktake of their operating and stakeholder environments, and their goals, and to select the strategies that are most appropriate to the situation.

While all writers comment on various aspects of the drivers of and inhibitors to effective coworking, there are a couple of aspects that are implicit in their arguments but not specifically addressed. Their identification may prove fruitful for further discussion and research.

In particular, the power to create change lies within each of us and motivating ourselves and others to challenge the status quo is a prerequisite for success. It is well acknowledged that a sudden crisis or emergency creates strong clarity of purpose (for example, to preserve life) and can be so powerful that people willingly put their differences and other priorities aside and work constructively together. An example of this is the introduction of gun control laws in Australia after the Port Arthur massacre in 1996. For nearly a decade, the federal government had been working with the states and territories in an effort to introduce stricter gun control laws. Despite some ongoing opposition, this was achieved within months of the tragedy in Tasmania.

How do we create the same sense of shared responsibility, passion and energy for the less dramatic, but entrenched and insidious problems that persist in our society? How do we shake ourselves and others out of accepting things as they are and unlock the drive to create change—particularly when it may take 20 years or longer to realise the changes? One answer might lie in the rapid improvement in information technology and our increased access to independent, reliable and real-time data. Good information can tell a stronger, more compelling story to those with power than case studies and anecdotes. It can also provide us with a quantifiable 'return on investment' that facilitates collaborative goal setting and enables measurement of alternative strategies and accurate evaluation of impact. Importantly, good data are a prerequisite for the expansion of access to private capital, such as social investment bonds.

While the focus of these chapters is cross-sector collaboration, there are also many examples of projects initiated and driven by those outside existing systems. Independent advocates can often achieve change where others cannot. Unlike those who have worked 'in the system' for some years, they usually have no association with previous policies nor are they limited by existing relationships, organisational structures or modes of thinking. Their loyalty is to solving the problem or to helping a specific population and, as an outsider, they can cut through bureaucracy when others cannot. On some occasions the best cross-sector leaders are those who can recognise when they are not the best person to lead change and who instead support someone better placed to create change.

With governments continuing to transfer the provision of human and other services from the public sector to the not-for-profit and for-profit sectors, and ongoing budget pressures, the need for more sophisticated collaborative processes and skills will continue to increase. The challenges of cross-sector working are not new, but by pooling the knowledge of experts, such as Keast, Seibert and Black, and by leveraging ever improving information technology and other resources (including innovative methods of fundraising), there are real opportunities to achieve step change for some of society's most entrenched problems.

6

Policy Impediments to Social Investments by Australian Businesses

Leeora D. Black[1]

The role of business in social investment

The term 'social investment' has been used loosely by Australian business to denote any philanthropic contribution to society, sometimes as part of corporate social responsibility (CSR) programs or corporate foundation grant making. Corporate social investment (CSI) can entail donations, managerial expertise or use of corporate infrastructure and resources (Cooke 2010).

Definitions of CSI are often very broad. For example, KPMG's report on *Unlocking the Value of Social Investment* (2014: 4) says social investment is '[a]ny investment a company makes to contribute to society that is not primarily motivated by generating a direct financial

1   I am grateful for the support and advice of a number of people in preparing this chapter: Jacqueline Hartford, intern, ACCSR (RMIT University); Corinne Proske, Director, Government, Education and Community, Head of Community Finance and Development, National Australia Bank; Daniel Madhavan, Chief Executive Officer, Impact Investing Australia; and Ainsley Lee, Head of Investments, NRMA Strategy & Investments.

return'. This includes donations, sponsorship, volunteering, matched giving and pro bono work, all of which are the traditional tools of corporate philanthropy.

This definition represents a traditional view of CSI. Newer definitions directly challenge the view that CSI is incompatible with financial returns. Social investment can unlock significant sums of private investment capital, according to the Global Impact Investing Network (www.thegiin.org) and local organisations such as Impact Investing Australia (impactinvestingaustralia.com/). Big Society Capital (bigsocietycapital.com/), a UK-based financial institution with a social mission set up to help grow the social investment market, defines social investment as 'the use of repayable finance to achieve a social as well as a financial return'. Compared with traditional views of CSI, the goal of social impact investment is very specific: to catalyse viable private markets to address pressing social needs.

Impact Australia estimates the market for social impact investment could reach $32 billion in a decade (NSW DPC 2015), whereas, in 2013, philanthropic donations from businesses in Australia amounted to more than $850 million (Philanthropy Australia n.d.). Social impact investment suggests a much more promising avenue for achieving significant social outcomes. Therefore, I have chosen in this chapter to use the Big Society Capital definition of social impact investment as the lens through which to examine social investments by Australian business, or CSI.

Social investments by Australian businesses that adopt an impact investment orientation are, so far, in their infancy. In this chapter, I will suggest three new opportunities for social investments by business and describe some potential roles for government in stimulating this innovative approach to achieving social outcomes. The concept of 'shared value' (Porter and Kramer 2011) holds promise for increasing social investments by business. I will then describe policy impediments to further social investment by business and suggest some potential solutions.

Three opportunities for social investments by business

There is significant potential to expand social investment by business through financial intermediaries, superannuation funds and CSR programs.

Banks and other financial intermediaries

Banks and other financial intermediaries such as credit unions or investment banks can use their financial strength to develop innovative approaches to funding social enterprises. A social enterprise is a business that aims to make a social impact as well as generate a financial return. There may be more than 20,000 social enterprises in Australia (Social Traders and QUT 2010).

One example is STREAT, a social enterprise that aims to address youth homelessness and disadvantage, bringing about social change through market-focused business activities, such as food services businesses. STREAT sought a bank loan of $1.5 million to develop a property to set up a food business. The property was leased from a private investor for a peppercorn rent of $1 a year. That kind of arrangement does not provide the collateral that a traditional bank loan requires. Most banks would have looked at it simply on a traditional commercial basis and said no.

STREAT's bank, however, the National Australia Bank (NAB), was very keen to support the organisation's vision due to their own CSR orientation, and worked to get the deal up for them.

More recently, NAB has signed a further $2.5 million loan for STREAT to help finance the construction of a new multimillion-dollar training facility for Melbourne's homeless youth (Christie 2015). The facility will train 250 young homeless Australians each year and give them the opportunity of a career in hospitality. Importantly, the deal will help STREAT transition to a fully self-funded business model. STREAT is not required to make any interest payments during construction, with the value of the property providing security during the building phase. After the facility has been built, the debt will be sold to investors.

Other successful impact investments in Australia are the Good Start Early Learning Centre, Australian Chamber Orchestra Instrument Fund, Barefoot Power and Hepburn Community Wind (Addis et al. 2013).

Intermediaries play an important role in bringing the supply of money and the demand for capital together in the social impact investment market (Burkett 2012; Addis et al. 2013). Financial intermediaries can take a wide range of forms and roles, from advisers to institutions that can assist with raising capital.

Impact Australia points out that intermediaries are particularly critical when the sector is still developing, as there are fewer established pathways to connect supply and demand, and there is a need for systemic ways for supply and demand to 'find' each other (Addis et al. 2013).

Skilled professionals who can match investors with social enterprises are required. A need for intermediation is a strong and consistent theme in the Australian market (Senate Economics References Committee 2011). There is potential for specialists to enter the sector and structure impact investment deals and products, and it is expected that demand for such intermediaries will increase (Addis et al. 2014).

Superannuation funds

It was not until the 2006 federal government report on *The Social Responsibility of Corporations* (CAMAC 2006) that it was made clear that it is in the interests of long-term investors such as superannuation funds to take social factors into account in their investment decisions. That same year the Parliamentary Joint Committee on Corporations and Financial Services report on corporate responsibility (PJC 2006) strongly encouraged superannuation trustees to consider companies' environmental and social responsibilities. The report stated, 'it is in fact so far bound up in long term financial success that a superannuation trustee would be closer to breaching the sole purpose test by ignoring corporate responsibility' (PJC 2006: s. 5.41). A decade on and about 50 per cent of Australian total assets under management now consider environmental, social and governance factors (RIAA 2015).

Involvement of the superannuation sector in social investment, however, remains all but non-existent. One exception is the industry superannuation fund HESTA. In September 2015, it announced a $30 million social impact investment fund brokered through Social Ventures Australia (Appell 2015). The fund will use a combination of debt, equity and social impact bonds to target deal sizes between $1 million and $10 million (Oppes 2015).

CSR programs

CSR programs have been moving to a more strategic orientation for many years; however, the use of innovative financial instruments to drive social as well as financial outcomes is not well established in corporate Australia. This is despite the fact that the biggest proportion of CSR budgets generally goes into community investment (ACCSR 2014).

Unlike most large businesses, NRMA Motoring, a New South Wales-based membership association, seeks social as well as financial outcomes from its investment portfolio. NRMA Motoring held three social investments, according to its 2015 sustainability report (NRMA 2015), including social benefit bonds (SBBs) and a direct investment in a social venture.

NRMA Motoring's approach is unusual, but may become more popular as business increasingly understands the role it can potentially play in driving better social outcomes by addressing social problems through business innovation.

Banks could play a positive role in stimulating social investment through CSR programs by creating new financial vehicles along the lines of climate impact bonds to enable other companies to invest a portion of their community spend in impact investments.

Shared value

The concept of shared value (Porter and Kramer 2011) holds promise for increasing social investments by Australian businesses. Shared value is a business strategy that delivers an improved profit formula or new market opportunity by addressing societal challenges. Its authors claim to be reshaping the traditional corporate response to societal issues. It calls for business to address social issues relevant to their business by innovating at scale through three potential pathways: redefining products and markets, redefining productivity and creating enabling local environments.

Nestlé's work with SA farmers to secure its supplies of oats for the Uncle Toby's brand is a good example of shared value. Nestlé worked with farmers and the South Australian Research and Development Institute to develop oat breeds that deliver better quality and yields, are disease and drought tolerant and contain higher beta-glucan content. This program not only gives Nestlé certainty of supply and a better-quality milling oat, it also gives farmers a guaranteed return and oats better suited to their conditions. It also gives consumers a more nutritious product.

This form of shared value has much in common with strategic CSR (Burke and Logdson 1996); however, rising interest in shared value in Australia may lead to more corporate social investments with significant economic and social benefits beyond the firm. Shared-value approaches are also compatible with social impact investments.

Obstacles to social investment by business

The barriers to further social investment by Australian business are numerous and well canvassed in several reports by the Senate Economics References Committee (2011), Impact Investing Australia and others (for example, Addis et al. 2013, 2014). They include: lack of access to early stage risk capital; lack of data; limited investments and high transaction costs; cultural barriers; lack of taxation incentives; the absence of clear policy to assist growth and encourage investment; and the lack of benchmarking and measurement.

The NSW Government identified barriers to the growth of social impact investment in New South Wales in its 2015 *Social Impact Investment Policy*. Barriers include:

> [L]imited proven models to build investor confidence, a lack of quality data to measure and quantify outcomes, diverse views on how to measure outcomes, the need for government to see genuine risk sharing in transactions, sufficient capability and capacity across government and social sector organisations, and economies of scale and diversification necessary for larger investors and funds to invest. (NSW DPC 2015: 3)

In a report written for the United Kingdom's Social Impact Investment Taskforce, Triodos Bank identified regulation as a barrier to impact investing by setting minimum investment levels too high and thereby restricting the pool of potential investors (Social Impact Investment Taskforce 2014). A further barrier is that the majority of tax incentives are aimed only at mainstream investments such as mutual funds and stock investments.

In Australia, the deductible gift recipient (DGR) rules of the taxation system mean that charities with DGR status can receive tax-deductible gifts from donors, but they must be established entities. Early stage social entrepreneurs are very unlikely to qualify for tax-deductible gifts or investments (Senate Economics References Committee 2011). Private ancillary funds (PAFs) can fund only DGR-status organisations and have poor incentives to make social investments (Senate Economics References Committee 2011). Further, the social sector is prohibited by DGR and PAF requirements from using grants for investment, and must buy 'stuff' (private communication, 2015).

The Australian Treasury (2014) has concluded that clarification of regulation would help facilitate market development. Such clarification might include financial obligations for superannuation companies and amendments to laws to facilitate private investors to access social impact bonds. Currently, social impact bonds are burdened by onerous disclosure requirements. The report recommends exploring ways to facilitate the development of the impact investment market and encouraging innovation for funding, and provide guidance to superannuation companies on impact investing.

It is frequently harder for social enterprises than for commercial enterprises to access funds. Social entrepreneurs' risk profile is too high for regular finance arrangements and too costly for banks to go the extra mile.

Finally, the mindset for CSR programs is not attuned to the concept of investment for a financial return, rather than grants. The result is a weak deal pipeline and poor capacity of social sector organisations to pursue social investments.

The role of government in social investment by business

Government can play a variety of roles in stimulating social action by business: mandating, facilitating, collaborating and endorsing (Fox et al. 2002). Governments in Australia have so far adopted a 'facilitating' approach. In a facilitating role, governments act as a driver for social and environmental change through enabling or providing incentives for organisations. There is also opportunity for governments to encourage participation from investors through raising awareness, as well as developing management tools, benchmarks and guidelines (Fox et al. 2002: 5). Governments can also act as underwriter, co-investor, regulator, procurer of goods and services or provider of subsidies and technical assistance (Wood et al. 2013).

The World Economic Forum (WEF 2013) has three recommendations for the role of government in social impact investing. The first is to 'provide tax relief for risky or early stage investments in which public benefit is created, but below-market returns are generated' (WEF 2013: 29). The purpose of this recommendation is to catalyse investment in projects that might provide below-market returns and may be avoided by investors unless there is an incentive. The second recommendation is to '[c]autiously revise regulations that restrict willing capital into impact investments' (WEF 2013: 29). If regulation is restricting investment, changes to regulation may reduce barriers and encourage increased capital flow. The third recommendation is to 'help de-risk the ecosystem through innovative funding mechanisms. Ways governments can do this are to provide access to capital, and take a subordinate position in a layered structured fund to attract mainstream investors (WEF 2013: 29).

Recently, some Australian state governments have announced programs, or their intention to establish programs, to facilitate social impact investment. This increased involvement by government has raised questions as to what role the public sector can play in breaking down barriers to impact investment in Australia.

In January 2015, the NSW Government released its *Social Impact Investment Policy*. The policy outlines the future direction for social impact investment, building on existing SBB programs such as Newpin and the Benevolent Society Bond.

In July 2015, the Queensland Government announced it would undertake a SBB pilot program (Pitt 2015). Three SBBs will be piloted, targeting early intervention in social issues such as reoffending, homelessness and childhood education. A Social Benefit Bonds Readiness Fund will also be set up to assist providers in the design phase of the pilot (Remeikis 2015).

Currently, the SA Government is moving towards trialling social impact bonds and received expressions of interest for social impact investment up to 20 February 2015, after releasing a discussion paper (SAG 2015).

The governments of Victoria, Western Australia and Tasmania are in various stages of developing social impact investment initiatives (Charlton et al. 2013). In response to recommendations arising from the 2015 *Review of Australia's Welfare System*, the then federal minister for social services, Scott Morrison (Mather 2015), has also outlined his enthusiasm and support for an increased role for social impact bonds in addressing social issues.

Policy options for Australia

In this section, I describe some policy options for government to consider to stimulate greater social investment by business.

New business structures

Currently, a company structure can be either for-profit or not-for-profit (NFP). NFP companies are prohibited from making distributions to members or paying fees to directors (ASIC 2011), meaning there can be no investments with financial returns. For-profit company directors are required to act in the best interests of the company, which does not exclude taking social impacts into consideration (PJC 2006); however, a permissive approach is not the same as encouragement.

In the United States, a new form of corporate structure has been authorised in 30 states and the District of Columbia: the 'B Corporation' (Wikipedia 2016). B corporations differ from traditional companies as they specifically seek a positive impact on society and the environment, in addition to returns for shareholders. While nothing in Australian corporations law prohibits social benefits as well as financial returns, neither is there much encouragement.

The B corporation movement established a presence in Australia in 2014 (B Lab n.d.) and is canvassing perspectives on the establishment of a new legal form in Australia that considers impacts not only on shareholders, but also on society and the environment. In Australia, B corporations are certified based on an assessment of the company's governance, transparency and environmental and social impacts, and not on a separate legal form.

Arguments for creating a legal form for B corporations in Australia include giving specific legal protection to directors and officers to consider the interests of all stakeholders, not just shareholders (that is, creating a safe harbour for directors), and helping mission-driven businesses to attract venture capital and command higher valuations.

But the more powerful and urgent argument is the ability to direct capital into business that can address social impacts at scale.

Encouraging shared value

Governments can play a significant role in changing mindsets, raising awareness and encouraging action (Fox et al. 2002). The Australian Government has so far used a shared-value approach to encouraging business investment in foreign aid through its 'Ministerial statement on engaging the private sector in aid and development: Creating shared value through partnership' (DFAT 2015), released on 31 August 2015. However, more could be done to stimulate business investment in addressing social problems in Australia through supporting shared-value education and training, partnering with business and establishing intermediary organisations with the capacity to bring investors and investees together.

Support for intermediary organisations

The UK Government, for example, established Big Society Capital in April 2012 to grow the social investment market. Big Society Capital's first annual report outlines the UK Government's policy development journey since 2000 that led to its establishment (Big Society Capital 2012). Big Society Capital makes direct investments as well as working with others to facilitate deals and raise awareness. Funding is provided from dormant bank accounts and banks. At 30 June 2015, Big Society Capital reported £370 million (A$713 million) invested in a portfolio of 39 charities and social enterprises.

An Australian body that undertakes a similar role to Big Society Capital would be an important enabler of the emerging social investment market.

Taxation

Unlike Australia, the UK Government provides some tax relief for investments (not just donations) in charities and social enterprises. In a submission to the federal government's tax White Paper process, Social Ventures Australia (SVA 2015) released a tax discussion paper that called for tax concessions for impact investments in social enterprises, social impact bonds and social and affordable housing projects.

The SVA submission recommended:

1. Investors be able to offset the amount invested in a social enterprise or social impact bond against their assessable taxable income in the year that the investment is made.
2. Investors receive a tax exemption for interest repayments or dividends as they are repaid during the life of the investment.
3. Capital gains tax should also be exempt when the impact investment is held for a minimum period.
4. A new social infrastructure tax offset scheme should be implemented using non-deductible/non-assessable social and affordable housing bonds so that investors can lend at submarket rates to developers building new social and affordable housing stock.

Sole-purpose test

The 'sole-purpose test' requires superannuation fund trustees to manage funds solely for the benefit of fund members' retirements (APRA 2011). This does not prohibit positive social outcomes (PJC 2006). Indeed, environmental, social and governance considerations are now mainstream (RIAA 2015). However, this is not the same as putting social impacts on a par with financial returns. It is possible for superannuation funds to seek positive social impacts, as demonstrated by the establishment of Good Super in 2013 (goodsuper. com.au), which has 100 per cent of funds in impact investments, and Christian Super in 1984 (christiansuper.com.au/), with about 10 per cent of funds in impact investments (Impact Investing Australia n.d.). As noted earlier, HESTA has committed to a $30 million social impact investment fund.

The sole-purpose test allows superannuation funds to invest for positive social outcomes where returns are comparable with commercial rates of return; however, others have argued that funds can invest in vehicles that provide a lower commercial rate although they generally avoid doing so (Senate Economics References Committee 2011). The committee called for clarification, if necessary, of the fiduciary duties of superannuation funds and their ability to engage with social impact investment opportunities (Senate Economics References Committee 2011: Recommendation 4.4).

A clear statement by government that positive social impacts are consistent with the sole-purpose test may help to embolden investors to participate in new types of social investments.

Conclusion

In this chapter, I have argued that greater social investment by business can be unlocked by adopting a view of social investment that encourages the pursuit of financial, as well as social, returns. I have suggested that banks, superannuation funds and CSR programs all have a significant role to play in unlocking this potential. Corporations law and our taxation system provide little encouragement for this type of social investment by business, but that could change with thoughtful policy approaches. Governments are beginning to welcome experiments with social impact investing but much more is possible. Some of the ways in which governments can encourage greater social investment by business are: the encouragement of shared-value approaches; the use of B corporation structures to unlock social entrepreneurship; capacity and pipeline-building initiatives along the lines of the United Kingdom's Big Society Capital; the use of taxation incentives; and clarification of the sole-purpose test.

References

Addis, R., A. Bowden and D. Simpson. 2014. *Delivering on impact: The Australian Advisory Board breakthrough strategy to catalyse impact investment*. Australian Advisory Board report to Impact Investing Australia, Melbourne.

Addis, R., J. McLeod and A. Raine. 2013. *IMPACT-Australia: Investment for social and economic benefit*. Canberra: Commonwealth Department of Education, Employment and Workplace Relations and JBWere.

Appell, D. 2015. 'Australia's HESTA commits A$30 million to social impact fund.' *Pensions & Investments*, 3 September. Available from: pionline.com (accessed 3 December 2015).

Australian Centre for Corporate Social Responsibility (ACCSR). 2014. 'The 10th year: Progress and prospects for CSR in Australia and New Zealand.' In *Annual Review of the State of CSR in Australia and New Zealand*, 12. Melbourne: ACCSR.

Australian Prudential Regulation Authority (APRA). 2011. *The sole purpose test*. Superannuation Circular No. III.A.4, February. APRA, Sydney.

Australian Securities Investment Commission (ASIC). 2011. *Registering not for profit or charitable organisations*. Information Sheet 81, November. ASIC, Sydney. Available from: asic.gov.au/for-business/starting-a-company/how-to-start-a-company/registering-not-for-profit-or-charitable-organisations/ (accessed 9 December 2015).

B Lab. n.d. *Developing Model Legislation for Australian B Corps*. Melbourne: B Lab. Available from: bcorporation.com.au/benefitcorp_au (accessed 9 December 2015).

Big Society Capital. 2012. *Annual Report*. London: Big Society Capital.

Burke, L. and J. M. Logsdon. 1996. 'Corporate social responsibility pays off.' *Long Range Planning* 29(4): 437–596.

Burkett, I. 2012. *Building Blocks for Action*: *Place based impact investment in Australia*. Canberra: Commonwealth Department of Education, Employment and Workplace Relations, NAB, Mission Australia and JBWere.

Charlton, K., S. Donaid, J. Ormiston and R. Seymour. 2013. *Impact Investments: Perspectives for Australian superannuation funds*. Sydney: Herbert Smith Freehills, Evans & Partners, The Ian Potter Foundation, Macquarie Funds Group, Macquarie Group Foundation and University of Sydney.

Christie, R. 2015. 'NAB expands social impact investment offerings.' *InFinance*, 9 June. Available from: finsia.com/news/news-article/2015/06/09/nab-expands-social-impact-investment-offerings (accessed 3 December 2015).

Cooke, D. 2010. 'Building social capital through corporate social investment.' *Asia-Pacific Journal of Business Administration* 2(1): 71–87.

Corporations and Markets Advisory Committee (CAMAC). 2006. *The social responsibility of corporations*. Report, December. Corporations and Markets Advisory Committee, Canberra.

Department of Foreign Affairs and Trade (DFAT). 2015. Ministerial statement on engaging the private sector in aid and development: Creating shared value through partnership. 31 August. Australian Government, Canberra.

Fox, T., H. Ward and B. Howard. 2002. *Public Sector Roles in Strengthening Corporate Social Responsibility: A baseline study*. October. Washington, DC: The World Bank.

Her Majesty's Government (HMG). 2014. *Growing the Social Investment Market: 2014 progress update*. London: Minister for Civil Society, United Kingdom.

Impact Investing Australia. n.d. *Impact Profile: Tim Macready*. Melbourne: Impact Investing Australia. Available from: impactinvestingaustralia.com/impact-profile-tim-macready/ (accessed 2 August 2015).

KPMG. 2014. *Unlocking the Value of Social Investment*. Sydney: KPMG Australia.

Mather, J. 2015. 'Scott Morrison keen to follow NSW into social impact bonds.' *Australian Financial Review*, 9 September. Available from: afr.com/business/banking-and-finance/investment-banking/scott-morrison-keen-to-follow-nsw-into-social-impact-bonds-20150909-gjifh6 (accessed 28 March 2016).

New South Wales Department of Premier and Cabinet (NSW DPC). 2015. *Social Impact Investment Policy*. Sydney: NSW Government. Available from: dpc.nsw.gov.au/__data/assets/pdf_file/0011/168338/Social_Impact_Investment_Policy_WEB.pdf (accessed 2 August 2015).

NRMA. 2015. *Preparing for the Future. NRMA corporate responsibility review 2014/15*. Sydney: NRMA. Available from: mynrma.com.au/images/About/NRMA_Corporate_Responsibility_Review_2015.pdf (accessed 2 December 2015).

Oppes, A. 2015. 'Implications of new growth phase in Australian impact investing.' *SVA Quarterly* 13.

Parliamentary Joint Committee on Corporations and Financial Services (PJC). 2006. *Corporate responsibility: Managing risk and creating value*. Report of the Parliamentary Joint Committee on Corporations and Financial Services, June. Australian Government, Canberra.

Philanthropy Australia. n.d. *Fast Facts and Stats*. Melbourne: Philanthropy Australia. Available from: philanthropy.org.au/tools-resources/fast-facts-and-stats/ (accessed 2 August 2015).

Pitt, C. 2015. Social benefit bonds explore new solutions to complex problems. Media Statement by Treasurer, Minister for Employment and Industrial Relations and Minister for Aboriginal and Torres Strait Islander Partnerships, The Honourable Curtis Pitt, 13 July. Parliament House, Brisbane. Available from: statements.qld.gov.au/Statement/2015/7/13/social-benefit-bonds-explore-new-solutions-to-complex-problems (accessed 28 March 2016).

Porter, M. and M. Kramer. 2011. 'Creating shared value.' *Harvard Business Review* (January–February).

Remeikis, A. 2015. 'Queensland Labor, LNP agree social benefit bonds are the future.' *Brisbane Times*, 13 July.

Responsible Investment Association Australasia (RIAA). 2015. *Responsible Investment Association Australasia Benchmark Report.* Sydney: RIAA.

Senate Economics References Committee. 2011. *Investing for Good: the development of a capital market for the not-for-profit sector in Australia.* Canberra: Australian Government. Available from: aph. gov.au/Parliamentary_Business/Committees/Senate/Economics/Completed_inquiries/2010-13/capitalmarket2011/report/index (accessed 27 July 2015).

Social Impact Investment Taskforce. 2014. *Impact Investing for Everyone: A blueprint for retail impact investing.* London: Social Impact Investment Taskforce. Available from: socialimpactinvestment.org/subject-papers.php (accessed 16 July 2015).

Social Traders and Queensland University of Technology (QUT). 2010. *Social Enterprise in Australia: A preliminary snapshot.* Brisbane: Social Traders and QUT.

Social Ventures Australia (SVA). 2015. *Re:think*. Tax Discussion Paper. Social Ventures Australia, Sydney. Available from: bettertax.gov. au/files/2015/03/TWP_combined-online.pdf (accessed 9 December 2015).

South Australian Government (SAG). 2015. *Building a stronger society. A discussion paper on social impact investment.* 18 December. Economic Analysis Division, Department of the Premier and

Cabinet, Adelaide. Available from: assets.yoursay.sa.gov.au/production/2013/12/18/00_24_24_430_Building_a_Stronger_Society_web_version_.pdf (accessed 28 March 2016).

Treasury. 2014. *Financial System Inquiry Interim Report*. Canberra: Australian Government. Available from: fsi.gov.au/publications/interim-report/ (accessed 21 July 2015).

Wikipedia. 2016. 'Benefit corporation.' *Wikipedia*. Available from: en.wikipedia.org/wiki/Benefit_corporation (accessed 28 March 2016).

Wood, D., B. Thornley and K. Grace. 2013. 'Institutional impact investing: Practice and policy.' *Journal of Sustainable Finance & Investment* 3(2): 75–94.

World Economic Forum (WEF). 2013. *From the Margins to the Mainstream: Assessment of the impact investment sector and opportunities to engage mainstream investors*. Geneva: World Economic Forum. Available from: iris.thegiin.org/research/from-the-margins-to-the-mainstream/summary (27 July 2015).

7

Navigating Reform in Contested Spaces: Reflections on not-for-profit sector regulatory reform in Australia, 2010–2013

Krystian Seibert[1]

Introduction

Historically, the not-for-profit (NFP) sector in Australia has not generally benefited from any strategic and wide-ranging NFP sector-specific regulatory reform. Although over the years certain subsectors have benefited from particular reforms, there has been a clear lack of broad-based and comprehensive reform focusing on the key structural components of NFP regulation.

At the Commonwealth level, where regulation of the NFP sector has generally been focused on taxation matters, reforms have mostly been ad hoc and piecemeal, resulting in a taxation framework that is extremely complex and in some respects inequitable (O'Connell 2008: 17; Treasury 2013: 22).

1   The author thanks Professor Ann O'Connell, Professor Myles McGregor-Lowndes OAM, Mr Robert Fitzgerald AM and Ms Susan Pascoe AM for their comments on a draft version of this chapter. The chapter reflects the author's own views and any errors are the author's.

The situation at the state and territory level is little different. This is most obvious in the case of fundraising regulation, which is fragmented and inefficient (Productivity Commission 2010: 138). Although fundraising regulation is reviewed from time to time, there has been little progress towards delivering widespread improvements, let alone any national consistency.

The establishment of the Australian Charities and Not-for-profits Commission (ACNC) was a major part of the NFP sector reform agenda that the Australian Government pursued between 2010 and 2013. It was an attempt to shift away from reform that was ad hoc and piecemeal or lacked substance and demonstrated a certain level of government indifference. With a specific focus on the NFP sector and charities in particular, it was strategic in nature and involved comprehensive and wide-ranging change rather than just tinkering around the edges.

At the time of the ACNC's establishment, former Assistant Treasurer David Bradbury (2012c) described the reform process in the following way:

> The establishment of the ACNC is the key component of the Gillard Government's objective to deliver smarter and more effective regulation of the NFP Sector.
>
> The ACNC is future-focused, structural reform, which the NFP Sector has long called for and has been recommended by review after review.
>
> As the NFP sector grows, it is critically important to support the sector through smarter regulation. This involves designing a regulatory framework which is suited to the NFP sector and addresses flaws in the current approach to NFP regulation.

This is not to say that the reform process was perfect, or that the outcome met the expectations of all stakeholders in full. That would be an impossible task, and, as with any new regulatory framework, there are often aspects that require 'tweaking' after the initial implementation phase has passed. Nor is it to say that the reform process addressed all of the wide variety of challenges confronting the NFP sector, which are the subject of recommendations in the Productivity Commission's 2010 report *Contribution of the Not-for-profit Sector*. The establishment of the ACNC was never put forward as a solution to all these challenges.

In this regard it is also important to emphasise that the ACNC reform process is ongoing, and will be until the elusive goal of a fully national approach to areas such as fundraising regulation is achieved.

As an adviser to the former Assistant Treasurer during 2012 and 2013, I was closely involved with the establishment of the ACNC and associated aspects of its regulatory framework such as its governance standards and financial reporting arrangements. My role included oversight of the development of the ACNC legislation and supporting the Assistant Treasurer's efforts to secure its passage through the Parliament. This involved working closely with officials within the Department of Treasury and engaging extensively with stakeholders within the NFP sector. The experience provided me with a unique perspective on the ACNC reform process 'on the inside'.

The purpose of this chapter, however, is not to recount the ACNC reform process in detail, nor to examine the background to the process. This is done well elsewhere (see, for example, Pascoe forthcoming; O'Connell et al. 2013). Nor is the purpose to examine the 'politics' of the process, including subsequent uncertainty about the ACNC's future after the 2013 election. Rather, the aim of this chapter is twofold. First, to illustrate why the ACNC reform process was a unique example of cross-sector working, which is the focus of this edited volume. Second, to reflect on the key insights from this process, which might inform future regulatory reform efforts, regarding regulatory reform as it relates to the NFP sector and beyond. These reflections are based on my own experiences and my discussions with the many stakeholders with whom I worked as part of the ACNC reform process.

The ACNC reform process: A unique case study of cross-sector working

As pointed out above, Australia's regulatory framework for the NFP sector has generally been characterised by a lack of strategic and wide-ranging reform. Where reform has occurred, it has largely been ad hoc and piecemeal. Reforming such a regulatory framework in a more strategic manner was a complex undertaking. This complexity, together with other unique and significant characteristics, makes it an interesting example of cross-sector working. These characteristics are discussed below and provide some useful context for the 'key insights' from the ACNC reform process that are examined in the following section of this chapter.

Focus, breadth and complexity

The establishment of the ACNC was the largest and most complex structural reform experienced by the NFP sector in Australia (and, in particular, the charitable sector, which forms part of the broader NFP sector).

Although reforms such as the introduction of Australia's Goods and Services Tax (GST) in 2000 had a big impact on charities and other NFPs, the GST was an economy-wide reform and not specifically focused on charities.

Charities in certain subsectors have certainly participated in large and complex reform processes. For example, disability charities are currently experiencing a major period of change with the introduction of the National Disability Insurance Scheme and its consumer-directed care model. However, these changes, as considerable as they might be, do not impact on or involve the entire charitable sector. That is one defining feature of the ACNC reform process: it was complex, and challenging at times, and it was focused on the entire charitable sector and therefore impacted on all charities. In this regard it is unique.

A response to sector advocacy

The ACNC reform process was also an interesting example of a regulatory reform process in that it involved establishing a regulator in response to prolonged advocacy by a large segment of those whom it would regulate. Advocacy in favour of regulation is not uncommon, especially where it can benefit certain actors in a regulated space to the detriment of other actors. But proactive advocacy in favour of establishing a regulator by a broad cross-section of those whom it would regulate is rarer—and rarer still where it involves a relatively large sector; at last count there were more than 53,000 charities in Australia (acnc.gov.au).

Many Australian charities and their peak representative bodies had been advocating for a national charities regulator for some time, and it was first recommended in 2001 by the *Report of the Inquiry into the*

Definition of Charity and Related Organisations (Sheppard et al. 2001). Until 2011, however, there had been reluctance from government to pursue such a course of action, and it is reasonable to assert that had it not been for the advocacy of a broad cross-section of the charitable sector and its influence on the findings of subsequent reports such as the Productivity Commission's *Contribution of the Not-for-profit Sector* (2010), the establishment of the ACNC would not have occurred.

Proactive reform to establish a facilitative regulator

When the then opposition's Shadow Minister for Families, Housing and Community Services, Kevin Andrews, announced in June 2012 that a Coalition Government would abolish the yet to be established ACNC, he commented that '[n]owhere has the mischief that requires this new monolithic regulatory structure been identified' (Andrews 2012). In one sense, Andrews was correct: the establishment of the ACNC was not a response to some sort of crisis of public confidence in Australian charities, such as that which has prompted the United Kingdom Government to give more powers to its Charity Commission (Chamberlain 2014).

But in another sense, the then shadow minister's comments overlooked the fact that reactive regulation in response to a crisis is not an ideal approach to developing regulatory policy. It can lead to kneejerk reactions involving disproportionate responses to real or perceived problems. Indeed, one rationale for the establishment of the ACNC was that it was meant to prevent such kneejerk regulation. The aim would be to try to avoid any crisis, rather than wait for one to happen, by proactively pursuing regulatory reform that would support the growth of Australia's NFP sector (Bradbury 2012c).

In this regard, the ACNC reform process intended to establish a 'facilitative' regulator. Facilitative regulation can mean different things to different people, but it is most commonly used to describe a regulator which focuses on not only enforcing regulations but also supporting those it regulates to assist them to meet their regulatory obligations. This is, however, a relatively narrow definition of the term. For the purposes of this chapter, 'facilitative' is used in a broader sense, describing a regulator which is established to foster

THE THREE SECTOR SOLUTION

or nurture the sector it will regulate. In so doing, the regulator can support organisations within the sector to achieve their objectives and maximise their contribution to the common good.

This facilitative role is a key purpose of the ACNC regulatory framework and is codified in the second object of the *Australian Charities and Not-for-profits Commission Act 2012* (*ACNC Act*), 'to support and sustain a robust, vibrant, independent and innovative Australian not-for-profit sector'. This is reinforced by some of the matters the ACNC Commissioner must have regard to in exercising their powers and functions under the *ACNC Act*, contained in Sections 15-10 (d) and (h), such as 'the maintenance and promotion of the effectiveness and sustainability of the not-for-profit sector' and 'the unique nature and diversity of not-for-profit entities and the distinctive role that they play in Australia'.

In *The Regulation of Organised Civil Society*, Garton (2009) dismisses the importance of such 'less tangible' reasons to regulate civil society organisations including charities. Garton cites other more important reasons such as the need to prevent anticompetitive practices, the need to coordinate the sector, the need to respond to philanthropic failures, the need to ensure accountability and the need to prevent the erosion of key civil society organisation characteristics (2009: 119). While a desire to promote accountability and transparency certainly formed part of the motivation for the establishment of the ACNC,[2] especially within the government, even this desire was framed within a context of establishing a 'facilitative' regulator, with the then assistant treasurer stating in his second reading speech for the Australian Charities and Not-for-profits Commission Bill 2012 (ACNC Bill) that '[e]nsuring that the sector can consolidate its standing in the community through enhanced transparency and accountability is essential to its ongoing growth and sustainability' (Bradbury 2012b).

Therefore, based on the experience of the ACNC reform process, Garton is somewhat unwise to dismiss the significance of supposedly less tangible reasons to regulate the charitable sector, such as a desire to foster or nurture the sector. The intention to establish a facilitative regulator had implications for the nature of the cross-

---

2   See *ACNC Act* (s. 15.10[b]).

sector collaboration involved during the ACNC reform process. This is a particularly relevant factor in the case of a number of the 'insights' discussed in the next section of this chapter.

Contested reform in a highly charged political environment

Although it is not the purpose of this chapter to examine the politics of the ACNC reform process, it is nonetheless important to highlight the broader political context in which the reform process occurred. The establishment of the ACNC took place during the Forty-Third Parliament (2010–13), which had a number of notable characteristics, including the relative instability associated with minority governments, which, although common in some other countries, are quite rare in Australia, especially at the federal level.

Overlaid on to this was the particularly adversarial nature of political engagement between the government and the opposition during this period. By its very nature, our parliamentary system is adversarial, but few would disagree with the conclusion that the Forty-Third Parliament was even more so than others. This particularly adversarial nature of political engagement was also witnessed in the context of the ACNC reform process—the establishment of the ACNC was a contested space, strongly opposed by the opposition. One need only review the Hansard transcripts of the debate on the ACNC Bill 2012 to see a number of heated exchanges that took place as the Bill and its associated ACNC (Consequential and Transitional Provisions) Bill 2012 were debated and ultimately passed. Progressing reform in such circumstances becomes even harder, especially when the numbers are so finely balanced in the Parliament and there is no prospect of support from the opposition. In spite of this, the ACNC Bills ultimately did become law.

Successful cross-sector working

The establishment of the ACNC was a large and complex structural reform that can be regarded as a success. Of course, this depends on how you define success.

For the purposes of this chapter, it is regarded as a success first because the ACNC *was established*. This is an achievement in itself because it was a very complex reform involving a diverse range of stakeholders both within and beyond the charitable sector. Furthermore, this reform was pursued in a highly charged political environment and subject to strong political opposition, as discussed above.

Second, it is regarded as a success because of the broad support for the ACNC as reported in published surveys. The Pro Bono Australia *State of the Not for Profit Sector Survey* (2015) found that nearly 60 per cent of respondents preferred the ACNC to be the charities regulator, with 30 per cent preferring co-regulation, 7 per cent preferring self-regulation and only 5 per cent preferring the Australian Taxation Office (ATO). Notably, 80 per cent of respondents recognised the ACNC's importance in developing a thriving Australian NFP sector (Pro Bono Australia 2015).

This is not to assert that the ACNC's work is complete. Indeed, part of the promise of the ACNC relates to streamlining the regulatory framework for the charitable sector. The regulation of charities comes from many sources, including the Commonwealth and the states and territories. In the words of the Productivity Commission (2010: xxiii), this regulation is 'complex, lacks coherence, sufficient transparency, and is costly to NFPs'.

The ACNC has much work ahead of it, and much expectation riding on it. The announcement by the Australian Government of its decision to retain the ACNC (Porter and O'Dwyer 2016) will greatly assist to progress this work.

The success of the ACNC reform process involved cross-sectoral collaboration between government and stakeholders from the NFP sector and beyond. This included multiple government agencies such as the Treasury, the ATO and the Department of the Prime Minister and Cabinet, as well as the ACNC Implementation Taskforce. It involved a diverse range of charities including social welfare, religious, arts, environmental, international development and philanthropic organisations—as well as their various peak bodies. It also involved the professional advisers to these organisations such as accounting and law firms, peak bodies representing accountants, company directors and company secretaries as well as academic experts and researchers. All of these actors contributed their effort and expertise, and the effectiveness of this cross-sectoral collaboration was crucial to the success of the ACNC reform process.

Reflections on the key insights from the ACNC reform process

As discussed above, the ACNC reform process had a number of unique and significant characteristics that make it an interesting example of cross-sector working.

Structural reform is generally difficult to deliver; but despite various challenges and the fact that the ACNC is effectively still a work in progress, it is a structural reform that was delivered. There are a number of key insights from the ACNC reform process that are worth reflecting on to inform future regulatory reform efforts. Many of these insights relate to factors that were pivotal in achieving such major reform in a relatively short time.

Demonstrating an intention to proceed with a new approach to collaboration and engagement

The ACNC reform process was underpinned by an intention to proceed with a new approach to government and NFP sector collaboration and engagement. This approach was formalised in the *National Compact*, which had as one of its 'shared principles' an aspiration to build 'a relationship between the government and the sector based on mutual respect and trust' (Department of the Prime Minister and Cabinet 2011: 7). The shared aspiration for the relationship between the government and the NFP sector involved a commitment to work together respectfully, based on mutual understanding, and to communicate openly with each other.

Traditionally, there has often been a relationship of mistrust between the NFP sector and government. It is inevitable, and perhaps even necessary, to have a degree of tension between the two sectors— especially given that a key role of the NFP sector is to undertake advocacy, and this means that the sector (or parts of it) and government will at times disagree on certain policy questions and have different views of how best to address particular social, economic and environmental challenges.

The widespread use of so-called gag clauses in Commonwealth funding agreements with NFP organisations under the Howard Government was an example of a policy that indicated a certain mistrust of the NFP sector within government, but also bred mistrust of the government within the NFP sector. Given this relationship of mistrust, some form of circuit-breaker was needed, and it is arguable that setting out shared principles and aspirations in a document such as the *National Compact* provided this.

There were tangible acts by the government, even before the *National Compact* came into force, demonstrating a desire to move in this direction. An example is the removal of gag clauses from Commonwealth funding agreements with NFP organisations in 2008 (Pro Bono Australia 2008). Such a commitment to proceed with a new approach to government and NFP sector collaboration and engagement was a prerequisite to the ACNC reform process. As discussed in the previous section, the establishment of the ACNC was not precipitated by any crisis of public confidence in Australian charities. Rather, it was a reform advocated for by the NFP sector, and hence it required not only the consent but also the support of the soon to be regulated sector to achieve the reform outcome.

So the *National Compact* played a critical role in facilitating the ACNC reform process—without both the government and the NFP sector 'starting afresh', it is highly doubtful the establishment of the ACNC would have been possible. Nevertheless, it is important to point out that during the ACNC reform process, the relationship between the government and the NFP sector was strained at times, and required recalibration.

On Senator Mark Arbib and then David Bradbury taking on the role of Assistant Treasurer in late 2011 and early 2012, respectively, there was a sense that the relationship was under some pressure. Some of the reasons for this are discussed in more detail below, but factors contributing to this included disagreements about the direction of the ACNC reform process, combined with short consultation times as well as some concerns about taxation measures the government was progressing alongside the ACNC reform process. In response to this, there was a renewed government focus on collaboration and consultation. This included increased engagement and involvement from the Assistant Treasurer and his office in the reform process, with support from the Minister for Social Inclusion (who had overall responsibility for NFP sector policy within the government) and his office.

Timelines for reform balanced with the window of opportunity for reform

Although lobbying for an independent regulator had taken place over many years, the actual establishment of the ACNC happened in a relatively short period.

Treasury (2011) published the *Scoping study for a national not-for-profit regulator* Consultation Paper in January 2011, the proposed establishment of the ACNC was announced on budget night in 2011 (Shorten and Plibersek 2011) and the ACNC was up and running by the end of 2012. While there was a desire to take advantage of the window of opportunity to progress reform, the pace of reform did present a challenge. This is evident from the chronology of ACNC reform process interactions in Table 7.1; the shaded areas indicate formal consultations undertaken involving submissions, face-to-face engagement or both.

Table 7.1: Chronology of the ACNC reform process

11 February 2010	Productivity Commission recommends a national Registrar for Community and Charitable Purpose Organisations
9 August 2010	The Australian Labor Party commits to a scoping study to establish a national not-for-profit regulator during federal election campaign
21 January 2011	Treasury publishes the Consultation Paper *Scoping study for a national not-for-profit regulator*
10 May 2011	Budget 2011–12 includes $53.6 million in funding over four years to establish the ACNC and to make related structural changes in the ATO
27 May 2011	Australian Government announces that Robert Fitzgerald AM will be the chair of the ACNC's Advisory Board
4 July 2011	*Final Report* of the scoping study released, and Susan Pascoe AM appointed the chair of the ACNC Implementation Taskforce
28 October 2011	Treasury publishes the Consultation Paper *A definition of charity*

8 December 2011	Treasury publishes the Consultation Paper *Review of not-for-profit sector governance arrangements*
9 December 2011	Treasury publishes the exposure draft of the Australian Charities and Not-for-profits Commission Bill and ACNC Implementation Taskforce releases a discussion paper on the functions and operations of the ACNC
January–February 2012	ACNC Taskforce conducts community consultations across the country
1 March 2012	Australian Government extends the start date of the ACNC to 1 October 2012
17 May 2012	Australian Government defers timing of proposed governance and external conduct standards and financial reporting to allow for further consultation
12 June 2012	ACNC Implementation Taskforce publishes its *Implementation Report*
5–6 July 2012	Revised exposure draft of the ACNC Bill and accompanying exposure draft of the ACNC Consequential and Transitional Bill published and referred to the House of Representatives Standing Committee on Economics
26–27 July 2012	House of Representatives Committee public hearings on the Bill
15 August 2012	House of Representatives Committee reports on Bill
23 August 2012	The ACNC Bill 2012 and its accompanying Consequential and Transitional Bill introduced into the House of Representatives and referred to the Senate Community Affairs Legislation Committee and the Joint Committee on Corporations and Financial Services
3 September 2012	Joint Committee public hearings on the ACNC Bill
4 September 2012	Senate Committee public hearings on the ACNC Bill
10 September 2012	Joint Committee report tabled
12 September 2012	Senate Community Affairs report tabled
18 September 2012	ACNC Bills pass the House of Representatives
31 October 2012	ACNC Bills pass the Senate
1 November 2012	Senate amendments passed by the House of Representatives
November 2012	NFP Sector Reform Council roundtable on ACNC Governance Standards discussion draft released
3 December 2012	Royal assent and ACNC commences operations
6 December 2012	Susan Pascoe AM appointed by the Governor-General as the inaugural commissioner of the ACNC
10 December 2012	ACNC officially launched by Assistant Treasurer David Bradbury
17 December 2012	Treasury publishes Consultation Paper Governance standards for the not-for-profit (NFP) sector and draft financial reporting regulations

December 2012 – March 2013	ACNC undertakes consultation on regulatory approach
8 April 2013	Treasury publishes Charities Bill exposure draft
1 July 2013	ACNC Governance Standards and Financial Reporting Regulations commence

Source: Adapted from ACNC (2013b).

Based on Table 7.1, between January 2011 and April 2013 (a little more than two years), there were 11 formal consultations undertaken involving submissions, face-to-face engagement or both. Some of these, particularly in December 2011, involved relatively short consultation time frames. This was in large part driven by the tight deadline for establishing the ACNC, which was originally meant to commence on 1 July 2012; and the tight deadline for establishing the ACNC was driven by a desire to take advantage of the window of opportunity to progress such a reform within the duration of the Forty-Third Parliament. However, it understandably led to some consternation among stakeholders, as evidenced by this statement from a stakeholder submission in response to the ACNC Bill exposure draft and governance arrangements discussion paper:

[W]e are concerned that the sector's hitherto support for the establishment of a national regulator is being undermined by the rapid process of drafting with key points of departure from the blueprint for a national NFP regulator set down by the Productivity Commission (2010); and by the inadequate amount of time provided for consultation on these changes, notably at a time when many organisations are closed or unable to consult with their members and boards on these important reforms. (ACOSS 2012: 3)

The pace of reform can be particularly challenging for NFP stakeholders, who might not have the resources available to business and other stakeholder groups but also often need to consult within extensive networks of member organisations. This was perhaps something that was not always fully appreciated, especially given the cumulative impact of multiple consultations over time, and the implications of this in terms of the resourcing of NFP stakeholders.

It quickly became apparent to the government that things needed to be slowed and therefore an extension was provided for the consultation process around the ACNC Bill exposure draft and governance arrangements discussion paper, and the date of the ACNC's commencement was pushed back to October 2012 (Arbib and Butler 2012). Further, not long after Bradbury took on the role of Assistant Treasurer in early 2012, a decision was made to phase in the ACNC regulatory framework, with the ACNC to commence operation in 2012 and the introduction of the ACNC's financial reporting and governance standards framework to be delayed by a year, commencing in 2013 (Bradbury and Butler 2012b).

The aim of this decision was to slow things a little and focus on progressing the primary foundational components of the ACNC regulatory framework before moving on to other components. It would not only allow for more time to consult on the ACNC's financial reporting and governance standards framework (discussed further below), but also provide more time for charities to transition into the ACNC regulatory framework and familiarise themselves with any new requirements. This staged approach was welcomed by NFP stakeholders (CSA 2012), and was a decision that assisted in holding together the reform process without losing reform momentum.

Maintaining reform clarity and focus

At the same time as the government announced its intention to establish the ACNC on budget night in 2011, it also announced a proposal to introduce a 'Better Targeting of NFP Sector Tax Concessions' (Better Targeting) measure (commonly referred to by stakeholders as the unrelated business income tax or 'UBIT') (Shorten and Plibersek 2011). This proposal would have restricted the use of charitable tax concessions for so-called unrelated commercial activities. Its announcement came as a surprise to the NFP sector and was the subject of considerable concern and uncertainty.

It is not the purpose of this chapter to discuss the merits or otherwise of the Better Targeting proposal in any detail (Turnour and McGregor-Lowndes 2012 provide a compelling argument for why Better Targeting was not necessary). However, with the benefit of hindsight, it is reasonable to conclude that progressing complex regulatory reform (the establishment of the ACNC) as well as contentious taxation reform (Better Targeting) alongside each other was not a good decision.

Better Targeting presented various challenges on a number of levels. It challenged aspects of the *National Compact*—for example, the shared aspiration to 'communicate openly with each other', given that it was announced on budget night in 2011 with no prior consultation. This placed considerable strain on the 'refreshed' relationship that the government had sought to form with the NFP sector through the *National Compact*.

Flowing on from this, the presence of Better Targeting made progressing the ACNC reform process more challenging. This was not only because the uncertainty and concern around Better Targeting shifted some of the focus away from the positive objectives of the ACNC reform process, but also because the possible imposition of additional red tape through implementing Better Targeting contradicted one of the key objectives of the ACNC, which was to reduce red tape over time. The announcement to implement Better Targeting represented a dilution of reform clarity and focus—and such clarity and focus are very important when seeking to undertake major structural reform such as the establishment of the ACNC. It was an unnecessary distraction, which shifted the focus off the main game.

On Bradbury taking on the role of Assistant Treasurer in early 2012, there was a conscious desire to maintain reform clarity and focus. A decision was taken to delay the introduction of Better Targeting for one year, and then again for two years in early 2013 (Bradbury and Butler 2013). This enabled the efforts of the government and NFP sector to focus on the ACNC reform process, with consideration of Better Targeting, including whether or not to proceed with it, deferred to a time after the ACNC was established.

There was clearly much happening. Given the importance of establishing the ACNC and some of the questions being raised about the Better Targeting proposal, the ACNC was given priority. The Better Targeting proposal was subsequently abandoned by the current government after the 2013 election.

Seeking to coproduce reform

In an environment characterised largely by constructive stakeholders who want to participate in the reform process in good faith, government should seek to coproduce reform where possible. This is particularly the case where, as with the establishment of the ACNC, the aim was to create a facilitative regulator, rather than one based on a presumption of wrongdoing and the need for heavy-handed compliance measures. It is also important in a reform context underpinned by an intention to proceed with a new approach to government and NFP sector collaboration and engagement—as evidenced in the *National Compact*.

Coproduction can come across as a buzzword—it sounds great and nobody can disagree with it—but the reality often does not live up to the ideal. However, the development of the ACNC governance standards provides a good case study of where this approach was adopted and proved to be beneficial.

As noted above, the introduction of the ACNC governance standards was delayed to allow for passage of the ACNC legislation and then to provide more time to consult on the content of the ACNC governance standards before they entered into force. The approach adopted in developing the governance standards involved preparing a discussion draft consultation paper outlining possible standards and the rationale for their inclusion. A NFP Sector Reform Council roundtable was then convened in Canberra, with council members and a wide range of other stakeholders and experts invited to attend. Attendees were provided with an advance copy of the discussion draft to formulate their views on it.

At the roundtable itself, the chair of the NFP Sector Reform Council led the discussion, which involved examining each draft governance standard and seeking the views and opinions of attendees. The discussion was very useful and informative and involved a number of changes to the draft governance standards (Treasury 2012). For example, initially there was a proposal to include a 'fit and proper' test for 'responsible entities' as part of the standards; however, the view of stakeholders at the roundtable was that this would be unworkable. Therefore, this proposal was not proceeded with. Other modifications and changes were also made before the discussion draft was finalised and a consultation paper was released for two months of public consultation (Bradbury and Butler 2012a). This process proved to be an effective way of introducing a degree of coproduction into the process of developing the governance standards.

Too often consultation consists of government preparing a consultation document with little or no direct input from stakeholders at an early stage. But this kind of early engagement can not only identify issues that can be rectified before wider public consultation takes place, it also cultivates an atmosphere of openness as well as mutual respect and trust, which was a shared principle of the *National Compact*. It is also not particularly difficult to do, in that a discussion draft can be distributed and a stakeholder roundtable organised relatively easily. Even if all stakeholders did not necessarily agree with every aspect of the governance standards in their final form, there was recognition of the benefits of this process—as evidenced by this statement contained in a stakeholder submission in response to the discussion paper that was released for broader public consultation: 'We acknowledge that these standards have already been the subject of consultation within the industry and we believe that they have been significantly improved from an earlier draft' (AICD 2013: 1).

The culture of the prospective regulator is critical

By their very nature, regulators are vested with various powers and discretions. The key personnel of a regulator are given decision-making powers and their decisions shape how the regulator is perceived by those it regulates and by the broader community. These decisions can range from regulatory decisions—for example, about whether an organisation is registered as a charity or how noncompliance is addressed—to decisions about how to implement the regulatory framework, such as how it engages and consults stakeholders about its regulatory approach or the type and tone of the guidance it produces.

These are all matters of regulatory culture, which is driven by the staff of a regulator and in particular its leadership; when it comes to establishing a regulator with a good regulatory culture, people do matter. This is one critical component of a new regulatory framework that is basically impossible to codify in legislation. You can set out certain matters that the regulator must have regard to in exercising their powers and functions, such as those contained in Section 15-10 of the *ACNC Act*, but even that has limitations in terms of its impact on regulatory culture.

This can be a source of some uncertainty among stakeholders. They might be satisfied with the legislative component of a regulatory framework, but then they might be uncertain and perhaps even concerned about how this legislation will be administered. Whether the regulator will operate with a heavy hand or be more of a 'light touch' regulator is an important question stakeholders ask themselves.

One way to address this uncertainty, and to provide a flavour of the culture of a prospective regulator before it has been formally established, is to effectively establish a 'regulator in waiting'. This is the approach that was adopted with the establishment of the ACNC. The assistant treasurer at the time, Bill Shorten, established the ACNC Implementation Taskforce in July 2011, with current ACNC Commissioner, Susan Pascoe, as the chair (Shorten 2011b), later to be referred to as the interim commissioner.

Just before this, in May 2011, it was announced that Robert Fitzgerald would be the first chair of the ACNC Advisory Board. Although the board would come into being only after the ACNC legislation was passed, the benefit of such an early announcement was that it enabled the Interim Commissioner and the taskforce to benefit from Fitzgerald's expertise and experience (Shorten 2011a).

The Interim Commissioner and the taskforce were charged with laying the groundwork for the ACNC, which initially involved extensive stakeholder consultation on matters such as the ACNC's proposed regulatory approach and other aspects of how the organisation would administer the ACNC legislation should it be passed.

To inform its work, the taskforce undertook extensive stakeholder consultation, which included one-on-one meetings with stakeholders, presentations at stakeholder events and hosting a range of open community consultations in early 2012. It released its *Implementation Report* in June 2012, summarising the outcomes of its consultations and setting out a roadmap for how the ACNC would operate (ACNC Taskforce 2012).

Through its work, the taskforce provided a clear indication to stakeholders of what to expect once the ACNC was formally established, and demonstrated that the ACNC reform process was truly about establishing a facilitative regulator. The taskforce embraced the principles of the *National Compact* in its own approach to engagement, and in this regard it played a critical role in holding together and maintaining confidence in the ACNC reform process. It is arguable that without the presence of the taskforce and the work it undertook, the establishment of the ACNC would not have been realised.

NFP sector regulatory reform in a federation

Regulation of the NFP sector is spread across both Commonwealth and state/territory governments. The Commonwealth, for example, regulates access to Commonwealth tax concessions and NFP companies limited by guarantee, while the states and territories regulate access to state/territory tax concessions, incorporated associations and fundraising. State and territory attorneys-general are also the nominal regulators of charitable trusts.

It is no wonder, then, that the Productivity Commission (2010: 138) concluded that this approach to regulation of the NFP sector is fragmented and inefficient. One of the rationales for the establishment of the ACNC was to address this complex regulatory mishmash and to drive a national approach to NFP regulation (Bradbury 2012a). However, the Commonwealth did not have the power to simply take over state and territory regulation, and therefore there were essentially two options available for implementing such a national approach.

Before committing to the establishment of the ACNC, the Commonwealth could have begun negotiations with state and territory governments. The aim would be to obtain an agreement that addresses the various inconsistencies and complexities of NFP regulation and involves either the transfer of certain responsibilities to the Commonwealth and a new Commonwealth regulator or some form of alignment between state/territory regulation and Commonwealth regulation. Alternatively, the Commonwealth could take the lead and establish the ACNC itself—and seek to engage with the states and territories parallel to this process.

If the first approach were adopted, it is probable that little progress, if any, would have been achieved. The political context within which the federation operates makes any reform through the Council of Australian Governments (COAG) very difficult. That is not to say that reform is impossible, as there are of course examples of reform efforts that have successfully progressed through COAG—just as there are many reform efforts that have failed.

Therefore, the approach adopted was to establish the ACNC as a platform for delivering a national approach to NFP regulation—with significant reductions to regulatory burdens to occur over time with the cooperation of the states and territories (Bradbury 2012c). This is a regulatory reform approach that was based on the notion of 'build it, and they will come'.

Of course, there were some critics of this approach and, not surprisingly, some state and territory governments were not happy. But realistically, it was the only option available if there was to be any movement towards a national approach to NFP regulation. Some early signs were positive—for example, in 2012 the South Australian Government announced it would make amendments to its incorporated associations and charitable collections legislation to harmonise reporting requirements with the ACNC (Bradbury et al. 2012), followed by the Australian Capital Territory in 2013 (Bradbury et al. 2013).

Unfortunately, uncertainty about the ACNC's future has restricted its ability to achieve further progress with other jurisdictions. However, given the Australian Government's decision to retain the ACNC, there is now immense potential to obtain the agreement of other states and territories to align their regulatory frameworks with that of the ACNC. Evidence of this is that in 2015 the NSW Government expressed in-principle support for aligning its fundraising regulation with the ACNC regulatory framework (OLGR 2015).

Although NFP sector regulatory reform is harder to progress in a federation, the argument against a 'build it, and they will come' approach to the ACNC reform process is weak. Some form of action with a firm objective in mind is better than endless negotiation with no realistic prospect of an outcome. Given there is now certainty regarding the ACNC's future, there is an opportunity to further test this conclusion and the effectiveness of the approach.

Understanding that considering NFPs and charities as a 'single homogenous sector' is a challenge

The NFP sector tends—as the name suggests—to be thought of as a single sector, when it really is a set of diverse subsectors unified under the principle that their purposes are not focused on private gain or, in the case of charities, are directed at public benefit. If we consider charities themselves, the diversity is considerable. Charities include large and small welfare organisations, universities, arts organisations, environmental organisations, large religious organisations and small community churches, charitable trusts and foundations, hospitals and aged care providers, housing cooperatives—and the list goes on.

These are all *very* different organisations. Each subsector has its own agendas, interests and institutional structures. Some might not even identify as being charities at all, despite being charities at law—for example, universities and some trusts and foundations. This challenges the notion that there is a coherent and homogeneous NFP sector with which the government can engage (Butcher 2015: 3).

The ACNC reform process effectively required maintaining a coalition of subsectors, which necessitated a very strong emphasis on stakeholder engagement but also an appreciation of how a common set of regulatory arrangements can have different impacts on different subsectors. This ultimately required modifications to the ACNC regulatory framework to seek to address these in part—for example, for small religious congregations, for non-government schools and for private ancillary funds. These modifications included targeted exemptions, tailored subsector-specific regulations and transitional arrangements. If a regulatory framework is sufficiently flexible, some of these different impacts can be managed administratively to minimise red tape, and the ACNC has been proactive in that regard—for example, in its work with non-government schools.

If we were to turn the clock back to before the ACNC reform process began, an alternative way of addressing this challenge might have involved phasing in the introduction of the ACNC regulatory framework to different parts of the NFP sector. For example, approximately 20 per cent of registered charities are either public benevolent institutions or health promotion charities (ACNC 2013a: 52). As a set of organisations, they would share relatively similar characteristics, although they will vary in size. They also benefit from the most generous set of tax concessions available to charities, including deductible gift recipient status and the fringe benefits tax exemption.

Perhaps these types of organisations could have been phased into the ACNC regulatory framework first, with others to follow over time. The option of phasing in such a manner was raised relatively early in the ACNC reform process (Not-for-profit Project 2011: 6). However, on balance, the flexible nature of the ACNC regulatory framework, as mentioned above, allowed for the tailoring of certain aspects of it to suit the unique situation and needs of particular subsectors within the NFP sector. The need for such flexibility does not appear to have been envisaged at the beginning of the ACNC reform process, but one lesson from the process is that when seeking to establish an interface with such a diverse sector, it is important to recognise the implications of this diversity for the development of the new regulatory framework, and manage these implications accordingly.

Conclusion

The establishment of the ACNC was a unique example of cross-sector working; it demonstrated that a diverse range of stakeholders from different sectors can work together collaboratively to implement a complex change. Like any reform process, the ACNC reform process was not perfect and had its challenges. Lessons were learnt along the way, and these insights are useful not only in the context of regulatory reform as it relates to NFP sector, but also might assist other regulatory reform efforts more broadly.

The ACNC reform process can be rightly described as a success— in that the ACNC was established and it has built an excellent reputation as a regulator. However, success in this regard is not static, but rather dynamic. The mere existence of the ACNC at any given point is indeed a testament to the efforts of stakeholders, as described above. But it is the ACNC's performance over time that will provide a richer and more elaborate picture of its effectiveness as a regulator. The ACNC is a work in progress, and over time it will be judged against a number of standards. One of these includes its ability to deliver on the promise of a smarter national approach to NFP regulation. But it is important to note that the responsibility for delivering this is not the ACNC's alone; it is a regulator, not a policymaker. It will therefore rely on both federal and state/territory governments to swing their support behind efforts to streamline and simplify NFP regulation.

The Australian Government's decision to retain the ACNC provides an opportunity for the next stage of cross-sector working to begin. This will involve the ACNC, policymakers at a federal and state/

territory level and stakeholders across the NFP sector ramping up efforts to implement the reforms necessary to address the fragmented and inefficient approach to NFP regulation we still currently have in Australia—for which the ACNC provides the solution.

References

Andrews, K. 2012. The Coalition's approach to the charitable sector: Empowering civil society. Address to the Menzies Research Centre, Melbourne, 15 June.

Arbib, M. and M. Butler. 2012. Gillard government listens to sector on not-for-profit reforms. Media Release, 1 March. Parliament House, Canberra.

Australian Charities and Not-for-profits Commission (ACNC) Taskforce. 2012. *Implementation Report*. Melbourne: ACNC.

Australian Charities and Not-for-profits Commission (ACNC). 2013a. *Australian charities 2013: The first report on charities registered with the Australian Charities and Not-for-profits Commission*. Report prepared by Curtin University Not-for-profit Initiative. Melbourne: ACNC.

Australian Charities and Not-for-profits Commission (ACNC). 2013b. *Not-for-profit Reform and the Australian Government*. Melbourne: ACNC.

Australian Council of Social Service (ACOSS). 2012. *Submission in Response to the ACNC Bill Exposure Draft and Governance Arrangements Discussion Paper*. Sydney: ACOSS.

Australian Institute of Company Directors (AICD). 2013. *Submission in Response to Development of Governance Standards Consultation Paper*. Sydney: AICD.

Bradbury, D. 2012a. Australian Charities and Not-for-profits Commission passes Senate. Media Release, 31 October. Parliament House, Canberra.

Bradbury, D. 2012b. Parliamentary Debates. House of Representatives. 23 August 2012, 9722.

Bradbury, D. 2012c. The NFP sector reforms: Moving towards smarter regulation. Address to the Thomson Reuters Not-for-profit Law and Regulation Conference, Sydney, 17 October. Available from: ministers.treasury.gov.au/DisplayDocs.aspx?doc=speeches/2012/011. htm&pageID=005&min=djba&Year=&DocType= (accessed 7 July 2016).

Bradbury, D. and M. Butler. 2012a. Public consultation on ACNC governance standards and financial reporting regulations. Media Release, 17 December. Parliament House, Canberra.

Bradbury, D. and M. Butler. 2012b. Staging the introduction of regulatory reform for the not-for-profit sector. Media Release, 17 May. Parliament House, Canberra.

Bradbury, D. and M. Butler. 2013. Later start date for better targeting of not-for-profit tax concessions. Media Release, 31 January. Parliament House, Canberra.

Bradbury, D., M. Butler and A. Barr. 2013. ACT signs up to new charities regulator. Media Release, 11 March. Parliament House, Canberra.

Bradbury, D., M. Butler and J. Rau. 2012. Government delivering real reductions in red tape for charities. Media Release, 11 October. Parliament House, Canberra.

Butcher, J. 2015. 'The third sector and government in Australia: Not-for-profit reform under Labor, 2007–13.' *Australian Journal of Political Science* 50(1): 148–63.

Chamberlain, E. 2014. Charity commission: Power and responsibility. NCVO blog, 14 February. National Council for Voluntary Organisations, London. Available from: blogs.ncvo.org.uk/2014/02/14/the-charity-commission-power-and-responsibility/ (accessed October 2015).

Chartered Secretaries Australia (CSA). 2012. Finally some sense in regulatory reform of the NFP sector. Media Release, 18 May. Chartered Secretaries Australia, Sydney.

Department of the Prime Minister and Cabinet. 2011. *National Compact: Working together*. Canberra: Australian Government.

Garton, J. 2009. *The Regulation of Organised Civil Society*. Oxford: Hart Publishing.

Not-for-profit Project. 2011. *Submission in Response to the Scoping Study for a National Not-for-profit Regulator Consultation Paper*. Melbourne: University of Melbourne.

O'Connell, A. 2008. 'The tax position of charities in Australia: Why does it have to be so complicated?' *Australian Tax Review* 37: 17.

O'Connell, A., F. Martin and J. Chia. 2013. 'Law, policy and politics in Australia's recent not-for-profit sector reforms.' *Australian Tax Forum* 28(2): 289–315.

Office of Liquor, Gaming and Racing (OLGR). 2015. *Regulatory Impact Statement: Charitable fundraising regulation 2015—Report on public consultation*. Sydney: NSW Government.

Pascoe, S. forthcoming. 'Sector advocated, sector supported: Australia's charity regulator.' In *Regulating Charities: The Inside Story*, eds M. McGregor-Lowndes and R. Wyatt. London: Routledge.

Porter, C. and K. O'Dwyer. 2016. Retention of the Australian Charities and Not-for-profits Commission. Media Release, 4 March. Parliament House, Canberra.

Pro Bono Australia. 2008. New Labor Government Removes 'Gagging' Clauses. Online article, 14 January. Pro Bono Australia, Melbourne. Available from: probonoaustralia.com.au/news/2008/01/new-labor-government-removes-gagging-clauses-2/ (accessed 6 July 2016).

Pro Bono Australia. 2015. *State of the Not for Profit Sector Survey*. Melbourne: Pro Bono Australia. Available from: probonoaustralia.com.au/wp-content/uploads/2016/02/2015_sector_survey.pdf (accessed 6 July 2016).

Productivity Commission. 2010. *Contribution of the Not-for-profit Sector*. Canberra: Australian Government.

Sheppard, I., R. Fitzgerald and D. Gonski. 2001. *Report of the Inquiry into the Definition of Charities and Related Organisations*. Canberra: Australian Government.

Shorten, B. 2011a. Next stage for not-for-profit reforms announced. Media Release, 27 May. Parliament House, Canberra.

Shorten, B. 2011b. Susan Pascoe appointed NFP reform implementation taskforce chair. Media Release, 4 July. Parliament House, Canberra.

Shorten, B. and T. Plibersek. 2011. Making it easier for charities to help those who need it. Media Release, 10 May. Parliament House, Canberra.

Treasury. 2011. *Scoping study for a national not-for-profit regulator.* Consultation Paper. Australian Government, Canberra.

Treasury. 2012. *Governance standards for the not-for-profit (NFP) sector.* Consultation Paper. Australian Government, Canberra.

Treasury. 2013. *Fairer, Simpler and More Effective Tax Concessions for the Not-for-profit Sector: Final report of the Not-for-profit Sector Tax Concession Working Group.* Australian Government, Canberra.

Turnour, M. and M. McGregor-Lowndes. 2012. 'Taxing charities: Reform without reason?' *Taxation in Australia* 47(2): 74–77.

8

Shining a Light on the Black Box of Collaboration: Mapping the prerequisites for cross-sector working

Robyn Keast

Introduction

Collaboration continues to be the go-to solution for government (Economist Intelligence Unit 2007; O'Flynn 2009; Keast 2011). Its allure is compelling. If only we could collaborate better we could overcome budget deficits, solve protracted and emergent complex social problems, overcome economic and environmental problems, deliver seamless and integrated services, reduce duplication and inefficiencies, develop coherent policies and programs and, finally, be more innovative and productive. The drive for 'collaborative advantage' (Huxham 1996) is not restricted to government, with both the community and the private sectors also relying on it to generate new and future-driven directions and resources.

Despite confidence that collaboration will deliver enhanced outcomes, its design and implementation are often treated as forming somewhat of a 'black box'—full of mystical properties and practices with little clear direction. Yet, over time, the spotlights of research and practice have uncovered substantial insights into and knowledge of what goes on in this black box to generate successful collaboration. For example, the different drivers and distinctive characteristics—that is, what makes collaboration different from other forms of working together—are well known, as are some of the processes and competencies required for authentic and successful collaboration (Gray 1989; Thomson and Perry 2006; Innes and Booher 2010). Even with this insight, research across several sectors suggests that more than 50 per cent of collaborations fail to achieve their purpose (Dacin et al. 1997; Fyall and Garrod 2009; Spyrisadis 2002; Kale and Singh 2009; Lunnan and Haugland 2008).

It has been well argued that these failures can be overcome or prevented by paying greater attention to the dynamics of collaborative working and, in particular, by focusing on the design and application of processes that facilitate the interactions needed for collaboration to work (Gray 1989; Wood and Gray 1991; Ring and Van de Ven 1994; Thomson and Perry 2006; Keast 2011). As Innes and Booher (2010: 10) succinctly state, 'it is the doing of collaboration'—the interaction processes—that is least understood. However, despite there being numerous exemplars of collaboration (see Appendix 8.1), rarely have the specifics of the processes been subject to detailed interrogation.

This chapter addresses this gap by drilling into the minutiae of collaborative processes to understand how they are selected and function. It begins by outlining collaboration's distinctive characteristics, illuminating the relational aspect as well as the supporting mechanisms. The secondary analysis research approach is then set out, followed by a discussion of the findings and their implications. Finally, a conclusion is presented that may provide a new focus to guide the work, particularly of network leaders and managers.

Differentiating collaboration

Governments and other bodies have long had available to them a range of interorganisational relationship forms to address their varying needs and challenges (Cropper et al. 2008). These options—summarised here as the 'five Cs' (competition, cooperation, coordination, collaboration and consolidation)—are set out schematically in Figure 8.1, which also highlights their key linking mechanisms and purposes (Keast 2016).

The close grouping of cooperation, coordination and collaboration (the 'three Cs') (Brown and Keast 2003; Keast et al. 2007) at the centre of this relational continuum has led to a tendency to use the three terms in an undifferentiated way, despite growing agreement that collaboration exhibits distinctive characteristics to the others (Himmelman 1994, 2002; Hogue 1994; Gray 1989; Wood and Gray 1991).

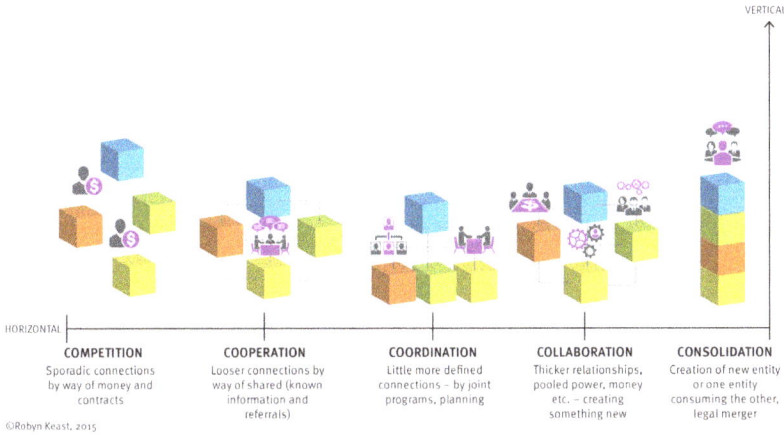

Figure 8.1: Continuum of interorganisational relationships: The five Cs
Source: Created by the author.

The differences pointed to in Figure 8.1 in relation to the three Cs are made more apparent below.

Cooperation is defined by short-term, mostly informal and largely voluntary relations between organisational entities or individuals (Hogue 1994; Cigler 2001; Lawson 2002). In cooperative arrangements, while participants might share basic information, space or referrals (Mulford and Rogers 1982), they remain autonomous and rarely share resources. Cooperative behaviours are established to achieve individual, rather than collective, outcomes (Mandell 2002). As Schermerhorn (in Mulford and Rogers 1982: 13) notes: 'cooperation entails the deliberate relations between otherwise autonomous organizations for the joint accomplishment of individual operating goals.'

Coordination is applied when there is a need to align resources or orchestrate people-tasks and specialised interventions in an ordered relationship to meet predetermined or set goals (Litterer 1973; Dunshire 1978). It does not rely on goodwill but rather has some force of a formal objective or mandate, with one organisation generally taking the lead responsibility for the work—that is, a lead department or central agency. Because it is located on both the vertical and the horizontal axes, coordination can draw on both influencing and compelling behaviours to act in desired ways (Dunshire 1978: 16–17). In practice, then, coordination moves beyond the basic information sharing of cooperation to involve joint planning and programming (Mulford and Rogers 1982). Coordination refers to the formalised institutional relationships among existing networks of organisations, while cooperation is 'characterized by informal trade-offs and by attempts to establish reciprocity in the absence of rules' (Mulford and Rogers 1982: 13).

Whereas cooperation and coordination are focused on doing the same things, although more efficiently, *collaboration* is about doing something new or different—for example, new programs, products or service models. Collaboration is about systems change (Cigler 2001; Keast et al. 2007; Innes and Booher 2010). This degree of change requires that members acknowledge their interdependencies—that is, they are reliant on each other to achieve individual and collective outcomes— and therefore must forge strong interpersonal relationships to work together more closely (Mandell 2001). Such relationships require comprehensive interactions: multiparty planning as well as dense and well-defined communication flows. A high level of trust is key and the relational time frame is longer, with some research indicating that it can take upwards of three years to build relationships of sufficient strength for collaboration to be successful and sustained (Annie E. Casey Foundation 1993; Keast 2004). Together, these factors position collaboration as a distinctive and higher-order level of collective action (Gray 1989).

Collaboration and process

As the above highlights, collaboration comprises a distinctive set of intersecting relational dimensions. While various distillations of these dimensions for collaboration exist (Gray 1989; Huxham and Vangen 2003; Ring and Van de Ven 1994), there is a consensus that the following are involved: an interpersonal orientation (trust, reciprocity, respect, reputation), interdependency (shared reliance on each other for results), mutuality (common vision, values and communication) and the undertaking of joint programs that meet both individual and collective goals (the collaborator's dilemma). Such elements are enabled by processes that address governance, administration, organisation, mutuality and norms (Wood and Gray 1991; Mattessich et al. 1992; Cropper et al. 2008).

To enact these relational elements and dimensions and deliver collaborative value creation, interactive processes and mechanisms that nurture, facilitate and leverage the connections need to be established and implemented. 'Process' here refers to a series of actions or steps needed to deliver the end result of collaborative actions and outcomes and can include, for example, procedures, activities and events (Vandeventer and Mandell 2011; Keast 2011). To guide the process orientation of collaboration, several authors have developed process-oriented models, with some adopting staged approaches in which members move through levels of intensity (Hogue 1994; Himmelman 1994); others, such as Gray (1989), suggest stepwise sets of actions such as problem setting, direction setting and implementation. Increasingly, however, the consensus is that collaboration emerges from synergistic interactions and is therefore more likely to be an iterative and cyclical process than following a direct plan of action (Ring and Van de Ven 1994; Thomson and Perry 2006). Adding to the challenges of prescribing collaboration processes are the different contexts and purposes that require divergent processes to meet various outcomes (Cigler 2001; Huxham 2000; Huxham and Vangen 2003, 2005). Gray (1989) identified two key process approaches: those designed for resolving conflict and those for advancing common vision.

Each of these process approaches proposes different types of interaction mechanisms. Specifically, the goal of achieving a common vision calls for events and actions that open up communication and encourage participants to facilitate a better articulation their ideas, visions and purposes. Process mechanisms best suited to this function are centred on appreciative planning and collective strategies, including, for example, community gatherings, world-café sessions and other similar forums. By contrast, the goal of resolving conflict requires actions that bring together disagreeing parties to explore their differences, clarify points of departure and convergence of agreement. Processes that open up the dialogue between participants, gather information, check facts and, through these steps, identify their shared interests. Mechanisms facilitating these process steps would include negotiated agreements, policy dialogues and community panels.

As the above suggests, far from being a neat set of defined processes, collaboration is often messy, unfolding and relies heavily on often emergent processes to mould relationships that create synergies to be leveraged. Understanding how these processes function and unfold is crucial to successfully managing the kinds of multiparty and multi-organisational relationships involved in collaborative arrangements.

From this it can be seen that collaboration requires a number of process factors to be addressed, including: the nurturing of new and building on existing relationships, implementing events and mechanisms that help to establish trusting relationships, forging agreements on what and how to work together and strategies for identifying and managing conflicts. How these tasks and relational issues and actions are handled is considered core for achieving effectiveness.

While offering many important insights, extant collaboration case studies do not always provide sufficient detail on the process to inform how or why they did or did not work.

This chapter unpacks and examines a set of collaborative endeavours to identify the processes employed and their impact, and comment on the adequacy of these to reach collaborative outcomes.

Research approach

Seven cases that have all been identified broadly as collaborative are examined specifically to uncover details on the processes employed. The cases differ in their scale, ranging from state to regional and local initiatives, and cover social as well as physical infrastructure topics. Thus, they provide some differentiation in terms of focus, participants, process designs and interactions.

The study uses a secondary analysis to re-interrogate data collected, collated and analysed previously on the selected cases: the Sacramento Water Forum (WF) (Connick 2003, 2006; Innes and Booher 2010), the Services Integration Project (SIP) (Keast et al. 2004, 2007; Boorman and Woolcock 2002; Woolcock and Boorman 2003; Klijn and Koopenjan

2015), Family and Youth Network (FYN) (Keast 2004; Ryan 2003), Gold Coast Homelessness Consortia (Keast 2004; Keast et al. 2008, 2012), Collaborative Research Network (CRN) (unpublished internal reports and participant interviews, 2012–15), the Adelaide Oval Redevelopment (CRC for Construction Innovation 2008) and the Pacific Motorway Project (Waterhouse et al. 2001). All cases were constructed from interviews and/or focus groups as well as being informed by extensive documentation including project reports, negotiation agreements, internal correspondence and minutes from meetings.

Secondary analysis of these existing datasets enabled different lenses to be applied to distil new or different insights that were related to, but not directly considered in, the original study (Heaton 1998; White 2010). Specifically, this study sought to more deeply examine the processes employed in each of these cases and how these worked in practice. Following the quality recommendations of Heaton (1998, 2004) and others (for example, Irwin and Winterton 2011), the author either had direct involvement in the original research design, data collection and analysis for the cases or was able to draw on readily available case background information. Thematic analysis was used to identify the process strategies applied in practice, their elements and impacts (Denzin 1984).

Findings and discussion

The findings show that all initiatives instituted some form of process or set of actions to facilitate the interactions needed for collaboration to take place. Table 8.1 outlines the array of processes applied across the cases. The primary processes identified ranged from the use of interest-based negotiation for the WF, a Graduate Certificate in Inter-professional Development for the SIP, different types of sense-making and consensus-building events, such as community gatherings and workshops for other social services groups (FYN and the Homelessness Consortia), to the use of collective orientation events (CRN) and pre-project workshops, coupled with relational contracts in the infrastructure arenas (Adelaide Oval and Pacific Motorway).

Table 8.1: Summary of the key presenting processes used

Case	Collaboration process mechanisms
Services Integration Project	Graduate Certificate in Inter-professional Development, breakfast meetings and gatherings, appreciative planning, structured meetings and agendas, dedicated facilitator
Family and Youth Network	Structured program of pre-workshops and sense-making conference, appreciative planning, memorandums of understanding (MOUs), colocation of services, joint projects
Homelessness Consortia	Coalition building, appreciative planning (strategy of inclusiveness), joint training events, symposia, MOUs and informal relational agreements
Collaborative Research Network	Contract, structured program of events (scheduled meetings, workshops), agreements and planning documents, strong previous relationships
Sacramento Water Forum	Interest-based negotiation, single text document, dialogic events, communication mediums, shared meals, expert facilitator
Adelaide Oval Redevelopment	Pre-project workshop, social events, computer-aided design (CAD) drawings providing neutral facts for shared understanding/agreement
Pacific Motorway	Pre-project workshops, relational contract, media and communication strategies, community stakeholder meetings

Process selection

The WF's selection of negotiation and consensus building reflected a long history of conflict over water in the region, for which planning was not a strong enough process. The process began with a conflict-assessment tool 'to see if the conditions were favourable for a consensus-based process and subsequently to identify the range of interests involved' (Innes and Booher 2010: 45). Following the negotiation path, the WF also used the strategy of a single text negotiation document as a way to keep track of their various agreements.

By contrast, the social services and research collaborations (SIP, FYN, Homelessness Consortia and CRN) started from a position of agreement and were focused on forging a plan for how to work together. Accordingly, these bodies used processes aimed at advancing their common visions and developing plans for action, including community meetings (SIP) and practitioner/researcher workshops (FYN, Homelessness Consortia and CRN) to articulate their values and establish agreement on how to go forward together. The value of these 'communicative' approaches in forging a collective view for going forward was captured in the following:

> A public meeting was subsequently called to which the general community service providers were invited … The Process was designed to facilitate general discussion and input for direction. Through the various processes of coming together, we were able to see the big picture, not just our little individual bits. (FYN in Keast 2004: 168)

> [B]efore we started putting things down on paper we went through a long process of talking and sharing to achieve that agreement on what our goals were for the work we agreed to do together and how to work together … The process allowed us to communicate, to share goals and understanding of what we are all about and what we are doing together. (SIP in Keast 2004: 195)

> The first thing we did was get together and say okay so we have set some targets … What are we going to do together to be able to achieve that? So we planned a series of writing fellowship programs … and other various workshops to build up our relationships and practices of working together. (CRN Interview 3, 2015)

The physical infrastructure projects also used communicative processes to smooth over different working approaches and facilitate different disciplines working together, with both opting for pre-project workshops, coupled with a relational contract (CRC for Construction Innovation 2006: 3). As Waterhouse et al. (2001: 9) explained of the Pacific Motorway Project, but equally relevant to the Adelaide Oval project, '[t]his type of approach seeks to alter the traditional adversarial relationship to one based on trust and the pursuit of common goals'.

The analysis highlighted a link between the choice of process adopted, the focus or purpose sought and the outcomes to be achieved. This suggests a level of strategic deliberateness in process choice or, as has elsewhere been noted, fit-for-purpose process designs (Keast et al. 2007; Innes and Booher 2010). For example, the cases looking to achieve systems change, such as the social services bodies and the WF, employed more relationally intense linking mechanisms than the infrastructure projects, which sought more of an adjustment to the normal business process than all-out change. The differences required in time and commitment between these two process models are evident below:

> The cooperative intentions of the contract were reinforced by a full-day workshop at the start of the project which aimed to encourage 'best-for-project' thinking ... backed up by regular collaborative meetings and ad hoc social events such as barbeques and cricket matches. (CRC for Construction Innovation 2006: 3)

> In this [Graduate Certificate] course SIP members spent 16 full days over two semesters learning new ways of working and unlearning old behaviour, developing shared language and skill sets ... we learnt about each other in ways that would not have been possible if we had just been going to meetings once a month for a couple of hours and having a cup of tea and a bit of a chat. (SIP in Keast 2004: 137–38)

Significantly, participation in the graduate certificate was not limited to core SIP members, but rather was eventually extended to many members of the broader community, providing an indication of the scope and scale of the change in behaviour sought and eventually achieved (Boorman and Woolcock 2002; Woolcock and Boorman 2003).

Supplementary process

Returning to Table 8.1, it can be seen that, alongside the 'primary or presenting' process, the cases also employed several supplementary processes, often run simultaneously. These ranged from the relatively conventional linking mechanisms, such as scheduled programs of meetings (SIP, WF and CRN) to the use of MOUs (FYN, Homelessness Consortia and WF) and contracts (CRN, Pacific Motorway and Adelaide Oval) that provided some parameters around the exchanges.

While they might seem counterintuitive, it is apparent that the use of strong administrative processes played a central role in many of the collaborations. Such processes included scheduled meetings and clear agendas as well as personnel and processes dedicated to monitoring inputs and outputs. As one SIP member explained: 'These keep us going—stick the pins in and keep us on track' (Keast 2004: 141). The FYN members developed the 'velvet glove' metaphor to describe their leader's monitoring approach, which was simultaneously gentle but directive.

Communication strategies and tools of various types were also used by all seven cases—some more extensively than others. Connick (2006: 31) provides some insight into the complexity of the WF's dynamics and therefore the reach and importance of the extensive communication process:

The group also addressed issues of communication and accountability that ultimately resulted in each caucus writing and adopting a detailed strategy for how its members would communicate with their constituents, keeping them apprised of Water Forum developments. This latter item was critical in developing participants' confidence that they were working with individuals who were able to negotiate on behalf of their organizations and, to a certain extent, broader constituencies.

Other processes followed more informal approaches—for example, relying on ad hoc social events such as barbecues and attendance at cricket matches, coffee/chat meetings or mentoring (CRN) as the means to build or extend their connections and keep people on the same page. The mix of relationship-building mechanisms variously undertaken by the cases are very similar to those outlined by Vandeventer and Mandell (2011: 57), who added to the list shared meals and structured team trust-building activities as well as field trips to neutral but mutually relevant settings.

The benefits of existing relationships in quickly building or 'turbocharging' collaborative teams were frequently noted across several cases, particularly within the research collaboration project. For instance, one of the CRN project leaders spoke of adopting a 'conscious partnering approach' (CRN Interview 5, 2015), while another noted that having existing relationships helped to smooth over some of the early 'getting to know you' steps and enabled easier transition into joint works (CRN Interview 6, 2015).

It is interesting to note that while those initiatives described as being more genuinely or more strongly collaborative (SIP and WF) did draw on conventional processes, they took care to reframe and rename these processes or events to better reflect and model the type of focus and behaviour sought. For example, SIP and FYN meetings often used the term 'rules of engagement' instead of 'terms of agreement' to signal the type of behaviour sought in their interactions.

The need to be careful with the implementation and rollout of processes was also stressed, particularly taking into consideration context and past relationships. The FYN leader made this evident in the following statement: 'There is a lot of history at play. So you have to move slowly. If you move too quickly they will think they have been railroaded … and you will go backward' (Keast 2004: 177).

This issue of pressure was also raised regarding government funding stipulations for collaboration and particular collaborative processes. For example, FYN and the Homelessness Consortia were obligated to enter into a collaborative arrangement as part of their funding agreements. Huxham and Vangen (2003: 15) warned of a relationship between process, power and funding, suggesting '[t]hose who choose who to involve are obviously powerful, but those who choose the process of who to involve may be more so'. It is interesting to note that while both cases acknowledged the potential influence of the funds on their practice, they stressed that they had entered into the collaborations because it was the 'right thing to do'; the funds were secondary.

Process impact and adjustments

It is evident from these cases that taking time to create and implement the right processes had a positive effect on the interactions and outcomes. As one SIP member noted:

> Everyone was involved in the setting of the protocols. So there were no surprises, demands or ideals that we did not think we could sustain. At the outset we made a commitment within the team around equity and quality input ... I felt that it was a very equitable, caring, supportive environment for the discussion of these difficult issues. (Keast 2004: 140)

In addition, there is some evidence from most cases to show that the more deliberate and strategic they were in their selection and implementation of processes, the more extensive and sustained were the results.

Noticeably, the priority of the processes sometimes shifted in accordance with the life-cycle stage of the collaborative endeavour. As an example, in the two infrastructure projects, early in the relationship-building stages greater attention was directed towards processes that brought members together, largely to establish 'best-for-project' procedures (CRC for Construction Innovation 2006). Once the relationships were established and consensus was reached on working arrangements, it was possible to implement the actions via the procedures outlined and agreed to earlier in the relational contract. A similar, if less dramatic, lessening in process intensity can be seen in the social infrastructure arena, where there was generally a strong investment up-front in events and mechanisms that built relationships and consensus of purpose, contribution and working arrangements. Over time, as processes and behaviours became embedded—frequently encapsulated in the phrase 'this is how we work together'—the need for such constant relational nurturing and oversight reduced. Nonetheless, more successful collaborations regularly and deliberately employed specialist facilitators and used other processes, such as check-back, to ensure they were 'still on the same page, still going forward together' (FYN and SIP).

A life-cycle explanation for the changes occurring in collaborative endeavours and associated shifts in process forms has been put forward (see, for example, Lowndes and Skelcher 1998). However, as Cropper and Palmer (2008) argue, and as this study attests, the social and contextual dynamics of collaborative interactions lead to processes that are iterative, intertwined and unfolding rather than linear or perfectly iterative and unfolding. Ring and Van de Ven (1994: 96) state that these processes 'are continually shaped and restructured by actions and symbolic interpretations of the parties involved'. This hybridity and fluidity are best encapsulated in the following: 'There are lots of things that we did ... there is no blueprint' (CRN Interview 6, 2015).

Together, the cases distil some important insights about macro-collaboration processes. First, it is apparent that a mix of processes is in play and that these often cut across and defy Gray's (1989) dual model. For example, several cases shaped their interactions using both communicative and negotiated processes. This hybridity adds to the complexity of collaborative working and calls for more dexterity in its management. Second, there is evidence of deliberate and strategic thinking in action regarding the selection of process as well as implementation. That said, the overwhelming sense is that collaboration and its processes continue to defy any prescriptive recipes for implementation. Each case, while having some similarities, remains highly individual and requires processes that match its unique purpose, context and features.

The importance of micro-processes

While the macro-processes of structure and procedures clearly are important to delivering collaboration, deeper analysis of the cases, especially those defined as more collaborative or successful, highlighted some additional characteristics located at what several authors have termed the micro or practice level (Huxham and Vangen 2005; Hibbert et al. 2008). The emphasis at this level seems to be less on the doing of collaboration and more on perfecting the different patterns of thinking and types of behaviours that enable the level of engagement for genuine collaboration. Here attention is directed to members' interaction with or treatment of others:

> At first the relationships … the dynamics were terrible. It took a lot of time and effort to really learn how to talk to each other, how to be present and listen and pay attention to how we treat each other. (SIP in Keast 2004: 165)

> WF members spent the first year learning about each other and how to deal with each other. (Mandell 2011: 183)

> How can I help you with that? How can I take a load off with that? Being careful with [the] use of language to re-enforce collaborative practice and model behaviours sought and gently instil the values. (CRN Interview 8, 2015)

By focusing on and strengthening relationships, understanding and appreciating colleagues, helping them out and not apportioning blame, actions emerge that help to smooth over differences and difficulties and prepare the ground for synergistic working.

It also seems that reaching out beyond superficial engagement to genuinely understand and appreciate others—or, as Mandell (2001: 142) says, 'step into each other's shoes'—is important. Case respondents perceived these micro-relational processes to be 'transformational'— that is, focused on moving relationships and behaviours beyond just going through the motions of talking and sharing to generate the space for reciprocity and mutual gain to emerge. These small, but powerful actions were seen to provide a push beyond the practice norm, as articulated here: 'It is the extra things you do because of the relationships that makes the difference. Having a coffee and a talk in an informal atmosphere and being completely honest and occasionally putting yourself out to help someone else meet their goals' (Homelessness Consortia in Keast et al. 2008: 80).

Several of the cases also posited that through their changed demeanour they were able to forge shared understandings: 'We just have an understanding between us that this is how things work' (FYN in Keast

2004: 162). Bohm (1996: 6) explains this phenomenon as a 'stream of meaning flowing among and between … which may emerge as new understanding'.

To be most effective, this new way of thinking and behaving has to become embedded or second nature (Mandell 2001; Innes and Booher 2010). Yet, from the cases it was apparent that collaborative competencies did not always come easily to members. One of the more powerful process tools to facilitate deeper dialogue was highlighted in both the SIP and the WF projects and centred on the use of a dedicated facilitator whose role was to help members reflect not only on their progress towards goals, but also importantly on their actions and behaviours in relation to each other. Innes and Booher (2010: 47) provide a telling insight into sometimes complex conflicts in collaborative arrangements and the importance of a neutral person, where the facilitator reminded the group that they were 'living in two worlds' and that they should 'check their guns at the door'. The importance of a process minder or process catalyst (Huxham and Vangen 2003; Mandell and Keast 2009) becomes central.

Implications

The unmistakable importance of both macro and micro-processes for collaboration has implications for both practice and research. First, at the macro level, more time and effort must be directed to following through on perfecting design and implementation. To support this, process variables need to be addressed in more detail and with greater regularity to identify those that are most effective in helping collaborators to reach intended outcomes, thus providing more informed key performance indicators.

Third, for authentic collaboration behaviours and thinking to be embedded in individuals and organisations, it requires regular practice and reflection (Hibbert et al. 2008; Huxham and Vangen 2003, 2005). Innes and Booher (2010) call this process 'praxis' and argue that it is based on extended practical experience deeply informed by theorising and reflection. Moon (1999: 63) describes reflective practice as a 'set of abilities and skills, to indicate the taking of a critical stance, an orientation to problem solving or state of mind'. Such reflection can be achieved through the directed efforts of an experienced facilitator or process minders or occur as a result of individuals' check-back and review of their behaviour and actions. All of these demand time and effort of people and organisations—not often acknowledged or provided for in collaboration design or budgeting.

Conclusions

This study confirms earlier propositions that successful collaboration relies heavily on good processes and their implementation. Key process factors to be addressed include: nurturing new and building on existing relationships, establishing trusting relationships, forging agreements on what to work on together and how to work together, building new leadership capacities and identifying and managing conflicts. The study also points out that the mix of processes selected is important, especially that they match the outcomes sought. Furthermore, the implementation of the processes has to be authentic and follow the intent of the collaboration itself. As Innes and Booher (2010: 9) succinctly stated, it 'very much matters what the collaborative process is and how it unfolds'.

By shining the light of research more deeply into the black box of collaboration, this study has also illuminated the existence of a complex set of micro-processes that underpin and anchor collaborative processes. These micro-processes, which include as an example the small interactions and interpersonal behaviours that occur between people who like and respect each other, facilitate deeper dialogue and in so doing allow synergies to be enacted and push beyond normal ways of working. While both macro and micro-processes are not new concepts, they are often overlooked in the push for action and outcomes. These findings serve as a reminder to pay attention to the detail of collaboration.

References

Annie E. Casey Foundation. 1993. *The Path of Most Resistance*. Baltimore: Annie E. Casey Foundation.

Bohm, D. 1996. *On Dialogue*. London: Routledge.

Boorman, C. and G. Woolcock. 2002. 'The Goodna Service Integration Project: Government and community working together for community well-being in Goodna.' In *Governing Local Communities, Building State and Community Capacity*, ed. T. Reddel, 57–81. Brisbane: University of Queensland.

Brown, K. and R. Keast. 2003. 'Citizen–government engagement: Community connection through networked arrangements.' *Asian Journal of Public Administration* 25(1): 107–32.

Cigler, B. 2001. 'Multiorganizational, multisector and multicommunity organizations: Setting the research agenda.' In *Getting Results through Collaboration: Networks and network structures for public policy and management*, ed. M. Mandell, 71–85. Westport, Conn.: Quorum Books.

Connick, S. 2003. The use of collaborative processes in the making of California water policy. Dissertation, Environmental Sciences, Policy and Management, University of California, Berkeley.

Connick, S. 2006. *The Sacramento Water Forum: A case study?* IURD Working Paper Series, WP-2006-06. Institute of Urban Regional Development, University of California, Berkeley.

Cooperative Research Centre (CRC) for Construction Innovation. 2006. *Better project outcomes with relationship management and 3D CAD: The Brite Project*. Innovation Case Study No. 11. QUT Digital Repository, Brisbane. Available from: eprints.qut.edu.au/27132/1/27132.pdf (accessed 22 April 2016).

Cooperative Research Centre (CRC) for Construction Innovation. 2008. *Brite Innovation Case Study No 11: Adelaide Oval Redevelopment— Better project outcomes with relationship management and 3D CAD*. Brisbane: Brite Project.

Cropper, S. and I. Palmer. 2008. 'Change, dynamics and temporality.' In *The Oxford Handbook of Interorganizational Relations*, eds S. Cropper, M. Ebers, C. Huxham and P. Ring, 635–63. New York: Oxford University Press.

Cropper, S., M. Ebers, C. Huxham and P. Ring. 2008. 'Introducing interorganizational relations.' In *The Oxford Handbook of Interorganizational Relations*, eds S. Cropper, M. Ebers, C. Huxham and P. Ring, 3–21. New York: Oxford University Press.

Dacin, T. M., M. A. Hitt and M. Levitas. 1997. 'Selecting partners for successful international alliances: Examination of US and Korean firms.' *Journal of World Business* 32: 3–16.

Denzin, N. 1984. *The Research Act*. Englewood Cliffs, NJ: Prentice Hall.

Dunshire, A. 1978. *Implementation in a Bureaucracy*. Oxford: Martin Robinson.

Economist Intelligence Unit. 2007. *Collaboration: Transforming the way business works*. Report, April. Economist Intelligence Unit, London. Available from: eiu.com/site_info.asp?info_name =Collaboration_Transforming_the_way_business_works&rf=0 (assessed 8 January 2016).

Fyall, A. and B. Garrod. 2009. *Tourism Marketing: A collaborative approach*. Bristol: Channel View Publications.

Gray, B. 1989. *Collaborating: Finding common ground for multiparty problems*. San Francisco: Jossey-Bass.

Heaton, J. 1998. *Secondary analysis of qualitative data*. Social Research Update, 22. University of Surrey, Guildford.

Heaton, J. 2004. *Reworking Qualitative Data*. London: Sage.

Hibbert, P., C. Huxham and P. Ring. 2008. 'Managing collaborations.' In *Oxford Handbook of Interorganizational Relations*, eds S. Cropper, M. Ebers, C. Huxham and P. Ring, 390–416. New York: Oxford University Press.

Himmelman, A. 1994. 'Communities working collaboratively for change.' In *Resolving Conflict: Strategies for local government*, ed. P. Herrman, 27–47. Washington, DC: International City/County Management Association.

Himmelman, A. 2002. (revised). *Collaboration for a change: Definitions, decision-making models, roles, and Collaboration Process Guide*. Himmelman Consulting. Available: depts.washington.edu/ccph/ pdf_files/4achange.pdf (accessed 1 July 2016).

Hogue, T. 1994. *Community Based Collaboration: Community wellness multiplied*. Corvallis, Ore.: Centre for Community Leadership, Oregon State University.

Huxham, C. 1996. 'Collaboration and collaborative advantage.' In *Creating Collaborative Advantage*, ed. C. Huxham, 1–18. Thousand-Oaks, Calif.: Sage.

Huxham, C. 2000. 'The challenge of collaborative advantage.' *Public Management Review* 2: 237–57.

Huxham, C. and S. Vangen. 2003. 'Working together: Key themes in the management of relationships between public and non-profit organizations.' *International Journal of Public Sector Management* 9(7): 5–17.

Huxham, C. and S. Vangen. 2005. *Managing to Collaborate: The theory and practice of collaborative advantage*. New York: Routledge.

Innes, J. and D. Booher. 2010. *Planning with Complexity: An introduction to collaborative rationality for public policy*. Abingdon, UK: Routledge.

Irwin, S. and M. Winterton. 2011. *Debates in qualitative secondary analysis: Critical reflections*. Timescape Working Paper Series No. 4. University of Leeds, Leeds. Available from: timescapes.leeds.ac.uk/assets/files/WP4-March-2011.pdf (accessed 22 April 2016).

Kale, P. and H. Singh. 2009. 'Managing strategic alliances: What do we know now, and where do we go from here.' *Academy of Management Perspectives* August: 45–62.

Keast, R. 2004. Integrated public services: The role of networked arrangement. Unpublished PhD Thesis. School of Business, Queensland University of Technology, Brisbane.

Keast, R. 2011. 'Joined-up governance: How the past informs the future international.' *Journal of Public Management* 34(4): 221–31.

Keast, R. 2016. 'Integration terms: Same or different?' In *Grass Roots to Government: Joined-up working in Australia*, ed. G. Carey, 25–46. Melbourne: Melbourne University Press.

Keast, R., K. Brown and M. Mandell. 2007. 'Getting the right mix: Unpacking integration means and strategies.' *International Public Management Journal* 10(1): 9–33.

Keast, R., K. Brown, M. Mandell and G. Woolcock. 2004. 'Network structure: Working differently and changing expectations.' *Public Administration Review* 64(3): 353–61.

Keast, R., J. Waterhouse, K. Brown and G. Murphy. 2008. *Place-based network analysis and case studies: Final report*. Prepared for the Queensland Department of Communities Responding to Homelessness Strategy, Brisbane.

Keast, R., J. Waterhouse, G. Murphy and K. Brown. 2012. *Pulling It All Together: Design considerations for an integrated homelessness services system—Place based network analysis. Brisbane: Department of Families, Housing, Community Services and Indigenous Affairs.*

Klijn, E.-H. and J. Koopenjan. 2015. *Governance Networks in the Public Sector*. London: Taylor & Francis.

Lawson, H. 2002. 'Improving conceptual clarity: Accuracy and precision and facilitating more coherent institutional design.' In *The Contribution of Interprofessional Collaboration and Comprehensive Services to Teaching and Learning. The National Society for the Study of Education Year Book*, eds M. Brabeck and M. Walsh, 30–45. Chicago: University of Chicago Press.

Litterer, J. A. 1973. *The Analysis of Organizations*. 2nd edn. New York: John Wiley & Sons.

Lowndes, V. and C. Skelcher. 1998. 'The dynamics of multi-organizational partnerships: An analysis of changing modes of governance.' *Public Administration* 76: 313–33.

Lunnan, R. and S. Haugland. 2008. 'Predicting and measuring alliance performance: A multidimensional analysis. *Strategic Management Journal* 29(5): 545–56.

Mandell, M. 2001. 'The impact of network structures on community-building efforts: The Los Angeles Roundtable for Children community studies.' In *Getting Results through Collaboration: Networks and network structures for public policy and management*, ed. M. P. Mandell, 129–53. Westport, Conn.: Quorum.

Mandell, M. 2002. 'Types of collaboration and why the differences really matter.' *The Public Manager* (Winter): 36–40.

Mandell, M. 2011. 'Water forum case study.' In *Negotiating the Business Environment: Theory and practice for all governance styles*, eds J. Waterhouse, R. Keast and K. Brown, 163–64. Melbourne: Tilde University Press.

Mandell, M. and R. Keast. 2009. 'A new look at leadership in collaborative networks: Process catalysts.' In *Public Sector Leadership*, eds J. Raffel, P. Leisink and A. Middlebrook, 163–78. Cheltenham, UK, and Northampton, Mass.: Edward Elgar Publishing.

Mattessich, P., M. Murray-Close and B. Monsey. 1992. *Collaboration: What makes it work?* St Paul, Minn.: Amherst Wilder Foundation.

Moon, J. A. 1999. *Reflection in Learning and Professional Development: Theory and practice*. London: Kogan Page.

Mulford, C. L. and D. L. Rogers. 1982. 'Definitions and models.' In *Interorganizational Coordination*, eds D. L. Rogers and D. A. Whetten, 9–31. Ames, Iowa: Iowa State University Press.

O'Flynn, J. 2009. 'The cult of collaboration.' *Australian Journal of Public Administration* 68(1): 112–16.

Ring, P. and A. Van de Ven. 1994. 'Development processes of cooperative inter-organizational relationships.' *Academy of Management Review* 19(1): 90–118.

Ryan, P. 2003. *I'm looking to the future: Final report Reconnect Project*. Department of Families, Housing, Community Services and Indigenous Affairs, Canberra.

Spyrisadis, A. 2002. 'Collaborative partnerships as strategic marketing tools of international hotel chains in pursuit of business development and competitive advantage.' *Journal of Travel and Tourism Practice* 9(3): 35–48.

Thomson, A. and J. Perry. 2006. 'Collaboration processes: Inside the black box.' *Public Administration Review* 66(6) (Supplement): 20–31.

Vandeventer, P. and M. Mandell. 2011. *Networks that Work*. 2nd edn. Los Angeles: Community Partners.

Waterhouse, J., K. Brown and C. Flynn. 2001. 'The Pacific Motorway: A case study examining public sector management dilemmas.' *Journal of Contemporary Issues in Business and Government* 7(1): 21–28.

White, P. 2010. 'Making use of secondary data.' In *Key Methods in Geography, eds* N. Clifford, S. French and G. Valentine, 61–76. Thousand Oaks, Calif.: Sage.

Wood, D. and B. Gray. 1991. 'Towards a comprehensive theory of collaboration.' *Journal of Applied Behavioral Science* 27(2): 139–62.

Woolcock, G. and C. Boorman. 2003. *Goodna Service Integration Project: Doing what we know we should—Final report.* The Community Service and Research Centre, University of Queensland, Brisbane.

Appendix 8.1

Table A8.1: Summary of collaboration exemplars

Case and region	Policy issue	Location	Initiator
Services Integration Project, south-east Queensland	Regional services integration and governance	Goodna, Queensland	State government agencies and university
Family and Youth Network, regional New South Wales	Integrated homeless services	Regional New South Wales	Government (funding requirement) and sectoral
Gold Coast Homelessness Consortia, south-east Queensland	Integrated homeless services	Gold Coast, Queensland	Homeless service providers (government and non-government)
Collaborative Research Network, regional New South Wales/ south-east Queensland	Regional research capacity building	Gold Coast, Queensland, and Lismore, New South Wales	Australian Government
Sacramento Water Forum, USA	Regional water planning	Sacramento region, California	Local government
Adelaide Oval Redevelopment, metropolitan South Australia	Infrastructure	Adelaide, South Australia	Private contractor
Pacific Motorway, south-east Queensland	Infrastructure	Brisbane, Queensland	State government and private operator

Part 3. Great Expectations: Outcomes and social impact

Overview

Nina Terrey

There is growing pressure for governments and not-for-profits (NFPs) to demonstrate social impact, driven by finite resources and increasing expectations from citizens and communities. The achievement of social impact comes from a complex set of accountabilities, services and interactions between government, NFP organisations, the community and other stakeholders. Among the many challenges with this expectation is the fact there is no clear and concrete set of practices or the necessary organisational arrangements within NFPs and government to conduct effective measurement of social impact. The chapters in this section tackle this very issue and present compelling arguments that answer such questions as: what if we were bold enough to say we could measure policy impact? What if we could demonstrate that there is a way to report incremental social impact? What if we rethought the relationship between government funders and NFPs to measure impact? All three chapters explore the delicate and fundamental relationship between NFPs, government and community in the achievement of measuring social impact.

In Chapter 9, Emma Tomkinson addresses a new frontier for reporting required of NFPs to government funders. Tomkinson explores the current limits of reporting, such as the capability of NFPs and limited sharing of lessons from social impact across a wide stakeholder base. She then explores what will be necessary to shift reporting from outputs to outcomes with a particular hypothesis on the role of the government funders in the activity of measuring social impact. Tomkinson emphasises a more active role for government funders in the prescription and tracking of social impact. Tomkinson purports that government funders and NFPs can work better together to generate measurement models and reporting and, by partnering, generate better-quality data to distil lessons and statements of social value achieved.

In Chapter 10, Dale Tweedie takes an NFP view of the observed disconnects between NFPs and key stakeholders such as government, boards and members, which impact on the ability to be accountable for the quality of their services. Tweedie draws attention to the classical tensions such as time spent on reporting on service delivery compared with time spent on improving service delivery. The finite resources of NFPs mean reporting is limited to the necessary requirements set by government funders, which are commonly output based rather than outcomes based. This is further compounded by the variability in reporting requirements between different government funders. Tweedie uncovers important insights about reporting social impact from the perspective of NFPs, and he offers important considerations for future reporting on social impact such as external evaluations. He presents such important ideas as challenging point-in-time formal reports with dynamic, ongoing dialogue-based interaction between funders and NFPs to better harness lessons and understand impacts. He further explores the better linkages between reporting impact and services delivered by NFPs and the tracking of both qualitative and quantitative measures. Tweedie also points to innovative NFP measurement activities that capture service delivery impacts and go beyond what funders expect to report. He pays attention to the variability of NFPs' skills and capacity to evaluate, including at the board level, and he suggests strategies such as drawing on third-party, external expert evaluation to provide feedback on the effectiveness of service delivery. Last, Tweedie addresses the issues of red tape reduction and the importance of striking the balance between removing unnecessary burdens and maintaining compliance with standards for effective service delivery.

In Chapter 11, Rodney Scott and Ross Boyd provide a detailed analysis of the lessons of measuring impact from the New Zealand 'Better Public Services' (BPS) reforms. Scott and Boyd take us through the evolution of performance management in the New Zealand public sector from an inputs focus, to an outputs focus and then to an outcomes focus. They then take us into a more progressive measurement framework, which focuses on collaborating for outcomes and results. Scott and Boyd discuss the 2011 New Zealand Government BPS reforms, which aimed to improve the lives of New Zealanders in 10 key social impact areas and which relied on collective accountability across multiple government and NFP organisations. The chapter explores the evaluation of the 10 social impact areas against five-year targets (2012–17). Most insightfully, the discussion points to the learning attitude applied to the measures that has meant in some areas targets have been changed to be more expansive or more specific. The authors discuss 10 lessons from the design, measurement and refinement of the targets and measures for collective social impact.

The lessons discussed by Scott and Boyd provide important considerations for future collective impact targets and measures. Some of the lessons discussed include getting the right language to define the targets and measures. The authors ask whether there is a material difference between 96 per cent participation and 100 per cent participation in early childhood education, versus focusing on a different target and measure such as quality of early childhood learning. A common feature of measurement is that once targets and measures are defined, increased reporting can reveal a more accurate picture and hence the baseline may appear to go backwards, which is what happened with the reporting of domestic violence—a social issue that is often under-reported—which saw an increase under the reforms. This implies that leaders need wisdom as they interpret results. The important observations the authors make are that the targets and measures across the 10 social impact areas are in a constant state of review and reflection because in complex systems the nature of our understanding and articulation is never perfect but rather an ongoing process of refinement through learning. This chapter is an excellent example of a government taking courage to define what it might mean to measure collective impact. There is a lot to learn from Scott and Boyd.

Common threads across the chapters point to a shared view that measurement is limited to current simple models, which can be too outputs focused. The results from measuring impact remain locked in formal reports and little is shared and learnt by the collective for sustainable improvements to service delivery across the NFP sector. Encouragingly, each of these authors points out that the choice to effectively measure social impact lies with government funders and NFPs because the approaches, specific measures and methods that are required should and can be refined and changed to work better for all involved. These chapters will give readers confidence that we can demonstrate, as a collective, that we are meeting great expectations of social impact.

9

Does Outcomes-Based Reporting Contribute to or Contradict the Realisation of Social Outcomes?

Emma Tomkinson

Introduction

Over the past two decades or more Australian and New Zealand governments have progressively shifted the locus of much human service provision from the state (government-owned entities) to non-state providers—especially not-for-profit (NFP) organisations. To satisfy the need for accountability, government 'purchasers' of services have also required reporting on outsourced services to ensure that public funds are well spent. But in the past few years, our perception of what it means to spend money 'well' has changed. Today we are witnessing a trend towards maximising not just *what* money was spent on or how much *activity* occurred, but how much people's lives were affected.

This chapter examines the value of reporting, both for NFP service providers *and* for their government funders, and looks at ways by which this value can be increased. It proposes that if funders are to truly focus on outcomes, the design of their reporting requirements and the manner in which reported information is used *must* be better aligned to the furtherance of the outcomes they pursue. It argues that reporting should be *for* outcomes, rather than just *on* outcomes—that is, reporting should not just describe the outcomes of a program, but also enhance or contribute to those outcomes. Likewise, it argues that reporting needs to serve all stakeholders who are in a position to use the information generated to further outcomes. Of necessity, this entails a much greater degree of reciprocity in reporting than is commonly seen at present. It is not sufficient for information to flow in only one direction (from service providers to purchasers/funders). It also argues the need for government funders to report back to NFP service providers and their clients.

Background

Over the past few decades the role of government—at least in the industrialised West—has steadily shifted from that of a 'provider' of services to that of a 'purchaser' of services (Collins-Comargo et al. 2011; Koning and Heinrich 2013; Martin 2005). This shift has been underpinned by the logic of competition and, unsurprisingly, has been accompanied by the application of competitive processes for the allocation of funding (NSW DPC 2009). Although Australian governments have, since the 1970s, provided funding to NFP organisations in the form of grants-in-aid to undertake activities complementary to state provision (effectively, a form of state philanthropy), the making of grants in the community social service space has largely given way to service procurement via contracts, especially in the human services space (Childs 2014; NSW Ministry of Health 2013).

Moreover, as illustrated in Figure 9.1, the shift from provider to purchaser has served to transform the nature of reporting on expenditure. When governments provide services directly—that is, when services are provided by government employees of a government-owned entity—reporting tends to be vertical and hierarchical. Furthermore, the emphases of such reporting tend to be on: 1) the acquittal of funds appropriated for particular purposes; and 2) the quantum of outputs provided (for example, bed days, hospital admissions, kilometres of road sealed and so on). The absence of separation between the purchaser and the provider can act to militate against accountability to executive government and the public.

When government purchases services from third parties, however, reporting can better serve the purpose of enhanced accountability: it can allow government to monitor what it is paying for, assess the quality of services provided, compare contractors and leverage value for money and innovation through competition, as well as validate that services are being delivered in accordance with contractual requirements.

Role of Government

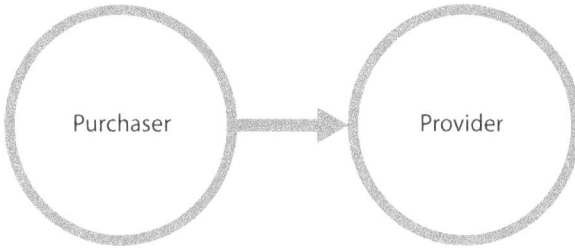

Mode of funding
for non-state actors

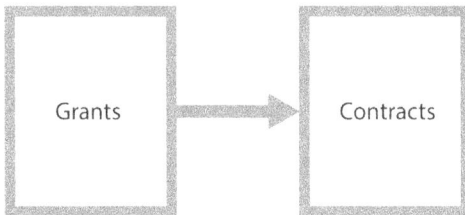

Reporting focus

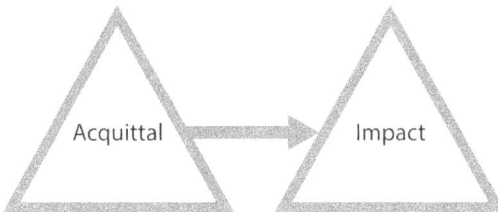

Figure 9.1: The changing role of government
Source: Created by the author.

In short, reporting helps government manage the varieties of risk associated with the outsourcing of services. Here, it is important to note that in policy areas such as disability and aged care the advent of individualised/person-centred funding is further transforming the role of government from a purchaser of services to a market steward (Easton 2015). This will almost certainly be the case with Australia's National Disability Insurance Scheme (NDIS) (see Nevile, Chapter 12; and Needham, Chapter 15 in this volume).

Just as the modus operandi of government service delivery is changing, so too are our expectations of government. Government services were once judged almost solely on broad criteria such as availability and accessibility. Measures of availability include the number of sites offering services, as well as opening hours, waiting times and how well locations match the geographical distribution of need. These are still important considerations for publicly funded services, but in recent years they have been augmented by measures of 'efficiency'. These tend to focus on activities and outputs such as the number of registered clients, the volume of service transactions, the number of appointments conducted or how long each phone call takes. They are often expressed as ratios of outputs to inputs. Of these ratios, the most common seeks to assign a cost per unit of service. Furthermore, a concern for efficiency lies at the heart of much government outsourcing: the belief that the cost structures of direct government provision are prohibitively high in comparison with the private and NFP sectors.

If, however, a concern for efficiency is unaligned with a concern for 'effectiveness', perverse outcomes can result: services that are inexpensive on a unit-cost basis that nevertheless fail to deliver desired impacts. For this reason, we have in recent years seen reporting frameworks broaden to embrace not just technical and economic efficiency, but also effectiveness (Goldsmith 2010). We are thus moving beyond asking how much government-funded services cost per unit of service provided to asking whether, and to what extent, funded services achieve positive outcomes for the people they serve (see Figure 9.2). This chapter focuses on government-funded services that are about producing 'outcomes' for people—usually the people with the greatest needs in our community—and considers how we might align every part of a service, including its reporting framework, towards improving outcomes.

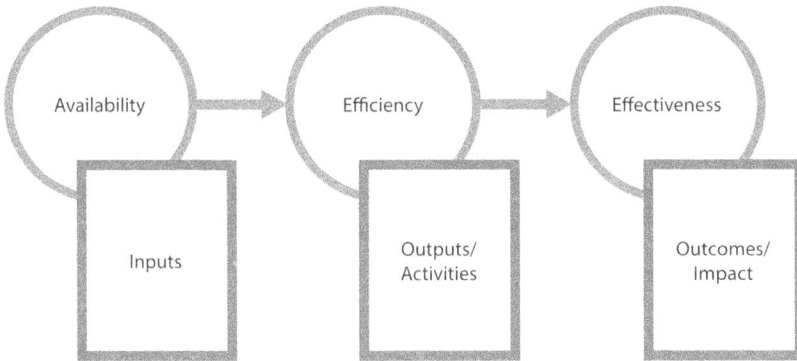

Figure 9.2: Changing expectations of government
Source: Created by the author.

The link between reporting and outcomes

To accommodate a focus on outcomes, government commissioners and purchasers of services are redesigning contracts to directly link payments with outcome improvements (NSW DPC 2015). This can include coupling incentives and sanctions with providers' performance in relation to prescribed outcomes, targets and associated measures. In 2009 the NSW Government announced its intention to move towards 'outcome based monitoring to assess compliance rather than financial reporting, where appropriate' (NSW DPC 2009: 14). Other Australian jurisdictions have followed suit. Examples include the Tasmanian Government's *Funded Community Sector Outcomes Purchasing Framework* (Community Sector Relations Unit 2014), the Queensland Government's *Outcomes Co-Design* framework (Department of Communities, Child Safety and Disability Services 2015), the Victorian Government's *Outcomes Framework* for human service system reform (Department of Health and Human Services 2015) and the Australian Capital Territory through its community sector reform initiative (KPMG 2016).

Reporting requirements can, however, conflict with the achievement of desired outcomes. Sometimes reporting requirements are onerous in terms of staff time commitment, resulting in staff spending a disproportionate amount of their time managing reporting systems rather than delivering services. For example, Considine and Lewis

(2010) found that in the first 10 years of outsourced employment services in Australia the proportion of time that caseworkers spent on administration increased while the proportion of time spent with jobseekers dropped from 50.1 per cent to 45.7 per cent. While one might well imagine that government contract administrators would want caseworkers spending as much time as possible helping jobseekers find work, they nevertheless designed systems of administration and reporting that worked against this.

Reporting regimes can also create perverse incentives (see Ronalds, Chapter 16, this volume) that lead service delivery staff to engage in activities that are contrary to best-practice service delivery. For example, call centre staff are often monitored according to how long their calls are, with shorter calls being more highly valued. However, some callers have more complex needs than others and require solutions that take much longer to put together. Where funding agreements place a higher value on throughput (measured as the number of discrete transactions), call centre staff are under pressure to limit the time they spend on complex cases.

It is worth remembering that an outcomes focus is not always the prime consideration for all services. Sometimes all that is desired is efficiency. For many government services—such as processing tax returns, renewing vehicle registrations, registering for benefits and verifying personal identification—citizens are not looking for their lives to change, they just want these things done right and fast.

Reporting: The definition

Understandably, organisations delivering services on behalf of government are expected to formally report back to the purchasing entity. This is partly for the purposes of ensuring contractual and legal compliance, as well as demonstrating accountability: to ensure that public funds have been spent in the manner for which they were intended. In practice, the bulk of reporting required by government purchasers focuses on the acquittal of expenditure and activity. The reporting landscape is changing, however, and government purchasers are increasingly looking to funded organisations to report on the outcomes produced for beneficiaries or clients so as to demonstrate the impact achieved by public policy (Westall 2012;

ACEVO et al. 2012). This chapter argues that reporting needs to be reframed as a process of strategic communication that helps inform and focus stakeholders on what is important and what can be learnt from prior service delivery. Reporting amounts to a great deal more than simply the public annual reports of an organisation; it includes *all* communication of results to *all* stakeholders. In this chapter, the concern is the subset of reporting that is focused on the changes in people's lives (outcomes) produced by social services delivered by social purpose organisations on behalf of government.

It is now broadly accepted that reporting on inputs (dollars, human resources, capital) and/or outputs (units of service produced, number of transactions, registered clients) is not sufficient to provide real insight into the impact that services have on people's lives. Any redesign of reporting frameworks to better support the purpose of improving the outcomes of services needs to encompass *what* is reported, *to whom* it is reported and *how often*. However, the business systems within which public sector purchasers of mandated services operate are steeped in a culture of compliance. Reporting is largely 'one-way traffic' with little in the way of feedback or value adding to service providers. Service provider organisations commonly observe that they expend precious time undertaking compliance activities that add little to the task of service delivery and result in reports that 'disappear' into a black hole of bureaucracy.

This chapter proposes that the onus is now on public sector purchasers to place their reporting frameworks in the service of achieving desired outcomes. In short, reporting frameworks can become an important tool for engagement as well as a *real-time* strategic resource for the ongoing management of services and adjustment of service delivery. To do this, reporting—as strategic communication—should serve the needs of a wider range of stakeholders, including: beneficiaries and clients, service managers and frontline staff, collaborative partners and ancillary service providers, executive management and boards, funders and regulators and affected communities (ACEVO et al. 2012). As mentioned previously, the advent of person-centred approaches to funding such as Australia's NDIS makes it even more important to recognise beneficiaries/clients as a key audience for reporting.

The burden of reporting

Reporting on outcomes is strongly coupled with methodologies for 'impact measurement'—the estimation and recording of the effect of a service or program. But who bears the costs associated with such a methodologically complex and potentially resource-intensive undertaking? In the United Kingdom, research undertaken in 2013 by New Philanthropy Capital (NPC) found that 75 per cent of funders claimed they provided support for impact measurement while 64 per cent of charities surveyed claimed that their funders did *not* pay for impact measurement (Kail et al. 2013: 4–5). This apparent discrepancy is strongly suggestive of a significant disconnect between funders and the organisations they fund around the burden of reporting. These findings are consistent with the commonly reported claims of Australian funded organisations that they are not compensated for the financial impost of reporting pursuant to their contractual obligations.

Reporting should not be about 'ticking the accountability box'. As Tweedie observes (Chapter 10, this volume), reporting frameworks can act to impair accountability even in organisations acting with the best of intentions. Indeed, Australia's NFP sector abounds with tales of reporting frameworks that are strategically unaligned with the purposes for which funding is provided and that add little reflexive value to policy. Furthermore, many NFP organisations claim they are subject to multiple reporting, compliance and accountability requirements. A NSW Government consultation undertaken in 2009 identified a number of reporting and contracting burdens claimed by funded NFP organisations (summarised in Figure 9.3). They used the umbrella term 'red tape', which included the reporting burdens of progress status reports, external audits, formal and informal monitoring and annual statements.

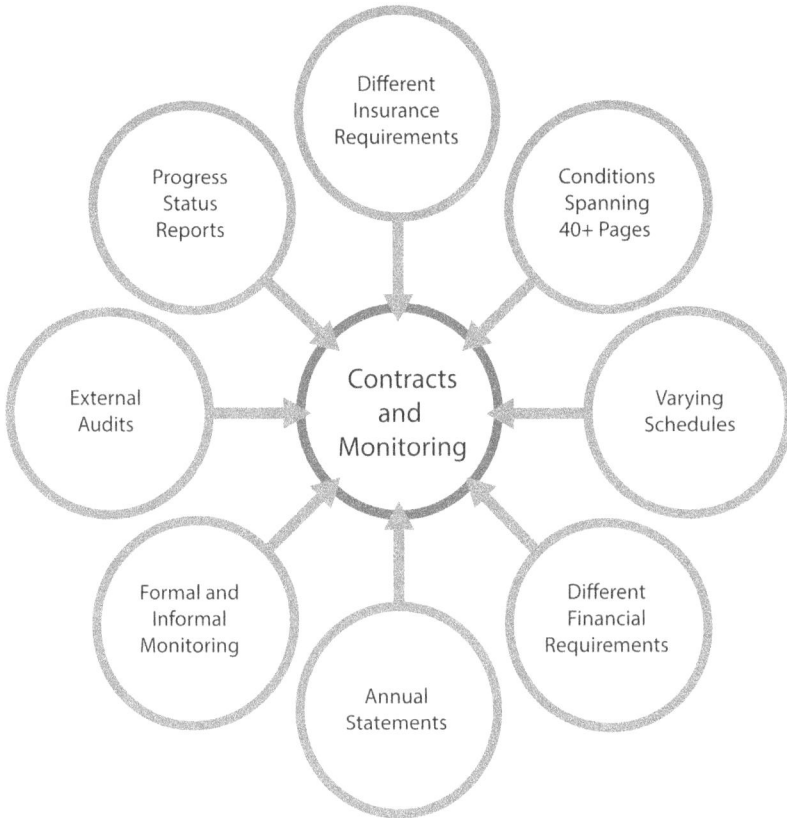

Figure 9.3: Red tape issues for NGOs
Source: After NSW DPC (2009: 8).

Leveraging wider benefits from reporting

Measuring and reporting on outcomes are not easy. A recent study published as part of the Bankwest Foundation Social Impact Series found that 'community sector organisations and funders' in Western Australia 'are struggling with outcomes measurement, and facing critical barriers at the organisational and systems levels that are impeding progress' (Bankwest Foundation 2015: 2). The study found that the areas in which NFPs struggle with their outcomes measurement include the articulation of outcomes, estimating cost–benefit ratios and making the best use of existing data (Pro Bono Australia 2015). At the organisational level, critical barriers to outcomes measurement included a lack of internal capacity, fragmented funding, problems with staff engagement and access to data and the use of inconsistent language (Pro Bono Australia 2015).

For an example of better practice in outcomes reporting let us consider a non-state funder in the United Kingdom, the Diana, Princess of Wales Memorial Fund.[1] Its journey illustrates how a funder can take a leading role in measurement and evaluation and work with grantees to improve outcomes. A strategic review undertaken by the fund in 2006 identified a failure to reap the benefits of their evaluations of the programs they funded. Although many evaluations were done, they were of variable quality and their findings were often not shared or acted on. The fund implemented a number of changes to leverage greater value from their evaluation and reporting practices. One critical innovation was to achieve a separation of 'compliance' from 'learning': 'Compliance answers the question, "Did you do what you said you would?" Learning focuses on asking, "What broader lessons can be draw from this project?"' (Rickey et al. 2011: 37–38).

Consequently, the fund's approach to 'learning' was to provide information that can be acted on to adjust and improve a grantee's activities. As observed by Rickey et al. (2011: 37–38): 'Before, there used to be endless reports and endless standard evaluations with a lot of detailed questions. The new approach has enabled staff to spend more time focused on improving the impact of projects, rather than simply on compliance monitoring.'

Not only did this benefit the fund (by providing assurance concerning impact) and their grantees and beneficiaries (by facilitating improved performance in relation to outcomes), the external sharing of learnings from the evaluation process also benefited other organisations.

---

1   The Diana, Princess of Wales Memorial Fund was established in 1997 as a grant-making charity to honour the late Princess's humanitarian work by supporting 'people on the margins of society and of the charities that work alongside them'. Between 1997 and December 2012, when the fund closed, 'it had awarded 727 grants to 471 organisations, and spent over £112 million [$212.6 million] on charitable causes'. See: dianaprincessofwalesmemorialfund.org/about-fund (accessed 8 April 2016).

Can the benefit overtake the burden?

According to Pritchard et al. (2012), charities often start down the impact measurement road only under pressure from funders. Although NFP service providers often find that an enhanced focus on outcomes/ impacts can lead to improved services (Pritchard et al. 2012), it is important to recognise that there can be significant cultural, financial and technical impediments that militate against the embrace of impact measurement. In an ideal world, the measurement of outcomes would be a strategic choice, rather than a response to the coercive actions of purchasers/funders.

Ideally, information systems are designed to aid the delivery of services by frontline staff. Staff should be encouraged to value the information stored in the system and this will create incentives to enter this information accurately and completely. One possible by-product of such a system might be automated reports for a range of stakeholders. Stakeholders will find the information useful and valuable and will help to complete the virtuous circle by providing positive feedback and suggestions for service and data improvement.

Although the barriers to the redesign of business processes to support impact measurement can be intimidating, there are examples of organisations whose investment in redesign of data systems has paid off. Daniel Leach-McGill described how one such investment in system redesign won over frontline staff at Australian children's charity Good Beginnings:

> The biggest hindrance is that it eats into the time our workers want to spend with clients. When staff have been able to find a direct use of the system, they interact more with it and data quality improves. Some sites are using reports straight out of the system for clients to take to court as evidence, for example when access to their children is being reviewed. They're able to generate a report of attendance and snapshot summary of sessions over time so that the client is able to use and own it. When they can see its use, the value of the system overtakes the administrative burden. (Tomkinson 2015a: 14)

Government funders need to be proactive about pursuing outcomes through measurement and reporting, but it does seem that practices are improving. In the most recent NSW state of the community services sector survey, more respondents reported that their relationships with the NSW Government in relation to reporting and compliance had strengthened (34 per cent) than said it had weakened (9.2 per cent) (Cortis and Blaxland 2015). This was consistent with the previous year's results (Cortis and Blaxland 2014).

'Ability Links' offers a good example of outcomes reporting expressly designed to work *for* service providers. An initiative of the NSW Department of Family and Community Services, in partnership with consulting firm Urbis, the Ability Links evaluation framework was developed in close consultation with service providers via an iterative process in which all results are published on a dedicated website (abilitylinksevaluation.com.au). Ability Links is a program to support people with disabilities to pursue their personal goals while helping local communities become more inclusive and supportive. Rather than specify the outcomes from the beginning, the evaluators asked participants and staff over the first couple of years what outcomes were achieved, and these are what are now reported on.

For service providers working with a few clients for a long period, reporting occurs as outcomes happen, rather than at a set frequency, resulting in a reduced reporting burden over the duration of the intervention. Outcomes reported are ascribed social, economic and environmental values and are used by the department in their decision-making for the future. In addition, not only are evaluation reports prepared and provided to the NSW Government, but also all providers are supplied with each report as it is developed (Tomkinson 2015b).

Who's reporting to whom? The value add

When information flows only in one direction—from funded organisations to their funders—much of the potential value of reporting is lost. For reporting to contribute to outcomes it needs to have a capacity to communicate with a range of stakeholders using a variety of platforms and methods, including:

- annual reports, annual reviews and impact reports
- management information, board reports and organisational reviews
- reports to funders, supporters, investors and commissioners
- internal communications with staff and volunteers

- communications materials, such as websites, brochures and leaflets
- fundraising materials
- key messages about the organisation
- communications with, and feedback and responses from, its beneficiaries (ACEVO et al. 2012).

There are many ways in which it would be possible for governments to add value to the data they receive and share it with stakeholders. Governments collect vast amounts of data in the course of running tendering processes for community-based human services, yet beyond using this information for the purposes of determining successful bidders there is little evidence that governments are capable of exploiting the full value of this rich mine of information. The data contained in tender documents and compliance reports could be enormously useful for identifying service gluts and gaps, biases in their own procurement processes, better practices that could be shared and opportunities for organisations to collaborate or learn from one another. At present, however, much of the value of the information collected by governments as purchasers of services is lost and is not used to contribute to better outcomes. This amounts to a failure on the part of public sector purchasers to realise their potential to add value as a key stakeholder in the service delivery supply chain.

The reporting process should reward organisations that are delivering and improving outcomes. Many funders in the public and private sectors have policies of funding an organisation only once or funding them forever, regardless of the outcomes they achieve. In addition, some funders have a policy of requiring the return of any surplus generated by improved efficiency. The failure to reward performance, or indeed to effectively punish good performance, results from the absence of any meaningful nexus between performance and funding. Under such conditions there is little incentive for organisations to report on outcomes (Pritchard et al. 2012).

It is important to reiterate that the definition, measurement, attribution and comparison of outcomes are complex and difficult undertakings. In some cases, claimed outcomes cannot be reliably attributed to particular interventions and instead reflect differences in populations or other factors external to the policies, programs or services in question (Cohen 2016; Lester 2016).

The way outcomes are defined affects how they are pursued

If we accept the desirability of reporting on outcomes, we ought to also accept the virtue of feedback loops through which the measurement of outcomes generates new insights that in turn inform refinements of the service delivery models that produced the outcomes in the first place. It can be argued that all measures of outcomes create incentives and, to the extent possible, when defining outcome measures it is also necessary to anticipate any incentives that might arise.

Let us consider two examples from the United Kingdom: 1) the contract for HMP Doncaster, a privately operated Category B prison managed by Serco; and 2) the contract for the HMP Peterborough Social Impact Bond. For Doncaster Prison, the outcome measure was the proportion of offenders who commit at least one offence in the 12 months after release and are convicted at court (Ministry of Justice 2014b). For Peterborough Prison, the outcome measure was the frequency of reconviction events, based on offences committed within 12 months of release from prison and convicted at court (Jolliffe and Hedderman 2014).

The Peterborough Prison measure encouraged service providers to work with the most prolific offenders over the entire 12 months post release, regardless of whether or not they were reconvicted in that time, as each offending event continued to be counted (Nicholls and Tomkinson 2013). In contrast, the Doncaster Prison measure encouraged the service provider to cease working with a prisoner as soon as they were reconvicted, as they immediately ceased to count for the outcome payments: 'The Alliance chose to withdraw community support for offenders who are reconvicted within the 12 month period post-release as they feel that this does not represent the best use of their resources' (Hichens and Pearce 2014).

It seems clear that the outcome measures adopted for each prison created quite different incentives with the potential for significantly different consequences for the reintegration of released offenders and observed rates of recidivism.

Objectives served by reporting

As has already been observed, it is generally accepted that funded organisations are required to report back to government to provide assurance that public money has been well spent. One might indeed go further and suggest that public money can only said to be spent well when such expenditure results in positive changes in people's lives (subject, of course, to the application of some reasonable test of value for money). If positive change—the production of outcomes—is indeed the goal of public policy and investments in social programs, decisions about the design and implementation of reporting regimes should be consistent with this goal.

Too often, however, the business systems underpinning the outsourcing of social programs and services have militated against the maximisation of outcomes. Examples abound of prescriptive contracts that restrict providers from adjusting the mode of service delivery to improve reporting systems, that force providers to repeatedly provide the same information, and digital reporting systems that will not integrate with provider systems or even allow providers to export the data for their own use. And yet, public sector funders are sometimes slow to accept that their business systems, operational policies and practices are what reduce the ability of providers to produce the outcomes they are funded for.

Reporting can also be used to support the benchmarking of external providers. One of the clearest examples of benchmarking in the Australian context is the 'star rating' system used by Job Services Australia to:

- enable jobseekers to assess the comparative performance of providers in their local area
- give providers a measure of their contractual performance
- allow the department to drive improved performance and allocate business share to providers (Department of Employment 2015).

The star ratings measure the relative performance of providers for each site across Australia by calculating a performance score for two contractual key performance indicators (KPIs) over the most recent three-year period: KPI1 'Efficiency' is the average time taken by providers in comparison with other providers to assist relevant participants into employment; and KPI2 'Effectiveness' is the proportion of relevant participants for whom placements and outcomes are achieved (Department of Employment 2015). These scores are then used to calculate a national average performance score and star ratings are subsequently allocated on the basis of the comparison of individual site performance scores with the national average (Department of Employment 2015). For example, all sites with scores 40 per cent or more above the national average are allocated five stars. Providers with one or two stars risk having their contracts suspended, terminated early or not renewed. The star ratings and their associated 'star percentages' are detailed in Table 9.1.

Table 9.1: Job Services Australia star rating and star percentages

Star rating	Star percentages
5 stars	40% or more above the average
4 stars	Between 20% and 39% above the average
3 stars	Between 19% above and 19% below the average
2 stars	Between 20% and 49% below the average
1 star	50% or more below the average

Source: Based on Australian Government (2012).

In 2002, the Productivity Commission reviewed the employment services system and concluded that 'it incorporates strong incentives—particularly through the star rating system—for providers to improve their performance without direction by government' (Productivity Commission 2002: xxxiv).

While the amount of variation between providers has narrowed over time, an unforeseen consequence of the star rating system has been that the number of employment services providers has dropped from 306 for the first round of contracts in 1998 (DEWR 1998) to only 44 for the 2015 round of contracts (Australian Government 2015).

Whose data?

The requirement imposed by government commissioners and purchasers of services on external service providers to demonstrate outcomes carries with it an implicit assumption that the data necessary to demonstrate impact necessarily originate at the point of service delivery. Sometimes, however, government entities are the custodians of records that are more detailed and reliable than any dataset held by an external service provider. Government-held records can represent a mine of invaluable information for the purposes of gauging the impact of policy and programs. This is particularly true in the criminal justice space where records arise through interactions with police, court appearances, sentences and incarcerations.

In the United Kingdom, the Ministry of Justice established the Justice Data Lab to calculate the effect on reoffending of programs for offenders using data drawn from the National Police Database. Using 'propensity score matching', the system compares offenders who have participated in a program with offenders with similar offending histories who have not participated in a program. The reoffending of the two groups is compared to calculate the 'effect size' of participation in an offenders' program. This service does not involve additional cost to providers and is available to both public sector and externally provided programs. One of the conditions of the lab is that results are published (Ministry of Justice 2014a).

The system is not fail-safe, as it is possible for providers to submit data for a subset of offenders that have improved the most. Despite such caveats, the Justice Data Lab marks an important innovation that enables external providers to obtain an estimate of the effect of their programs without huge expense. Since the Justice Data Lab was established, the UK Department of Work and Pensions has announced it will pursue a similar initiative. As far as results have gone, the majority of programs submitted to the Justice Data Lab have not shown statistically significant effects. Of those that did show an effect, most appeared to reduce reoffending, although several were associated with an increase in reoffending.

There is an abundance of data held by governments and external providers that are never used by anyone. Although we are good at collecting data, we have not been nearly as good at creating meaning from data collected in the course of social service delivery. Barriers to the creation of meaning include failures to invest in (including disinvestment in) analytical capability, contracts that fail to make financial provision for data collection and systematic evaluation and the prevalence of rules-based organisational cultures that are concerned more with compliance than with continuous learning and improvement.

Shifting the focus from compliance to learning

So, how might the shift from a 'compliance culture' to a 'learning culture' be accomplished when it comes to the commissioning and procurement of publicly funded human services? This is a complex and multifaceted question. Certainly, a greater appetite for experimentation and risk-taking is a prerequisite—qualities not strongly in evidence in the Australian Public Service, according to Peter Shergold (Chapter 2, this volume). We are, therefore, obliged to look further afield for inspiration.

The Education Endowment Foundation, funded by the UK Government, supports an evidence-based approach, with experiments conducted in hundreds of schools across the United Kingdom. These experiments home in on components of programs, such as mentoring or homework, to identify factors and variables that contribute to positive outcomes for students. The results of the experiments are published in an easily accessible digital format. This enables teachers to make informed decisions about teaching strategies and practices they might want to bring into their own classrooms (Education Endowment Foundation 2016).

A key barrier to achieving outcomes in our changing world is our attachment to certainty. If we can let go of needing to be certain that we are doing the right thing, we open ourselves up to being able to adjust and adapt to the context, populations and localities we are serving (Schorr 2016).

As Tony Fujs of the Latin American Youth Center says, 'continuous improvement is the key to performance management. It's the idea of the continuous dynamic learning, positive feedback loop that you put in place' (cited in Leap of Reason 2016).

The Leap of Reason initiative in the United States offers one example of an organisation that seeks to 'influence a mindset change among leaders who play a significant role in the social and public sectors and who are motivated to create meaningful, measurable, and sustainable improvement in the lives of individuals, families, and communities' (Leap of Reason 2016). This it aims to do by inspiring leaders to expect and support:

- highly effective, high-performing organisations
- mission-focused, performance-driven leadership
- disciplined, informed management
- talented staff functioning within a culture of continuous improvement
- funding based on reason and results rather than blind faith or photogenic anecdotes (Leap of Reason 2016).

The Leap of Reason initiative provides resources and case studies to inspire leaders of social purpose organisations to raise their performance through a focus on mission, information and evidence.

Another organisation—this time from the United Kingdom—that has implemented a similar approach is Social Finance (2016a), which is 'a not for profit organisation that partners with the government, the social sector and the financial community to find better ways of tackling social problems in the UK and beyond'. The models used by Social Finance are driven by social *and* financial returns: 'We provide high quality financial and data analysis, create robust financial and delivery models and we build relationships between different sectors to produce better solutions to societal problems. We focus on delivery and what works' (Social Finance 2016b).

The cycle of information and analysis in Figure 9.4 is based on practices pioneered by Social Finance.

Figure 9.4: The impact analysis cycle
Source: Tomkinson (2015a).

The six components of the cycle in Figure 9.4 are broken down as follows:

1. As a service is delivered, the participants in the service not only give consent for their data to be collected, they also consent to it being analysed by providers and shared between them.

2. The data are entered into a case management system that allows client records to be accessed by service delivery personnel employed by all relevant organisations engaged in providing the subject program or intervention service. The system should be designed in close consultation with frontline staff in order to mirror the service that is being delivered. The nature of the data and the manner of its collection will be driven by the requirements of service delivery with analysis undertaken by a dedicated performance analyst.

3. Performance analysts 'drive' the data sharing and collection system through developing close relationships with all stakeholders, front-line staff in particular. It is their role to extract meaning from the data and communicate it to the relevant stakeholders.

4. It is entirely possible for service delivery staff working at the coalface to directly observe apparent patterns, trends or effects amongst a small cohort of clients. Having the ability to work with an analyst to test and validate their 'field observations' using data drawn from hundreds, or even thousands of cases can give them unprecedented insight and a basis for service improvement.

5. The analysts are also responsible for feedback loops and reporting, but this is reporting that is a consequence of the system, not the purpose of the system. They report to funders, to government, to other collaborators, to managers, and to all frontline staff members. For frontline staff members these reports are individualised, so each staff member receives useful information about their own clients.

6. Gathering and analysing data, and maintaining strong networks of stakeholders, is pointless without the capacity to adjust the mode of service delivery in response to new information and new insights. This is perhaps the hardest part of this system. To be effective, it needs to be an iterative and collaborative process so that changes are sensible, supported and continue to be analysed for their effect. (Tomkinson 2015a)

In closing

If the foregoing discussion has a somewhat discursive character the reader might consider that this is not unlike the nature of impact reporting itself—or at least, as it is too often practised. This volume and most of the chapters it contains adopt as their pivotal theme the existence and persistence of gaps and disconnects—between rhetoric and reality, between social investment and social return and between effort and impact. So, what are some of the take-home messages?

First, we have a situation in Australia that sees governments routinely gathering and archiving massive amounts of information generated by the delivery of services and yet failing to fully exploit the unrealised potential of this goldmine of data. In one sense, this could be seen as an inevitable consequence of a pervasive compliance culture more concerned with fiscal discipline than with organisational learning and systems redesign. It might also be argued that over the past two decades or more the inexorable embrace of outsourcing has been accompanied by the divestment of the internal analytical capability necessary to meaningfully interrogate the metadata generated by externalised service provision for strategic purposes. Indeed, there is ample colloquial testimony inside and outside the Australia public sector that such 'hollowing' is a reality. For example, outsourced employment services in Australia have produced an extraordinary amount of data from hundreds of service providers over almost two decades, but there has been little analysis to add value to those data and feed the lessons back to the organisations delivering services and their staff, let alone to people accessing services who might benefit from reflective analysis.

Second, the purchaser–provider dichotomy reinforced by purist procurement approaches to outsourcing in the social policy space has tended to reinforce a hierarchical, vertical command-and-control mentality that serves to impair strong relationships of reciprocity and trust between government entities and external service providers. In addition, government is not the only game in town when it comes to investing in third parties to deliver public benefit. There are many large charities and foundations both in Australia and (especially) overseas that channel hundreds of millions of dollars to NFP organisations from whom governments might learn a great deal about reporting for impact, working collegially across sectoral and organisational boundaries and transmitting learnings. This represents a huge—and, to this point, unrealised—opportunity for government to learn from other funders.

I will conclude by sharing four powerful ideas proposed by Buteau et al. (2015) that offer valuable guidance to organisations from *any* sector engaged in the business of financing social benefit. Although developed initially for foundations funding grantees, these ideas are equally applicable to governments funding contracted service providers:

Idea #1

Engage in more and deeper discussion with grantees about their performance assessment and management efforts.

- Understand how grantees are investing in their capacity for assessment.
- Ask grantees what performance information they are collecting to assess their organisation's performance, and what else they would like to be able to do in these efforts.
- Talk with grantees about how they are using the results of their performance assessments.

Idea #2

Fund nonprofits' efforts to measure their performance.

Idea #3

Reflect on how well your performance data requirements for grantees align with the goals of your grants and the organisations you fund.

Idea #4

Help nonprofits share with other organisations what they have learned through their performance assessments—about what does and does not work. (Buteau et al. 2015: 19)

Of the four ideas set out above, perhaps number three offers government the most viable pivot for change? Indeed, good public governance demands that government entities reflect carefully on how well their performance data requirements for externalised service providers align with the goals of their service funding agreements and the organisations they fund.

According to Hedley et al. (2010: 1):

[W]hen surveyed, donors consistently say that the two most important factors in trusting charities are how the money is spent and what it achieves …

[T]he informed donor will become increasingly important to charities as they struggle to survive the coming storm of public spending cuts, and pressures on individual, foundation and corporate giving. Those charities that equip themselves now to communicate with these donors will be better prepared to compete in these difficult times. And while measuring outcomes and impact is rarely straightforward, we believe that charities can communicate their impact successfully by following a simple formula of five key questions:

1. What is the problem we are trying to address?
2. What do we do to address it?
3. What are we achieving?
4. How do we know what we are achieving?
5. What are we learning, and how can we improve?

These five questions set out an intellectual framework so obvious that it is difficult to understand why it is so seldom evidenced in practice. For outsourced services, the first question should be answered in the original tender document written by the public sector entity charged with the procurement task. The second should be answered in the responses to the tender (rather than being prescribed with no possibility of alteration from the outset). The final three should prompt organisations delivering services to articulate the outcomes they aim to achieve and formulate appropriate and comparable methodologies for measuring impact and strategies for documenting and sharing learnings. For that matter, systematically attending to each of the five questions could be transformative even for the dwindling share of mandated public services that continue to be delivered directly by government.

As a final note, as reasonable as the above schema appears on the surface, we also need to accept that there will be barriers: government entities will be loathe to relinquish control; systems for compliance will be subject to path-dependent resistance to change; and, in increasingly commercialised and competitive human service markets, service providers will be reluctant to share commercially sensitive information. This, alas, is the nature of the complex and often uncertain policy and organisational landscape in which we find ourselves. There is, however, some comfort to be found in the knowledge that reporting can increasingly contribute to social impact and that the tools exist to chart a mutually beneficial course forwards.

References

ACEVO, Charity Finance Group, Institute of Fundraising, NCVO, New Philanthropy Capital, Small Charities Coalition, Social Enterprise UK and SROI Network. 2012. *The Principles of Good Impact Reporting*. London: ACEVO, Charity Finance Group, Institute of Fundraising, NCVO, New Philanthropy Capital, Small Charities Coalition, Social Enterprise UK and SROI Network. Available from: thinknpc.org/publications/the-principles-of-good-impact-reporting-2/ (accessed 8 April 2016).

Australian Government. 2012. *Job Services Australia Star Ratings Methodology from July 2012 to June 2015*. Canberra. Available: docs.employment.gov.au/node/31825 (accessed 27 June 2016).

Australian Government. 2015. *Request for Tender for Employment Services 2015–2020: Employment provider sites by employment region*. Canberra: Australian Government. Available from: docs.employment.gov.au/node/34721 (accessed 8 April 2016).

Bankwest Foundation. 2015. *Supporting development and growth in the WA community sector*. Bankwest Foundation Social Impact Series. Bankwest Foundation, Perth. Available from: csi.edu. au/media/uploads/Bankwest_-_Research_Highlights_2015.pdf (accessed 8 April 2016).

Buteau, E., R. Gopal and J. Glickman. 2015. *Assessing to Achieve High Performance: What nonprofits are doing and how foundations can help*. Cambridge, Mass.: The Center for Effective Philanthropy. Available from: effectivephilanthropy. org/wp-content/uploads/2015/04/Assessing-to-Achieve-High-Performance.pdf (accessed 8 April 2016).

Childs, T. 2014. *NCOSS Funding Reform and Procurement Process Case Study Report*. Sydney: NSW Council of Social Service.

Cohen, M. K. 2016. 'Evaluation of foster care agency should look beyond "performance scorecard".' *The Chronicle of Social Change*, 20 January. Available from: chronicleofsocialchange.org/featured/ ill-conceived-benchmarks-can-bad-consequences-kids/15177 (accessed 8 April 2016).

Collins-Camargo, C., B. McBeath and K. Ensign. 2011. 'Privatization and performance-based contracting in child welfare: Recent trends and implications for social service administrators.' *Administration in Social Work* 35(5): 494–516.

Community Sector Relations Unit. 2014. *DHHS Funded Community Sector Outcomes Purchasing Framework*. Hobart: Tasmanian Department of Health and Human Services. Available from: dhhs. tas.gov.au/__data/assets/pdf_file/0013/161005/DHHS_Funded_ Community_Sector_Outcomes_Purchasing_Framework_Final.pdf (accessed 8 April 2016).

Considine, M. and J. M. Lewis. 2010. 'Front-line work in employment services after ten years of new public management reform: Governance and activation in Australia, the Netherlands and the UK.' *European Journal of Social Security* 12(4): 357–70.

Cortis, N. and M. Blaxland. 2014. *The State of the Community Service Sector in NSW 2014*. Sydney: NSW Council of Social Service. Available from: sprc.unsw.edu.au/media/SPRCFile/State_of_the_community_ service_sector_in_NSW_2014.pdf (accessed 8 April 2016).

Cortis, N. and M. Blaxland. 2015. *State of the Community Service Sector in NSW 2015*. Sydney: NSW Council of Social Service. Available from: sprc.unsw.edu.au/media/SPRCFile/SPRC_Report__ State_of_the_Community_Service_Sector_in_NSW_2015.pdf (accessed 8 April 2016).

Department of Communities, Child Safety and Disability Services. 2015. *Outcomes Co-Design*. Brisbane: Queensland Government. Available from: communities.qld.gov.au/gateway/funding-and-grants/outcomes-co-design (accessed 8 April 2016).

Department of Education, Employment and Workplace Relations (DEEWR). 2013. *Job Services Australia Star Ratings Methodology from July 2012 to June 2015*. Canberra: Australian Government. Available from: docs.employment.gov.au/node/31825 (accessed 8 April 2016).

Department of Employment. 2015. *Job Services Australia Star Ratings Methodology from July 2012 to June 2015*. Fact Sheet. Australian Government, Canberra. Available from: docs.employment.gov.au/system/files/doc/other/jsa-star-ratings-methodology-july-2012-to-june-2015-fact-sheet.pdf (accessed 8 April 2016).

Department of Employment and Workplace Relations (DEWR). 1998. New job network to replace the CES. Media Release. Parliament House, Canberra. Available from: parlinfo.aph.gov.au/parlInfo/search/display/display.w3p;query=Id%3A%22media%2Fpressrel%2FBXR30%22 (accessed 8 April 2016).

Department of Health and Human Services. 2015. *Outcomes Framework*. Melbourne: Victorian Government. Available from: www.dhs.vic.gov.au/for-service-providers/for-funded-agencies/services-connect/what-is-services-connect/services-connect-outcomes-framework (accessed 8 April 2016).

Easton, S. 2015. 'CEO's lessons from the NDIS: scaling individualised services.' *The Mandarin*, 29 October. Available from: themandarin.com.au/56316-ndia-chiefs-lessons-market-stewardship-front-lines/ (accessed 14 December 2015).

Education Endowment Foundation. 2016. *About Us*. London: Education Endowment Foundation. Available from: education endowmentfoundation.org.uk/about/ (accessed 8 April 2016).

Goldsmith, S. 2010. 'Defining the Role of Government.' Blog, Governing.com. Available from: governing.com/blogs/bfc/defining-role-government-budget-battles.html (accessed 8 April 2016).

Hedley, S., S. Keen, T. Lumley, E. N. Ogain, J. Thomas and M. Williams. 2010. *Talking About Results*. London: New Philanthropy Capital. Available from: thinknpc.org/wp-content/uploads/2012/09/Talking-about-results.pdf (accessed 8 April 2016).

Hichens, E. and S. Pearce. 2014. *Process Evaluation of the HMP Doncaster Payment by Results Pilot: Phase 2 findings*. London: Ministry of Justice. Available from: socialwelfare.bl.uk/subject-areas/services-client-groups/adult-offenders/ministryofjustice/162313hmp-doncaster-pilot-evaluation-report.pdf (accessed 8 April 2016).

Jolliffe, D. and C. Hedderman. 2014. *Peterborough social impact bond: Final report on cohort 1 analysis*. Prepared for the Ministry of Justice by QuinetiQ/University of Leicester, London. Available from: gov.uk/government/uploads/system/uploads/attachment_data/file/341684/peterborough-social-impact-bond-report.pdf (accessed 8 April 2016).

Kail, A., A. Van Vliet and L. Baumgartner. 2013. *Funding Impact: Impact measurement practices among funders in the UK*. London: New Philanthropy Capital. Available from: thinknpc.org/publications/funding-impact/ (accessed 8 April 2016).

Koning, P. and C. J. Heinrich. 2013. 'Cream skimming, parking, and other intended and unintended effects of high-powered, performance-based contracts.' *Journal of Policy Analysis and Management* 32(3): 461–83.

KPMG. 2016. *Development of a Community Services Industry Plan in the ACT*. Canberra: Community Services Directorate.

Leap of Reason. 2016. 'About Us.' Website. Available from: leapofreason.org/about-us/ (accessed 8 April 2016).

Lester, P. 2016. 'The Promise and Peril of an "Outcomes Mindset".' *Stanford Social Innovation Review*, 13 January. Available from: ssir.org/articles/entry/the_promise_and_peril_of_an_outcomes_mindset (accessed 8 April 2016).

Martin, L. L. 2005. 'Performance-based contracting for human services: Does it work?' *Administration in Social Work* 29(1): 63–77.

Ministry of Justice. 2014a. *Justice Data Lab User Journey Document*. London: HMG. Available from: gov.uk/government/uploads/ system/uploads/attachment_data/file/392927/justice-data-lab-user-journey.pdf (accessed 8 April 2016).

Ministry of Justice. 2014b. *Peterborough Social Impact Bond, HMP Doncaster: Payment by results pilots final re-conviction results for cohorts 1*. London: HMG.

National Audit Office. 2015. *Outcome-Based Payment Schemes: Government's use of payment by results*. London: National Audit Office. Available from: nao.org.uk/wp-content/uploads/2015/06/ Outcome-based-payment-schemes-governments-use-of-payment-by-results.pdf (accessed 8 April 2016).

New South Wales Department of Premier and Cabinet (NSW DPC). 2009. *Non-Government Organisation Red Tape Reduction*. Sydney: NSW Government. Available from: adhc.nsw.gov.au/__data/ assets/file/0006/238272/NGO_Red_Tape_Reduction_Report.pdf (accessed 8 April 2016).

New South Wales Department of Premier and Cabinet (NSW DPC). 2015. *Outcomes Measurement*. Sydney: NSW Government. Available from: dpc.nsw.gov.au/programs_and_services/social_impact_investment/ outcomes_measurement (accessed 14 December 2015).

New South Wales Ministry of Health. 2013. *Partnerships for Health: A response to the Grants Management Improvement Program Taskforce report*. Sydney: NSW Government. Available from: health.nsw.gov.au/business/partners/Publications/gmip-taskforce-report-response.pdf (accessed 8 April 2016).

Nicholls, A. and E. Tomkinson. 2013. *Case Study: The Peterborough Pilot Social Impact Bond*. Oxford: Saïd Business School, University of Oxford. Available from: emmatomkinson.files.wordpress. com/2013/06/case-study-the-peterborough-pilot-social-impact-bond-oct-2013.pdf (accessed 8 April 2016).

Pritchard, D., E. N. Ogain and T. Lumley. 2012. *Making an Impact*. London: New Philanthropy Capital. Available from: thinknpc.org/publications/making-an-impact/ (accessed 8 April 2016).

Pro Bono Australia. 2015. 'Outcomes measurement hits barriers in WA.' *Pro Bono Australia*, 1 October. Available from: probonoaustralia.com.au/news/2015/10/outcomes-measurement-hits-barriers-in-wa/ (accessed 8 April 2016).

Productivity Commission. 2002. *Independent review of the Job Network*. Report No. 21, AusInfo. Productivity Commission, Canberra.

Rickey, B., T. Lumley and E. N. Ógáin. 2011. *A Journey to Greater Impact: Six charities that learned to measure better*. London: New Philanthropy Capital. Available from: www.thinknpc.org/publications/a-journey-to-greater-impact/ (accessed 8 April 2016).

Schorr, L. B. 2016. 'Reconsidering evidence: What it means and how we use it.' *Stanford Social Innovation Review*, 8 January. Available from: ssir.org/articles/entry/reconsidering_evidence_what_it_means_and_how_we_use_it#sthash.xn7UN9EB.dpuf (accessed 8 April 2016).

Social Finance. 2016a. 'About Us.' London: Social Finance. Available from: socialfinance.org.uk/about-us/ (accessed 8 April 2016).

Social Finance. 2016b. 'Impact.' London: Social Finance. Available from: socialfinance.org.uk/impact/ (accessed 8 April 2016).

Tomkinson, E. 2015a. Delivering the promise of social outcomes: The role of the performance analyst. Online article. Available from: deliveringthepromise.org/ (accessed 8 April 2016).

Tomkinson, E. 2015b. *SIMNA NSW Event Recap: An iterative evaluation design*. November. Sydney: Social Impact Measurement Network of Australia. Available from: simna.com.au/simna-nsw-event-recap-an-iterative-evaluation-design/ (accessed 8 April 2016).

Westall, A. 2012. *Measuring social value, social outcomes and impact*. Social Value Briefing 2. National Association for Voluntary and Community Action, London.

10

Not-for-Profit Accountability: Addressing potential barriers

Dale Tweedie[1]

Introduction

This chapter analyses barriers that not-for-profit (NFP) organisations face in meeting public demands to be accountable and considers possible responses, based on a study of NFP staff, directors and regulators in Australia. While 'accountability' has many possible meanings, the chapter focuses on barriers to NFPs being accountable for the *quality* or *impact* of their services *even when* they are motivated to do so. Of course, there are many other ways that accountability can break down, including through conflicts of interest and outright fraud. However, given the complexity of accountability demands, there are numerous obstacles to being accountable even with the best intentions. A key finding of this study is that many NFP staff and directors want to be accountable, but encounter various barriers to doing so. The chapter explores three such barriers: 1) reporting

1   Thank you to all participants in this study for their time, trust and insights. Thank you also to Dr Karina Luzia for her collaborative work in conducting the research on which this chapter draws, and to Professor Nonna Martinov-Bennie for her support for, and contributions to, this research agenda.

that does not improve service quality; 2) NFP boards that lack active members; and 3) red tape reduction that might threaten minimum service standards.

The chapter has three main sections. Section one briefly outlines the research approach and method, which include in-depth interviews with 23 staff, directors and regulators in the Australian NFP sector. Section two summarises the barriers to accountability that emerged from these interviews and analyses how each barrier can impede even well-motivated NFPs' capacity to be accountable. Section three explores potential responses to each barrier, drawing on both NFPs' experiences and relevant research. The chapter particularly emphasises how accountability entails not only formal reporting and policy, but also effective communication. Consequently, improving accountability may require changes to reporting and governance processes and the relationships in which these processes are set.

Research approach and method

NFPs face growing public demands to be accountable (Productivity Commission 2010: xxx; Treasury 2011), but what accountability means is increasingly complex and unclear. Accountability was once almost synonymous with financial reporting (Gray 1983; Carnegie and Wolnizer 1996); however, its meaning has expanded to encompass a much wider set of expectations about how organisations plan, assess and justify their activities. Academic research typically defines accountability very broadly as the 'giving and demanding for reasons for conduct' (Roberts and Scapens 1985; Sinclair 1995; Unerman and O'Dwyer 2006) or, more strongly, as 'the process of holding actors responsible for actions' (Ebrahim 2003: 814; Fox and Brown 1998: 12; see also Stewart 1984). So defined, accountability extends from traditional governance concerns about board structure and financial reporting and controls to demonstrating effective use of public funds. While there is widespread consensus that NFPs need to be accountable, there is little consensus on which accountability practices are most important and, therefore, what accountable NFP organisations should look like in practice.

This chapter analyses one aspect of accountability—accountability for service quality—based on a 2014 study of the demands NFPs face to be accountable and how NFP staff and stakeholders are managing these demands. The study conducted in-depth interviews with 23 NFP staff, directors and regulators, who occupied roles at 30 different NFPs at the time of the study. Participants were drawn from all organisational levels, including: four directors in their primary NFP role (nine directors of any NFP); five chief executive officers (CEOs) (or equivalent);[2] four managers; four frontline service workers; four regulators; and two participants who preferred their primary roles to remain anonymous. A cross-section of participants was selected on the basis that accountability demands are not limited to CEOs and boards, but extend across organisational hierarchies—for example, 'downward accountability' (Edwards and Hulme 1996: 967) of service staff to clients. Since no funders were interviewed, the analysis of the NFP–funder relationship is necessarily one-sided. Nonetheless, understanding NFPs' perspectives on this relationship provides an important, albeit partial, perspective. The majority of participants (14, or 61 per cent) worked at large NFPs (more than $1 million in revenue); three participants (13 per cent) worked at medium-sized NFPs ($250,000 – $1 million in revenue); three (13 per cent) were regulators; and three (13 per cent) did not state the size of the organisation or the size was not applicable.[3] Interviews were semi-structured—that is, grouped around key themes but open-ended—to avoid constraining participants' possible views. All interviews were coded using computer-aided analysis (NVIVO 10) to identify common themes and challenges, and the three barriers to accountability outlined below emerged from this analysis.

---

2   Some NFPs use the term 'director' to designate the senior executive officer, who then reports to a management committee or board. To avoid confusion, all participants in the most senior executive role are termed CEO, while 'director' refers only to board members.

3   The typology of large, medium and small NFPs is from the Australian Charities and Not-for-profits Commission (ACNC). To compare this breakdown with the composition of the NFP sector in Australia more broadly, see Knight and Gilchrist (2014). As Knight and Gilchrist (2014) highlight, while the majority of NFPs are small, a core of larger organisations collects most revenue.

Three potential barriers to accountability for service quality

NFP staff and directors in this study most strongly endorsed being held accountable for their organisations' capacity to deliver its key service or mission:

> I think that society as a whole has become a bit more litigious and accountable … But I see some of those accountabilities as being a positive thing; I don't think just anybody can educate children. So this level of accountability moves us away from inappropriate people looking after and caring for and educating young children. (Participant [P] 6, CEO, medium-sized childhood education NFP)

> There's not a lot of trust in delivery of funding and in flexible use of funding and reporting that appropriately. So I think then what happens is that people think that they'll use that reporting as a kind of lever to make everybody do what they want to do instead of allowing some level of autonomy. But I don't think there should be autonomy in things like regulations and standards for education care settings. That can't be compromised and it's not a burden. It's what people do with it that makes it a burden. (P13, CEO, large childhood education NFP)

Both statements above support external accountability mechanisms that enforce service quality, even while recognising that not all accountability demands serve this end. Since many NFP directors and staff join their organisation to serve its particular mission (see, for example, Light 2002: 109), their commitment to service quality is not surprising. However, recognising that many NFP staff are committed to being accountable for service quality does frame NFP accountability differently to the mainstream governance literature. This literature largely represents accountability as being concerned with managing conflicts of interests—paradigmatically, compelling for-profit managers to serve shareholders' interests (for example, Fama and Jensen 1983a, 1983b; see also Brennan and Solomon 2008; Olson 2000). Of course, NFPs also face conflicts of interests, especially since they are often accountable to multiple stakeholders (Ebrahim 2003; O'Dwyer 2005), and also are susceptible to fraud (BDO 2014). Yet the focus of NFP staff and directors on being accountable for service quality suggests that NFP accountability can also break down in different ways. In particular, the three barriers explored below are predominately cases where people *intend* to be accountable for service quality, but various reporting, governance or regulatory practices create impediments.

Barrier one: Reporting that is weakly linked to service quality

Since most participant NFPs are highly dependent on external funding, what NFPs report is strongly influenced by funders' actual or perceived reporting requirements:

> Our focus is on being accountable to the government department that let the contract and gave us the money. (P5, director, large social services NFP)

> Interviewer: Are there particular groups that figure in those [board] conversations, as these are the people we really need to be concerned about?

> P1: Yes, it's organisations so it's always funders. (P1, director, large social services NFP)

> P12: All we measure at the moment is activities. You know, the number of people in beds on a particular night, etc.

> Interviewer: Those kinds of things, are they being measured because that's what …

> P12: Government requires. (P12, manager, large social services NFP)

It has been widely observed that reporting and regulatory requirements can sap NFPs' limited time and resources (for example, Productivity Commission 2010); however, participants in this study were not primarily concerned about time spent reporting as such. Rather, participants were predominantly concerned with reporting that did not adequately measure or evaluate the quality or impact of their services, in at least three interrelated respects.

The first was reporting to funders that did not ask for *enough* information to genuinely assess a program's quality or impact:

> This is the only program that I've ever worked in where the reporting is so minimal. And accountability—incredibly—almost non-existent … When I first started I thought it was like any other government contract and I was logging everything that I was doing and they came in and said there is too much in there. Stop it. Just key actions or key progress …

> If we had those things in place it would probably be a bit better because it seems like whilst we're doing such minimal reporting it feels as though the reporting that we do has no value whatsoever. (P14, manager, large community development NFP)

To be clear, this quote does not reflect all participants' experiences; many have stringent and extensive reporting requirements. It does, however, speak to the *variability* of funders' reporting requirements, which range from very detailed to almost non-existent for even multimillion-dollar programs. The quote above also indicates how too little reporting can sometimes be a greater imposition on NFPs than more rigorous reporting. Poor-quality reporting still takes time and resources, but may not deliver useful information:

> [M]aybe this [lack of detailed reporting] has something to do with why the program hasn't been funded beyond this year … When you look at the success of the program it's very hard to see where the success is because it hasn't been evaluated, no-one has been held accountable. Some organisations are doing really fantastic things and some are really, really poor. (P14)

This quote illustrates how rigorous reporting on service quality not only enables funders to discharge their oversight role, but also may have more tangible value to NFPs by enabling them to demonstrate the value their services deliver.

A second way reporting to funders became detached from service quality was when measured outputs were weakly linked to service outcomes:

> At the moment all we do is measure how many people come in and how many supports we give them. That doesn't tell us if we're actually doing anything that has any lasting change. (P12)

> Everyone likes the idea of results-based accountability—it's just how you actually do [it] that is important. (P15, service worker, large community development NFP)

These quotes highlight the continued reliance on measuring outputs despite several decades of discussion about more outcomes-based measures (for example, Plantz et al. 1997; Kaplan 2001). However, they also point towards the ongoing difficulties of using alternative measures, as one director explained:

> We have all these program reports that come up that we've done this and we've done that and here are our stats for this month. Here's the café's income and stuff. Does that fundamentally tell me whether we're doing a good job or not? I don't really know … I do think that compliance starts being the easy thing to focus on because you can't quite work out how to have a conversation about whether we're doing something well or not. (P1)

This quote suggests that boards themselves are not necessarily aware of how best to measure their organisations' outcomes. There can also be external structural impediments to measuring outcomes, such as the need to demonstrate *some* results to funders even if these results are weakly linked to the program's ultimate goals:

> We still need to have a minimum amount of quantitative [measures] because … it still provides us with that base because it takes a long time to get outcomes. So those quantitative measures are usually outputs, activities and we need to show that we've done something with the money, not wait 10 years when there are some outcomes from it. Because it can take that long for real sustainable measurable outcomes from a continuous improvement approach. (P12)

This implies that a potential barrier to adopting more outcomes-based measures is providing results that are compatible with short to medium-term funding cycles.

A third way reporting became detached from service quality was when NFPs received little *feedback* on, or *oversight* of, the information they reported. Feedback can enable NFPs to use the information they report to assess and improve their services. On this basis, several participants strongly supported even extensive external evaluation of their services provided that funders or evaluators also returned the information and analysis to them:

> P14: As part of that [external funding] they actually employ external evaluators to assess, which makes it so much easier because all the reporting is up to them.
>
> Interviewer: So that's positive for you, is it, having external assessors?
>
> P14: Yes … because they're people that are trained in that area, so it's really great data that you get back. (P14)

In discussing the lack of *oversight* of NFP reporting, the term 'oversight' refers to funders or other agencies with capacity to investigate and intervene when service providers are not meeting reasonable standards. Many NFP participants in this study supported strong oversight of their sector's services, either because they are committed to their particular service sector (for example, ensuring all children receive a quality education) or because they had a broader interest in ensuring that all providers were effectively using public funds. Several participants reported *less* external oversight than they would like:

> They [the funder] don't seem to be auditing us regularly … There were members of departments turning up and questioning us and I think that's died off over the last three years … So we're concerned that we're not delivering the programs as best we can because there's no apparent measurement of it outside the systems I described that we have set up ourselves …

> I'm a taxpayer. I'd like to know that my money's being spent properly … I'm on the board of the organisation and I don't really know how good our delivery of that [service] is. I'm sure that government doesn't know. (P5)

As discussed further below, these findings suggest that many NFP sector directors and staff may welcome reporting that is focused on service outcomes—and that is properly designed, monitored and enforced, rather than perceiving such reporting as an onerous imposition.

Barrier two: Boards without informed and active members

A second potential barrier to accountability is when boards lack oversight of, or feedback on, their own performance. This issue was most apparent in member-based organisations whose boards are nominally elected by, and report to, a broader membership. Prior research has identified 'democratic accountability' of elected boards to members as one foundation of NFP legitimacy (Edwards and Hulme 1996). In Australia, Governance Standard 2 issued by the ACNC establishes 'accountability to members' as a minimum requirement of registered charities: 'Charities must be open and accountable to their members. This standard allows members to be in a position to understand their charity's operations and raise questions they may have about its governance (for example, about where future activities will be focussed and its financial position)' (ACNC 2013: 6).

Several member-based organisations in this study either had no active members or lacked a membership base that was engaged and knowledgeable enough to question either the board's decisions or the operational and strategic guidance the board provides:

> We call a meeting, we're flat out getting half of them to turn up … We've got to personally invite all our members to come and only half of them turn up and it's probably only for the cup of tea …

> The membership aren't into making sure we're doing our job, like shareholders, perhaps, in a commercial operation or something like that. I'm not quite sure who we report to, really, from a point of view of somebody else keeping an eye on us and making sure that we're doing the jobs. (P5)

> P11: Our membership is fairly small … The members can go to the annual general meeting where the board is elected …

> Interviewer: Does that get much of a turnout?

> P11: I don't think it's huge, no. Otherwise, they get a copy of the annual report. Apart from that, I don't know that they have a huge involvement. (P11, senior staff member, social services NFP)

In several cases, the board was largely self-perpetuating. Since the board's operation can affect NFP performance as well as governance (Ranson et al. 2005), the broader issue these cases raise is the extent to which NFP boards have a clear sense of to whom they are accountable and how this accountability is discharged:

> I think the board thinks it's accountable for itself or to the chairperson. I don't know that it feels accountable to the client base, but I don't think we're evaluated by the client base …

> The effectiveness of the board is not measured. I can't see how it is measured … Are any boards effectively measured? (P18, director, large social services NFP)

Ideally, an active membership should prompt boards to review and evaluate their own performance. In the absence of such a membership, a key question is who is able to ask NFP boards the 'tough questions' about their processes and strategy that they might not have thought of themselves?

Barrier three: Maintaining minimum standards while reducing red tape

The third potential barrier is maintaining minimum service standards across the sectors NFPs service while also reducing regulatory red tape. In Australia, this potential barrier is linked to the recent debate about whether the ACNC should be retained or disbanded. Paradoxically, both critics and supporters of the ACNC have cited reducing red tape as a primary motivation. Critics have argued that the ACNC adds an unnecessary layer of bureaucracy to the NFP sector (for example, Rittelmeyer 2014). Yet the ACNC's proponents have observed that the commission has reducing red tape as one of its three main mandates, and has repeatedly emphasised that reducing red tape for NFPs is a priority (ACNC 2014; Ernst & Young 2014).

Amid the underlying consensus about the importance of eliminating red tape, several participants in this study were concerned that the red tape reduction agenda might undermine minimum service standards, especially in service areas such as child care that have especially vulnerable clients:

> I know a lot of people say that there's too much red tape in child care but if you didn't have the red tape then people would take the shortcut. (P9, CEO, medium-sized childcare/education NFP)

> My view is that any society, wherever you are, needs some sort of framework and guidelines … so I have no problem with the regulations being in place at all. The red tape that we constantly hear about is more about the systems. It's not the reg[ulations] themselves. If you look at the reg[ulation]s, a lot of them are common sense. You know, children need so much space. (P17, CEO, large childhood education NFP)

These participants indicate the difficulty of distinguishing red tape—presumably 'bad legislation' or standards—from effective legislation. In their ACNC-sponsored report on red tape, Ernst and Young (2014: 56) state that red tape is: 'Regulatory and reporting obligations that are *excessive*, *unnecessary* or *confusing*. Given this definition, determining what constitutes red tape is open to being highly subjective to an individual or organisation and is highly dependent on the unique circumstances of the charity involved' (emphasis added).

The clearest examples of what participants in this study viewed as red tape were duplicative reporting and accreditation requirements. One NFP undertook three separate accreditation processes for essentially the same service. Another participant described the overlapping standards in homelessness services:

> We have the National SHS Standards—the National Specialist Homelessness Services Standards—that are still in draft form. You've got the NSW SHS Standards. You've also got the NSW Good Governance. You've got the Queensland Human Service Standards … You've got all of these standards that are very, very similar and people have got to measure their work against often two or three of them when they're all very similar … Why can't we just have one set? (P12)

While eliminating duplication is an important and widely shared objective, what constitutes *unnecessary* regulation is less clear:

> What concerns me about this red tape issue is [that] some people refer to it, the red tape, as … documenting children's learning. We've got a really strong stance that that is a basic teaching tool for any teacher no matter what age group you're working with. That's not the regulatory burden. (P17)

The example of whether or not requiring childhood education providers to document children's learning is red tape illustrates the difficulty of determining when regulation or accreditation standards are *unnecessary*. To categorise a requirement to document children's learning as red tape necessitates a substantive judgement about whether such documentation improves learning outcomes, and about whether it is possible to enforce this practice. These judgements require expertise in the specific service area—in this case, childhood education—rather than broad-based policy expertise. In essence, participants were concerned that the policy consensus on removing duplicative red tape might facilitate watering down service standards that are deemed 'unnecessary', but without the substantive discussion or debate—especially with sector experts and stakeholders—that more rigorous and responsible reform would require.

A broader issue here is that the shift towards market-based funding models makes legislated minimum service standards *more* rather than *less* important to ensuring sectorwide accountability on service quality. In this study, the participants who were most concerned about the potential for deregulation to decrease service quality were concentrated in sectors facing growing competition from for-profit providers. However, actual or proxy market systems can pressure both for-profit and NFP providers to cut costs. While competitive pressures may lower prices for end users, the risk is that pressures to reduce costs will drive declining service quality if minimum standards are not carefully monitored and actively enforced. This risk is especially serious in core public services such as childhood education and health that also have vulnerable clients and significant—and arguably intractable—information asymmetries between service 'buyers' and 'sellers'.

Addressing barriers to NFP accountability: Prospects and possibilities

Given the diversity of the services NFPs provide, and the differences in NFP size and structure (see Knight and Gilchrist 2014), there are likely to be many possible responses to the barriers identified above. Moreover, some issues—most notably, distinguishing 'necessary' from 'unnecessary' regulation—require sector-specific expertise rather than generic principles. Nonetheless, participants' own experiences, and relevant academic research, suggest possible responses to each barrier.

Reconnecting reporting to services

Funders have considerable power to modify their reporting requirements (Oakes and Young 2008), and could more closely link reporting to service outcomes in several practical ways. The most obvious include: 1) requiring sufficiently detailed reporting; 2) including outcomes as well as output measures; and 3) ensuring reporting data are fed back to NFPs. The ACNC has particularly stressed the last point, with one senior regulator arguing that funders and regulators should either assess reports and disclose their findings or remove the reporting requirement:

If you cannot locate its [the report's] necessity and also then its effectiveness to meet that necessity, you've got an unnecessary piece of [reporting]. So every year someone puts in their association's report to a state regulator, and it's put into that filing cabinet and locked. It's not made available to the public. No-one ever looks at it. There's no assessment of its worth. What is being achieved by filling out that form? Absolutely nothing. (P21, senior regulator)

The study findings also imply, however, that practical improvements in NFP reporting requirements may need a broader shift in how both funders and NFPs conceptualise accountability—namely, a shift from largely formal reporting towards an ongoing relationship of interaction and dialogue. There are various impediments to this transition, such as the constant rotation of contract managers (Ernst & Young 2014: 53). Nonetheless, the most effective reporting relationships this study found were part of an open and reciprocal discussion between the NFP, their funder and key stakeholders:

We feel that they [the funder] are approachable, that they know what we're going through so we can trust them … Essentially, we need to talk to each other at the end of the day … That's one of the biggest things, I'd say: opening up the communication between governments and NFPs. Having a one-off consultation meeting isn't enough. That's not open communication, that's a consultation. (P10, manager, large social services NFP)

This particular NFP held quarterly meetings with key stakeholders that the funder would attend, and the funder encouraged meetings between different providers to discuss shared concerns. This NFP's reporting also included open-ended narrative as well as quantitative metrics, and the NFP was able to negotiate—within boundaries—which performance metrics their clients completed and how. One reason reporting contributed to service quality in this case was the broader relationship of communication and trust between NFP and funder. This suggests that any review of funders' reporting requirements should include and *retain* NFPs, and also other key stakeholders such as clients, as part of this ongoing process.

While funders have more scope to change the accountability relationship, NFPs may also be able to improve their reporting practices by measuring and disclosing important service outcomes, even when funders do not require this information. Several NFPs in this study had initiated performance metrics to capture aspects of their services' value that their funders' reporting templates overlooked. One example was from a counsellor in a neighbourhood centre whose professional body encouraged members to survey and track clients' well-being over their counselling sessions:

> The management committee here's not asking me to do these things, the funding body's not, but our peak body's way of thinking [is that] you want to prove to them things that they [providers and funders] haven't even thought of asking … This is a social justice issue to keep the money where it belongs. (P15)

The peak body that promoted these surveys was clearly advocating continued public funding for the services their members provide. But provided the measures are reliable and rigorously used, these initiatives tend to reinforce rather than challenge public accountability. Thus, while funders' power over NFPs creates a strong responsibility for funders to more closely link reporting to service quality, NFPs may also be able to instigate closer links between reporting and service quality.

Linking boards to members

According to one senior regulator, board accountability requires that NFP members have *opportunities* to question the board, but not necessarily that they regularly do so: 'I don't mind if no-one turns up to the annual general meeting [AGM], and I don't mind if anyone asks any questions at the AGM, as long as they have the opportunity to do so' (P21).

This participant noted that two NFP structures, trustees and member-constituted boards, lack any formal external constituency. However, he argued that NFPs typically have a broader stakeholder community—termed 'moral stakeholders'—who are committed to the organisation and are likely to intervene in cases of severe governance failure:

> [NFPs are] no longer simply a proprietary ownership of shares and money; it is a sense of responsibility to the wider community for delivering public good. The moral stakeholders have a legitimate interest in ensuring that occurs. So they don't need this proprietary— they don't need to hold a share. They may not even need to hold a membership. They are the people around—the stakeholders around—who will intervene if they suspect something is wrong. (P21)

Clearly, accountability to moral stakeholders requires *public* transparency mechanisms, such as the ACNC's charities register, because moral stakeholders do not necessarily have access to the same information as formal members.

However, even given sufficient public transparency, moral stakeholders are at best able to set boundaries on NFPs' governance practices, rather than providing ongoing feedback on board performance. Consequently, in the absence of active members, boards need to find processes or practices that perform a comparable function. One possible substitute—albeit imperfect—for an active membership is to more rigorously assess board performance against external best-practice governance standards, which could at least provide an external reference point for boards' decision-making processes. While several standards have been proposed, there is no agreed standard of NFP board best practice, despite board members requesting such standards or guidance: '[What I would like is] to be able to say, here's your best governance guidelines, best practice in the organisation of not-for-profits' (P16, director, large social services NFP).

One large NFP in this study had voluntarily adopted several governance standards and practices from incorporated for-profit organisations, and thereby appropriated an external benchmark to guide their own operation. However, this is unlikely to suit smaller NFPs, and may not apply to other service areas.

A second potential approach is for boards to actively cultivate other stakeholder groups to more regularly question, and provide feedback on, their performance and strategic guidance. P21's concept of moral stakeholders emphasises that NFPs are often located within a broader community who are interested in their activities. The practical challenge is to engage this broader community in more regular discussion of the organisation's direction, and of the board's role in guiding this direction, rather than having moral stakeholders emerge only in organisational crises. External consultants can be used to structure engagement with stakeholders, but this can be both expensive and fraught (O'Dwyer 2005). More regular facilitated meetings with key external stakeholders might play a similar role.

Red tape and minimum service standards

Participants' concerns about eliminating red tape reveal a potential tension between removing *duplicative* and *unnecessary* regulatory constraints and preserving sector-wide service quality benchmarks. As section two observed, judgements about what service standards are *necessary* require sector-specific experience and expertise. Inter alia, this suggests that while *duplicative* red tape might be identified and removed at a national policy level, deciding what constitutes *unnecessary* service quality regulation or standards will require far-reaching engagement and consultation, including with NFPs who deliver these services and the clients who receive them.

In determining what regulation affects service standards, it is important to recognise how minimum qualifications for NFP staff may enhance accountability as well as improve service quality. In several participant organisations, especially those without a well-informed and experienced board, NFP staff described holding each other accountable to shared professional standards and norms. Professional standards and norms do not replace external reporting and oversight; however, they do illustrate how minimum staff qualifications may also support workplace-level accountability. At the same time, staff qualification requirements are attracting close scrutiny due to tighter public budgets and more market-based funding, both of which can pressure organisations to employ staff who are less qualified and therefore cheaper to employ. While the merits of mandating particular minimum qualifications would need to be addressed at the service-sector level, this study suggests that it would be misleading to debate these minimum qualification standards solely within a red tape framework. Rather, since professional qualifications can also support accountable service delivery, regulated minimum qualifications are part of a broader debate about the right *balance* between accountability and cost.

Conclusion

This chapter has reviewed three potential barriers to NFPs being accountable for the quality or impact of their services. First, NFPs' reporting to funders may not provide sufficient information or feedback on the quality or impact of their services. In response, the chapter suggests not only that funders may need to adapt their reporting requirements, but also that NFP reporting may need to be set within a more open and ongoing dialogue between NFPs, funders and other stakeholders. Second, while board accountability to members is central to governance theory and standards, many NFP boards lack members who can effectively question their performance. The challenge this poses to NFPs' boards is to introduce external standards or relationships that perform a comparable function. Third, the chapter illustrates how agendas to reduce red tape could impede sector-level accountability if they undermine minimum service standards, especially in increasingly cost-sensitive funding environments. To mitigate this risk, red tape reduction that bears on service standards will need extensive sector-level engagement. More generally, while the shift towards more market-based funding systems can expand client choice, it also makes it more important to carefully preserve minimum service standards and qualifications against inevitable cost-driven critiques.

References

Australian Charities and Not-for-profit Commission (ACNC). 2013. *ACNC Governance Standards Guidance*. Melbourne: Australian Government and ACNC.

Australian Charities and Not-for-profit Commission (ACNC). 2014. *Forum Report: Measuring and reducing red-tape in the not-for-profit sector*. Melbourne: Australian Government and ACNC.

BDO. 2014. *BDO Not-for-Profit Fraud Survey 2014*. Sydney: BDO Australia Limited.

Brennan, N. and J. Solomon. 2008. 'Corporate governance, accountability, and mechanisms of accountability: An overview.' *Accounting, Auditing and Accountability* 21(7): 885–906.

Carnegie, G. D. and P. W. Wolnizer. 1996. 'Enabling accountability in museums.' *Accounting, Auditing & Accountability Journal* 9(5): 84–99.

Ebrahim, A. 2003. 'Accountability in practice: Mechanisms for NGOs.' *World Development* 31(5): 813–29.

Edwards, M. and D. Hulme. 1996. 'Too close for comfort? The impact of official aid on nongovernmental organizations.' *World Development* 24(6): 961–73.

Ernst & Young. 2014. *Research into Commonwealth regulatory and reporting burdens on the charity sector*. A Report prepared for the Australian Charities and Not-for-profits Commission. Ernst & Young, Canberra.

Fama, E. F. and M. C. Jensen. 1983a. 'Agency problems and residual claims.' *Journal of Law and Economics* 26(2): 327–49.

Fama, E. F. and M. C. Jensen. 1983b. 'Separation of ownership and control.' *Journal of Law and Economics* 26(2): 301–25.

Fox, J. A. and L. D. Brown (eds). 1998. *The Struggle for Accountability: The World Bank, NGOs and grassroots movements*. Cambridge, Mass.: The MIT Press.

Gray, R. 1983. 'Accounting, financial reporting and not-for-profit organisations.' *AUTA Review* 15(1): 3–23.

Kaplan, R. S. 2001. 'Strategic performance measurement and management in nonprofit organizations.' *Nonprofit Management and Leadership* 11(3): 353–70.

Knight, P. A. and D. J. Gilchrist. 2014. *Australian Charities 2013: The first report on charities registered with the Australian Charities and Not-for-profits Commission*. Melbourne: ACNC.

Light, P. C. 2002. *Pathways to Nonprofit Excellence*. Washington, DC: The Brookings Institution Press.

Oakes, L. S. and J. J. Young. 2008. 'Accountability re-examined: Evidence from Hull House.' *Accounting, Auditing & Accountability Journal* 21(6): 765–90.

O'Dwyer, B. 2005. 'The construction of a social account: A case study in an overseas aid agency.' *Accounting, Organizations and Society* 30(3): 279–96.

Olson, D. E. 2000. 'Agency theory in the not-for-profit sector: Its role at independent colleges.' *Nonprofit and Voluntary Sector Quarterly* 29(2): 280–96.

Plantz, M. C., M. T. Greenway and M. Hendricks. 1997. 'Outcome measurement: Showing results in the nonprofit sector.' *New Directions for Evaluation* 1997(75): 15–30.

Productivity Commission. 2010. *Contribution of the Not-for-Profit Sector*. Canberra: Productivity Commission. Available from: pc.gov. au/inquiries/completed/not-for-profit (accessed 14 August 2014).

Ranson, S., C. Farrell, N. Peim and P. Smith. 2005. 'Does governance matter for school improvement?' *School Effectiveness and School Improvement* 16(3): 305–25.

Rittelmeyer, H. 2014. *Independent Charities, Independent Regulators: The future of not-for-profit regulation*. Sydney: Centre for Independent Studies.

Roberts, J. and R. Scapens. 1985. 'Accounting systems and systems of accountability: Understanding accounting practices in their organisation context.' *Accounting, Organizations and Society* 10(4): 443–56.

Sinclair, A. 1995. 'The chameleon of accountability: Forms and discourses.' *Accounting, Organizations and Society* 20(2–3): 219–37.

Stewart, J. 1984. 'The role of information in public accountability.' In *Issues in Public Sector Accounting*, eds A. Hopwood and C. Tomkins, 13–34. Oxford: Philip Allan.

Treasury. 2011. *Scoping Study for a National Not-for-Profit Regulator*. Canberra: Australian Government. Available from: archive.treasury. gov.au/contentitem.asp?ContentID=2054 (accessed 14 August 2014).

Unerman, J. and B. O'Dwyer. 2006. 'Theorising accountability for NGO advocacy.' *Accounting, Auditing & Accountability Journal* 19(3): 349–76.

11

Results, Targets and Measures to Drive Collaboration: Lessons from the New Zealand Better Public Services reforms

Rodney Scott and Ross Boyd

Introduction

Performance measurement is a hotly contested topic in government (Brignal and Modell 2000) and the not-for-profit (NFP) sector (Kaplan 2001) and in interaction between the two (Macpherson 2001). This chapter presents lessons from the use of impact measures in the New Zealand Government as examples to be applied in other contexts. The use of impact measures is complicated by problems of control and attribution (Smith 2009). Many organisations have instead resorted to output measures, or even input and activity measures, which may promote efficiency but do not address the effectiveness of interventions (de Lancer-Julnes and Holzer 2001).

The history of performance measurement in the New Zealand Government has gone through several stages. Until the new public management (NPM) reforms of the late 1980s and early 1990s, reporting focused on inputs. Government departments and the managers therein would diligently record how money was spent and how department staff used their time (Boston et al. 1996). This contributed to a public service that was seen as overly bureaucratic and process oriented.

The NPM reforms introduced management concepts from the corporate centre: decentralisation, managerialism, contractualism and accountability. Departments planned to deliver a range of goods and services and reported their achievement to parliament (Scott 2001). This was seen as improving the efficiency and responsiveness of the public service, but the focus on outputs meant that the services provided were not necessarily the most effective.

The 'Managing for Outcomes' reforms required departments to describe how the outputs they produced contributed to outcomes through an outcomes framework or intervention logic. Starting in 2002, departments produced *Statements of Intent* that replaced the *Departmental Forecast. Statements of Intent* described the intent behind the outputs produced. This was seen as contributing to increased effectiveness in cases where responsibility for the outcome fell to a single department (SSC 2011). Where responsibility for outcomes crossed departmental boundaries, departments were encouraged to coordinate with each other under the 'Managing for Shared Outcomes' initiative (SSC 2004); however, this was seen as less successful. Agencies were grouped into 'sectors', but interdepartmental groups at a sectoral level were seen as lacking focus and direction (SSC 2011).

In 2011, the New Zealand Government created the Better Public Services (BPS) Advisory Group to provide advice on how to improve the performance of government. One area of attention was improving government effectiveness in addressing persistent crosscutting social harms. The resulting 'Better Public Services' reforms included the selection of 10 'Results' to improve the lives of New Zealanders, which relied on collective accountability between multiple departments for achieving a specified social impact (SSC 2015a). While individual departments did not operate a sufficiently broad array of levers to effect change in crosscutting problems, groups of departments had greater control. The 'Results Approach' could therefore be described as collaborating for outcomes. These four stages are necessarily a simplification of a large number of complex changes and describe the public management system in terms of its performance measures only, ignoring concurrent changes in governance, finance and structural arrangements. The decadal transitions are shown in Figure 11.1.

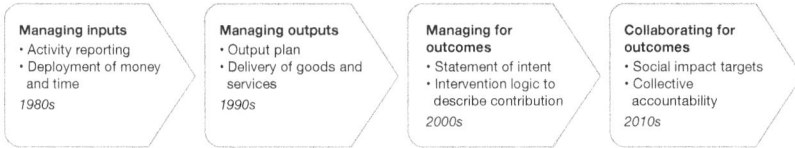

Managing inputs
• Activity reporting
• Deployment of money and time
1980s

Managing outputs
• Output plan
• Delivery of goods and services
1990s

Managing for outcomes
• Statement of intent
• Intervention logic to describe contribution
2000s

Collaborating for outcomes
• Social impact targets
• Collective accountability
2010s

Figure 11.1: Stylised representation of performance management in the New Zealand Government
Source: Created by authors.

The following sections of this chapter describe the Results Approach to impact measurement and identify lessons for how to select impact measures to drive and support collaboration.

The Results Approach

The 10 Results were initially scheduled to run for five years from 2012 to 2017. The Results Approach is designed to retain the strengths of the current public management system while addressing weaknesses such as fragmentation, lack of prioritisation and obstacles to collaboration. The Results Approach has five key features: agencies organising around outcomes (an extension of the sectoral approach); focusing on a small number of results; specifying the outcomes at a manageable level; appointing leaders and making them responsible for achieving results; and using data and performance information to drive action. The result areas cross agency and ministerial portfolio boundaries. A focus on achieving outcomes requires agencies to find ways to work together and to combine capabilities and resources. Each outcome requires a different approach, acknowledging different existing arrangements, capability and readiness.

These Results were selected because they were important and long-standing problems that had proven resistant to previous attempts at change, and because making meaningful progress would require collaboration between multiple organisations. The rationale for selecting each of the 10 Results is described briefly in the paragraphs below.

Result 1 aims to reduce long-term welfare dependence. Being out of paid work and on a benefit for extended periods increase the risk of poverty, social dislocation and deteriorating overall health. It can also have negative effects on the children of people on a benefit long term. The cost of paying benefits to working-age people is now more than NZ$8 billion (A$7.15 billion) a year, with much higher lifetime costs. Reducing long-term welfare dependence is about supporting people to better their lives, managing the government's future financial liability and supporting the New Zealand economy by ensuring it has a skilled and productive workforce.

Results 2–4 aim to better support vulnerable children. Early childhood experiences are linked with adult mental health issues, drug and alcohol abuse, poor educational outcomes and unemployment. Many children are at risk of poor outcomes because they do not get the early support they need. Remedial spending is thought to be less effective and more costly than preventative action. For example, treating rheumatic fever alone costs NZ$40 million (A$35.7 million) per year in New Zealand.

Results 5–6 aim to boost skills and employment. Success in education is essential for the government's goal of building a productive and competitive economy. It also helps New Zealanders develop the skills needed to reach their full potential and contribute to the economy and society.

Results 7 and 8 aim to reduce crime in New Zealand. Crime is associated with substantial economic and social costs. Crime is a complex, multifactorial social problem that requires different agencies to work together; previous attempts to address crime through the actions of a single agency have been largely unsuccessful.

Results 9 and 10 target improved interaction with government. Interacting with government is harder than it should be for both businesses and individuals. Businesses report that they find government services complex and fragmented, and that interacting with government takes more cost and effort than it should. The time and cost of dealing with government affect businesses' competitiveness and productivity and thereby have a negative impact on economic growth. Individuals want to deal with government in new and different ways and government needs to respond to that. New Zealanders increasingly expect service delivery from the government that is digital, responsive and personalised.

Each of these outcomes consists of a 'Result', a 'target' and a 'measure'. The Result describes the outcome that is desired, such as 'reduce the incidence of rheumatic fever'. The target specifies the degree of change required, such as 'reduce the incidence of rheumatic fever by two-thirds by 2017'. The measure specifies how the target will be calculated and assessed. In the case of rheumatic fever, the actual incidence is unknown, but the rate of hospitalisation can be assessed through hospital data. The measure is the incidence of first-episode hospitalisations for rheumatic fever per 100,000 population occurring in the previous 12 months. Where historical data were available, this was used to predict the outcome without the changes introduced. The measure is reported publicly every six months (see SSC 2015b: Results Snapshot). Table 11.1 shows the 10 Results, targets and measures (note that Result 3 consists of two targets and Result 7 consists of three targets).

Table 11.1: Results, targets and measures

Result area	Result	Target	Measure
Reducing long-term welfare dependence	1. Reduce the number of people who have been on a working-age benefit for more than 12 months	Reduce the number of people continuously receiving working-age benefits for more than 12 months by 30%	The number of people continuously receiving Jobseeker Support benefits for more than 12 months
Supporting vulnerable children	2. Increase participation in early childhood education	98% of children starting school will have participated in quality early childhood education	Percentage of children starting school who regularly participated in early childhood education before starting school
	3. Increase infant immunisation rates and reduce the incidence of rheumatic fever	Increase infant immunisation rates so that 95% of eight-month-olds are fully immunised *and* Reduce the incidence of rheumatic fever by two-thirds	Percentage of children aged eight months who are fully immunised *and* number of first-episode rheumatic fever hospitalisations in previous 12 months, per 100,000 population

Result area	Result	Target	Measure
	4. Reduce the number of assaults on children	The 10-year rise in children experiencing physical abuse will be halted and current numbers reduced by 5%	The number of children who experienced substantiated physical abuse in the previous 12 months
Boosting skills and employment	5. Increase the proportion of 18-year-olds with NCEA[1] level two or equivalent qualification	85% of 18-year-olds will have achieved NCEA level two or an equivalent qualification	Percentage of population aged 18 years who have achieved NCEA level two or equivalent
	6. Increase the proportion of 25–34-year-olds with advanced trade qualifications, diplomas and degrees (at level four or above)	55% of 25–34-year-olds will have a qualification at level four or above	The proportion of 25–34-year-olds with a qualification of NZQF[2] level four and above, captured in the Household Labour Force Survey
Reducing crime	7. Reduce the rates of total crime, violent crime and youth crime	Reduce the crime rate by 15% *and* reduce the violent crime rate by 20% *and* reduce the youth crime rate by 25%	Number of reported crimes in previous 12 months *and* number of reported violent crimes in previous 12 months *and* number of court appearances by 14–16-year-olds
	8. Reduce reoffending	Reduce the reoffending rate by 25%	Percentage of reimprisonment among prisoners within 12 months of their release and of reconviction among community-sentenced offenders within 12 months of the start of their sentence, based on previous 12 months' data
Improving interaction with government	9. New Zealand businesses have a one-stop online shop for all government advice and support they need to run and grow their business	Business costs from dealing with government will reduce by 25%	Survey questionnaire administered to 1,200 businesses, in which respondents are asked to rate their average level of effort in dealing with all the government agencies they had contact with during the previous 12 months, on a 10-point scale

Result area	Result	Target	Measure
	10. New Zealanders can complete their transactions with the government easily in a digital environment	An average of 70% of the most common transactions with government will be completed in a digital environment (up from 29.9% baseline)	Percentage of service transactions completed digitally in previous three months, of 10 common services

[1] NCEA = National Certificate of Educational Achievement
[2] NZQF = New Zealand Qualifications Framework
Source: Adapted from State Services Commission (2012).

All 10 Results have made progress towards their targets, and exceed both the 2012 baseline and the historical trend data where this information was available (SSC 2014). These successes have been achieved in areas that have been resistant to previous attempts at change.

In response to this success, the government has revised the targets in Results 1, 6 and 7 to make them more difficult. Result 1 aims to reduce working-age client numbers by 25 per cent to 220,000 from 295,000 as of June 2014, and to reduce the long-term cost of benefit dependency by $13 billion (as measured by an accumulated actuarial release) by June 2018. The target for Result 6 was increased from 55 per cent to 60 per cent and the target date extended by one year. The target for Result 7 has been made more challenging, changing from a 15 per cent reduction in total crime by 2017 to a 20 per cent reduction by 2018.

The Results Approach consists of several elements, each of which may contribute to its success (Scott and Boyd 2015). The use of targets and measures of social impact is believed to have been critical in making the Results Approach successful where past approaches have failed. The targets appear to have contributed to the success of the Results Approach in four important ways, explained below: focus, commitment, urgency and momentum.

Focus

Previous attempts at interdepartmental collaboration had delivered information sharing and some policy coordination, but lacked a guiding purpose (SSC 2011). The Results provide a focus—or 'common agenda' (Kania and Kramer 2011)—to these interactions, aligning the perspectives of participating departments towards a common goal. The Results Approach encouraged a kind of action-learning perspective (Revans 1980), where participating departments would constantly ask themselves and one another whether any particular action brought them closer to the goal. For this purpose, the targets had to be simple, intuitive and memorable.

Commitment

The New Zealand public management system is focused particularly on accountability (Schick 1996; Vitalis and Scott 2015). By communicating to chief executives that they would be held collectively accountable for progress towards a measurable target, the Results Approach built commitment to the successful achievement of the desired outcomes. Accountability is felt through relationships with ministers, performance assessment by the State Services Commission (SSC) and public scrutiny. The six-monthly reporting of progress towards the targets attracts some media attention (see, for example, Kirk 2015).

Urgency

The Results provide a direction of travel, but the targets quantify the required change. The targets were carefully chosen with the intention that they would be very challenging, but not so hard to achieve that participating departments would give up hope. When the target provided the right degree of challenge, this created a sense of urgency and encouraged participating departments to think at scale. Where Results have slipped behind their progress goals, this has stimulated challenging conversations among responsible chief executives and ministers.

Momentum

Finally, the six-monthly reporting provided a tangible sense of progress. Collaboration seems to benefit from a kind of positive feedback loop, where success breeds commitment to further working together (Black and Andersen 2012; Scott et al. 2014). This was more effective in the Results where there was only a short delay between actions and results. Despite these generally observed benefits, some Results, targets and measures have been more successful than others.

Lessons on Results, targets and measures

The Results, targets and measures were co-created through careful dialogue between ministers, participating departments and the three central agencies: the State Services Commission, Treasury and the Department of the Prime Minister and Cabinet. On the whole, they have worked very well, but each has its own strengths and weaknesses, with implications for generalised theory on constructing collaborative social impact targets and measures.

Strategic alignment

Result 1—reducing long-term welfare dependence—has been criticised for focusing on government expenditure rather than on social outcomes (Chapple 2013; Stuart 2014; Fletcher 2015). The government saw long-term unemployment as a social harm that limits social participation and predicts a range of long-term outcomes, and used long-term receipt of the Jobseeker benefit as a proxy for long-term unemployment. It may be that an alternative framing of the issue, around employment rather than welfare benefits, would have been more motivating to a wider range of parties. This suggests that it is important to carefully select the words used in setting Results.

Of more direct implication to the collaborative efforts in Result 1, there was a mismatch between the Result and the strategy of the leading department, the Ministry of Social Development. The Ministry of Social Development (2012) is currently using an actuarial approach to prioritising social investment, which calculates the expected forward liability to the Crown of benefit recipients and targets investment in the areas that will make the biggest reduction in forward liability. There is a tendency for the cases with the most expensive forward liability to have the best marginal return on investment. This strategy ran into conflict with the Result 1 measure, which counted the number of people continuously receiving the Jobseeker benefit for a year or more, counting a reduction in the number of people equally, with no regard to their future liability. This mismatch between the measure and the organisational strategy caused tension in the management of the Result. Consequently, as noted above, the Result 1 target has now been broadened to include an actuarial measure of forward liability, aligned to the social investment approach.

Setting the challenge

Result 2—increasing participation in early childhood education—is a clear and easily understandable Result, with an equally clear target and measure. The target is to increase participation from 95 per cent to 98 per cent by 2016. The participating departments developed new ways of working to target population groups that had lower rates of participation, and increased participation rates to 96.5 per cent. Two years into the five-year Result period, it seemed that Result 2 would reach its target. However, these first gains to get from 95 per cent to 96.5 per cent are likely to be much easier than the shift from 96.5 per cent to 98 per cent, and progress has flattened.

The Result 2 target shows the fine balance required in setting social impact targets. Setting the target to be too easy risks complacency; setting the target to be too hard risks despondency. Progress cannot always be expected to be linear; Results with long lag times may be expected to make greater progress in later years, but those such as Result 2 that move into the more complex and hardest-to-reach cases may be expected to slow as each successive case becomes more difficult. Beyond the difficulty of setting an appropriate rate of change, there is a further consideration as to what level of compliance with a public policy is a reasonable expectation. At some point between the current 96.5 per cent and 100 per cent, efforts to increase participation rates in early childhood education will reach those individuals actively resisting involvement, and the marginal cost for each new success will become very high. Setting targets too high risks wasted effort that could be better spent on other problem areas.

Lagging indicators and late completions

Result 3 has two targets and two measures. The first target is to increase immunisation rates from 85 per cent to 95 per cent by 2014 and maintain that through to 2017, and the measure reports on immunisation rates at eight months of age. As of the end of 2014, the rate of full immunisation at eight months was 93.5 per cent. However, by 12 months, this had risen to 95 per cent. Delaying immunisation increases the time that children are potentially at risk of contracting childhood diseases. The timeliness component of the measure has had a focusing effect on agencies involved in Result 3, where recent actions have been targeted at ensuring vaccinations are completed earlier.

The immunisation measure is a time-sensitive one, and gives up-to-date feedback to the Results team on progress towards the target. By contrast, the rheumatic fever part of Result 3 uses an annualised measure, reporting the number of incidences of rheumatic fever in the previous 12 months. This was chosen because rheumatic fever is seasonally variable, so comparing full-year data was the easiest way to make like comparison. However, this also means that the Results team does not fully understand the progress that has been made until a full year after an intervention has been made.

Increased reporting

Result 4—reducing assaults on children—was targeted at stabilising an alarming upward trend in reports of physical abuse against children. Ending a worrying trend is a more complicated story than producing an absolute reduction in harm. It was perhaps for that reason that the target was set not at halting the increase, but at reducing substantiated physical abuse against children by 5 per cent by 2017. It was recognised at the time of setting this target that this would be a very difficult target to meet.

Family violence is often a hidden problem, with reported cases representing only a fraction of total cases. Many initiatives designed to reduce the actual incidence of family violence cause increased reporting rates. In this regard, Result 4 could be successful in reducing family violence, while being unsuccessful in reducing reported incidences. Where possible, measures should not rely on reporting rates, though this is sometimes unavoidable. This is also an issue for Results 7 and 8.

Confusion of responsibility for performance and assessment

Result 5—increasing the proportion of 18-year-olds with National Certificates of Educational Achievement (NCEA) level two—has been used to provide targets for each secondary school in the country. This has put direct pressure on schools to improve their achievement rates. NCEA level two includes internal assessment components, and the application of the target at school level provides an incentive for grade inflation (McNaughton 2015). While no direct evidence of grade inflation has been presented, the existence of this perception suggests that it may be beneficial to maintain a separation between responsibility for performance and for assessment.

Population cohorts versus milestone indicators

Result 6—increasing the proportion of 25–34-year-olds with New Zealand Qualifications Framework (NZQF) level four or above— is measured by a population survey, the Household Labour Force Survey. The intention behind the use of a population survey rather than administrative data on qualification achievement was to drive closer coordination between the business, education and immigration sectors to improve the skills and productivity of the labour force. A cohort survey ensured that immigrants would be included in the data, whereas a milestone indicator, such as that used in Result 5, would have missed individuals who arrived in the country after that age milestone or who gained qualifications overseas. One consequence of using a cohort measure is that age-specific interventions can take a long time to affect the entire cohort—for example, an intervention targeting 25-year-olds would take 10 years to impact all individuals in the age group.

One additional limitation to the Result 6 measure stems from the use of random sampling in the Household Labour Force Survey. The small number of 25–34-year-olds captured in this survey means that there is a larger error margin for the reporting of this Result, and levels tend to vary from quarter to quarter due to random noise. Results 6 and 9 are the only ones that rely on sampling.

Changing goalposts

Result 7—reducing the rate of total crime, violent crime and youth crime—has three targets and three measures. For two of these— total crime and youth crime—the original target proved to be less challenging to achieve than originally expected. The government was faced with two options: either declare victory on Result 7 and move on or change the target to make it more difficult. If the government chose not to change the target, this may have the effect of reducing the urgency with which that Result team tackled the problem. Conversely, changing the target could be seen as punishing the Result 7 team for their early success (though the team did not see it this way). The government ultimately decided to introduce revised and more challenging targets for Results 1, 6 and 7, as discussed above.

Perverse incentives

Result 8—reducing reoffending—is a simple statement of the desired change. However, the two-word title hides a more nuanced picture. The measure takes into account the rate of re-imprisonment among prisoners within 12 months of their release and the rate of reconviction among community-sentenced offenders within 12 months of the start of their sentence. Community-sentenced offenders have typically committed crimes with lesser social harm than those facing imprisonment, and also represent an easier target for rehabilitation intervention. By combining the measure for re-imprisonment with reconviction of community-sentenced offenders, this may provide an incentive to target interventions towards the cases that are associated with the least social harm.

This incentive may not be merely theoretical. The reduction in reoffending in Result 8 has come largely from community-sentenced offenders, and this has received some media attention (Brooking 2014).

Organise around outcomes rather than solutions

Result 9—New Zealand businesses will have a one-stop online shop for all government advice and support they need to run and grow their business—describes a proposed solution to make it easier for businesses to interact with government. Collaboration is a complex social problem and addressing complex problems typically requires adaptive solutions (Kurtz and Snowden 2003). The use of social impact measures provides feedback to collaborators to allow them to adapt their practice. By specifying a solution rather than a problem, the Result 9 team is more restricted in what practices it can consider.

In response, the Result 9 team has focused instead on the target and measure. The target is to reduce costs to business from dealing with government by 25 per cent by 2017. The measure is that businesses will perceive that their effort has reduced (as measured in a perception survey). Therefore, the Result, target and measure each describe different things: an online hub, reduced costs and increased ease, respectively. This mismatch between Result, target and measure has caused some distraction and debate within Result 9. Collaboration to achieve social impact is a challenging proposition at the best of times; where there is confusion about the objective, this difficulty is magnified.

Result, target and measure mismatch

Result 10—that New Zealanders can complete their transactions with government easily in a digital environment—also suffered from a mismatch between the Result, the target and its measure. There was not a convenient measure for ease of interaction with government, so Result 10 developed a volume target instead, setting a target that 70 per cent of New Zealanders' most common transactions with government will be completed in a digital environment by 2017. It was not cost-effective to measure all government transactions, so Result 10 then selected a basket of transaction types to use as indicators.

Focusing on ease of interaction (the result) can lead to different actions compared with focusing on the channel of interaction (the measure). In many cases, a transactional service can be delivered more easily in person, or automatically, compared with having to complete the service through a digital channel. Result 10 has recently started to target life events for which interaction with government is particularly difficult, such as the birth of a child. This difficulty is caused by a person having to deal with multiple agencies, which can be confusing and often involves providing the same information multiple times. In many cases, the best solution for customers is integration of services to reduce complexity and redundancy, rather than simply transferring services to a digital environment. Making it easier for New Zealanders to complete transactions with government may not affect the Result 10 measure at all, and therefore the measure is not serving its purpose as a focusing or rallying call to participating agencies.

Additionally, there has been some internal discussion about whether Results 9 and 10 are comparable to the other eight, and whether they are suitable for the Results Approach. Results 1–8 describe a social impact. Results 9 and 10 describe a measure of service quality. Additionally, while Results 1–8 can often be addressed by two to four agencies working together, Results 9 and 10 involve many agencies. The experiences of those working on Results 9 and 10 have been significantly different to those working with Results 1–8, and it is not yet clear how this should be managed or resolved. The experiences for Results 9 and 10 are providing valuable lessons for implementing government-wide change, but these have not yet been fully explored and are beyond the scope of this chapter.

Conclusions

Outcomes measures often break down at an individual organisation level, because outcomes are beyond the control of that organisation and because change is difficult to attribute to any given action. However, when several organisations combine their efforts, their combined effect may be easier to see.

The Results Approach has helped New Zealand make progress on 10 previously intractable problems, where numerous previous attempts have failed. The use of publicly reported measurable social impact data has been important in driving focus, commitment, momentum and urgency to support interdepartmental collaboration. When compared with previous New Zealand attempts at using measurement to drive performance, the Results Approach uses more explicit targets, simpler measures and greater public accountability.

While each Result has been successful, no measure is perfect. The experience of the Results Approach has provided many lessons for the New Zealand Government on how to design impact measures to drive collaboration. With the benefit of hindsight, we remain pleasantly surprised with how well the Results, targets and measures have fared. However, each has its own challenges, and it is the intention of this chapter to highlight the strengths and weaknesses of the Results to help others to design effective impact measures that improve performance.

In using shared targets for driving collaboration, the Results Approach demonstrates the importance of carefully choosing a Result (the outcome you want to achieve), a target (the degree of change) and a measure (how progress will be calculated). These need to be closely aligned, otherwise there is the opportunity for perverse incentives or distraction and debate between conflicting goals. It appears important to select outcomes, rather than solutions, to allow the collaboration to develop their own innovative practice.

If targets are going to change behaviours, they need to be sufficiently challenging to disrupt complacency. Publicly setting challenging targets is risky, because failing to achieve those targets causes reputational damage. The Results Approach benefited from the government being willing to take a portfolio approach to 10 areas, accepting from the beginning that it was unlikely the target would be achieved in all 10 areas. If organisations are going to replicate aspects of the Results Approach, it will be important to establish conditions where it is acceptable to set difficult targets and risk failure. The inverse is targets that are too ambitious and that act to decrease motivation because they appear unachievable. This does not appear to have been a problem in the Results Approach so far, but it may be a risk as the target dates draw nearer.

Most social outcomes are the product of complex interrelationships between social conditions, arising over time. Targets appear more effective in driving performance if they can measure more immediate impacts: educational achievement instead of subsequent employment outcomes or immunisation rates rather than incidence of vaccine-preventable disease. However, this is not always the case, as shown in Results 7 and 8. Crime is a complex multi-factorial problem, often representing the culmination of a lifetime of social disadvantage and negative environmental factors. Results 7 and 8 show that significant changes to crime and criminal reoffending rates are possible in only two years.

Applicability to other sectors

Any case study research must consider the extent to which the findings may be generalised. The Results Approach uses impact measures to drive performance in the public sector. We assume that the lessons are most directly transferable to other government settings, particularly those jurisdictions with a strong focus on accountability. Some of the benefits and drawbacks of this approach are likely to apply equally to other sectors, and some are not. The following paragraphs provide some suggestions for how impact measures may work differently in different types of organisations, and then justify why collaborators from all sectors should be cognisant of the lessons from the Results Approach.

Targets are likely to work differently in mission-driven versus performance-driven organisations (Osborne 1993). Organisations within the public sector are often driven by a mix of personal commitment to the mission and managerial accountability for performance. Within upper management levels, performance accountability tends to be a strong driver (Schick 1996).

Public policy targets usually function as a combination of symbolic signalling and management accountability (Boswell 2014). The Results are important symbolically in that they signal the importance of particular issues and indicate a sense of commitment to addressing them. The targets set the degree of aspiration to that goal. These factors are likely to be important for mission-driven organisations, such as those in the community and NFP sectors.

The management accountability functions may appear more foreign to the community and NFP sectors. As discussed in this chapter, the New Zealand public sector has a strong focus on accountability. Departments could not be held responsible for the actions of other departments, so no one was responsible for problems that spanned multiple departments. Collective accountability for the achievement of crosscutting targets provided a means to drive performance in these areas. In archetypal mission-driven organisations, things get done because individuals see them as important and worthwhile, not because someone is being held responsible (Osborne 1993). In these settings, collective accountability for achieving targets may be a less useful concept. By extension, these mission-driven organisations may not face the same risks of gaming or perverse incentives that come with the use of targets.

There are at least two reasons why even the most pure mission-driven organisation should still be thinking about the management accountability functions of targets. First, community and NFP organisations usually rely on some sort of external funding, such as philanthropic donations or government service contracts. Both philanthropists (Leadbeater 1997) and governments (Fox and Albertson 2011) are increasingly looking for evidence of impact.

These external funders will bring the assumptions of behaviour from their own performance-driven backgrounds, and community and NFP organisations will need to be able to navigate the same challenges of accountability and transparency attributed to performance-driven organisations above.

There is a second and perhaps more immediate reason that other sectors need to understand how collective accountability for impact measures can drive performance in the public sector. Significant attention in recent years has been dedicated to the collective impact (Kania and Kramer 2011) that can occur when different sectors work together (Selsky and Parker 2005; Bryson et al. 2006). In cross-sectoral collaboration it is important to understand motivations and anticipate the behaviour of collaboration partners. By understanding the benefits and potential pitfalls in public sector targets, other sectors can help design successful impact measures for use in cross-sectoral collaboration.

Where to next?

The 10 Results were initially designed for target achievement in 2017 (three have been revised, with additional and more challenging targets set for 2018). At the end of this period, the government will need to decide what to do with the 10 Results. These will be decisions for the elected government of the day, and the following paragraphs are purely speculative.

The Results appear very successful to date. Assuming this remains the case until 2017, one option would be to continue with the approach, largely unchanged. The government would need to consider which small number of problems were important priorities and amenable to the Results Approach. Some of the existing Results could be retained with new targets or some could be retired and replaced with other important problems.

The Results Approach has benefited from its tight focus on only 10 Results and, while there is no reason to suspect that 10 is a magic number, it is likely that the Results Approach would be less effective if extended to a much larger number. Chief executive and ministerial attention is a finite resource, which can only be extended to a few key priorities at any one time.

Some consideration has been given to how the Results Approach could be applied to problems in other contexts. One possibility is to apply it regionally. New Zealand is facing particular challenges in two of its largest metropolitan areas. Christchurch was severely damaged by earthquakes in 2010 and 2011 and efforts to rebuild and revitalise the city are ongoing. Auckland is New Zealand's largest city, is rapidly expanding, faces housing and transport challenges and has areas with persistent social harms. It is possible that the use of impact targets could be used to drive collaboration and performance in Christchurch and Auckland.

Another possibility would be to apply the Results Approach in other outcome areas. When the government set the 10 Results, they intentionally excluded economic targets as these were included in a separate program, the *Business Growth Agenda* (Ministry of Business, Innovation and Employment 2015). It may be possible to use a small number of impact targets to improve performance in addressing several economic problems. Natural resource problems were originally excluded from the Results Approach, in part because many natural resource management challenges were captured in the *Business Growth Agenda*, and in part because of the nature of natural resource problems. Many of the most important resource management issues in New Zealand have long lag times and require a consistent focus that extends well beyond five years. Measurement in the natural resource sector remains an important area of ongoing debate, and a new measurement and report regime has just been introduced (Ministry for the Environment 2015). How the Results Approach could be adapted for the natural resources sector is a possible area for future exploration.

The Results Approach has left the government with a predicament: it appears to be a very successful tool for improving performance and driving meaningful collaboration; however, part of its success appears to be linked to keeping the number of Results small. The temptation to use it everywhere must be balanced with careful consideration of how to keep it tightly focused. This consideration likely applies to the use of impact measures everywhere: the best measurement regimes consist of a small number of simple measures.

This chapter is based on one component of a broader evaluation program that explores and triangulates the effectiveness of the Results Approach from several angles (Scott and Boyd 2016).

References

Black, L. J. and D. F. Andersen. 2012. 'Using visual representations as boundary objects to resolve conflict in collaborative model-building approaches.' *Systems Research and Behavioral Science* 29(2): 194–208.

Boston, J., J. Martin, J. Pallot and P. Walsh. 1996. *Public Management: The New Zealand model.* Auckland: Oxford University Press.

Boswell, C. 2014. 'The double life of targets in public policy: Disciplining and signalling in UK asylum policy.' *Public Administration* 93(2): 490–505. DOI: 10.1111/padm.12134.

Brignall, S. and S. Modell. 2000. 'An institutional perspective on performance measurement and management in the "new public sector".' *Management Accounting Research* 11(3): 281–306.

Brooking, R. 2014. Corrections cuts crime with selective use of statistics. Blog. Available from: brookingblog.com/2014/08/03/corrections-cuts-crime-with-the-selective-use-of-statistics/ (accessed 21 July 2015).

Bryson, J. M., B. C. Crosby and M. M. Stone. 2006. 'The design and implementation of cross-sector collaborations: Propositions from the literature.' *Public Administration Review* 66(s.1): 44–55.

Chapple, S. 2013. 'Forward liability and welfare reform in New Zealand.' *Policy Quarterly* 9(2): 56–62.

de Lancer-Julnes, P. and M. Holzer. 2001. 'Promoting the utilization of performance measures in public organizations: An empirical study of factors affecting adoption and implementation.' *Public Administration Review* 61(6): 693–708.

Fletcher, M. 2015. 'Australia should think twice before adopting NZ welfare model.' *The Conversation*, 9 March.

Fox, C. and K. Albertson. 2011. 'Payment by results and social impact bonds in the criminal justice sector: New challenges for the concept of evidence-based policy?' *Criminology and Criminal Justice* 11(5): 395–413.

Kania, J. and M. Kramer. 2011. 'Collective impact.' *Stanford Social Innovation Review* 9(1): 36–41.

Kaplan, R. S. 2001. 'Strategic performance measurement and management in nonprofit organizations.' *Nonprofit Management and Leadership* 11(3): 353–70.

Kirk, S. 2015. 'Crime and welfare-dependency down – Government report card.' *Stuff.co.nz*, 6 July. Available from: stuff.co.nz/national/politics/70005112/crime-and-welfare-dependency-down-government-report-card (accessed 21 July 2015).

Kurtz, C. F. and D. J. Snowden. 2003. 'The new dynamics of strategy: Sense-making in a complex and complicated world.' *IBM Systems Journal* 42(3): 462–83.

Leadbeater, C. 1997. *The Rise of the Social Entrepreneur*. No. 25. London: Demos.

McNaughton, S. 2015. Broader issues of RCTs. Address to the Institute for Government and Policy Studies Symposium: Using Randomised Control Trials in Public Policy. Institute for Government and Policy Studies, Wellington.

Macpherson, M. 2001. 'Performance measurement in not-for-profit and public-sector organisations.' *Measuring Business Excellence* 5(2): 13–17.

Ministry for the Environment. 2015. *About Environmental Reporting in New Zealand*. Wellington: New Zealand Government. Available from: mfe.govt.nz/more/environmental-reporting/about-environmental-reporting-nz (accessed 17 July 2015).

Ministry of Business, Innovation and Employment. 2015. *Business Growth Agenda*. Wellington: New Zealand Government. Available from: mbie.govt.nz/what-we-do/business-growth-agenda (accessed 21 July 2015).

Ministry of Social Development. 2012. Investment approach refocuses entire welfare system. Media Release. New Zealand Government, Wellington. Available from: msd.govt.nz/documents/about-msd-and-our-work/newsroom/media-releases/2012/welfare-reform-paper-e-social-obligations.pdf (accessed 21 July 2015).

O'Leary, R. 2014. *Collaborative Governance in New Zealand: Important choices ahead*. Wellington: Fullbright New Zealand.

Osborne, D. 1993. 'Reinventing government.' *Public Productivity & Management Review* 16: 349–56.

Revans, R. 1980. *Action Learning: New techniques for management*. London: Blond & Briggs.

Schick, A. 1996. *The Spirit of Reform: Managing the New Zealand state sector in a time of change*. Wellington: State Services Commission of New Zealand.

Scott, G. 2001. *Public Sector Management in New Zealand: Lessons and challenges*. Wellington: The Australian National University.

Scott, R. J. and R. Boyd. 2015. 'The New Zealand Better Public Services results: A comparative analysis linking inter-agency collaboration with outcome performance.' In *Proceedings of the 2015 Australia and New Zealand Academy of Management Conference*. Brisbane: Australia and New Zealand Academy of Management. Available from: anzam. org/conference-material/past-event-material/ (accessed April 2016).

Scott, R. J. and R. Boyd. 2016. 'Collaborating for results in New Zealand: Evaluation using mixed methods and triangulation.' In *Proceedings of the 2016 International Public Management Network Conference*. St Gallen, Switzerland: International Public Management Network.

Scott, R. J., R. Y. Cavana and D. Cameron. 2014. 'Mechanisms for understanding mental model change in group model building.' *Systems Research and Behavioral Science* 33(1): 100–18. DOI: 10.1002/sres.2303.

Selsky, J. W. and B. Parker. 2005. 'Cross-sector partnerships to address social issues: Challenges to theory and practice.' *Journal of Management* 31(6): 849–73.

Smith, P. C. 2009. *Performance Measurement for Health System Improvement: Experiences, challenges and prospects*. Cambridge: Cambridge University Press.

State Services Commission (SSC). 2001. *Report of the Advisory Group on the Review of the Centre*. Wellington: State Services Commission. Available from: ssc.govt.nz/roc (accessed 17 July 2015).

State Services Commission (SSC). 2003. *Managing for Outcomes: Guidance for departments*. Wellington: State Services Commission.

State Services Commission (SSC). 2004. *Getting Better at Managing for Shared Outcomes: A resource for agency leaders*. Wellington: State Services Commission.

State Services Commission (SSC). 2011. *Better Public Services Advisory Group Report*. Wellington: State Services Commission. Available from: ssc.govt.nz/bps-background-material (accessed 17 July 2015).

State Services Commission (SSC). 2012. *Better Public Services: Results*. Cabinet Paper CAB (12)19. New Zealand Government, Wellington.

State Services Commission (SSC). 2014. *Better public service results: 2014 end-year progress report (with annexes)*. Cabinet Paper SEC (15)2. New Zealand Government, Wellington.

State Services Commission (SSC). 2015a. *Better Public Services: Results for New Zealanders*. Wellington: State Services Commission. Available from: ssc.govt.nz/bps-results-for-nzers (accessed 17 July 2015).

State Services Commission (SSC). 2015b. *Better Public Services: Snapshot of results at 19 Feb 2015*. Wellington: State Services Commission. Available from: ssc.govt.nz/bps-snapshot (accessed 17 July 2015).

Stuart, M. 2014. 'Future liabilities: Solutions to the "problem of welfare"?' *Open Review of Educational Research* 1(1): 183–92.

Vitalis, H. and R. J. Scott. 2015. 'Joint ventures in the public sector: Translating lessons from the private sector to New Zealand government departments.' In *Proceedings of the 2015 Australia and New Zealand Academy of Management Conference*. Brisbane: Australia and New Zealand Academy of Management. Available from: anzam. org/conference-material/past-event-material/ (accessed April 2016).

Part 4. New Tools for Policymakers and Practitioners

Overview

Ursula Stephens

What are the necessary preconditions for exploring alternative approaches to addressing social need?

In this section, there are four eminent contributors, bringing unique perspectives to addressing complex social problems. Each is concerned with citizen and client-controlled provision and consumer-directed care, using a variety of approaches, some of which are disruptive, others collaborative. All the perspectives offer innovation through cross-sector collaboration and public engagement.

The chapters share several themes.

The first is the need for evidence-based success and the challenges of substantiating policy success over time. Short-term decision-making that coincides with an electoral cycle or, indeed, a change of government makes it very difficult to develop key performance indicators of enduring success. Australia has strong examples, such as the Communities for Children program, which has endured over four governments and has demonstrated the strength of long-term investment. Ann Nevile's Chapter 12, using the example of disability employment services, advocates a person-centred approach. Nevile highlights that the current contracting regime for disability employment continues to constrain the capacity of agencies to deliver flexible, individualised services for those with disability, particularly those who want to work in open employment.

While personalisation of services allows service users to exercise some degree of choice and control in the new National Disability Insurance Scheme, and in aged care and health care, that sense of control is something that still eludes most jobseekers. Nevile challenges us to consider how best to address information asymmetry and design a funding model that is an enabler rather than a constraint.

Creaming, parking and churning clients are all risk-selection practices built into the disability employment funding model. Nevile examines the challenges of the licensing and accreditation processes, and how difficult it is to both enter and exit this market. The regulatory burden is heavy and the transaction costs of compliance are significant. How much should government regulate employment service providers? Nevile calls for a new approach to the payments system in this important policy area—one that will reward interim milestones towards achieving outcomes. Such an approach will encourage innovation and new partnerships. It provides opportunities for client choice and higher expectations being met, and it would enable pathways to be developed that lead people into the open employment market.

The second theme developed is how best to quantify and qualify what we mean by 'value for money'. Do we consider the concept of 'best value' as something that involves not just least cost, but also 'public benefit'? This is an important argument when dealing with early intervention and prevention programs: how do we quantify the opportunity cost of *not* intervening? Here, alliance contracting is examined by Cassandra Wilkinson (Chapter 13), who draws on the experience of the New Zealand health alliances to demonstrate how effective alliances are in preventative health and in dealing with complex social problems—such as drug dependency, mental health and homelessness—through a foyer approach. She highlights that alliances share risks and rewards, and that government must fund and understand the nuances of such an approach, rather than burdening the model with massive administrative costs and poorly defined program delivery and outcomes. Alliances can help to reduce fragmentation of services, but this model is necessarily expensive because of its intensive intervention, and there is not a one-size-fits-all solution. Wilkinson argues that there is an evidence deficit about outcomes and a need for strong evidence tools to be developed. Her call is for governments to announce funding in the language of 'results' rather than 'effort'.

The third theme is acknowledging that there are competing vested and political interests in the complex environment, where the challenges being addressed are perceived and defined in different ways by stakeholders and policy actors. Melina Morrison and Cliff Mills (Chapter 14) explore how the concept of mutuality is disrupting the status quo. They describe how mutuality is growing in Australia as an alternative approach to a market-based economy. The role that mutuals and cooperatives can play in the future of public services is explored, as employee share ownership and cooperatives emerge as innovative ways to address concerns about energy, waste and food quality. Mutuality is powerful in promoting localism through local coops, farmers' markets and cottage industries. Morrison explores how these approaches are highly professional, but also draw on community capacity building and volunteerism, building social inclusion and innovation. International experience highlights how cooperatives are playing a growing part in the future of public services.

A fourth recurring theme is focused on managing risk in public policy: shifting risk from government, responding to policy or programmatic failure, delivering efficiencies, dealing with competitive neutrality and how that impacts on service providers. Here we are able to consider transactional costs and shifting administrative burdens from the public to the private or non-governmental sectors, and how public accountability is managed. Catherine Needham pursues this issue in Chapter 15 about the boundaries of budgets: why and how should individuals make spending choices about their health and social care? As the state shifts from being a purchaser or provider of services, Needham highlights the challenges for government, service providers and citizens.

Each of the contributors identifies opportunities for innovation and recognises the importance of having champions for change within government and bureaucracies, teasing out how compliance regimes stifle the opportunities that can exist for driving social change agendas. Needham also encourages her readers to consider the implications of thin markets and underfunding, which can mean that while ostensibly there may be a choice of providers, citizens have limited choice over outcomes.

All four chapters call for putting citizens at the centre of policy frameworks, focusing on what these policies are seeking to achieve and highlighting the importance of building relationships in a value chain. Finally, there is a shared emphasis on developing a strong narrative and a shared understanding of what these approaches really mean. Morrison describes this as understanding who 'we' are and who 'they' are in the service mix.

Redesigning Procurement Strategies for Complex Policy Spaces

Ann Nevile

Introduction

In her summing up speech on the National Disability Insurance Scheme (NDIS) Bill, the then parliamentary secretary for disability noted that giving people choice and control over the care and support they receive is one of the ways in which Australia will give effect to the *UN Convention on the Rights of Persons with Disability* (McLucas 2013). The right to choose is enshrined in the design of the NDIS, under which, for the first time, individuals with disability will be given a choice over the type of services they receive and who delivers those services. However, the NDIS is not designed as a 'stand-alone' system and is expected to operate in conjunction with 'mainstream' disability services, such as employment. In this chapter, I argue that, despite commitments from successive Australian governments to reduce the administrative burden placed on disability employment service providers, the current contracting regime continues to constrain agency capacity to deliver flexible, individualised services—a situation that needs to change if Australians with disability who wish to work in open employment are to realise the economic, social and health benefits of employment that the majority of Australians take for granted.

The remainder of this chapter briefly discusses the design features of the current system, before presenting the evidence base for the assertion that introducing a person-centred approach will lead to better employment outcomes. The chapter then considers the suitability of an explicit voucher system, identifying three policy preconditions that need to be met before such a system can provide the requisite levels of choice and control.

Disability employment services

In Australia, government provision of mainstream employment services has been delivered through a mix of commercial and community or not-for-profit agencies since 1998. Since its inception, the Job Network[1] has been an active labour market program in that unemployed individuals are required to actively look for work and accept suitable work if offered. Providers are selected through a competitive tender process and funded by an outcome-based funding model that requires achievement of milestones before payment is made. Agencies are contracted to provide services in a designated employment service area (ESA) and allocated a certain market share within that ESA. Future contracts and percentage of market share are dependent on an agency's ranking relative to other agencies, not just within their ESA, but also across the whole of Australia. As well as assisting unemployed individuals to find work, employment service providers are required to report breaches of government requirements by jobseekers to Centrelink, a central government agency that manages all social security payments and provides residual employment services such as referrals to employment service providers. Unemployed individuals who are required to look for work are able to choose a service provider from among those operating within their ESA; however, the amount of publicly available information on the comparative performance of employment service providers is limited and Centrelink refers the majority of jobseekers to a particular provider. Service providers are obliged to accept all referrals from Centrelink unless they have reached 120 per cent of their allocated market share. Public spending

---

1   The Job Network was replaced in 2009 with a new generation of employment services known as Job Services Australia and, on 1 July 2015, Job Services Australia was replaced with jobactive, but the basic design elements remain the same.

on labour market programs decreased after the introduction of the Job Network, and the prioritisation of cheaper, shorter interventions has led to a decrease in the cost per client (Wright 2008: 17). In a system where financial viability is achieved by adopting a 'high-volume/low-value' business model, agencies feel they are no longer able to make long-term investments in jobseekers or engage in truly innovative practices (Fowkes 2011: 8).

The international literature recognises that quasi-markets are subject to risk selection (Bonvin 2008; Struyven and Steurs 2005) and, in Australia, where continued funding is dependent on performance relative to all other agencies—as opposed to meeting agreed 'best practice' benchmarks or standards, for example—there are even greater incentives for agencies to engage in risk selection. Thus, despite ongoing efforts by the relevant Commonwealth Government department to eliminate such behaviour, risk selection continues to characterise employment services in Australia (Nevile 2013b: 67–68).

The introduction of quasi-markets for agencies whose work focuses on providing employment services for people with disability has lagged behind mainstream employment services, but, since 2004, when policy responsibility for open employment services was transferred from the social services department to the employment department, administrative and funding arrangements for disability employment have been gradually aligned with those of mainstream employment services. Consequently, despite new contracting arrangements introduced on 1 March 2010—designed to provide 'all eligible job seekers with access to individually tailored and comprehensive services … to help participants obtain and maintain suitable employment' (Australian Government n.d., cited in Nevile and Lohmann 2011: 22)—agency capacity to deliver flexible, individualised services has decreased because aligning the administrative and funding arrangements of disability employment services (DES) with those of mainstream employment services has led to a complex, prescriptive and constantly changing administrative system and a funding structure that encourages agencies to focus on jobseekers who are more work ready (Nevile 2013a).[2]

Those working in the sector fully support the government's focus on outcomes, but remain concerned that despite successive government commitments to increase the participation of people with disability in open employment, the gap between participation rates for Australians without disability and those with disability has not decreased significantly for women and men with mild disability and has increased slightly for women and men with severe and profound disability (Kavanagh et al. 2013: 4–5). Only 40 per cent of DES jobseekers manage to obtain employment, and only 23 per cent manage to maintain their employment for 26 weeks (DSS 2014). At the same time, there is increasing recognition beyond the disability employment sector that services for people with disability should take a 'person-centred' approach (Nevile 2013a).

Needham (2011: 43) defines 'personalisation' as 'mechanisms that tailor services to specific circumstances of the individual', and goes on to note that '[p]ersonalised approaches share a common focus on outcomes rather than processes or outputs, often encompassing less quantitative aspects such as befriending, building relationships and broader quality of life issues'. However, an emphasis on building relationships means that processes cannot be ignored because processes mandated by a particular contracting regime may inhibit the development of beneficial and valued relationships. For example, those working in DES agencies report that:

> We used to be able to get to know our clients on a different level. Now they are just—and it is horrible to have to say—but they are just like cows that are waiting—'next', 'next'. You don't have time to get to know them and what motivates them. (Employment consultant, cited in Nevile 2013a: 154)

---

2   In February 2014, policy responsibility for DES was transferred back to the Department of Social Services (DSS). DSS is currently considering the nature of DES post 2018. The extent to which DSS is prepared to move DES funding and administrative arrangements away from those regulating mainstream employment services is not yet clear.

While DES jobseekers value being treated 'as a person, not a number' (Nevile 2013b: 73), for government, the importance of taking a person-centred approach lies in the fact that achieving desired outcomes in coproduced services such as disability employment is, at least partly, dependent on how jobseekers and workers are assisted to find work and sustain their employment.

The relationship between personalisation and achieving desired outcomes

As part of an Australian Research Council (ARC) Linkage Project (LP130100288), which developed indicators of service quality for disability employment services, DES jobseekers were asked what they valued. What was very clear from the survey results was that jobseekers highly valued outcomes (92 per cent identified that they wanted a job), but they also highly valued how those outcomes were achieved, and an important element in the process of finding employment was their relationship with the service provider. For example, 86 per cent said they valued having a choice about the sort of work they did. Jobseekers also valued employment consultants who listened to what they had to say (78 per cent) and helped them to feel confident about their abilities (74 per cent). The fact that jobseekers valued being given a choice about the sort of work they do is hardly surprising. A recent study by Burchardt et al. (2015: 61) on the degree of autonomy individuals experience in various aspects of their life concluded that disability was associated with low levels of choice and control across all domains, including employment; and evaluations of direct payments and other forms of personal budgets or consumer-directed care report high levels of satisfaction from service users because they are able to exercise some degree of choice and control (see, for example, Netten et al. 2012: 1563; Needham 2011: 49; Stevens et al. 2011: 266; Fisher et al. 2010: viii; Ottmann et al. 2009: 471; Daly et al. 2008: 20; Kremer 2006: 399).

The economic, social and health effects of employment are well documented, as are the negative effects of unemployment on feelings of well-being, with the negative effects of unemployment occurring at the onset and during extended periods of unemployment (Courts et al. 2014: 466, 469). Thus, the longer individuals are unemployed, the higher is the psychological cost of job search activities (Krueger and

Mueller 2011: 46). In other words, because the majority of jobseekers want to work, continued unsuccessful job search activity leads to increased feelings of sadness or depression:

> Maybe I shouldn't say this, but I suppose I can understand because Centrelink put so much pressure on you to get a job, I can understand why there are so many suicides, because you tend to get so depressed about sending out resume after resume and getting [rejection] letters back. (Jobseeker, cited in Nevile 2013a: 152)

At the same time, individuals with higher levels of subjective well-being are more likely to be successful in gaining employment than those with lower levels of subjective well-being (Saloniemi et al. 2014: 533; Andersen 2008: 451).

While different theories have been put forward to explain the relationship between unemployment and subjective well-being, the loss of control that accompanies unemployment has been identified as a major reason for its negative effects on subjective well-being (Creed et al. 2012: 697). General psychological theories that have been applied to unemployment shed further light on the links between loss of control, decreased levels of subjective well-being and a reduced probability of re-employment. Expectancy-value theory is a cognitive motivation theory that relates the strength of an individual's motivation to strive to achieve a certain goal to their expectations of success (Vansteenkiste et al. 2005: 270). In the labour market context, expectancy-value theory predicts that unemployed jobseekers who have confidence (expect) that they will perform well in a job interview will put more effort into job search activities than those with lower expectations. A meta-review of studies that test the expectancy-value theory in relation to labour markets confirms this hypothesis (Vansteenkiste et al. 2005: 270–71). Furthermore, jobseekers who have confidence in their ability to search for jobs are more likely to be successful in gaining employment than jobseekers with lower levels of self-efficacy (Duffy et al. 2013: 55).

The implication of these findings is that employment assistance that includes activities designed to enhance jobseekers' confidence in their own abilities will be more effective than programs that do not contain such elements: 'The challenge for practitioners is to provide strategies for unemployed people that will allow them to maintain high levels of job seeking, while at the same time maintain their psychological health and optimism. Increasing feelings of control are likely to be helpful with this' (Creed et al. 2012: 698).

Recent studies provide support for Creed et al.'s (2012) assertion that interventions that address psychological barriers will increase the probability of jobseekers gaining employment (see, for example, Maguire et al. 2014: 309).

While expectancy-value theory highlights the importance of motivation in achieving desired behaviours, and hence outcomes, self-determination theory argues that different types of motivation will lead to different outcomes. When applied to unemployed individuals, self-determination theory predicts that individuals who are intrinsically motivated will put more effort into job search activities and persist for longer than individuals who undertake job search activities because they feel obliged to do so (Vansteenkiste et al. 2004: 346).

What is particularly important for countries such as Australia with compliance-centred regimes is that when extrinsic motivation comes to be accepted by an individual as personally important (identified autonomous motivation), it has the same effect as intrinsic autonomous motivation (Vansteenkiste et al. 2005: 272). In other words, increased employment outcomes are possible in compliance-centred regimes that rely on controlled motivation if employment consultants/support workers are given the opportunity to assist jobseekers and workers turn controlled motivation into identified motivation. With its dual focus on both outcomes and processes that increase the likelihood of desired outcomes, personalisation is one way in which controlled motivation can be turned into identified autonomous motivation.

Operationalising person-centred approaches

Personalisation can be put into effect through direct cash payments or some form of voucher system whereby eligible service users are able to 'purchase' social goods in a competitive market. Allowing service users to choose their service provider should, in theory, make service providers more responsive to the needs of individual service users and hence lead to the provision of more flexible, responsive services. Thus, in theory, voucher systems also allow more choice for service providers in terms of how policy goals are achieved.

In the area of DES, the potential benefit of a voucher system—the provision of more flexible and individualised services—is uncontroversial. As noted earlier, this is an explicit goal underlying previous changes in contracting arrangements and something that service providers would like to be able to provide. Furthermore, a quasi-market in DES already exists, as do design elements, such as eligibility criteria and a payment structure that reflects differing levels of need and type of service, and the government has already transferred significant financial risk on to service providers in that it does not guarantee a specific number of referrals and service provider agencies face the real prospect of contract termination or reduction in market share if their performance falls relative to all other agencies. Indeed, the level of financial risk service provider agencies are now expected to bear has meant a reduction in the number and diversity of service delivery agencies. For example, over the years the number of DES providers has fallen from about 350 to about 100.

Voucher systems, or proposals to introduce such systems, often attract vociferous debate, much of it ideological (Belfield and Levin 2005)—in part, because vouchers are simply a policy tool that can be used to expand or contract the welfare state (Daniels and Trebilcock 2005: 2). In other words, vouchers or other forms of person-centred approaches are not, in themselves, a remedy for inadequate funding, nor will they overcome supply constraints that arise from low population density. For example, in the United Kingdom, cost saving was a key theme in the personalisation narrative (Needham 2011: 51) and, over the years, critics of individual budgets have argued that the promise of improvements in service quality has been undermined by a funding model that simply reallocated 'generally inadequate funding within arbitrary and unhelpful eligibility criteria and means testing' (Beresford 2011–12: 40). In 2010, the UK Audit Commission concluded that 'personal budgets are unlikely to result in significant cost savings for councils' (cited in Wilberforce et al. 2012: 255)—a conclusion that echoes findings from a broader evaluation of personal budgets that additional transaction costs were associated with personal budgets, with service providers arguing that the only way they could offer more personalised services was if they were able to determine the price for their services, rather than the price being set by the local authority (Wilberforce et al. 2012: 253). As well as potentially affecting service quality, underfunding also constrains the salaries available to those providing personalised care, which in turn increases the difficulties involved in recruiting sufficient staff, particularly in rural areas (Baxter et al. 2013: 405; Glendinning 2012: 297; Cowen et al. 2011: 34).

Thus, as a comparative study of cash-for-care programs in four European countries noted, 'merely switching from direct service provision … to cash payments does not in itself enhance choice and control' (Timonen et al. 2006: 468). The extent to which voucher systems deliver more choice to service users and more flexible, individualised services depends on the way in which such schemes are regulated. Active restriction of choice is often justified on the grounds of accountability, while passive restriction of choice occurs through information asymmetry, and as a consequence of the particular funding model adopted. The next section discusses these issues in more detail.

Policy preconditions

The relationship between choice and accountability

The concept of choice is central to the discourse surrounding personalisation, with choice seen as important—both as an end in itself and as a means to other policy-oriented ends. Many people with disability value choice for intrinsic reasons: in choosing, they are able to exercise control and agency, and being able to exercise control and agency is valued in itself, regardless of the policy outcome (Nevile 2009: 82; 2013a: 152). Theoretical approaches that value choice for intrinsic reasons are based on a range of philosophical positions, from neoliberal or libertarian perspectives to Amartya Sen's capability approach. For example, in an address to the National Press Club in November 2013, Mitch Fifield, then assistant minister with responsibility for disability in the Liberal National Party (LNP) Coalition Government, noted that 'the design at the heart of NDIS—the individual at the centre and in control being able to choose the supports of their choice—could not rest more easily with the philosophy of my party' (Fifield 2013).

For some, intrinsic justifications of choice sit easily with particular extrinsic justifications. For example, many people with disability, academics and commentators have argued that choice is a fundamental prerequisite for realisation of social inclusion, citizenship and human rights (Hall 2009: 46; Glendinning 2008: 459; Spandler 2004: 192).

Those who care for a family member with disability tend to value choice for instrumental reasons—that is, if carers are given a choice and provided with the means to realise that choice, they can access services that best suit the needs of their family member: 'Having control over the money is the best way of giving people power. Otherwise we are forever fitting (or not fitting) into programs and services that might not suit us but which are all that is on offer' (Sally Richards, cited in Productivity Commission 2011: 354).

Or they can provide experiences for their family member that enrich that person's life:

> Tim turned 21 and, like any young man, he's entitled to … a 21st birthday. [Under self-directed funding,] I was able to employ [someone] … to do some social education informally with him in preparation for his 21st birthday. It worked sublimely. He got the issue, even though his cognitive capacity is quite limited … and he had a ball. (C. Quinn, cited in Productivity Commission 2011: 371)

For politicians and bureaucrats, instrumental justifications for choice can be particularly powerful. For example, politicians in the United Kingdom have embraced the notion that to attract and secure political legitimacy, public services need to offer service users (consumers) the same level of choice as is offered by the private sector (Glendinning 2008: 458). In its Inquiry Report, *Disability care and support*, the Productivity Commission (2011: 357) argued that 'an absence of genuine choice tends to result in lower quality and more costly services, less product variety and less innovation' because the ability of service users to act like consumers broadens the scope for competition and hence provides greater pressure for responsive, high-quality services.

Policy narratives that succeed in legitimising a certain course of action and that mobilise support across different national and international agencies by taking bits and pieces of different agendas and burying differences do not, however, provide good guides to action because the logic of political mobilisation and the logic of implementation are different (Mosse 2004: 663). For this reason, the implications of differing justifications usually manifest when broad policy goals (more choice) are translated into specific program design parameters. As Burchardt et al. (2015: 47) noted, the dominance of instrumental justifications in policy discourse means that governments are happy to give service users a choice between different providers, but choice over outcomes is usually limited or non-existent. For example, an evaluation of 13 individual budget trial sites in the United Kingdom found that while individual budget holders reported greater feelings of control over daily life, choice was constrained by decisions made by service delivery staff over what constituted a legitimate use of public funds (Stevens et al. 2011: 268). When the Netherlands introduced the option of personal budgets for individuals receiving care in the home in 1995, concerns about the accountability of clients meant that the scheme was tightly regulated. The resulting complexity discouraged some individuals from participating in the program and one-third of those who did participate outsourced all administrative requirements associated with the personal budget to care professionals paid by the state (Kremer 2006: 391).

Choice can also be restricted by concerns about the capacity of service users to exercise choice or a concern that they may make 'suboptimal' choices. For example, in the United Kingdom, the low rate of participation of people with learning disabilities in direct payments was due to the belief in some social service departments that people with learning disabilities do not have the competence or capacity to manage direct payments, with the result that people with learning disabilities were not actively encouraged to participate in the scheme (Hall 2009: 49). Similarly, in the Netherlands, when people with disabilities were first provided with a personal labour re-integration budget, some case managers did not inform eligible clients about the voucher scheme because they believed they were not capable of managing their own budget (Bosselaar and Prins 2007: 115). In Australia, information from those involved in the NDIS trial sites indicates that low expectations are, at times, restricting the choices of those involved in the scheme (De Natris 2015). In other words, an overly cautious approach to accountability and risk management concerns may result in 'individuals not being supported to make choices and take control' (Carr 2011: 16).

Information asymmetry

Passive restriction of choice occurs when service users do not have sufficient information to make an informed choice about which service provider is best for them. As noted earlier, there is little publicly available information on the performance of disability employment agencies. The star ratings system was originally developed for this purpose, but has only ever been used as a performance management tool. While the star ratings system provides a simple, composite measure of performance, the method by which ratings are generated is complex, opaque and difficult to understand for both service providers and users. A further problem with the star ratings system is that it contains no information about the way in which outcomes are generated—information that is important for service users. In other words, confronted with a single number, service users have no idea whether a five-star service provider achieved this ranking through engaging in risk selection or whether they do indeed provide high-quality services. In addition, the comparative nature of the star ratings system is of little use to service users who are only interested in the relative performance of service provider agencies in the city or local area in which they live (Wright 2008: 27).

In the case of DES, the problem of information asymmetry is relatively easy to overcome. The new indicators of service quality developed through LP130100288, and based on what jobseekers and workers value, together with information on employment outcomes, provide clear, simple and easy to understand information on both process and outcomes.[3] While service provider agencies could publicise information that was not a true reflection of agency performance, dissatisfied service users are free to leave the agency and, over time, word of mouth would mean an agency that consistently inflated performance measures would suffer reputational damage. As one UK service provider observed when asked whether a move away from

---

3   Service provider agencies could make the following information publicly available and update it annually or every six months: the percentage of jobseekers and workers who feel able to take control of their lives in relation to seeking, gaining and maintaining work; the percentage of jobseekers and workers who feel confident about their abilities in relation to seeking, gaining and maintaining work; the number of jobseekers who have been placed in a job in the past six months; and the number of workers who have remained in that job for 13 weeks, 26 weeks or longer than 26 weeks.

block contracts would mean a loss of business: '[t]he people who need to worry are those who are currently providing rubbish services' (cited in Wilberforce et al. 2012: 254).

Being supported to make choices and take control involves the provision of information about different service providers, but it also involves providing the opportunity for individuals to think about what it is they want, 'based on a rich understanding of what might be possible' (Burchardt et al. 2015: 62). As the NDIS example indicates, providing such opportunities may require training frontline staff involved in assessment and decision-making processes and establishing service delivery systems that are person-centred and relationship-based rather than systems that focus on process auditing and administration (Carr 2011: 15).

The funding model

Passive restriction of choice can also occur when procurement strategies restrict supply—for example, having a limited number of licensed or accredited providers from which service users can choose (Carr 2011: 13) or funding models that do not provide incentives to tailor services to individual needs (Wilberforce et al. 2011: 596). For this reason, the continued development of quasi-markets is essential. In the case of DES, the current quasi-market needs to be deregulated, with agency ability to continue operating dependent on business decisions taken by the agency rather than by government. Entry into the market would be dependent on passing a licensing or accreditation process, as is currently the case with aged care facilities.

As noted earlier, person-centred approaches raise particular accountability concerns in relation to potential choices made by service users, but also encompass concerns about the actions of service providers in terms of providing quality services. Concerns about the actions of service providers are particularly prevalent in debates over the effectiveness of school voucher programs, with government regulation seen as necessary to maintain service quality in the form of national education standards (Ladd 2003: 20). While public interest in the outcomes of various social care programs is not as intense as interest in educational outcomes, the existence of risk selection means that the question of whether governments should regulate the behaviour of service providers needs to be considered.

Under the current contracting regime for DES, government control over the actions of service providers significantly restricts the ways in which service providers can assist jobseekers. Conceptualising their relationship with service providers in terms of agency theory means that governments fail to recognise the fact that DES staff see themselves as professionals with responsibility for acting in accordance with professional standards (Nevile 2013b: 68). The strength of these professional standards is clearly evident in the understanding DES staff have of the importance of relationships in terms of achieving desired outcomes, and the processes that allow those respectful, supportive relationships to be developed and maintained:

> My clients respond to being treated with respect because this is one of the few places they're actually going to get it. If I'm going to make someone believe that they can do something, that takes time and it also requires me listening to them and knowing that. (Employment consultant, cited in Nevile 2013b: 74)

The desire of service providers to be treated as professionals requires a recalibration rather than an abandonment of accountability mechanisms. All DES agencies are required to comply with national disability service standards and are audited by independent quality-assurance auditors every three years to ensure compliance with all standards. Surveillance audits against some, but not all, of the standards are carried out in the intervening two years. Because the disability service standards were developed and updated through a consultative process that included service providers and service users, they are consistent with service providers' professional norms, and hence service providers are happy to be held to account through the national standards.

As noted earlier, the performance management framework can significantly affect the incentives to engage in risk selection, as can the payment structure. For example, when Germany introduced placement vouchers for jobseekers who had been unemployed for more than three months or who signed up for a job creation program, the private placement agency received half the value of the voucher once the jobseeker had been in work for six weeks, with the remaining amount paid when the individual had been in employment for six months. A payment system that only rewards outcomes creates incentives for agencies to focus attention on easier to place jobseekers, with the German Federal Audit Court concluding that the placement vouchers 'could be seen as windfall gains for recruitment agencies, since they would have placed the job seeker in question even if the bonus had not been available' (Bruttel 2005: 394). Payment systems that include payments on completion of interim milestones, such as improvements in confidence, are more likely to reduce the possibility of risk selection.

However, even when interim milestones are rewarded, there remains the issue of the weighting attached to the interim milestones compared with outcome payments. While there is no risk-free solution to this question, one possible solution is to allocate 40 per cent of an individual's payment to interim milestones, specified through a joint planning process, and 60 per cent to outcomes.

The difficulties involved in determining the level of assistance needed by each individual raise the question of whether agencies should be free to charge more for their services than allocated by government. The majority of DES users are obliged to look for work and, being dependent on government payments, have little or no capacity to top-up allocated entitlements. Under the current system, DES agencies are able to assist people who are not eligible for employment service support (for example, individuals who are assessed as having a work capacity of zero to seven hours per week) but who come to the agency through direct registrations. That is, they are not referred by Centrelink, but choose to come because they want to work and have heard about the agency or have had contact with the agency while still at school. It is important that the ability of DES agencies to assist such individuals is not diminished, particularly when the NDIS is rolled out across Australia. Giving agencies the autonomy to determine the price of their service for direct registrations could be one way of increasing economic participation for all Australians with disability.

An explicit voucher system in the form of a smart card would facilitate payment on completion of agreed milestones and outcomes and would also make it easier for service users to move to another provider if they become dissatisfied with their current provider. While use of a smart card has the potential to reduce the transaction costs associated with voucher schemes, it would not eliminate them entirely. Under the current contracting regime, however, service providers have to spend a significant amount of time meeting departmental reporting requirements and it is likely that the introduction of a voucher system in a deregulated market would lead to a reduction in time spent on administration and compliance activities.

Conclusion

In this chapter I have argued that the introduction of an explicit voucher system for DES with entry into the market through a licensing or accreditation process will increase the capacity of service providers to deliver what government, service providers and service users want: flexible, individualised services and improved employment outcomes.

References

Andersen, S. H. 2008. 'The short- and long-term effects of government training on subjective well-being.' *European Sociological Review* 24(4): 451–62.

Baxter, K., P. Rabiee and C. Glendinning. 2013. 'Managed personal budgets for older people: What are English local authorities doing to facilitate personalized and flexible care?' *Public Money and Management* 33(6): 399–406.

Belfield, C. and H. M. Levin. 2005. 'Vouchers and public policy: When ideology trumps evidence.' *American Journal of Education* 111(4): 548–67.

Beresford, P. 2011–12. 'Are personal budgets necessarily empowering for service users? If not, what's it all about?' *Research, Policy and Planning* 29(1): 37–43.

Bonvin, J.-M. 2008. 'Activation policies, new modes of governance and the issue of responsibility.' *Social Policy and Society* 7(3): 367–77.

Bosselaar, H. and R. Prins. 2007. 'Personal return to work budgets for persons with disabilities: Demand-based delivery of re-integration services in The Netherlands.' *European Journal of Social Security* 9(2): 111–25.

Bruttel, O. 2005. 'Delivering active labour market policy through vouchers: Experiences with training vouchers in Germany.' *International Review of Administrative Sciences* 71(3): 391–404.

Burchardt, T., M. Evans and H. Holder. 2015. 'Public policy and inequalities of choice and autonomy.' *Social Policy and Administration* 49(1): 44–67.

Carr, S. 2011. 'Personal budgets and international contexts: Lessons from home and abroad.' *Journal of Care Services Management* 5(1): 9–22.

Courts, A., K. Lehmann and M. Hood. 2014. 'The health and wellbeing effects of active labor market programs.' In *Interventions and Policies to Enhance Wellbeing: A complete reference guide. Volume VI*, eds F. A. Huppert and G. L. Cooper, 465–82. Chichester, UK: Wiley Blackwood.

Cowen, A., P. Murray and S. Duffy. 2011. 'Personalised transition: A collaborative approach to funding individual budgets for young disabled people with complex needs leaving school.' *Journal of Integrated Care* 19(2): 31–36.

Creed, P., M. Hood and L. Y. Leung. 2012. 'The relationship between control, job seeking, and well-being in unemployed people.' *Journal of Applied Social Psychology* 42(3): 689–701.

Daly, G., A. Roebuck, J. Dean, F. Goff, M. Bollard and C. Taylor. 2008. 'Gaining independence: An evaluation of service users' accounts of the individual budgets pilot.' *Journal of Integrated Care* 16(3): 17–25.

Daniels, R. J. and M. J. Trebilcock. 2005. *Rethinking the Welfare State: The prospects for government by voucher*. London: Routledge.

De Natris, P. 2015. Address to the NDS Disability at Work Conference. Melbourne, 19 May.

Department of Social Security (DSS). 2014. *Evaluation of Disability Employment Services 2010–2014*. Canberra: Australian Government.

Duffy, R. D., E. M. Bott, B. A. Allan and C. L. Torrie. 2013. 'Examining a model of life satisfaction among unemployed adults.' *Journal of Counselling Psychology* 60(1): 53–63.

Fifield, M. 2013. Address to the National Press Club. Canberra, 20 November.

Fisher, K., R. Gleeson, R. Edwards, C. Purcal, T. Sitzek, B. Dinning, C. Laragy and D. Thompson. 2010. *Effectiveness of individual funding approaches for disability support*. Occasional Paper No. 29. Department of Families, Housing, Community Services and Indigenous Affairs, Canberra.

Fowkes, L. 2011. 'Rethinking Australia's employment services.' *Perspectives*. Whitlam Institute, Sydney.

Glendinning, C. 2008. 'Increasing choice and control for older and disabled people: A critical review of new developments in England.' *Social Policy and Administration* 42(5): 451–69.

Glendinning, C. 2012. 'Home care in England: Markets in the context of under-funding.' *Health and Social Care in the Community* 20(3): 292–99.

Hall, E. 2009. 'Being in control: Personal budgets and the new landscape of care for people with learning disabilities.' *Mental Health Review Journal* 14(2): 44–53.

Kavanagh, A., L. Krnjacki, A. Beer, A. La Montagne and R. Bentley. 2013. 'Time trends for socio-economic inequalities for women and men with disabilities in Australia: Evidence of persisting inequalities.' *International Journal for Equity in Health* 12(73): 1–10.

Kremer, M. 2006. 'Consumers in charge of care: The Dutch personal budget and its impact on the market, professionals and the family.' *European Societies* 8(3): 385–401.

Krueger, A. B. and A. Mueller. 2011. 'Job search, emotional well-being, and job finding in a period of mass unemployment: Evidence from high-frequency longitudinal data.' *Brookings Papers on Economic Activity* (Spring): 1–81.

Ladd, H. F. 2003. 'Introduction.' In *Choosing Choice: School choice in international perspective*, eds D. N. Plank and G Sykes, 1–23. New York: Teachers College Press.

McLucas, J. 2013. Senate summing up speech, National Disability Insurance Scheme Bill. 20 March. Parliament House, Canberra.

Maguire, N., V. C. Hughes, L. Bell, A. Bogosian and C. Hepworth. 2014. 'An evaluation of the choices for well-being project.' *Psychology, Health & Medicine* 19(3): 303–15.

Mosse, D. 2004. 'Is good policy unimplementable? Reflections on the ethnography of aid policy and practice.' *Development and Change* 35(4): 639–71.

Needham, C. 2011. *Personalising Public Services: Understanding the personalisation narrative*. Bristol: The Policy Press.

Netten, A., K. Jones, M. Knapp, J.-L. Fernandez, D. Challis, C. Glendinning, S. Jacobs, J. Manthorpe, N. Moran, M. Stevens and M. Wilberforce. 2012. 'Personalisation through individual budgets: Does it work and for whom?' *British Journal of Social Work* 42(8): 1556–573.

Nevile, A. 2009. 'Values and the legitimacy of third sector organisations: Evidence from Australia.' *Voluntas* 20(1): 71–89.

Nevile, A. 2013a. 'Reframing rights as obligations: Implications for service users' ability to exercise their rights.' *Australian Journal of Human Rights* 19(2): 147–64.

Nevile, A. 2013b. 'The curse of accountability: Assessing relationships in the delivery of employment services.' *The Economic and Labour Relations Review* 24(1): 64–79.

Nevile, A. and R. Lohmann. 2011. *'It is like they just don't trust us': Balancing trust and control in the provision of disability employment services*. Available from: crawford.anu.edu.au/sparc/pdf/2011/20110621_final_report.pdf (accessed 28 June 2016).

Ottmann, G., C. Laragy and M. Haddin. 2009. 'Experiences of disability consumer-directed care users in Australia: Results from a longitudinal qualitative study.' *Health and Social Care in the Community* 17(5): 466–75.

Productivity Commission. 2011. *Disability care and support*. Productivity Commission Inquiry Report No. 54, July. Productivity Commission, Canberra. Available from: pc.gov.au/projects/inquiry/disability-support/report (accessed 7 January 2014).

Saloniemi, A., K. Romppainen, M. Strandh and P. Virtanen. 2014. 'Training for the unemployed: Differential effects in white- and blue-collar workers with respect to mental well-being.' *Work, Employment and Society* 28(4): 533–50.

Spandler, H. 2004. 'Friend or foe? Towards a critical assessment of direct payments.' *Critical Social Policy* 24(2): 187–209.

Stevens, M., C. Glendinning, S. Jacobs, N. Moran, D. Challis, J. Manthorpe, J.-L. Fernandez, K. Jones, M. Knapp, A. Netten and M. Wilberforce. 2011. 'Assessing the role of increasing choice in English social care services.' *Journal of Social Policy* 40(2): 257–74.

Struyven, L. and G. Steurs. 2005. 'Design and redesign of a quasi-market for the reintegration of job seekers: Empirical evidence from Australia and the Netherlands.' *Journal of European Social Policy* 15(3): 211–29.

Timonen, V., J. Convery and S. Cahill. 2006. 'Care revolutions in the making? A comparison of cash-for-care programmes in four European countries.' *Ageing & Society* 26(3): 455–74.

Vansteenkiste, M., W. Lens, H. De Witte and N. T. Feather. 2005. 'Understanding unemployed people's job search behaviour, unemployment experience and well-being: A comparison of expectancy-value theory and self-determination theory.' *The British Journal of Social Psychology* 44: 269–87.

Vansteenkiste, M., W. Lens, S. De Witte, H. De Witte and E. L. Deci. 2004. 'The "why" and "why not" of job search behaviour: Their relation to searching, unemployment experience, and well-being.' *European Journal of Social Psychology* 34: 345–63.

Wilberforce, M., K. Baxter and C. Glendinning. 2012. 'Efficiency, choice and control in social care commissioning.' *Public Money and Management* 32(4): 249–56.

Wilberforce, M., C. Glendinning, D. Challis, J.-L. Fernandez, S. Jacobs, K. Jones, M. Knapp, J. Manthorpe, N. Moran, A. Netten and M. Stevens. 2011. 'Implementing consumer choice in long-term care: The impact of individual budgets on social care providers in England.' *Social Policy and Administration* 45(5): 593–612.

Wright, S. 2008. *Contracting our employment services: Lessons from Australia, Denmark, Germany and the Netherlands.* CPAG Policy Briefing. Child Poverty Action Group, London.

13

Alliance Contracting: How to progress in a world of uncertainty

Cassandra Wilkinson

Introduction

Australian governments spend billions of public dollars every year tackling 'wicked problems'. It is likely most of that money is put to good use. Unfortunately, we cannot say for sure if every dollar is used well or if it could have been used better. Despite having led the world in social services contracting, Australian governments have learned far too little about what money achieves once it leaves the balance sheet. Despite decades of discussion about inputs, outputs and outcomes, we have a poor evidence base with which to analyse what works and what does not and what might be done better.

This is consistently the advice of the Productivity Commission, the Australian National Audit Office (ANAO), various auditors-general and independent reviewers of public performance. Productivity Commission Chairman, Gary Banks (2009), summed up a substantial part of the problem in his introduction to the commission's report *Challenges of Evidence-Based Policy-Making*, noting that 'social policy is notoriously difficult to design and evaluate'. Discussing the *Overcoming Indigenous Disadvantage Report*, he noted that identifying things that work 'has proven challenging, to say the least; not necessarily because there are few things that are "working", but because in most cases the information available to substantiate their effects is lacking' (Banks 2009).

The problem of our poor evidence base extends far beyond the Indigenous policy realm. Banks (2009) gave the following examples of counterintuitive evidence based on Productivity Commission reviews:

- immigration and higher birth rates have little impact on the ageing population
- the presumption that road use is subsidised relative to rail is not borne out by the facts
- the objective of zero solid waste is not only costly, but also environmentally unsound
- bidding wars for investment and major events by state governments generally constitute not only a negative sum game nationally, but also often a zero sum game for the winning state
- tax concessions for research and development (R&D) do not encourage new research
- binary views as to whether child care is good or bad are both wrong
- reducing class sizes has little empirical support, while the importance of teacher performance and the link to pecuniary incentives are neglected although backed by strong evidence.

Why this occurs is of course a matter of debate, but Australian Public Service Commissioner, Lynelle Briggs, also writing in *Challenges of Evidence-Based Policy-Making*, provided a thoughtful view:

> In the real world, policy is developed in a fluid environment, is subject to competing vested and political interests, and can be driven by pressure to act quickly to solve headline-grabbing problems. Ideally, we need systems that are informed by evidence at each stage of policy development, from when an issue is first identified, to the development of the most appropriate response, and subsequent evaluation of its effectiveness. (Banks 2009)

Governments often announce funding in the language of results rather than effort. This has the effect of politically banking gains that are yet to achieved—for example, a claim that $x made available to a program will deliver specific results for every client in the program over the project period. One never hears, for instance, an announcement that $x will likely have an effect on half a given treatment cohort with effects lasting an average of six months before program effects begin to degrade. Even more rarely are these claims evidenced by reference to high-quality trials; more often their credentials are borrowed from their provider. To the extent that reputable charities are the program deliverers, there is some comfort that expertise and effort will be brought to bear. But having spent time on the bidding side in these situations, I am aware of how often genuine best-evidence practice is not within the budget of the contract being sought.

This makes it very difficult for providers, public servants and their political masters to let the results speak for themselves over time. Programs that perform poorly may be quietly defunded, but even if this is possible (which it often is not) results cannot inform future spending if they are not reported transparently due to fear of contradicting previous announcements about expected results. Reporting is also not likely to be frank if parties cannot openly say that failure to achieve results will lead to changes over the program period. Providers are given a do-or-die responsibility with little room to innovate over the life of the contract. The lack of control added to unreasonable expectations leaves many providers seeing evaluation as a sword of Damocles.

A similar position is advanced by Kerry Schott in her final report for the NSW Commission of Audit (2012), which advised the government that it had not placed sufficient emphasis on evaluating the programs it funds. 'To the degree that program evaluations occur at present, they are incorrectly viewed as a potential threat to the continuance of programs and funding' (NSW Commission of Audit 2012). The report advised that evaluation was hampered by:

- a lack of performance information, cost, goals and objectives, linkages and program history
- evaluations being done by the agency and people involved in running the program
- insufficient resources being devoted to program evaluations
- the results of program evaluations being undermined by vested and sectoral interests that inevitably develop in support of programs.

All of these factors conspire against the development of an evidence base. This means that each time an additional dollar is made available to solve a given problem, we know less than we should about how to spend it.

With public sector reform increasingly focused on commissioning and other forms of active purchasing, this lack of an evidence base means there is too little to purchase 'off the shelf'. As policymakers shift to a preference for integrated social services, there is a growing requirement to identify multidimensional models of care and new kinds of contracts with which to purchase them. Given the need to innovate, these contracting models will need to support co-design through experimentation, review and adaptation. In the United Kingdom (ACEVO 2015) and New Zealand (New Zealand Treasury 2014), one model being used to develop new social service products is alliance contracting.

How can alliances solve the evidence deficit?

The social sector cannot easily provide better programs than they currently do because too often the cost per client they are allocated through government tenders is insufficient to apply best practice. It is almost always insufficient to undertake evaluation, review and reflection either during or after program delivery. The current approach of sporadically reviewing results post hoc means that funders do not know until all of the money is spent whether the money was spent well. More importantly, clients who underwent the program cannot benefit from insights delivered after the program has ended.

The private sector can scale up and deploy models with a strong evidence base under social benefit bonds (SBBs) or similar reward-based payments where they assume a delivery risk. The private sector is unlikely to take on the additional risk of product R&D without an obvious pipeline of profitable work to be won at a scale sufficient to pay back their investment. This may change, but probably not soon. If the private sector was capable and incentivised to develop effective intervention methodologies, there would be important questions as to intellectual property rights. While there are legitimate foreseeable arguments that creating property rights could spur innovation in the field, the prudent path, at least in the short term, favours creating a public domain evidence base with open-source policy prescriptions. In the testing phase, the high transaction costs, including lawyers and financial advisers, associated with SBB-style products are unlikely to represent good value for small experimental projects with a high risk profile.

Academics and consultants have a role to play but they are essentially evaluation service providers who are not in a position to change the total number of opportunities to perform evaluations. They are also disconnected from the service delivery, which means their insights are unlikely to support methodological improvement over the life of the project.

Traditional contracting cannot deliver this outcome because the product and therefore the price may need to change over time as results inform adaptations. Contracting specifications often have the perverse outcome of reducing service quality by acting as a barrier to innovation. When governments spend large sums quickly under input or even output-based contracts they are sentencing future service users and providers to nothing better than the best thinking available when the contract was signed. It would be better for payers and providers to be frank about the limits of current evidence and agree to contracts that allow them to work in collaboration to test, refine and redeploy continuously improving service methodologies.

What is needed is an approach to spending money on social programs that procures R&D in a scientific manner that can be shared as public domain knowledge to improve social policy through better evidence. Contracting must balance effort and reward, but, more importantly, must support an agile approach to program deployment based on open collaboration between purchaser, provider and client.

Happily, such a model has been used in the infrastructure sector for many years and is being adapted for use in the social sector. Alliance contracting is an arrangement in which parties work cooperatively, sharing risk and reward. The payer and the provider work as a single governance team to deliver the results the purchaser wants and which merit the provider being paid an agreed rate of return.

How do alliances differ from standard contracts?

Fundamentally, alliances are built to resolve uncertainty. They are a model designed for situations where neither the payer nor the provider can be sure what problems they will have to address to reach their goal. What they do know are the skills required, what kind of experience will help and what a fair rate of return should be if the private partner does a good job.

The Commonwealth Department of Infrastructure and Regional Development's *National Alliance Contracting Guidelines: Policy Principles* sets out the following rules for alliance contracts:

- The project has risks that cannot be adequately defined or measured in the business case or prior to tendering.
- The cost of transferring project risks to the contractor is prohibitive.
- The project needs to start as early as possible before the risks can be fully identified and/or project scope can be finalised, and the project client (as well as the project investor) is prepared to take the commercial risk of a sub-optimal price outcome.
- The client has superior knowledge, skills, preference and capacity to influence or participate in the development and delivery of the project, including for example, in the development of the design solution and construction method.
- Where taking a collective approach to assessing and managing project risks will produce, in special and rare circumstances, a better outcome than contracted allocation risk. (DIRD 2015)

The social policy sector has many challenges that meet the above criteria of requiring immediate action to be taken in an area where the risks cannot be fully identified and where people outside government have superior knowledge, skills and capacity. There are always too many clients who need immediate help to allow services to stop delivery while we define more perfect treatments. Purchasers cannot wait for perfect models to be available for purchase off the shelf. A collaborative contract is needed to learn while doing and share the risks associated with innovation.

There are currently too many knowledge gaps to write effective contracts for many kinds of social service provision. While an increasing number of analysts and advocates are excellent at benefit analysis, costs present a far trickier problem. This is because while we have a good understanding of the impacts of disadvantage, exclusion and other ills on clients and the community, we have less clarity about the costs of effective solutions. This is usually because we do not know enough about the therapeutic models that work effectively.

For instance, we may know that a homeless person needs case management, housing services, health care and a brokerage budget; we cannot say as easily how many hours of which practitioner's time are required in what balance between the various services.

We may know that a homeless teenager needs housing, physiotherapy, health services and re-engagement with school and family; we do not know how many hours of caseworker time are needed, what qualifications the caseworker needs to be most effective and therefore their hourly rate, which of the school re-entry programs represents value for money within our teen's case management budget or how many hours a week of visits to their emergency housing are required.

This may sound too hard to fix but some programs do go into this level of detail. Defined methodologies such as 'multidimensional treatment foster care' are specific about the level of training for staff, the composition of multispecialty teams, the duration of treatment and other elements. There is a range of treatment methodologies that have rigorously defined delivery systems and which are licensed by their developers to ensure fidelity to their treatment model. Interestingly, a common feature of such refined treatments is that they are substantially more expensive than more commonly contracted services.

What government gets in return for the extra cash is a greater certainty of likely success rates. The Washington State Institute for Public Policy's cost–benefit comparator tables suggest that these defined methods regularly outperform generic service contracts (WSIPP 2015).

Without knowing which unit cost achieves which likely success rate, the purchaser cannot enter into a contract with genuine confidence. Thinking about this from a market design point of view, we can see that for some services there is not enough information in the marketplace to allow best-value contracts to be struck.

One way of thinking about this is to start with the different types of problem definition, which fall broadly into three groups.

1. **Preventing future expense:** For example, integrated health management for sufferers of chronic illness prevents avoidable hospital admissions. Effective family therapy prevents foster care costs. Housing for the homeless can avoid substantial justice system and health costs. There is information available about direct costs to public agencies such as health and justice, as well as plenty of good estimates by the Productivity Commission, among others, regarding lifetime costs of income losses, welfare transfers, tax losses and gross domestic product (GDP) losses due to lower participation and productivity.

2. **Preventing unconscionable harms:** In some cases, solving a problem is not cost effective but we have a moral duty to do it anyway. For example, prison is in some cases a relatively less expensive 'service' cost for some people with chronic comorbidity and disadvantage challenges compared with the cost of social housing, mental health services, drug treatment, employment assistance and casework, that might be required to successfully re-engage the person with the community. Nonetheless, most people would agree that society cannot simply imprison the mentally ill and chronic reoffenders for fiscal reasons. We act in this case to reduce social harm.

3. **Preventing social exclusion:** There is a range of programs addressing challenges at the less acute end of the spectrum for which a clear cost–benefit case cannot easily be made, but which we nonetheless seek to deliver at good value to the taxpayer. These may include sports, arts and community grants that are generally desired by the population as contributors to social cohesion. The case for funding a free public opening night party for the Sydney Festival is not likely to stack up fiscally or economically, but it certainly makes a lot of people happy and adds to a sense of community and social well-being for those who attend. There are some economic benefits ascribed to arts events associated with tourism and recreational spending, but the returns on this 'investment' are not generally to taxpayers. It may never be possible to accurately assess the costs of social and cultural exclusion, but society has a strong moral view that a community should encourage social and cultural integration and exchange.

In each case, we have to determine a good-value price for the 'treatment' based on a slightly different approach to our analysis.

- **Treatments to prevent expense** can be assessed with traditional cost–benefit analysis (CBA). The 'treatment' should ideally work for a large enough number of the treated group and the 'cure' should persist long enough to cover the period in which costs would have been incurred. If this happens, any price less than the prevented expense represents value for money. Transaction costs come in to play but can be incorporated into the efficient price.

- **Treatments to prevent harm**, such as prisoner rehabilitation programs, can also be assessed using CBA, to compare relative value *with each other* rather than to determine a net positive CBA. It bears repeating that a positive or negative CBA should not determine whether something is funded. It merely serves to inform choices about which approach will deliver better value. Much effort can be wasted pursuing strategies to get to the magic number greater than one when all we really need to know is the relative performance of different programs solving a similar problem.

- **Treatments to prevent exclusion** have increasingly been the subject of efforts to design value assessment tools. There are plenty but they are largely sets of qualitative measures. Similar to the above argument about net value, too much time is spent trying to value expenditure on things such as art to reach a magic number that unlocks formal economic permission to proceed. It would be simpler to focus on getting a good unit price for whatever activities are desired.

The right contract model for a program depends on which kind of prevention we are doing and what kind of treatment is involved.

The kinds of treatment fall roughly into three groups.

1. **Treatments:** These are the most robust methods with clear program logic and defined delivery methodologies. Examples include functional family therapy, drug courts and parent–child interaction therapy. Treatments:
   - can be compared with a control
   - outputs and outcomes are predictable
   - unit costs are clear
   - can be purchased competitively
   - can be funded on pay by results
   - can be funded through social bonds.

2. **Services:** These include community food services, job placement, respite care, social and community housing, arts and sports services. The advantage of assessing services is that unit costs such as wages, capital, administration overheads and brokerage fees are relatively constant and transparent.

3. **Approaches:** These are evidence-based professional practices such as case management and mediation, which can be purchased but with less certainty about the 'dosage' strength and duration required to gain a desired result. However:
   - results cannot be predicted with certainty
   - scalability is unknown
   - replicability in new jurisdictions is unknown
   - metrics are often qualitative
   - efficient price is not known
   - effective price could be higher than funded.

Many of our social services are more like approaches than treatments. That is often not the fault of the providers. As discussed above, purchasers are not going to market with opportunities that allow for the use, testing or development of these more intensive service models. In the case of approaches, purchasers have a strong interest in helping the provider perfect their method and better understand their costs. An alliance model allows the parties to operationalise evidence-based approaches within a shared risk framework to test and refine therapeutic interventions. Once refined, both will better understand and predict likely outcomes and reasonable prices.

How it might work

The alliance model entails three phases of activity, described below:

Hypothesis testing phase

- Consult on proposed method with payer, provider, clients and stakeholders.
- Roll out as agreed.
- Monitor inputs, outputs, outcomes and impacts.
- Review and refine treatment method as often as required to meet client needs within budget.
- Assess whether current budget envelopes are reasonable.

Definition phase

- Document the cohort, their needs and reasonable service commitments.
- Agree on unit costs and measurement approach.
- Document the treatment methodology.
- Revise contracts to reflect revised costs and outcomes.

Performance management phase

- Service provider managed for results by funder.
- Robustness-tested regarding unit costs, results and reporting.
- Value-for-money testing becomes possible.
- Pay for results becomes possible.
- Reports and evaluations can be shared to add to the stock of evidence.

Importantly in this context, changes made due to initial approaches falling short of expectations can be shared without putting the parties into an adversarial contract-remedy scenario. The adversarial nature of standard contracting undermines honesty between the parties and with the wider community of practice. In a project where both parties are learning and will make mistakes, it is vital that a positive attitude to change is a shared legal responsibility.

How it has worked: The Sea Cliff Bridge

The beautiful Sea Cliff Bridge connects Coalcliff and Clifton, just north of Wollongong in New South Wales. It replaced an old road that ran along the cliff and was increasingly subject to rockfall. The road replacement was urgent and the task complex. Instead of competitively tendering, the Roads and Traffic Authority entered into an alliance with multiple partners including Laing O'Rourke.

The geography is challenging: there are five distinct geotechnical domains along the cliff line. The area was subject to multiple environmental, community and Indigenous heritage complexities. Twenty-six different options were considered with the final construction requiring two bridges: the first composed of five spans requiring four piers and a second multiple-span bridge built on a continuous curve to bypass the middle headland. The bridge contains an electric current to prevent sea spray deterioration. The bridge was completed for $52 million instead of the forecast $48 million but was delivered on time, giving the community back their connections with the least possible disruptions.

All parties praised the alliance model as contributing to the pace and professionalism but also the ingenuity of the project, which delivered innovations in health and safety, project management, community engagement and technical and construction challenges. The project won a slew of awards, including the 2006 Austroads Bridge Conference Award for large structures, the 2006 Case Earth Awards NSW, the International Quality & Productivity Centre (IQPC) Alliance Contracting Excellence (ACE) Awards and the 2006 Engineers Australia Engineering Sydney Division Award.

The project was complex, involved multiple constraints and stakeholders and was time critical and highly politically sensitive because the original road was closed in the lead-up to an election in a marginal seat. The alliance model gave the parties a contractual structure to be innovative, collaborative and responsive to the community. These features are common in social services and the alliance model can bring similar benefits to addressing them.

Certainly some alliances fail to deliver on expectations. The Commonwealth Department of Defence received poor assessments, including from its own minister, regarding the performance of its Air Warfare Destroyer alliance with Raytheon. Notwithstanding this persistently cited example of failure, the total value of alliance projects in the road, rail and water sectors in Australia from 2004 to 2009 was $32 billion (Department of Treasury and Finance 2009), which suggests many infrastructure purchasers are happier than the Defence Department with the model.

It is worth noting in this context that a joint guidance paper authored by representatives of the treasury departments of Western Australia, Queensland, New South Wales, Victoria and the federal government suggests there are pitfalls to be avoided in alliances including the temptation to cede thought leadership to the non-governmental partner (Department of Treasury and Finance 2014). A previous study, by Melbourne University and Evans and Peck and commissioned by the Victorian Treasury, found that 'there is a possible imbalance in the value proposition for alliancing' (Department of Treasury and Finance 2009: 9). While the model is theoretically sound, active management for value on the part of government is clearly required.

This is arguably a further benefit of the model. While competitive tendering allows government to notionally pass its responsibility to a third party, alliances require ongoing engagement and assertive pursuit of value and results by the government payer.

Maintaining the benefits of competition under alliance contracting

A common concern with alliance contracts is that they provide less certainty about funding requirements. Alliances arguably destroy the key advantage of contracts: risk transfer. Because the contracts are signed before unit costs are understood, it is difficult for finance departments to budget with certainty. However, the certainty of expenditure under any contract that is poorly understood can only be an illusion. If government contracts service X to provide Y clients with employment support at $Z per client, but it really costs Z+$10, the program will simply underperform.

This is arguably what happens much of the time. Having consulted for the non-governmental organisation (NGO) sector, this author is aware of many large NGOs that bid to win despite knowing the per capita costs are insufficient to undertake best-practice work. Their position is understandable; the work is only available at the inadequate price so they do the best they can. However, no one benefits from maintaining the illusion that inadequate funds can achieve an agreed outcome with certainty. In these cases, the public purchaser is buying activity and best efforts but is not really transferring risk because, ultimately, if the social problem persists, government will remain the party responsible for trying once again to fix it.

Having said that, it is important to maintain where possible the healthy disciplines associated with competitive tendering. This can be achieved within an alliance framework. Tendering can be used for determining alliance partners, and contract review rights can be used to determine whether to proceed after milestones such as determination of unit costs. Staying within budget is possible if non–price variables are well understood and not ruled out too early as factors that can change. In particular, the number of clients who can be assisted should not be fixed before unit costs, effect sizes and persistence rates are understood. If the number of clients to be assisted must remain fixed then the nature of the service has to be open to change. Differential treatment intensity is already effectively a feature of current contracts management as resources are balanced across a cohort rather than equally divided.

The need for such learning systems is growing

The need for contracting models that support innovation and risk sharing will likely grow. The Commonwealth Government's primary health reforms are focused on integrated care services, which Australia's health market does not currently offer at scale. In mental health, it is increasingly clear that integrated housing, employment, health and social services will need to be developed. Government will need to collaborate with providers to get these new services for clients.

The transition from volume-based contracting to value-based contracting and commissioning will require adaptive models that allow all parties to innovate services. If government is to develop 'choice-based markets', as recommended by the National Commission of Audit (NCOA 2014), or social purpose capital markets and social enterprises, as recommended by the McClure report, *A New System for Better Employment and Social Outcomes* (DSS 2015), government will need to work with its partners to innovate current models of care contracting. The present system is too opaque for either customers or investors to drive change.

Alliances offer an opportunity to develop the new treatments we need in an open-book partnership that supports transparency and grows the knowledge base for policymakers and providers. Most importantly, alliance models provide a mechanism to build better services for clients with their active collaboration.

References

ACEVO. 2015. *Alliance Contracting: Building New Collaborations to Deliver Better Healthcare*. Association of Chief Executives of Voluntary Organisations, London. Available: www.acevo.org.uk/sites/default/files/ACEVO%20alliance%20contracting%20report%202014_final-print-friendly-2.pdf (accessed 29 June 2016).

Banks, G. 2009. *Challenges of Evidence-Based Policy-Making*. Canberra: Australian Public Service Commission.

Brittain, K., A. Singh and M. Winter. 2014. *Alliance Contracting: Building new collaborations to deliver better healthcare*. London: Association of Chief Executives of Voluntary Organisations. Available from: acevo.org.uk/sites/default/files/ACEVO%20alliance%20contracting%20report%202015%20web-2.pdf (accessed 22 April 2016).

Department of Infrastructure and Regional Development (DIRD). 2015. *National Alliance Contracting Guidelines: Policy principles*. September. Canberra: Australian Government.

Department of Social Services (DSS). 2015. *A New System for Better Employment and Social Outcomes: Final report of the Reference Group on Welfare Reform*. Canberra: Australian Government.

Department of Treasury and Finance. 2009. *In Pursuit of Additional Value: A benchmarking study into alliancing in the Australian public sector*. Melbourne: Victorian Government.

Department of Treasury and Finance. 2014. *Alliance and Traditional Contracting*. Melbourne: Victorian Government.

National Commission of Audit (NCOA). 2014. *Towards Responsible Government: Appendix to the report of the National Commission of Audit. Volume 2*. Canberra: NCOA.

New Zealand Treasury. 2014. Briefings to incoming ministers. Information Release, November 2014, Updated May 2015 and August 2015. New Zealand Government, Wellington.

NSW Commission of Audit. 2012. *Government expenditure*. Final Report, 4 May. NSW Treasury, Sydney.

Washington State Institute for Public Policy (WSIPP). 2015. *Benefit–Cost Results*. Olympia, Wa.: WSIPP. Available from: wsipp.wa.gov/BenefitCost (accessed April 2016).

Expanding the Role of Cooperative and Mutual Enterprises in Delivering Public Services: Disrupting the status quo

Melina Morrison and Cliff Mills

Introduction

One could argue that many policy initiatives are based on a flawed (even arrogant) assumption—namely, that *we* can somehow *work out how to change things* by *getting people and institutions to do things differently*; where:

1. 'we' are those who consider that we have a duty, responsibility and right (government, important people in business, academia and civil society) to try to change things

2. 'working out how to change things' is based on a post-Enlightenment rationalist (we *can*), somewhat imperialist (*we* need to), but also modern nation-state (we *must*) way of thinking

3. 'getting people and institutions to do things differently' involves prescriptively *making things happen* to solve the problems that *we* have identified.

A counter narrative might start like this: 'Who do we think "we" are, and who are "they"?'

Should we reflect on whether we have the ability, the authority/ legitimacy and justification to intervene? And, might *they* have something to say, a part to play and possibly a different suggestion?

This is a brutal caricature of contemporary policymaking, but it fairly describes the experience of the mutual and cooperative sector in Australia.

Explaining mutuality

Mutuality has its origins in collective self-help: people doing things for themselves, their families and their communities because there is no one else to do it for them. Cooperatives were set up because there was a market failure in the availability of basic food and provisions (the private sector inflating goods prices, selling contaminated food and cheating on measures). Agricultural cooperatives were set up when farmers needed to collaborate to capture more value from the supply chain for the farm gate. Friendly societies and mutual insurance were established when there was no access to support in times of personal misfortune; and building societies were created when individuals aspired to provide for their own housing but could not do so (save by accident of birth) because there were no financial services available to them.

Because it is an alternative approach—alternative to private business, philanthropy and government—the whole dynamic, motivation, process, culture and governance of mutuality differs quite markedly from all of these. So, introducing the idea of mutuality and cooperation into this discussion about cross-sector working poses a challenge at the very least.

'Self-help' and mutuality occur because of something within each of us, which can emerge when we meet up with like-minded or similarly motivated people. Self-help emerges; you cannot do it to people.

This profound point has not been understood by many, including politicians, public servants and an army of professionals advisers who have been very busy doing something called 'mutualisation' to create 'public sector mutuals'. This is true even in the United Kingdom, where the mutual sector has been on this journey for the past 15 years or more.

Those of us who spend our working lives in the cooperative and mutual sector view the possibility of some form of mutual ownership of public services with huge excitement. We devote our energies to this approach because we believe there is something transformative and 'right' about ordinary people owning and influencing their essential services, and about essential services being run for community or public benefit, rather than for the private benefit of investors.

We also know that in both the United Kingdom and Australia, the origins of public services—and of their ethos of providing for the vulnerable, the disadvantaged and the marginalised (universality, fairness and so on)—were not legal statutes, but communities and individuals. Before the state stepped in in the mid-twentieth century, there was already a rich tapestry of services provided by mutual (self-help) and philanthropic organisations, which individuals and communities were providing. The state took over because these services were too good and too valuable to be available just on a patchwork basis; states like ours wanted them to be universal.

So those of us from a mutual and cooperative background are excited to think that the ideas and principles that have survived in our current organisational types could become mainstream again. We also know that you cannot create mutuals from the top down, by government diktat or by simply commissioning private sector professionals who have no actual experience of mutuality to somehow convert existing public organisations into something different.

Indeed, there are many in the United Kingdom who believe that the so-called process of mutualisation or the creation of 'public service mutuals' has simply been a mask for privatisation, because the objective is to reduce the number of individuals on the state's payroll, and mutualisation is politically much more acceptable than privatisation (Gosling 2014). It could be argued that some of what the Community and Public Sector Union (CPSU) says about the UK experience in its submission to the recent inquiry into cooperative, mutual and member-based firms is broadly correct (Senate Standing Committees on Economics 2015).

There is ideology and spin—on both sides—and this has led to some missed opportunities and mistakes. Some really good things have happened in the United Kingdom recently, but we do not want to make those 'mistakes' that have undermined the successes, and we have the knowledge and opportunity to make sure that we do not.

Asking the right question

If we are interested in mutual and cooperative ideas playing some part in the future of public services, we need to make sure we ask the right questions, before thinking about the answers.

The first question is not 'what legal structures could we use'. Legal structures do not create new types of organisations; people do. We need to address the question of what legal structure is used, but much later. First, we need to work out what we are aiming to do. Form follows function.

Nor should the question be: 'how do we turn our public services into public service mutuals?' Mutuality is not a magic wand or panacea. If income does not exceed expenditure, packaging a service up as mutual will not make it sustainable—nor will shoehorning a service into a mutual ownership structure somehow turn it into an actual mutual. Transactions processed by professionals do not create mutuals; people do.

If we want 'different' public services—where those using and those providing the services have a more engaged relationship and role in deciding how those services are provided and how they should evolve; where those services are economically sustainable with sound financial management, but where optimising the service for the benefit of the public is the fundamental purpose, not maximising profitability for investors—if we would like to see real change, not just the rearrangement of deckchairs, we need to realise that leaders and organisations like us do not make it happen. Ordinary people do— by changing the way they behave.

If there are bold people who are willing to be pioneers in doing things differently, if workers and trade unions are willing to make common cause with users and citizens in communities and if there is appropriate leadership (Mills and Yeoman 2013) available to take these people with them, we might be able to help them solve some problems. We can share mutual ideas that have worked before and support them in developing the essentials of mutuality such as establishing a membership, building engagement and involvement and learning how to manage and govern differently. Perhaps we can sit alongside them as they develop their own scaffolding to support their new vision—an ownership and governance structure (the legal bits)—which draws on what others have been doing, both two centuries ago and in this new millennium.

From the English experience (and it is English rather than UK; Scotland and Wales are on similar journeys, but via different routes), the first question is: *What are the services where those involved in providing them want to deliver differently and want to work more closely with users and citizens?*

And then: *Can mutual and cooperative principles help to inform a new vision for the next stage of development of those services?*

That might seem to be a strange place to start, but the reason is this: the ownership and governance models of public services are not the only things due for an update; rather, the way we plan and deliver those services needs to be re-examined, because it is no longer working as well as it could and, it is argued, it cannot continue to be funded on the current basis. Simply changing ownership and governance will not solve the problem. This, and the emergence of what is usually thought of as the 'public sector', needs to be explained further.

The postwar settlement

The publication of the Beveridge report in 1942 was a watershed moment for the United Kingdom and other states focused on the emerging role of what was to become the modern welfare state. It was in the postwar settlement based on Beveridge that the UK National Health Service (NHS) was born and a range of other services established as public services provided by the state and funded by central taxation. But public services, and their underlying ethos, were not created by statute. In short, the postwar settlement was the result of decades of development, thought and planning, because there was widespread recognition that the huge amount of existing services provided through self-help and philanthropy needed to be universally available, and the state was the best mechanism to achieve this.

In Australia, as observed by Alex McDermott in his history of Australian Unity (2015: 86), Robert Menzies freely conceded in his 1942 'forgotten people' radio broadcasts that after the war 'the functions of the State will be much more than merely keeping the ring within which the competitors will fight'. Our social and industrial obligations would be increased.

In the second half of the nineteenth century, Australians pioneered mutuals and friendly societies across the six colonies. Found in every community, these institutions were voluntary and self-regulating. By the eve of World War I, about 400,000 friendly society members helped to fund benefits for more than one million Australians (Andrews 2014). Self-help and philanthropy were the forerunners of the modern welfare state.

The problem today for many countries is that the state-based and tax-funded model has become economically unsustainable, due to demographic factors and spiralling demands on service provision at a time when many states are experiencing economic crises. But there is another fundamental cause of the current lack of sustainability and this is the whole approach to 'service delivery'.

Public services were born at a time when people did not live as long as they do today, when medical science was in its infancy and when people largely expected to have to provide for themselves. The decision by states to take on responsibility for providing a range of essential services to its citizens occurred at the end of World War II. Following a military campaign waged successfully through command and control and central coordination, the establishment adopted a similar organisational model to deliver public services to and for citizens.

Over the following decades, the introduction of performance management techniques from commercial manufacturing, of other market-based approaches, of new public management and of competitive tendering did not change the 'done-to' binary model of service delivery; however, it served to build a narrative that public servants and public services were (allegedly) inefficient, unaccountable and unimaginative, and it was used to drive arguments for privatisation and the commodification of services that are anything but commodities.

The United Kingdom now has examples of electronically tagged care workers tied to 15-minute time slots to 'deliver care' within a commercial framework seeking to maximise profits for investors.

Services that once were provided by and within communities have become something aimed at generating economic growth, rather than caring for people. Changing the ownership and governance structure of such commoditised services will not solve the issues. The whole approach to service delivery (now we have only binary language from the perspective of 'the provider') needs to be rethought, reimagined and redesigned to suit a different world.

We need a public *health* service not a public repair service, which is accessed only whenever our health is broken. We need to take responsibility as citizens for living healthier lives on the advice of health professionals, making better use of the money available for repairs. Service users and care professionals need to work together cooperatively to optimise health and well-being (Mills and Swarbrick 2014).

This is the starting point for modern mutual innovation: envisaging wholly new relationships as a context for more enlightened services, supported by a modern business and organisational model. There will be different approaches in different sectors and services, reflecting fundamental differences in the nature of those services, the context in which they are made available, the balance of relationships between those involved and many other key factors. But the common thread is always the people involved at the grassroots, how those people are connected to the service and how, by enabling different and new human relationships between those people, something more collaborative, more efficient and more focused on what is best for those people and their families and communities can emerge.

Crucially, those involved at the grassroots must include workers (and their unions). Their involvement and participation in developing a new vision is essential. Not only are workers also users themselves in another context; without appropriate terms and conditions and a fulfilling role that is fair to them as well as to citizens and users, any solution will be second best. Historically, there is much shared heritage between cooperatives and unions, and they need to make common cause again today in the public interest (Co-operative Heritage Trust 2016).

Working out a radically new approach requires a disruption to the historical way of seeing things, and a significant transfer of power. An example of such disruption is the National Disability Insurance Scheme—a big step towards giving users real power and choice. But will this alone disrupt the current marketplace of commoditised provision and turn it into something better? Will it help those trying to make a living as professional carers? Perhaps the concept of personalised budgets needs to go a step further. Individuals making individual choices can be relatively powerless; some do not necessarily find it helpful or advantageous, and some even find it stressful.

Individuals making choices collectively, however—collaborating for mutual support, maybe pooling budgets and seeking together to meet their own needs and the needs of others affected—is a transformative idea. A cooperative of personal budget holders, with a voice for family and friends, professional carers and local citizens? That would be disruptive.

This is the sort of new thinking needed to face today's challenges. A review of Australia's historical contribution to new thinking about the role of community, the role of the modern state and the role of individuals working collectively (please read McDermott 2015; it will inspire you) tells us that it is in our history, our heritage and our DNA to be pioneers and explore new thinking.

The English experience

Without wanting to be downbeat about what is going on elsewhere— because some of it is very good—here are some of the headline points from a review of what has been happening in England in relation to the mutualisation agenda.

Use of language

The word 'mutual' has been devalued, many people have been confused and misled and the historical mutual and cooperative sector has had its reputation tarnished.

For example, the Cabinet Office (2015) says: 'Although the [mutual] sector has varying definitions, a public service mutual has three key characteristics: An organisation that has spun out of the public sector … and continues to deliver public services … and involves a high degree of employee control.'

This reveals a limited understanding of mutuality. As you will see from our White Paper (BCCM 2014: 4), our definition is rather more demanding: 'an organisation which wholly or in part delivers public services through a co-operative or mutual governance structure, whereby members of the organisation are able to be involved in decision-making, and benefit from its activities, including benefits emanating from the reinvestment of surpluses.'

There has also been constant use in the United Kingdom of the phrase 'employer-owned/led mutuals' without a deeper understanding of the term and its inappropriateness.

Language is important. If it has the effect of misleading users, workers, communities and funders of services, disappointment will follow. Mutuals are based on trust and trusting personal relationships. Trust cannot be built up without clear and honest language—from the first conversation.

'Mutualisation'

As explained above, mutuality emerged from within communities as a self-help response to hardship. Communities, not consultants, public servants and governments, create mutuals.

The UK Cabinet Office approach has led to a number of professional firms with no experience or understanding of mutuality entering the business of 'creating' mutuals. Many have adapted the traditional consultancy and transactional approach used in privatisation (and in private sector sales and acquisitions) and then labelled the process 'mutualisation'.

This creates the wrong impression of what is being established, and the short time scales involved based on electoral cycles and accounting years can make it very difficult to achieve something worthwhile from a mutual perspective, at times frustrating the sincere attempts by those involved to do something 'mutual'.

The interesting stuff

Some good and interesting things, however, are happening. There have been some pioneering individuals and organisations who have been captivated by what a mutual or cooperative approach could do for their services, and who have been passionate about creating the opportunity for their service users and employees to play a major role in re-establishing a bottom-up approach focused on what is best for those in need of services and those involved in providing them.

We have some great examples of such initiatives in Australia, including the consumer-owned medical practice business, National Health Co-operative, which was established in the Australian Capital Territory in 2010, and Co-operative Home Care, a non-residential, home care agency in Sydney that is owned by its employees, which was set up in 2012 (BCCM 2014).

What are the leading examples of this in the past few years in the United Kingdom and how have they been successful?

How?

Having said that mutuals cannot be created from the top down and that they emerge from communities, how can opportunities be captured, or even created, to enable new member-owned enterprises to emerge from public services?

Leadership

The first requirement is for visionary leadership within a service that instinctively or with some encouragement understands the possibilities. No previous experience of mutuality is needed, just an open mind, a willingness to learn and courage.

A crucial element of that visionary leadership is a willingness to give away power. For many people and institutions, there is an instinct to hoard power and continue to seek to retain control even while expressly using the language of empowerment and localism. Within traditional mutual organisations, power starts from the membership, who, through some democratic and constitutional process, delegate most of that power to elected representatives and appointed executives. Changing to being member owned and controlled involves giving up a certain amount of power.

This is unlikely to happen without the existence of significant trust, which itself takes time and is based on personal relationships. Not only does the leadership need to have built up trust, it also needs to be willing to take risks based on that trust, to adopt a different leadership style and to take part in significant cultural change.

Unlike more traditional and hierarchical forms of management and governance, developing a user and worker-based sense of ownership requires a collaborative, collegiate approach to leadership, rather than the more traditional heroic 'alpha male' style. The grassroots membership is unlikely to put its efforts into making the whole venture more efficient and more successful and collectively 'taking ownership' unless it feels that it is sharing in something worthwhile, where its voice is heard and respected and where there is a sense of shared success.

Type of service

The second requirement is for an understanding of whether and, if so, how a cooperative approach to service delivery can substantially contribute to a better, more appropriate and relevant way of providing/accessing that service. Mutuality is not a panacea or a magic wand, but it may have something significant to offer where the real engagement and participation of users, employees and citizens will transform a service from a binary, done-to approach to something much more dynamic and productive, to reduce costs or generate additional income or produce other substantial benefits and savings.

This may be the case where there is a significant involvement of unpaid support, volunteers or individuals giving their time and skills with no expectation of financial reward—for example, some types of care, working with young people, leisure services and so on. Whether their motivation for this is based on generosity of spirit, faith, a passion for something, lack of fulfilment elsewhere or simply boredom, where their organised contribution and engagement can make a difference to economic viability, some form of mutual ownership may provide a stabilising mechanism and an appropriate basis for such relationships.

Funding and process

In the United Kingdom, there are extensive European regulations governing the spending of public money and essentially requiring the promotion of competition. This can make it difficult if not impossible for a mutual approach to emerge. If a public body is required to put out to public tender a service it is currently providing in-house, it is virtually impossible for the in-house team to construct a credible bid that has any chance of defeating the highly professional and competitive skills of large external private sector bidders.

A mechanism is needed to enable those individuals and teams of people currently operating within public ownership to emerge as part of a mutually based initiative to operate outside state ownership. Such an initiative is very challenging, requiring its own cultural change for people who are not used to operating in a commercial and competitive environment and who have to become responsible for both earning income and controlling expenditure. It takes some time to acquire the skills to do this, and they therefore need a three to five-year start-up period in which to prepare for fully independent, commercial operation.

The well-established concept of splitting commissioning from provision can often be a hindrance to the emergence of new mutual services. The commissioner/provider split is a mechanism for using competition between potential contracting parties to drive the best bargain for the public purse. As already mentioned, this leads to the commodification of services by breaking them into parcels of work that businesses can price, but which bears no relationship to what is needed in many areas of public service—namely, a personal relationship.

This means it might be easier to explore the possibility of mutual and cooperative ideas where there is no commissioner or commissioning arrangements. In the United Kingdom, this has occurred successfully in the context of social housing, where the structure of state support is via housing benefits allocated to individuals. In Australia, the growing availability of personalised budgets may create opportunities, but, where commissioning is a legal requirement, some 'work-around' is needed to enable a mutual approach to emerge.

Creating the environment

It is worth adding that governments can do a number of things to make it more likely that cooperative and mutual ideas will be considered. Legislation is one possibility, but it should be approached cautiously. A good example of this is in Wales, where recent legislation in health and social care requires the promotion of cooperatives and social enterprise in the provision of care and support.[1] This has been well received, but it remains to be seen if it is effective.

In England, legislation such as the *Localism Act* has created a series of rights, including the right to provide and the right to challenge. The *Social Value Act* has helped to raise awareness among public bodies, but more important from the point of view of cooperatives and mutuals is for the law establishing such organisations to be reviewed and modernised. This tends to happen every couple of decades for companies, but rarely if ever for mutuals.

Other positive legislative steps include things such as creating financial or fiscal advantages to encourage different types of businesses to emerge. Other legislative initiatives might focus on removing barriers or blockages. Sometimes statutory bodies can establish companies for certain purposes; this should be broadened to include mutual societies.

Most important is the removal of barriers to the emergence of self-help and cooperation, whether between individuals or corporate entities. Where competition law has the effect of inhibiting cooperation, this should be examined to check whether it is operating against the public interest.

A variety of other steps can be taken by governments to encourage the growth of mutuality, if they wish to do so (Mutuo 2010, 2015). The recommendations in the White Paper aim to promote, support

---

1   Available from: legislation.gov.uk/anaw/2014/4/pdfs/anaw_20140004_en.pdf (accessed 18 April 2016).

and create an enabling environment for the establishment of 'public service mutuals' (BCCM 2014: 21–27); however, their establishment is not the objective. The objective is to make citizens and communities much more engaged in the way services are available to citizens and to support the emergence of something that is a sustainable and better option than state-based or marketised public services.

Direct action taken by government to 'create mutuals' can become another mechanism for delivering some other government objective. Only people in communities can create and 'own' mutual organisations; today's challenge is how, through education, inspiration, support and guidance, people can be stimulated to take such steps.

The financial crises since 2007 have probably been the biggest generator of cooperative and mutual initiatives in more developed economies in recent years, and this suggests we should focus more on how to support people who wish to pursue self-help solutions than on seeking to impose our preferred solution.

What are the good examples in the United Kingdom?

It is in social housing that some of the most significant progress has been made. This dates back more than 10 years to the development of a tenant member-based model for housing for the Welsh Assembly Government (the Community Housing Mutual).[2] A number of housing providers have adopted this form in Wales (see, for example, Welsh Government 2014).

More recently and of greater interest has been the example of Rochdale Boroughwide Housing (RBH 2016), which developed a new tenant and employee-based model that went fully live in 2013 (see also Mutuo 2011b). A housing provider in South Wales is now adopting this approach and others are known to be interested in exploring it.

There have been significant developments in health care. A new member-based corporate model known as a 'public benefit corporation' (more popularly known as a foundation trust) was created by legislation

---

2   RCT Homes was the first to adopt this model, but not until 2007. See RCT Homes (2016).

in 2003, and now more than half of NHS trusts (hospitals, mental health trusts and other specialist health providers) have adopted this format. It is a step in the direction of mutuality, but only partially because the state retains substantial powers in relation to the price at which foundation trusts sell their services and the mechanism for procuring services. Many see it as a step towards complete privatisation, but that has not happened yet.

In community health services, however, more significant steps have been taken, with the establishment of a number of care providers which are mainly employee owned and controlled, although actually set up as community interest companies or community benefit societies. These include Care Plus Group, Anglia Community Services and Medway Community Services (Mutuo 2011a).

There have been some interesting developments in other areas, including youth services (Knowsley Youth Mutual 2016; CCfC 2013), library services (Explore York 2014; Powell 2015) and leisure and culture (Salford Community Leisure Limited 2016).

At a national level, the approach begun by the previous (UK) Coalition Government in relation to the potential transfer of Post Office out-of-state ownership to some kind of member-based model provides an illustration of an intelligent government-supported approach to the exploration of transition to mutual status by a national organisation (Co-operatives UK 2015).

References

Andrews, K. 2014. 'Foreword.' In *Public service mutuals: A third way for delivering public services in Australia*. White Paper, August, 3–4. Business Council of Co-operatives and Mutuals, Sydney.

Business Council of Co-operatives and Mutuals (BCCM). 2014. *Public service mutuals: A third way for delivering public services in Australia*. White Paper, August. Business Council of Co-operatives and Mutuals, Sydney.

Cabinet Office. 2015. *Mutuals Support Programme*. London: HMG. Available from: gov.uk/mutuals-support-programme (accessed 18 April 2016).

Circle Crew for Change Limited (CCfC). 2013. Website. CCfC, Consett, UK. Available from: circlecrewforchange.com/ (accessed 18 April 2016).

Co-operative Heritage Trust. 2016. *National Co-operative Archive*. Manchester: Co-operative Heritage Trust. Available from: archive. coop/hive/common (accessed 18 April 2016).

Co-operatives UK. 2015. *Mutual options for Post Office Ltd*. Report to the Department for Business Innovation and Skills. Co-operatives UK, Manchester. Available from: uk.coop/resources/mutual-options-post-office-ltd (accessed 18 April 2016).

Explore York. 2014. *Explore York Libraries and Archives*. York, UK: Explore York. Available from: exploreyork.org.uk/client/en_GB/ default (accessed 18 April 2016).

Gosling, P. 2014. 'When "mutualisation" of public services is actually privatisation.' *Co-operative News*, 26 August. Available from: thenews.coop/88845/news/general/when-mutualisation-of-public-services-is-actually-privatisation/ (accessed 18 April 2016).

Knowsley Youth Mutual. 2016. Website. Knowsley Youth Mutual, Liverpool. Available from: youthmutual.co.uk/ (accessed 18 April 2016).

McDermott, A. 2015. *Of No Personal Influence: How people of common enterprise unexpectedly shaped Australia*. Melbourne: Australian Unity.

Mills, C. and G. Swarbrick. 2014. 'Going with the grain: Organising for a purpose.' *London Journal of Primary Care (Abingdon)* 6(1): 3–7. Available from: tandfonline.com/doi/abs/10.1080/17571472.2 014.11493404 (accessed 18 April 2016).

Mills, C. and R. Yeoman. 2013. 'The civic reinvention.' *RSA Journal* (3): 32. Available from: thersa.org/discover/publications-and-articles/ journals/issue-3-2013/ (accessed 18 April 2016).

Mutuo. 2010. *The Mutuals Manifesto 2010*. London: Mutuo. Available from: mutuo.co.uk/mutuals-manifesto-launched/ (accessed 18 April 2016).

Mutuo. 2011a. *Community Health Services: Made mutual*. London: Mutuo. Available from: mutuo.co.uk/wp-content/uploads/2011/10/Community-Health-Services-Made-Mutual1.pdf (accessed 18 April 2016).

Mutuo. 2011b. *Social Housing: Made mutual*. London: Mutuo. Available from: mutuo.co.uk/wp-content/uploads/2011/10/Mutuals-social-housing1.pdf (accessed 18 April 2016).

Mutuo. 2015. *The Mutuals Manifesto 2015: Business for people*. London: Mutuo. Available from: mutuo.co.uk/news/business-for-people-the-mutuals-manifesto-2015/ (accessed 18 April 2016).

Powell, J. 2015. 'Suffolk Libraries celebrates its 3rd birthday.' *Suffolk Libraries Announcements*, 31 July. Available from: suffolklibraries. co.uk/announcements/suffolk-libraries-celebrates-its-3rd-birthday (accessed 18 April 2016).

RCT Homes. 2016. *More Than a Landlord*. Mid Glamorgan, Wales: RCT Homes. Available from: rcthomes.co.uk/main. cfm?type=MORETHANALANDLORD&object_id=2594 (accessed 18 April 2016).

Rochdale Boroughwide Housing Limited (RBH). 2016. Website. RBH, Manchester. Available from: rbh.org.uk/ (accessed 18 April 2016).

Salford Community Leisure Limited. 2016. Website. Salford, Manchester. Available from: salfordcommunityleisure.co.uk/ (accessed 18 April 2016).

Senate Standing Committees on Economics. 2015. *CPSU (PSU Group) submission to the Inquiry into Cooperative, Mutual and Member-Owned Firms*. July. Parliament House, Canberra.

Welsh Government. 2014. *Allowing Fully Mutual Housing Associations to Grant Assured Tenancies*. Cardiff: Welsh Government. Available from: chcymru.org.uk/en/about-us/useful-links/welsh-has-community-mutuals-and-other-members/ (accessed 18 April 2016).

The Boundaries of Budgets: Why should individuals make spending choices about their health and social care?

Catherine Needham[1]

Introduction

The postwar welfare states of many countries set up a division between cash transfers and state services, based on the assumption that citizens were the best purchasers of some services (for example, food and clothing) and that the state could purchase others more effectively on their behalf (for example, health and social care). However, a number of interrelated developments have increased the scope of services that are allocated in a cash form or via a notional budget—for example, personal budgets for care in England and the National Disability Insurance Scheme (NDIS) in Australia. As the NDIS is at an early stage of implementation, this chapter draws on the longer established English experience of personal budgets to consider the underlying

---

1   This chapter was first published as an article for the London-based think tank The Centre for Health and the Public Interest. It is reproduced here with kind permission from the centre.

rationale for transferring financial control down to the level of the individual. In particular, the chapter interrogates four claims that are made about individualised budgets:

1. They improve outcomes for individuals.
2. They extend choice and control to citizens, which they should have as a matter of right.
3. They make citizens more financially literate, contributing to service efficiency.
4. They correct system-level failings in public services.

Personal budgets in England

In England, initiatives to transfer resources to disabled people as direct payments began in the 1980s and were given legal endorsement in the *1996 Community Care (Direct Payments) Act*. Local governments, which have responsibility for social care, are now expected to move all eligible users on to a personal budget, which may be in the form of a direct payment to the individual, a managed budget (with funds remaining with the local authority) or a combination of the two. This is part of the broader personalisation agenda within social care to increase choice and control, improve prevention, enhance social capital and improve access to universal services (HMG 2007; Needham 2011). Personal budgets are now held by more than 50 per cent of older and disabled people, although take-up of direct payments has been much lower: 7 per cent of older people are in receipt of a direct payment, as are 25 per cent of people with learning disabilities (Age UK 2013).

The individualised funding agenda is not confined to social care. Personal health budgets have been trialled in the National Health Service (NHS) for people with a range of conditions such as diabetes and asthma and for users of mental health services (DH 2009; Forder et al. 2012). These budgets are now being rolled out nationally and localities are being encouraged to offer them to people with long-term conditions. Patients can choose to manage the money themselves, following new legislation on direct payments in health. Alternatively, they can work with health professionals or a third party to identify how to allocate a notional or managed budget. Budgets are also being introduced for the parents of children with disabilities and special educational needs, and are being proposed for a range of sectors such as adoption services and rough sleepers. Individualised budgets are also part of the Department of Work and Pensions' Right to Control initiative to make it easier for disabled people to access work (DWP 2008). The consolidation of a range of benefits, including housing benefits, into a monthly 'universal credit' paid directly to tenants (rather than the housing element going directly to the landlord) could arguably be seen as part of the same trend (Brown 2012). This builds on the earlier model of the Local Housing Allowance (LHA) through which eligible tenants in private rented accommodation receive their housing benefit directly. If tenants were able to secure a cheaper rent they could keep the additional money or they could top up the rent to access more expensive accommodation (DWP 2006).

The increasing disaggregation of budgets down to the individual level in the form of cash or a notional allocation has generated intense debate in the various sectors in which it has occurred. The most extensive debates to date have been within social care, where the policy is furthest advanced and where a set of recurring themes dominates the academic and practitioner literatures: do personal budgets turn care recipients into consumers or do they offer the means for people to become active citizens? Do personalised care services empower the budget holder or do they offload responsibilities from the state to the individual? Can the rights of older and disabled budget holders be respected at the same time as the rights of carers and care workers? Such debates are inherently recursive because the terminology (citizen, consumer, and so on) is unstable, experiences are heterogeneous and hard to measure and policy and funding contexts are constantly shifting.

To contribute to these debates without repeating them, this chapter interrogates the various rationales that have been put forward to justify the devolution of budgets down to the individual. While neoliberal retrenchment of the state is a catch-all explanation often proffered within the literature, the discussion here will focus on a range of claims that go beyond that rather simplistic account. Four claims are examined here: individualised budgets improve outcomes for individuals; budgets extend choice and control to citizens, which they should have as a matter of right; budget holding has an important educative function for individuals, enabling them to share in a common citizenship; and budgets correct system-level failings in public services. The discussion below argues that individual budgets have proven value in meeting claims one and two, but not in meeting claims three and four. The discussion focuses primarily on personal budgets in social care since this is the sector in which the evidence base is most mature, but also considers the existing or likely impacts in other sectors where possible.

Personal budgets lead to better individual outcomes

There is a growing body of evaluative data from social care indicating that people derive benefits from holding a personal budget to make care choices. The Individual Budgets Evaluation Network (IBSEN) funded by the UK Department of Health found that '[p]eople receiving an IB [individual budget] were significantly more likely to report feeling in control of their daily lives, welcoming the support obtained and how it was delivered, compared to those receiving conventional social care services' (IBSEN 2008: 2). These findings were strongest for people using mental health services and weakest for older people (Glendinning et al. 2008). The National Personal Budget survey conducted by Think Local, Act Personal, Lancaster University and the social innovation network In Control found that 'substantial majorities of people reported personal budgets having a positive impact' (Hatton and Waters 2011: 22). People receiving their social care budget as a direct payment have more transformative outcomes than people whose budgets are managed on their behalf by the local authority or a third party. According to the National Personal Budget survey: 'Whilst all personal budget holders reported positive outcomes, those managing the budget themselves as a direct payment reported significantly more positive outcomes than people receiving council managed budgets' (Hatton and Waters 2011: 4).

Within the health sector, a large government-funded evaluation of personal health budgets found that such budgets produced 'valued well-being benefits' (Forder et al. 2012: 156). These benefits came not from improved health outcomes (where the evaluation did not find statistically significant improvements) but from improvements in care-related quality of life and psychological well-being, which the researchers refer to as 'higher-order' aspects (Forder et al. 2012: 78). The psychological benefits of giving people more control are well known. As Glasby and Littlechild put it:

> There is a large literature in the field of psychology to suggest that control is essential to wellbeing and an important element in shaping people's lives and their susceptibility to stress … For many direct payments recipients, enhanced choice and control increased their self-confidence, morale and emotional and psychological health in a range of areas. (Glasby and Littlechild 2009: 117–18)

The mechanism through which personal budgets improve well-being and other outcomes is often assumed to be the purchasing power that comes with financial control (Tyson 2007). A member of In Control, a social enterprise set up to promote personal budgets, told the author in an interview: 'Until I've got hold of the money, or at least I'm directing the way that that money's spent, that provider is never going to listen to me. It is the power of the pound, the power of having the money is the bit that makes the difference' (Needham 2011: 55). A feature of the evaluations of budget holding across social care, the NHS and rough sleepers is, however, the value people place on the support planning process in which they sit down with a professional or other support worker and talk about their needs, preferences and capabilities. As a participant in the rough-sleepers' pilot put it:

> I've got to be honest here, it wasn't just the individual budget, it was the fact there was [a coordinator] there as well … We was meeting [regularly] to discuss it, and I'd actually gone from the stage of wanting nothing to do with these people, to actually looking forward to seeing them. (Hough and Rice 2010: 8)

Similar findings—about the value of building relationships with care providers—have emerged from the social care and health budget evaluations, highlighting that the one-to-one support that accompanies a budget is at least as important to improving well-being as the money itself (Needham 2014).

A matter of right

A second rationale for personal budgets is a rights-based argument—namely, that such budgets are designed to allow people to make the sorts of choices about their health and social care that are theirs by right to make. Within social care, people are choosing the times they get up and go to bed, the timing and content of meals, how they receive personal care, as well as how they spend their days—issues on which they can reasonably expect to have autonomy. The personalisation reforms are premised on an assumption that people are 'experts on their own lives' (Poll 2007), and social workers are expected to work within that paradigm. Within the health sector, the boundaries between clinical knowledge and patient knowledge have not shifted so far, but the rise of expert patient programs highlights a growing confidence that there is a range of health conditions on which patients have a normative claim to expertise and autonomy.

This is of course not to claim that making spending choices about health and social care is not a complex and uncertain process in which people need support. The National Personal Budget survey found that the 'single most commonly commented upon issue in the survey was a lack of clarity, often regarding how money could or couldn't be used, but also concerning other aspects of personal budgets as well' (Hatton and Waters 2011: 19). Inequalities in the capacity of citizens to navigate complex care systems have been a concern raised by many people, particularly in the context of personal budgets (Riddell et al. 2005; Barnes 2008; Glendinning 2008; Slasberg and Hatton 2011). Advocates of personalisation argue that the care systems that predated personal budgets were themselves characterised by complexity, lack of transparency and inequity. Hatton points out that these issues have not been created by personal budgets and should not be a reason to reject them: 'Plenty of evidence exists that social care services tend to be directed towards those with the skills, tenacity and resources to negotiate byzantine systems. However, this is not a specific issue concerning direct payments—it is a pervasive one found throughout social care' (Slasberg and Hatton 2011). The aim of personalisation advocates was to simplify the complex process of social care assessment and allocation of services into a transparent series of steps; an ongoing frustration for reformers has been the tendency of government to overly bureaucratise the allocation and monitoring of budgets (Routledge 2011).

Financial inclusion

A feature of welfare reform in the United Kingdom over several decades has been the encouragement of individual financial literacy and responsibility with the avowed aim of incorporating people into a common citizenship (Finlayson 2009). The New Labour Government's Child Trust Fund was an exemplar of this approach. Efforts to give citizens more direct control over financial resources through personal budgets could be seen as an extension of this educative function. The government sets out the rationale for the LHA, for example, as follows:

> By paying LHA direct to the customer it ensures they take on the personal responsibility of paying the rent to the landlord and helps develop the budgeting skills unemployed people will need when they move into the workplace. It also plays a part in the wider cross Government strategy of greater 'financial inclusion'. (DWP n.d.)

Personal budgets and health budgets can, similarly, be linked to the enhancement of financial literacy and the promotion of financial inclusion. The payments give people choices that may previously have been denied to them and incentivise careful budgeting since people can benefit directly from more frugal use of resources. Writing in a social care setting, Spandler (2004: 193) notes that '[p]owerful personal incentives exist for recipients to use their money wisely, efficiently and prudently because their survival and independence depend upon it'. As well as being more frugal, the service user may take on some of the hidden costs of the system, 'because the user often acts as an employer and budget holder, he/she soaks up much of the administrative and management costs. This may mean that recipients can get greater levels of social care at no greater cost' (Spandler 2004: 193).

Welfare reforms that purport to build civic inclusion and financial literacy through individualised financial labour and increased exposure to risk have, however, drawn widespread criticism (Ferguson 2007; Barnes 2008; Beresford 2008; Finlayson 2009). Writing in a care context, Scourfield (2007: 113) notes that '[d]irect payments fit comfortably with the project to transform the culture of the public, private and informal care sectors around principles of innovation, risk taking and enterprise'. This can perhaps be understood as a distortion of the citizen's income arguments put forward by the left, with financial inclusion being promoted not as part of an equal citizenship but on condition of compliance with activation policies around work and the family (Yeatman et al. 2009).

Fixing the system

There is great optimism among personalisation advocates about the potential for personal budgets to fix the problems that are evident in the existing system of social care support. The ambition of social enterprises like In Control, which developed much of the early thinking and design of personal budgets, has been very much system-wide, recognising the limitations of the social care market. Personal budgets are seen as a way in which individuals can tackle some of the many limitations of existing social care provision, whether it is risk-averse professionals limiting people's choices, large block contracts proving too restrictive to meet people's support needs or private companies providing a very poor standard of care (Land and Himmelweit 2010). The vulnerabilities of a care market funded by venture capital were starkly demonstrated with the collapse in 2011 of the Southern Cross Group, a large private provider of residential care homes in the United Kingdom. Many homes closed and others had to be picked up by state or other providers at very short notice, creating uncertainty and distress for many older people and their families (BBC 2011).

These structural problems have a knock-on effect on the social care workforce, which, it is well known, is low paid, with poor training standards and insecure working conditions (Ungerson 1997; Low Pay Commission 2009). A report into social care by the Equality and Human Rights Commission (EHRC 2011: 7) found 'serious, systemic threats to the basic human rights of older people who are getting home care services'. This conclusion echoed the findings of the *Time to Care* report into the home care sector, published by the Commission for Social Care Inspection (CSCI 2006: 2), which found 'the sector itself is a fragile one, that is struggling already to provide services of sufficiently high quality for those who need them now … A gap appears to be developing between what people themselves want and need, and what is on offer from statutory services'.

Despite the widespread recognition of these systemic failings, there is only limited scope to fix them through the market power of individual budget holders. Workforce changes may be brought about as more people shift to employing a personal assistant, rather than using social care agencies. Personal assistants have been found to have higher job satisfaction than agency workers (IFF Research 2008); however, they again can be a poorly paid and isolated workforce with little access to training (Ungerson 1999). Innovative third-sector organisations providing quality care services are expected to benefit from the market stimulus of lots of individual commissioners but may simply be unable to operate on the basis of such an insecure funding stream (Dayson 2011).

To understand the limitations of individualised budgets as a way to challenge system-level inadequacies, it is useful to study the experience of self-funders in the care system. Unlike 'early adopters' of personal budgets and direct payments, who may have characteristics that make them particularly well suited to managing care spending (and therefore from whom it may be difficult to generalise about mainstream impacts), self-funders include all those who are ineligible for means-tested local authority funding, which may say little about their support networks or financial acumen. They are large in number—40 per cent of older people are estimated to make some financial contribution to their care costs (Forder 2007)—and many have purchased care over a long period, making them a useful comparator group. Self-funders have not been well studied and have rarely been evoked in personalisation debates to inform understandings of how financial control intersects with care, perhaps because the drive for direct payments has come from younger disabled people for whom self-funding is less prevalent (Lloyd 2010).

A report on self-funders commissioned by the Putting People First Consortium noted:

> For some people there was a profound sense of 'powerlessness' and lack of control over their own financial resources, coupled with some real fear over what would become of them if their savings ran dry … It is clear that having sufficient resources to be a self-funder does not automatically give people greater control over their situation, and meaningful choices are often lacking. (Melanie Henwood Associates 2010: 48, 50)

It is certainly the case that the existence of a large bloc of self-funders has not led to the emergence of affordable, good-quality care for older people, as the endemic problems in the quality of home care services attests (EHRC 2011). A poorly regulated market intersects with the intimate nature of social care (and its complex interaction with vulnerability and dependence) to make individual market efficacy relatively weak (Rummery and Fine 2012).

The need for a system-wide fix is very apparent in social care, but much less so in health, where international measures indicate that the NHS continues to perform well in terms of quality (Commonwealth Fund 2014). The problems that personal health budgets seem designed to address are the growing financial pressures of the rising numbers of people with chronic health conditions and the value (normative and financial) of recruiting them as self-managers of those conditions. The funding landscape in health is also so different to that in social care that it is hard to read across, given that the NHS is a universal service whereas social care is means tested. There are currently no NHS analogues to social care self-funders, although with the likelihood of an increasingly commercial basis for many NHS services, there is an increased possibility of top-up payments being introduced to supplement a core set of NHS services, exposing health budget holders to the same market vulnerabilities that are very familiar from social care. The personal health budget evaluation noted: 'Policy makers should anticipate that the use of personal health budgets is likely to result in a higher level of expenditure going to "non-conventional" [that is, non-NHS] providers. Further research is required to better understand the scale of these changes' (Forder et al. 2012: 155).

Conclusion: Arguing for budgets

Personal budgets have been a hugely positive intervention for some people using social care services, particularly those who have been able to self-manage the money as a direct payment. There have also been benefits for people holding personal health budgets. The tentative nature of these findings, however, should be noted: they have tended to be observed among groups of 'early adopters', the benefits have been more around well-being than around health outcomes and they may be more attributable to the time spent on support planning than the time spent on the spending choices made. Nonetheless, there are sufficient data to see that there are some positive individual outcomes for people who choose to make care and health spending choices themselves.

There is also a rights-based rationale for including people more directly in choices about health and social care. Making choices via a budget is a complex process and the ability to do so is not shared equally, but there are intrinsic and instrumental reasons for believing that individuals—with families and communities—ought to play a key role in making those choices when they want to do so. The difficulties people face in making effective decisions about care should be a reminder of the importance of ensuring that people are well supported, particularly through peer support and advocacy networks that can draw on shared experience. It is also important to reaffirm that people's care choices and eligibility criteria do not have to be located in ever more complex bureaucracies, which even experienced observers find difficult to fathom.

The claim that controlling money is a valuable educative process is harder to sustain, having its roots in a view of 'active welfare' that is premised on forcing people to take on responsibilities. Not everyone will welcome the risks and complexities of being a budget holder, and making this compulsory is anathema to the principles that animated the independent living campaigns for direct payments.

The argument that budgets themselves will fix systemic problems in care provision is also unconvincing. There are distinctive attributes of care that act as important intervening variables in understanding how market changes play out. The self-funder experience highlights the complex interplay of market and social norms in a sector in which system-level marketisation is well established. A highly commodified sector has delivered a poor quality of care to those with and without their own purchasing power, largely because neither local authorities nor individuals have sufficient resources to meet the real costs of quality care or to demand effective accountability from providers.

Rather than seeing budgets as a way of giving people leverage to fix the problems of the social care market, they can be viewed as an effective tool to deliver change for some service users, although probably at the fringes rather than in the mainstream. Mainstream benefits may be best harnessed through focusing on the relational aspects of support planning, drawing on a series of evaluation findings about the value people derive from talking at length to a professional or peer planner about their capabilities and aspirations. The implementation of individualised budgets in England at a time when austerity so dominates the welfare terrain makes it hard to imagine that these relational benefits can be sustained. As the NDIS gathers momentum in Australia amid promises of a massive and sustained increase in funding, it is vital that good-quality information and advocacy are in place so that people with budgets can build relationships and communities and not just pick care items off a shopping list.

References

Age UK. 2013. *Making Managed Personal Budgets Work for Older People*. London: Age UK. Available from: ageuk.org.uk/professional-resources-home/services-and-practice/care-and-support/personalisation-hub/making-personal-budgets-work-for-older-people/ (accessed 29 July 2015).

Barnes, M. 2008. 'Is the personal no longer political?' *Soundings* 39: 152–59.

Barnes, M. 2011. 'Abandoning care? A critical perspective on personalisation from an ethic of care.' *Ethics and Social Welfare* 5(2): 153–67.

Beresford, P. 2008. 'Whose personalisation?' *Soundings* 40: 8–17.

British Broadcasting Corporation (BBC). 2011. 'Southern Cross set to shut down and stop running homes.' *BBC News*, 11 July. Available from: bbc.com/news/business-14102750 (accessed 29 July 2015).

Brown, C. 2012. 'Tenants on direct payment pilots pay rent on time.' *Inside Housing*, 17 August.

Commission for Social Care Inspection (CSCI). 2006. *Time to Care*. London: CSCI.

Commonwealth Fund. 2014. *Mirror, Mirror on the Wall, 2014 Update: How the US health care system compares internationally.* Washington, DC: Commonwealth Fund. Available from: commonwealthfund.org/publications/fund-reports/2014/jun/mirror-mirror (accessed 29 July 2015).

Dayson, C. 2011. 'The personalisation agenda: Implications for organisational development and capacity building in the voluntary sector.' *Voluntary Sector Review* 2(1): 97–105.

Department for Work and Pensions (DWP). n.d. *Local Housing Allowance: Frequently asked questions.* London: DWP. Available from: dwp.gov.uk/local-authority-staff/housing-benefit/claims-processing/local-housing-allowance/faqs/ (accessed 29 July 2015).

Department for Work and Pensions (DWP). 2006. *A New Deal for Welfare: Empowering people to work.* London: Her Majesty's Stationery Office.

Department for Work and Pensions (DWP). 2008. *Raising Expectations and Increasing Support: Reforming welfare for the future.* London: Her Majesty's Stationery Office.

Department of Health (DH). 2009. *Personal Health Budgets: First steps.* London: Department of Health.

Department of Health (DH). 2010. *A Vision for Adult Social Care.* London: Department of Health.

Equality and Human Rights Commission (EHRC). 2011. *Close to Home: An inquiry into older people and human rights in home care.* London: Equality and Human Rights Commission.

Ferguson, I. 2007. 'Increasing user choice or privatizing risk: The antinomies of personalization.' *British Journal of Social Work* 37(3): 387–403.

Finlayson, A. 2009. 'Financialisation, financial literacy and asset-based welfare.' *British Journal of Politics and International Relations* 11(3): 400–21.

Forder, J. 2007. *Self-funded social care for older people: An analysis of eligibility, variations and future projections.* PSSRU Discussion Paper 2505. Personal Social Service Research Unit and CSCI, University of Kent, Canterbury.

Forder, J., K. Jones, C. Glendinning, J. Caiels, E. Welch, K. Baxter, J. Davidson, K. Windle, A. Irvine, D. King and P. Dolan. 2012. *Evaluation of the Personal Health Budget Pilot Programme.* London: Department of Health.

Glasby, J. and R. Littlechild. 2009. *Direct Payments and Personal Budgets: Putting personalisation into practice.* Bristol: Policy Press.

Glendinning, C. 2008. 'Increasing choice and control for older and disabled people: A critical review of new developments in England.' *Social Policy and Administration* 42(5): 451–69.

Glendinning, C., D. Challis, J. Fernandez, S. Jacobs, K. Jones, M. Knapp, J. Manthorpe, N. Moran, A. Netten, M. Stevens and M. Wilberforce. 2008. *Evaluation of the Individual Budgets Pilot Programme.* York, UK: Social Policy Research Unit.

Hatton, C. and J. Waters. 2011. *National Personal Budgets Survey 2011.* London: Think Local, Act Personal, In Control and University of Lancaster.

Her Majesty's Government (HMG). 2007. *Putting People First: A shared vision and commitment to the transformation of adult social care.* London: HMG.

Hough, J. and B. Rice. 2010. *Providing Personalised Support to Rough Sleepers.* London: Joseph Rowntree Foundation. Available from: jrf.org.uk/publications/support-rough-sleepers-london (accessed 29 July 2015).

IFF Research. 2008. *Employment Aspects and Workforce Implications of Direct Payment.* Leeds: Skills for Care.

Individual Budgets Evaluation Network (IBSEN). 2008. *The national evaluation of the individual budgets pilot programme.* Summary Report. Social Policy Research Unit, York, UK. Available from: york.ac.uk/inst/spru/pubs/pdf/IBSENSummaryReport.pdf (accessed 17 April 2016).

Land, H. and S. Himmelweit. 2010. *Who Cares: Who pays?* London: Unison.

Lloyd, L. 2010. 'The individual in social care: The ethics of care and the "personalisation agenda" in services for older people in England.' *Ethics and Social Welfare* 4(2): 188–200.

Low Pay Commission. 2009. *National Minimum Wage Report 2009.* London: Low Pay Commission.

Melanie Henwood Associates. 2010. *Journeys Without Maps: The decisions and destinations of people who self-fund—A qualitative study from Melanie Henwood Associates.* London: Putting People First.

Needham, C. 2011. *Personalising Public Services: Understanding the personalisation narrative.* Bristol: The Policy Press.

Needham, C. 2014. 'The spaces of personalisation: Place and distance in caring labour.' *Social Policy and Society* 14(3): 1–13.

Poll, C. 2007. 'Co-production in supported housing: KeyRing living support networks and neighbourhood networks.' In *Research Highlights in Social Work: Co-production and personalisation in social care. Changing Relationships in the Provision of Social Care. Volume 49*, 49–66.

Putting People First. 2011. *People Who Pay for Care: Quantitative and qualitative analysis of self-funders in the social care market.* London: Putting People First.

Riddell, S., C. Pearson, D. Jolly, C. Barnes, M. Priestly and G. Mercer. 2005. 'The development of direct payments in the UK: Implications for social justice.' *Social Policy and Society* 4(1): 75–87.

Routledge, M. 2011. 'Let's not allow bureaucracy to derail personalisation.' *Community Care*, 25 May.

Rummery, K. and M. Fine. 2012. 'Care: A critical review of theory, policy and practice.' *Social Policy & Administration* 46(3): 321–43.

Scourfield, P. 2007. 'Social care and the modern citizen: Client, consumer, service user, manager and entrepreneur.' *British Journal of Social Work* 37(1): 107–22.

Series, L. and L. Clements. 2013. 'Putting the cart before the horse: Resource allocation systems and community care.' *Journal of Social Welfare and Family Law* 35(2): 207–26.

Slasberg, C. and C. Hatton. 2011. 'Are personal budgets improving outcomes?' *Community Care*, 6 October.

Spandler, H. 2004. 'Friend or foe? Towards a critical assessment of direct payments.' *Critical Social Policy* 24(2): 187–209.

Tyson, A. 2007. *Commissioners and Providers Together: The citizen at the centre*. London: In Control and Care Services Improvement Partnership.

Ungerson, C. 1997. 'Give them the money: Is cash a route to empowerment?' *Social Policy and Administration* 31(1): 45–53.

Ungerson, C. 1999. 'Personal assistants and disabled people: An examination of a hybrid form of work and care.' *Work, Employment and Society* 13(4): 583–600.

Yeatman, A., with G. Dowsett, M. Fine and D. Guransky. 2009. *Individualization and the Delivery of Welfare Services: Contestation and complexity*. Basingstoke, UK: Palgrave Macmillan.

Cross-Sector Working: Meeting the challenge of change

16

The Challenge of Change

Paul Ronalds

The conveners of the workshop 'Cross-Sector Working for Complex Problems: Beyond the rhetoric' invited Paul Ronalds, the Chief Executive Officer of Save the Children Australia, to give the closing address enunciating the core cultural and structural hurdles that must be overcome if cross-sector working is to become the 'new normal'. Paul's cogent analysis perfectly complements Peter Shergold's opening address and neatly bookends the presentations given in the four themed sessions. The chapter that follows is from the approved text of Paul Ronalds' address. This can also be viewed on the ANZSOG YouTube channel: youtube.com/watch?v=hORnOb1JE2o.

Introduction

This is an extremely timely workshop: now, more than ever, the three sectors of our society must collaborate effectively if we are to solve some of the most complex social, economic and environmental challenges we face.

When I joined the Department of the Prime Minister and Cabinet in 2010, I had spent more than 10 years advocating to government. I had a strong grasp of constitutional law and had been an active student of politics all my life. I was confident I knew how government worked. However, once on the inside, I quickly realised that I had not really understood how public policy decisions were made in practice: who had real influence over decisions or an effective veto to stop policy ideas from progressing; the constraints that public servants and politicians faced; and, importantly, the implicit incentives that governed all of the actors' actions. It is this last issue of implicit incentives that I think is particularly important and that I want to make the focus of my address today.

Let me begin by relaying a conversation I had recently with one of Save the Children's youth workers involved in juvenile justice in New South Wales. We know that a trusting relationship with this client group is critical as they transition out of detention. Yet, different funding streams can mean that there is a different worker inside a facility to the one in the community, breaking the relationship with the young person at the most critical time.

We also know that housing is the bedrock on which progress is made with this group. To pay for housing, the young person will need to obtain housing support from Centrelink. To access housing support, you need a bank account, which means you need sufficient identification. Yet, many of these kids do not have even a birth certificate. Who will help them to get a birth certificate, open a bank account, apply for a tax file number, navigate Centrelink, give them driving lessons, help them with a driver's licence and so on, so that they can maintain housing and have any chance of getting a job? The housing provider, the employment agency, the juvenile justice worker, Centrelink? All of these agencies and many more are funded to assist with some of these tasks but young people leaving detention face a dauntingly fragmented system. Is it any wonder that many decide it's easier to return to crime?

Today, I want to suggest to you that the problem we face in overcoming many complex social policy problems is clear. There has also been no shortage of trials and evaluations of approaches that can achieve substantial change in disadvantaged communities.

We know, for example, that services need to be joined up. People with multiple disadvantages need to simultaneously access a number of services to make progress, so services must be integrated (Vinson 2007; McArthur et al. 2010: 33–35). We know interventions must be contextualised to the local community's needs and leverage the strengths and assets that a local community may have. This requires local people to be empowered to respond to local conditions. We know we must integrate the social aspects of any solution with economic aspects. And we know that funding, measurement and accountability mechanisms must support a joined-up, long-term solution.[1]

There has been no shortage of government and community-supported trials that have adopted some or all of these characteristics (for examples, see Wilks et al. 2015). At the federal level, Communities for Children were established in 2004 and now operate in 45 locations around Australia. They use facilitating partners to develop and implement a whole-of-community approach to enhancing early childhood development.

The *Remote Service Delivery National Partnership Agreement* was established in 2009 to focus on 29 remote service delivery priority communities. It was based on a collaborative working arrangement with state and territory governments and local communities to improve access to and coordination of services, develop better governance and leadership and increase economic and social participation.

During the Rudd and Gillard years, Centrelink established a plethora of place-based trials around Australia to test collaborative approaches to improve access to services. Each of the initiatives focused on specific groups. For example, the Fairfield (in New South Wales) and Broadmeadows (in Victoria) initiatives focused on young refugees, while the Morwell trial in Victoria focused on the very long-term unemployed and youth.

There have also been a large number of state and local government and community-led initiatives. These include Victoria's Neighbourhood Renewal Program, Scanlon Foundation's work in Broadmeadows, the Opportunity Child initiatives around Australia and the Indigenous-led Empowered Communities initiative.

If we have a good understanding of the problem and there have been so many successful pilots, why has progress, as Peter Shergold said this morning, been so 'painfully slow'?

---

1 A range of reports has identified these types of problems—for example, APSC (2007); Australian Social Inclusion Board (2011); Walker et al. (2012).

Our problem is the challenge of change

There are many reasons why change in this area is so difficult.

First, achieving breakthroughs in complex policy problems is hard. I cannot think of a single Organisation for Economic Co-operation and Development (OECD) country that has made significant progress on breaking intergenerational cycles of disadvantage. A good example of the difficulty is illustrated by the recent reforms to the federal government's Indigenous Advancement Strategy.

Tony Abbott promised he would be a prime minister for Indigenous Australia. While I do not doubt the sincerity of this commitment, to make the promise look real, provide a sense of urgency and ultimately achieve some change within the constraints of a three-year electoral cycle, on his election, Abbott immediately set about making massive machinery of government changes, taking responsibility for Indigenous affairs into the Department of the Prime Minister and Cabinet. At the same time as these public service changes were being implemented, and as public servants were understandably concerned about the impact of changes on them personally, the government announced massive funding and service delivery changes.

As Fred Chaney (2014) suggested in his recent Button Oration:

> [H]old in your minds the administrative complexity of what the government is undertaking and the management challenge it faces. In the space of one year it is to take 150 existing programs which involve I understand some 1400 organisations and redirect expenditure into five broad streams while at the same time changing the geographic and hence jurisdictional basis of the administrative framework.

Is it surprising that such massive change in one of the most complex policy areas, implemented within a very short period (the electoral cycle), with limited buy-in from stakeholders and conducted in an adversarial political environment where views on what will work are strong and diverse, would have a limited chance of success?

Second, we all focus too little on supporting robust monitoring and evaluation. As a result, we lack the data to support robust policy and program implementation decisions. This was one of the findings of a recent meta-evaluation of place-based trials by the Australian

Institute for Family Studies on behalf of the Department of the Prime Minister and Cabinet (Wilks et al. 2015: 53). It found: 'High-quality evaluations of international [place-based initiatives] do show that they can be effective and can realise significant cost savings to government. However, among Commonwealth [place-based initiatives], the causal effects and cost-effectiveness of programs have rarely been evaluated.'

There are a number of reasons for this systemic failure.

Program evaluation is not routinely required by governments nor undertaken by non-profits and there are structural barriers that discourage it. In particular, funding to conduct evaluations is often not included in overall program budgets. Save the Children often finds that we have to seek philanthropic support to meet the costs of rigorous evaluation. There is also limited evaluation capability within the Australian Public Service.

Most program evaluations that do occur focus on process, inputs or outputs, rather than outcomes. These evaluations usually begin at the end of a program, rather than being planned during program design and integrated into the program logic and intended outcomes. Evaluations are often of poor quality—because of a lack of independence, transparency and dissemination of results.[2]

Third, there is a skills issue. It is no easy matter to:

- successfully negotiate agreements across governments, communities and the private sector
- provide genuine opportunities for communities to contribute to the design and delivery of local solutions to local issues
- manage the implementation of programs designed to achieve complex social and economic outcomes, often in very difficult physical or politically charged environments.

The 2010 *Ahead of the Game* report into the Australian Public Service (Advisory Group on Reform of Australian Government Administration 2010) provided a plethora of recommendations to improve government service delivery, enhance the Australian Public Service's policy

---

2   For a useful overview of the methodological, budget, administrative and political constraints of conducting robust evaluations in the Australian setting, see Cobb-Clark (2013). See also Ronalds (2015).

and implementation capability and facilitate cross-sector working. However, after the retirement of Terry Moran as secretary of the Department of the Prime Minister and Cabinet, these recommendations were largely put aside.

As important as these issues are, however, today I want to argue that what we need most of all to make progress is to change the current system's incentives. Only by changing the incentives of politicians, public servants, civil society and the private sector can we hope to achieve the type of progress we are all seeking.

Australia's twenty-first prime minister, Gough Whitlam, once said '[t]he punters know that the horse named morality rarely gets past the post, whereas the nag named self-interest always runs a good race' (Tookey 1989: 18). I think this quote neatly summarises our largest obstacle, but also our most significant opportunity, in achieving real progress in solving complex policy problems through cross-sector collaboration. Too often, we have sought to use rational policy arguments, evidence and moral suasion to argue for improved ways of working. When these fail, we double our efforts, futilely believing that by simply arguing harder, conducting further pilots or gathering more evidence things will change.

They will not.

It's not that these things are not important. It's just that they will not be sufficient. We need to change the system's incentives. This is the challenge of change to making progress with complex problems.

Government incentives

What is preventing change in government? It's not that public servants do not know that the system can be improved. In a recent global survey of public servants, only 1 per cent of Australian public officials agreed with the option that government was 'highly effective—little room for improvement' (Centre for Public Impact 2015). Interestingly, however, public servants in non-policy roles were less likely than their counterparts in policy positions to answer that government was highly effective or effective.

Those in more senior jobs were more likely to see government as being effective, with those in lower positions most likely to choose the options somewhat or highly ineffective. These findings certainly resonate with my own experience in government. Policy roles were more likely than implementation roles to support career progression. This created a strong incentive for the most capable public servants to move into policy roles. It also created an incentive for senior people to spend more time on policy issues than implementation issues.

In my view, this is the complete opposite of what is required. We need our best staff and most of their effort focused on policy implementation. Our efforts in solving complex policy problems should look like an iceberg, where 10 per cent of the effort goes into developing the policy and 90 per cent into its implementation. Of course, civil society organisations often make the same mistake. As soon as someone shows promise, they are promoted from program implementation to head office. The highest paid roles are not those dealing with program implementation.

It's also not the lack of opportunity

Accounting firm PricewaterhouseCoopers (2015) estimates that the 'social services market' totals $420 billion. The Australian and state governments are the two largest primary contributors to this market, providing $224 billion and $112 billion in services and funding, respectively. Given the size of this market even a small improvement in productivity would yield enormous returns.

But the incentives are wrong

At the political level, our politicians are elected based on policy promises, often with very limited investigation of the implementation challenges. Once they are elected and obtain advice on these challenges, they are faced with the choice of abandoning or at least modifying their promises or seeking to implement a policy with little chance of success. Often they decide to do the last, to avoid giving their political opponents an opportunity to claim a broken election promise.

Our Westminster system of government makes ministers responsible for the actions of their departments. This is reinforced by the media. Collaboration with other departments, other governments or non-governmental organisations can reduce control without changing responsibility. Asking a minister to pool administered funds, for example, increases risk while at the same time reducing political pay-offs such as the opportunity of opening new facilities or the kudos from success.

What about genuine engagement with community?

Giving communities early involvement in the policy process can create significant political risks: half-formed ideas can be misinterpreted, expectations may be raised, government priorities may change and you are left holding the policy baby. In addition, genuine collaboration requires the investment of significant time and resources—hard for politicians to do in our 24/7 media cycle. Instead, oppositions and even governments are seeking to be 'small targets'—anathema to genuine reform.

Similar challenges confront public servants

As a public servant, I was often asked to speed up program implementation to meet a politically convenient deadline at the expense of more careful policy implementation and improved collaboration. I also saw time and time again the system's disincentives for public servants to push a reform agenda. Public servants quickly understand that Machiavelli (1961: 51) was right when he argued that '[t]here is nothing more difficult to take in hand, more perilous to conduct, or more uncertain in its success, than to take the lead in the introduction of a new order of things'. We know that the long lead times to achieve impact, lack of robust evaluations, policy churn and the turnover of public servants and politicians all mean public servants are unlikely to be held accountable for the failure of programs to achieve outcomes.

Why attempt the difficult task of service delivery reform?

On the other hand, public servants will be held accountable for the mismanagement of funds or for a failure to follow process. This promotes a risk-averse, compliance-focused culture. The budget rules also act as a strong disincentive. I was astounded when I found out that the fiscal benefits of the outcomes that I was seeking to achieve—

reduced welfare dependence, improved education and employment outcomes, for example—were prohibited from being taken into account by Cabinet on the basis that they were 'second-round effects'. Can you imagine a private sector reform making investment decisions by ignoring the financial return? As perverse as it may seem, politicians and public servants are generally acting quite rationally in supporting a system that generally fails to deliver the outcomes we seek.

Community incentives

Are the incentives any better for community organisations? The same system of Westminster government combined with the behaviour of many private funding bodies means that community groups face enormously fragmented funding arrangements. These arrangements themselves promote 'community and organisational dysfunction' (Dillon and Westbury 2007: 191).

One of the best descriptions of the system's structural impediments is contained in the collective impact research work by John Kania and Mark Kramer (2011: 38):

> Most funders, faced with the task of choosing a few grantees from many applicants, try to ascertain which organizations make the greatest contribution toward solving a social problem.

> Grantees, in turn, compete to be chosen by emphasizing how their individual activities produce the greatest effect.

> When a grantee is asked to evaluate the impact of its work, every attempt is made to isolate that grantee's individual influence from all other variables.

The result is that thousands of community organisations 'try to invent independent solutions to major social problems, often working at odds with each other and exponentially increasing the perceived resources required to make meaningful progress' (Kania and Kramer 2011: 38). On the other hand, we know that collaboration is the best way to solve many social problems in today's complex and interdependent world.

Government tendering also often provides disincentives to collaboration. The recent Department of Social Services and Prime Minister and Cabinet tenders are good examples. The Department of Social Services grants round opened on 19 June 2014 and closed on 24 July 2014. The Prime Minister and Cabinet Indigenous Advancement Strategy tenders opened on 8 September 2014 and closed on 17 October 2014.

As Robyn Keast argues in her chapter, real collaboration takes far more time to negotiate than the month allowed by these tender periods. In fact, Save the Children found that such short periods increased the strain on local relationships, particularly those with Indigenous organisations.

It is also costly for the organisations involved. In a context where there is significant uncertainty about the outcome, intense competition and a reduced funding pool, devoting time to improved collaboration is a highly questionable investment. Add to this the profoundly negative impact of short-term funding cycles on staff retention and productivity. For Save the Children, the result of the Prime Minister and Cabinet Indigenous Advancement Strategy tenders was uncertain for six months after submission. This created significant anxiousness for staff and communities. Not surprisingly, where opportunities arose, staff decided to seek jobs elsewhere, undermining program delivery.

Even if community organisations succeed in building effective partnerships and demonstrating impact, community sector leaders know that there is at best only a weak correlation between delivering outcomes and increased government funding. Nous Group once undertook a comprehensive review of all of the evidence of homelessness interventions around the world. They ranked the research according to its robustness and developed a clever way to compare the cost effectiveness of different interventions. They found that there was a 250 times difference between the most and least cost-effective intervention.

Armed with such evidence, you would think governments would jump at the chance to increase funding to the most cost-effective programs. Instead, the recommendations were ignored because of the political implications of defunding such a large number of community groups.

Community groups themselves often encourage such inertia

Community groups can fail to respond to shifting community need and create political pain for politicians and public servants who, despite the barriers, seek reform. Community groups are often not sufficiently economically literate and seldom do they engage with funders in a robust, honest way. We know there are too many community organisations yet there are few real incentives for management and boards to negotiate mergers. None of this behaviour should be a surprise given the incentives that community organisations confront.

Private sector incentives

What about the private sector? Let me start with some good news. We have come a long way in this area. Many companies today do have strong incentives to improve collaboration around complex social and economic problems. Compare, for example, the Indigenous engagement of today's mining companies with the campaign against land rights in Western Australia in the 1980s, a campaign that saw a black hand building a brick wall across Western Australia to represent the threat to our enjoyment of our mineral riches (Chaney 2014). However, the private sector faces many of the same perverse incentives as the community sector. They face the same fragmented funding with the same pressure to demonstrate their own isolated influence on a desired outcome. The private sector also has little appreciation of how government or the community sector works.

I recently spoke at a private sector forum on shared value and many of the attendees implied in one way or another that we would make progress on complex policy problems if only government would get out of the way. Nonsense on stilts, as Jeremy Bentham once said. The United States has both the largest and most robust community sector and the most global corporate head offices, yet ranks at the bottom of the OECD for solving social problems. Despite the attractiveness of the idea of unleashing the potential of the private sector and local communities through more empowered civil society, we should not lose sight of the fact that government policies are still the main driver of well-being.

We need government to be actively involved in solving entrenched disadvantage, not passive funders of community-based organisations. We also need to overcome the deep disconnect between social and economic policy in this country. This disconnect starts with the lack of coordination (and sometimes disdain) between social and economic departments and is reinforced by a community sector that is often sceptical of the role of the private sector in community, further exacerbated by poor economic literacy.

The way forward

In the face of such a bleak picture, what is the way forward?

I am very interested in the behavioural insights work of the UK Government, recently also adopted by the NSW Government. Behavioural insights draw on research into economics and psychology to influence choices in decision-making. It seeks to identify subtle changes to the way decisions are framed and conveyed to achieve big impacts on behaviour. One wonderful example of the power of this approach is the toilets at Amsterdam's Schiphol Airport. The image of a small fly etched into each urinal significantly improved the accuracy of men's aim, reducing 'spillage' by 80 per cent (Thaler and Sunstein 2009: 4).

We need to stop simply repeating what we have done before hoping for a different outcome. More pilots of place-based initiatives will not take us forward if we do not address the systemic barriers to improved public sector service delivery. Instead, we need to continue to push for reform of the 'governance of government', particularly funding arrangements.

The actuarial approach being adopted by the National Disability Insurance Scheme is a promising example. It's one of the very few examples in public policy of where a strong incentive has been created to invest in early intervention. Another is the commissioning of outcomes approach discussed a number of times at this conference. Provided governments are prepared to step back from accounting for inputs, it has real promise.

We need tender processes that encourage, rather than discourage, collaboration and make investment worthwhile. A more transparent and consultative process, with longer lead times and longer contracts, is critical. We need to reward community organisations that invest in robust monitoring and evaluation.

We need government and philanthropists to support capacity building and sector consolidation.

We need to ensure we are thinking about the economic underpinnings of social interventions and vice versa.

We need more 'boundary riders' in government, in the community sector and in the private sector—people who understand the capacity and limitations of each sector and can successfully navigate them to achieve improved collaboration.

One way to change the incentives would be to require senior public servants to demonstrate significant cross-sector experience before being eligible for promotion. By changing the incentives, non-governmental organisations like Save the Children would be inundated with requests for secondments. Not only would this improve the skills and experience of public servants, it also would simultaneously enhance understanding in the private sector and civil society.

The pressures provided by a difficult fiscal environment may actually help

A recent speech by New Zealand's Deputy Prime Minister and Minister of Finance, Bill English (2015), to the Menzies Research Centre argued that the best way to achieve smaller government is to deliver better government. There is a strong case to be made that by focusing on the most disadvantaged—the government's most expensive clients—and investing more in them, significant savings can be made. Kevin Andrews (2014), as social services minister, highlighted the benefits of such an investment approach, where actuarial calculations of the lifetime cost of social support are used to more 'effectively target resources up-front'.

Increased transparency will also help

This starts with more and better evaluations.

During the late 1980s and early 1990s, Australia developed a reputation for a strong evaluation culture in the federal government. Since then, the quality of monitoring and evaluation has deteriorated markedly (Lopez-Acevedo et al. 2012). More and better evaluations, however, will not be sufficient. It also requires increased transparency about outcomes to help change the system's incentives.

Governments around the world have been increasing the amount of data available online. The United States' data.gov website was launched in May 2009; the UK site was publicly launched in January 2010. Australia's efforts were launched following the release of the Rudd Government's Government 2.0 Taskforce report in late 2009 but have proceeded slowly. Given the capacity for increased transparency to change system incentives, we need to provide greater support for this agenda.

We need to do more to highlight successes. This will give politicians more cover to implement reforms. As the evidence mounts and as it becomes easier to access, it will improve the incentives for politicians to lead the sort of service delivery reform that is required—and bring us closer to solving the challenge of change in public sector service delivery.

References

Advisory Group on Reform of Australian Government Administration. 2010. *Ahead of the Game: Blueprint for the reform of Australian government administration*. Canberra: Australian Government.

Andrews, K. 2014. Keynote Address to the Committee for Economic Development of Australia. Melbourne, 10 November.

Australian Public Service Commission (APSC). 2007. *Solving Wicked Problems: A public policy perspective*. Canberra: Australian Public Service Commission.

Australian Social Inclusion Board. 2011. *Governance Models for Location Based Initiatives*. Canberra: Department of the Prime Minister and Cabinet.

Centre for Public Impact. 2015. *Impact Imperative Survey*. USA: Centre for Public Impact. Available from: centreforpublicimpact. org/making-impact/impact-imperative/ (accessed 11 August 2015).

Chaney, F. 2014. A road to real reconciliation with Aboriginal Australia. Button Oration. Melbourne, 23 August.

Cobb-Clark, D. 2013. *The case for making public policy evaluations public*. Policy Brief No. 1/13, January. Melbourne Institute, Melbourne.

Dillon, M. and N. Westbury. 2007. *Beyond Humbug: Transforming government engagement with Indigenous Australia*. Adelaide: Seaview Press.

English, B. 2015. The 5th John Howard Lecture. Grand Hyatt Hotel, Melbourne, 25 June.

Kania, J. and M. Kramer. 2011. 'Collective impact.' *Stanford Social Innovation Review* (Winter).

Lopez-Acevedo, G., P. Krause and K. Mackay. 2012. *Building Better Policies: The nuts and bolts of monitoring and evaluation systems*. Washington, DC: The World Bank.

McArthur, M., L. Thomson, G. Winkworth and K. Butler. 2010. *Families' Experiences of Services*. Canberra: Department of Families, Housing, Community Services and Indigenous Affairs.

Machiavelli, N. 1961. *The Prince*. Trans. G. Bull. London: Penguin Classics.

PricewaterhouseCoopers. 2015. *Australia's Social Purpose Market: Understanding funding flows and exploring implications*. Melbourne: The Centre for Social Impact and PricewaterhouseCoopers.

Ronalds, P. 2015. 'Federal Government and non-profit relations in Australia.' In *Rebalancing Public Partnership: Innovative practice between government and non-profits from around the world*, ed. J. Brothers, 109–28. Surrey, UK: Gower.

Thaler, R. and C. Sunstein. 2009. *Nudge: Improving decisions about health, wealth and happiness*. London: Penguin.

Tookey, Christopher. 1989. 'Palin for Prime Minister'. *The Daily Telegraph*, 19 October: 18.

Vinson, T. 2007. *Dropping off the Edge*. Melbourne: Jesuit Social Services & Catholic Social Services Australia.

Walker, B. W., D. J. Porter and I. Marsh. 2012. *Fixing the Hole in Australia's Heartland: How government needs to work in remote Australia*. Alice Springs, NT: Desert Knowledge Australia.

Wilks, S., J. Lahausse and B. Edwards. 2015. *Commonwealth place-based service delivery initiatives: Key learnings project*. Research Report No. 32. Australian Institute of Family Studies, Melbourne.

17

Conclusion

John R. Butcher and David J. Gilchrist

An appetite for change

The workshop 'Cross-Sector Working for Complex Problems: Beyond the rhetoric' amply demonstrated that there is an appetite for more effective collaboration and engagement across sector boundaries. Some in the audience might have gone away somewhat deflated or disappointed because they came looking for ready-made solutions to long-standing and entrenched systemic, institutional, political and cultural barriers to cross-sector working. This is not because the presenters confined themselves to the task of setting out problems; indeed, solutions to vexing problems of meeting complex needs— or, at the very least, pathways *towards* solutions—figure strongly in the chapters contained in this volume.

Rather, it is more likely because each of the contributors has also been clear that failures to implement *effective* cross-sector working are largely due to the twin effects of institutional inertia and path dependence. Each of the contributors spoke to the constraints imposed by an authorising environment that privileges process over results. A number alluded to the difficulty of driving and sustaining a change agenda in the face of political timidity, a combative political culture and a hyper-vigilant media.

This was not the first time these issues have been aired, nor will it be the last. However, a number of authors discussed examples of change too, indicating that experiments are at least being made. We should take heart in the knowledge that while progress might be slow, the conversation will continue. So, let us take this opportunity to reflect on some of the critical gaps and disconnects that make the task of working across sector boundaries so difficult.

Gaps and disconnects

The 'disconnect' between words and actions is a central concern for each of the authors contributing to this volume. Also of concern are the gaps and disconnects that frequently plague the understandings and expectations of the community, legislators, the public service, non-state policy actors and those whose lives are directly affected by public policy; the legislative and regulatory architecture within which institutions and organisations are obliged to function; the rules and values that guide the behaviour and shape the perceptions of policy actors; as well as the aims and practical consequences of policy interventions.

These gaps and disconnects have greater consequence in today's reality of institutional and cross-sectoral interdependence. In Chapter 10, Dale Tweedie, for example, considers the varieties of disconnect that can occur in relation to accountability frameworks. Tweedie observes that despite the *intentions* of not-for-profit (NFP) organisations to be accountable for service quality, accountability can be impaired by the very reporting, governance or regulatory practices designed to provide assurance. This is reinforced by David J. Gilchrist in Chapter 4, highlighting the difficulty policymakers have in meeting the demands of red tape reduction in the context of increasingly complex individualised service delivery funding arrangements.

Gaps and disconnects are not confined to the realm of praxis; they also affect our understandings of sectoral relations at the meta-institutional level. In effect, NFP researchers and policymakers are hobbled by concepts and terminology that do not adequately or accurately represent the contemporary institutional or policy landscape. Furneaux and Ryan (2014) observe, for example, that existing conceptualisations and characterisations do not capture the complexity and variability of observed government/NFP relationships in contemporary Australia.

It is also important to recognise that policymaking in the NFP space is frequently plagued by an unhelpful tendency to conflate policies aimed at strengthening civil society (volunteering policy, social inclusion, self-reliance) with those aimed at ensuring that NFP service providers have the requisite capacity and capability to act as reliable partners to government (Dalton and Butcher 2014).

An abundance of rhetoric

Joined-up government, crosscutting solutions, networked governance, collaboration and cross-sector working—language such as this has been employed since the closing decades of the previous century to accentuate the importance of policy actors engaging across institutional, domain and sectoral boundaries to address complex policy problems. However, cross-sector working requires an appetite for risk that is often lacking in the public and NFP sectors, where conservatism, risk aversion and path dependence are well entrenched.

Peter Shergold made this point powerfully in his opening address to the workshop that provided the catalyst for this volume. Reflecting on lessons drawn from a distinguished career as a senior public servant and on his later experiences advising the WA and Victorian governments on more effective engagement across sectoral boundaries, Shergold suggested that the potential for cross-sector working had been 'sold short'. He offered this stark observation: 'Cross-sector working has been marked by failure—failure of implementation, but much more important, failure of imagination and failure of nerve' (Butcher and Gilchrist 2015).

At the outset of his address, in his personal acknowledgement of country, Shergold made the following 'confession': 'I, too, acknowledge that we meet on Aboriginal land. But more importantly, I acknowledge my part in helping to design and deliver programs over many years in the public service that did so little to address the gap of disadvantage that still exists.'

This was a poignant admission, and it spoke powerfully to the organising theme of the workshop: bridging the gap between policy rhetoric and policy reality.

The dynamics of dependence

It has long been recognised that NFP organisations—particularly those operating in the community social services space—are vulnerable to resource dependence on government. Fifteen years ago, Froelich (1999: 246) reflected—almost wistfully—that 'in our casual, naive, or maybe wishful thinking', we prefer to think of the NFP organisation 'as traveling an unfettered path in pursuit of its goals, free of mundane concerns associated with resource acquisition'. For this reason, she suggests:

> [W]e are troubled by the digressive efforts and peripheral activities associated with revenue-seeking behaviour. We worry and speculate about mission dilution and legitimacy erosion as distractions emerge from the necessary economic endeavours. Yet, these are and always have been the facts of life for a nonprofit organisation. (Froelich 1999: 246)

Few Australian non-profit scholars or policy practitioners today would disagree with Froelich's observation that:

> As nonprofits strive to reduce their vulnerability to income uncertainties and the influence of resource providers, they have moved away from concentrated dependence on a single revenue strategy. Revenue diversification brings new concerns and greater complexity. The wider variety of management tasks diverts more resources from mission-oriented efforts, and the growing number of constraints requires a delicate balance of often conflicting demands. (Froelich 1999: 263)

Froelich was, of course, writing about the experience of the NFP sector in the United States, where purchase-of-service contracting by government was already well entrenched by the late 1990s. Indeed, Jennifer Wolch, in her prescient book *The Shadow State: Government and voluntary sector in transition* (1990), warned that contracting almost inevitably lead NFP organisations to commodify their services and, as a consequence, transform their values.

Although Australian governments were somewhat slower to divest themselves of responsibility for the direct provision of community-based social services, the transition to a near total reliance on contracted service delivery in this country is almost complete. And it has to be said that the ascendancy of competitive tendering and contracting—particularly in the human services space—has had a transformative effect on the operations of many NFP organisations (Considine et al. 2014). As a result, there is in Australia today widespread concern in the NFP sector about the potential for 'mission drift'.

For example, the Director for Strategic Engagement at UnitingCare NSW & ACT, Doug Taylor, has suggested in an online post that the mission of many NFPs has become 'defined by the sum total of their Government contracts', leaving 'no place for working collaboratively with the community' (Taylor 2015). He went on to say:

> A symptom of this disease is the way in which many organisations conduct their strategic planning. I've been in organisations who plan on the basis of where they can get their next Government contract instead of looking at the community and discerning opportunities to meet unmet needs in line with their inherent mission and capability. (Taylor 2015)

Taylor's views give expression to widely shared fears about a debasement of the 'civil' in 'civil society' as a consequence of a triumph of market logic over the traditional values-driven missions of NFP organisations.

Any fears about the hollowing out of NFP 'values', however, need to be weighed against the implications of the hollowing out of state capacity and capability. Arguments in favour of externalised service provision are usually framed in terms of highly desirable ends such as value for money to taxpayers, improved efficiency and effectiveness or more choice and 'agency' for service users. There are concerns, nevertheless, among policy scholars and policy practitioners about the implications of a degraded capacity within the public sector to deliver the depth of thinking necessary to steer the kind of policy development and adaptation required to meet the challenges of problem complexity.

Australian governments—in particular, state and territory governments—depend as never before on external service providers to deliver a variety of public services via structured procurement processes (Alford and O'Flynn 2012; Davidson 2011). It is estimated that in Australia today more than $26 billion of public services are delivered by NFP organisations each year (Knight and Gilchrist 2014). Furthermore, competitive procurement processes have largely displaced grant-based funding as the preferred form of government investment in the NFP sector. Is the function of the public sector to become merely that of a contract manager? Is this what is necessarily implied by the contemporary enthralment with 'commissioning'?

This does not necessarily imply—as some might fear—the inexorable transfer of responsibility for the provision of human services and/ or public goods to the NFP sector. The state might be vacating the field of direct provision, but it is not relinquishing the financial or the policy reins. Salamon has observed an international trend towards the 'nonprofitization' of the welfare state in which governments 'turn increasingly to nonprofit organizations to assist in carrying out publicly funded functions' (Salamon 2015: 2154). Of this process, Salamon says:

> To be sure, the state is not surrendering its role as a guarantor of public wellbeing. Nor is it totally eliminating its service delivery role. But something quite significant is still afoot, suggesting a growing realization of the limitations facing exclusive reliance on state institutions in the delivery of important human services and of the special qualities that nonprofit organizations can bring to the social welfare arena as an active collaborator of the state. (Salamon 2015: 2154)

Salamon's observations are consistent with Bell and Hindmoor's portrayal of 'state-centric relational governance' in which:

> [T]he involvement of a wider range of actors in the process of governing has not been at the expense of the pivotal role played by governments. Our argument here is that even when governments have chosen to govern in alternative ways the state retains a pre-eminent position. On this basis we argue that states and governments are critical players in governance and that governance is also about state–society relationships, whatever the governance arrangements in place. (Bell and Hindmoor 2009: 153–54)

As Bell et al. (2010: 864) suggest, 'by developing closer relations with non-state organizations governments can enhance their capacity to achieve preferred goals'. That said, we ought to be mindful of

Peter Shergold's warning in Chapter 2 that governing cross-sector relationships is too important a matter to be left entirely in the hands of governments and the public service.

In the United States, governments have, over the past 30 years, come to rely on complex arrangements of networked external providers for the implementation of public policy (Milward 2014: 71). It should not be accepted as a given that externalised service provision is a panacea for the perceived shortcomings of public sector provision. According to Milward: 'Governance of cross-sectional, multi-level networks that deliver government services is an enormous task that is often poorly specified and has the potential to shape public policy and, to some extent, the citizen's relation to the state' (Milward 2014: 71).

Millward (2014: 71) observes that examinations of privatisation schemes have tended to omit any discussion of what contracting might mean to the legitimacy of the state. In a network of third parties operated by contract, Milward argues, the state can 'go missing'. This, according to Milward (2014: 72), is the 'hollow state'. This is a world in which 'non-governmental entities essentially govern, manage and deliver services that are paid for by taxpayer's dollars'—a world that gives rise to problems of democratic accountability (Milward 2014: 78).

Networked service delivery strategies employed here in Australia are not immune to problems associated with democratic accountability. The extent to which the terms of third-party procurement arrangements enjoy the shield of commercial confidentiality has been the subject of considerable debate in Australia for some time (see Barrett 1999). In 1997, the Australasian Council of Auditors-General (ACAG) offered the following concerns: 'Recent experiences in Australia would indicate that Government agencies are tending to use the pretext of commercial confidentiality as a shield against the disclosure of information which is commercially embarrassing to the Government or which raises issues of probity' (ACAG 1997).

More recently, O'Flynn (2014) has examined the legal instruments used by the Australian Government to procure offshore detention services for asylum-seekers attempting to reach Australia by boat. She observed that successive governments have seen fit to 'outsource their immigration problems not only to large for-profit security companies, but to other nations' (O'Flynn 2014). This, according to O'Flynn (2014):

> [N]ot only confuses the boundaries, but makes accountability and responsibility for various parts of this operation ambiguous …

> When we combine the power of the contract with intense competition in provider markets, governments should be big winners with lower prices and higher quality. In reality, the situation is much more complicated with profound challenges in specifying services, either an unwillingness or inability of purchasers to wield a big stick, and highly contorted supplier markets in some areas.

Thus, the dynamics of dependence—of the NFP sector on income from contracts and of government on non-state providers of mandated public services—contribute directly to the emergence of gaps and disconnects: between organisational behaviour and organisational values, between organisational mission (or purpose) and organisational capacity/capability and between community expectations and operational practices.

The regulatory gap

It has long been recognised that the regulatory environment in which NFPs operate—nationally and subnationally—needs to be modernised (Lyons 2003). In Chapter 7, Krystian Seibert considers the establishment of the Australian Charities and Not-for-profits Commission (ACNC), which was a key plank in a broader reform agenda characterised by its complexity, its pace, its political context and challenges associated with a diverse charitable sector. Seibert characterises the establishment of the ACNC as the largest and most complex structural reform experienced by the NFP sector in Australia (and by charities specifically). Moreover, the government's efforts to create a smarter regulatory framework for Australian charities occurred in response to active and prolonged advocacy by a large segment of those organisations that would be subject to regulation.

Seibert also suggests, however, that the Rudd and Gillard governments perhaps failed to fully appreciate that the NFP sector is not, as the name suggests, a single unitary sector. Rather, the NFP 'sector' is really a set of diverse subsectors comprising large and small welfare organisations, universities, arts organisations, environmental organisations, large religious organisations and small community churches, charitable trusts and foundations, hospitals and aged care providers, housing cooperatives—and the list goes on. Moreover, each subsector has its own agenda, interests and institutional history. This complexity is accentuated when we consider that some charities, such as the majority of Australian universities, are also state instrumentalities.

According to Seibert, the ACNC reform process effectively required maintaining a 'coalition' of subsectors, which necessitated a very strong emphasis on stakeholder engagement but also an appreciation of how a common set of regulatory arrangements can have different impacts on different subsectors. Seibert suggests that if we were to turn the clock back to before the ACNC reform process began, an alternative way of addressing this challenge might have involved phasing in the ACNC regulatory framework for different parts of the NFP sector (although he concludes that, on balance, the approach adopted by the government was sufficiently flexible).

The establishment of the ACNC was, nevertheless, a policy success insofar as the regulator was able to earn the respect of large parts of the charitable sector—in no small part due to the leadership of its inaugural commissioner, Susan Pascoe. However, the election in 2013 of the Abbott Coalition Government arrested and threatened to reverse the implementation of key measures (Butcher 2015b; Murray 2014). The inability of the former Abbott Coalition Government to pass legislation abolishing the ACNC suggests that the Coalition had misread the attitude of the sector. A portfolio reshuffle in December 2014 saw then Minister for Social Services—and principal champion for the abolition of the ACNC—Kevin Andrews, replaced in the portfolio with Scott Morrison, who quickly declared that abolition of the national charities regulator was no longer a priority (Jacks 2015).

In March 2016, the Turnbull Government announced its intention to retain the ACNC (Porter and O'Dwyer 2016). Hopefully, this means that the unravelling of sensible policy reform in the NFP space has been abandoned. Even so, unless new life is breathed into NFP sector reform, government commissioners and their NFP 'partners' will continue to navigate a complex and sometimes dysfunctional policy terrain. In such circumstances, the default practice of government(s) becomes, effectively, regulation by contract and regulation by administrative edict.

The relationship gap

The need for more effective policy frameworks for cross-sector engagement has occupied the attention of policymakers for some time (Saunders 2009; Shergold 2008). Furneaux and Ryan (2014) speculate about the range of factors that might lead to an improvement in government/NFP relations. While noting the 'conflicted service delivery context' and the 'estrangement' between NFPs and governments in Australia, they nevertheless conclude that it is entirely possible to achieve an alignment between the values/objectives of government and those of the NFP organisations with which they work (Furneaux and Ryan 2014: 1135). Among the range of factors that characterise successful relationships are clarity, trust, predictability, flexibility, collaborative intent and investment in capacity building (Furneaux and Ryan 2014: 1125).

In Chapter 4, David J. Gilchrist forensically examines Western Australia's Delivering Community Services in Partnership (DCSP) Policy. The DCSP Policy was hailed at the time of its commencement in 2012 as a thoroughly pragmatic approach to cross-sector relations (Butcher 2015a), but, three years on, Gilchrist finds that the sector's view of the success (or otherwise) of the policy is mixed, owing to 'frustration with inconsistent approaches being used across agencies and a perception of increased administrative burden'.

It should be noted that the DCSP Policy is only one of a number of instances in which state and territory governments have attempted to forge a new settlement with those parts of the NFP sector on which they depend. All states and territories have, for instance, flirted with the development of framework agreements or compacts with the NFP sector (Butcher 2015a). In recent times, compacts appear to have lost some of their allure, leading governments (and the sector) to focus their efforts on practical matters affecting their operations, such as streamlining tendering processes and/or reducing red tape (McGregor-Lowndes and Ryan 2009; Department of Family and Community Services 2012).

The evidentiary gap

A persistent problem in this policy space is the relative absence of a strong evidentiary base. Much peer-reviewed scholarly research is not 'policy relevant' and although there exists a significant 'grey literature' this is generally not peer reviewed and is therefore of uncertain value. Policy decisions are often based on anecdotal information and/or interpretations of data collected primarily for administrative purposes (as opposed to data collection designed to support policy deliberation), and there is relatively little in the way of benchmarking, information exchange or knowledge transfer between jurisdictions (on the part of either government or the NFP sector).

The experimentation gap

A recurring issue in any discussion of impediments to a more effective and collegial relationship between government and the NFP sector is the problem of risk-averse behaviour, especially on the part of public sector organisations. Peter Shergold calls for government to be 'adaptive, flexible and experimental—driven by trials, subject to errors' (Butcher and Gilchrist 2015).

Emma Tomkinson (Chapter 9) and Cassandra Wilkinson (Chapter 13) challenge policymakers and public sector managers to think differently about outcomes and the means to achieve them.

Tomkinson points out that as Australian governments have outsourced service provision to NFP organisations, they have also imposed reporting requirements to ensure that public funds are well spent. She also observes that in the past few years the perception of what it means to 'spend money well' has changed. According to Tomkinson, the trend has been towards maximising not just what money was spent on or how much activity occurred, but also what outcomes resulted. Her chapter examines the value of reporting for NFPs and their government funders and looks at ways in which this value can be increased. She argues that for funders to further the outcomes they pursue requires their reporting architecture to be redesigned so that it serves all stakeholders, including government funders, NFP staff and clients.

Whereas Tomkinson illustrates how the redesign of a business process might result in a more effective focus on outcomes, Cassandra Wilkinson goes further and offers a more radical proposal. Wilkinson suggests adapting the 'alliance contracting' model for use in the social sector. Long used in the infrastructure sector, alliance contracting is an arrangement wherein the payer and the provider work cooperatively as a single governance team, sharing both risk and reward. Alliances, says Wilkinson, are designed for situations of uncertainty. They might be well suited, she argues, for many areas of social service provision in which knowledge gaps make it difficult to write effective contracts.

The governance gap

In announcing his new ministry after his anointment as Prime Minister, Malcolm Turnbull declared that his would be a twenty-first-century government (Turnbull 2015). Turnbull spoke of the importance of 'human capital' and indicated that innovation would be a keystone of his government:

> If we want to remain a prosperous, first world economy with a generous social welfare safety net, we must be more competitive, we must be more productive. Above all we must be more innovative. We have to work more agilely, more innovatively, we have to be more nimble in the way we seize the enormous opportunities that are presented to us. We're not seeking to proof ourselves against the future. We are seeking to embrace it. (Turnbull 2015)

To embrace innovation implies an increased appetite for risk in policymaking; whether this is what Turnbull intended remains to be seen. Nevertheless, if we accept at face value that innovation will be encouraged and rewarded (as opposed to being thwarted and even punished by the application of prescriptive, rules-bound reporting and acquittal processes), it implies a need to renegotiate the terms of engagement between the public sector and non-state providers of publicly funded services.

Managers in the public and NFP sectors will need to adopt new forms of governance if they are to adaptively manage the transformations wrought by the implementation of game-changing reforms like the National Disability Insurance Scheme. In his opening address to the workshop, Peter Shergold predicted that in the public service of the future:

[P]ublic servants will continue to serve, faithfully, successive elected governments. They will continue to provide robust advice on the complex and wicked problems of public policy, but they will confidently eschew aspiring to have a monopoly in that regard and they will no longer depend on situational position or authority to command and control. Rather, public servants will see themselves as the facilitators of cross-sector working. Public services in this world will actively involve others in the design of policy, and in the legislative and administrative structures which give it effect. (youtube.com/watch?v=bUskU0X4_To)

As Helen Dickinson (Chapter 3) informs us, the academic literature offers 'a compelling narrative of government and public services, suggesting that traditional hierarchical arrangements have, over time, been replaced with more effective and efficient mechanisms of governance'—a narrative she describes as 'rather simplistic'. Instead, Dickinson finds that 'the transition between governance arrangements is rarely as clear-cut and straightforward as the academic literature typically presents this to be'. Although she suggests that, in reality, 'hybrid forms of governance prevail, with a complex overlay of different governance arrangements', she also draws our attention to the lack of research in relation to the unique challenges that hybridity creates.

Peter Shergold and Paul Ronalds, meanwhile, point out that the NFP sector also needs to reflect critically on its modus operandi. Again, in his opening address, Peter Shergold offered the following reflection on the potential for contestability in consumer-driven care:

This could be pretty tough for not-for-profit organisations. Get over it! I don't want to hear the benefits of block funding being argued because it's more convenient to the not-for-profit providers. Let's remind ourselves, what are the not-for-profits providing? They're providing services to those in need. That's what should determine [funding]. I envisage a day in the near future when aged people wanting home care services will not only be saying 'I don't want a service from provider x, I want to move to provider y.' Or say, 'I don't want to get my services from this not-for-profit community provider, I prefer to go and get it in the private sector.' That's, in a way, the potential, I think, of consumer directed care. (youtube.com/watch?v=bUskU0X4_To)

Paul Ronalds, in his concluding address, suggested that a 'risk-averse, compliance-focused culture', a 'dauntingly fragmented system' and a lack of understanding of the decision-making processes in government and civil society combine to work against breakthroughs on complex policy problems. Ronalds said the NFP sector has helped to create the inertia that has given rise to many of the systemic and institutional deficits that are acting as a brake on progress, citing a lack of economic literacy in the sector and a system of implicit incentives that reinforce maladaptive organisational behaviours. Ronalds added, 'we need to overcome the deep disconnect between economic and social policy in this country', concluding that 'we need to reform the governance of government'.

The trans-Tasman gap

In his opening address, Peter Shergold lamented that not only does New Zealand consistently 'wallop' Australia in rugby union, it also consistently outperforms Australia in 'just about every test of public administration'. Shergold pointed to the ability of political leaders across the Tasman to explain bold policy to the electorate, to positively market risk-sharing with non-state partners and to lead successful policy implementation. Shergold offered a 'genuflection' to New Zealand policymakers like Prime Minister, John Key, and Deputy Prime Minister, Bill English, who clearly and consistently sell the message that 'assessing risk and managing risk are precisely what is necessary to be experimental and adaptive'. This point was acknowledged by Prime Minister, Malcolm Turnbull, when he observed of the New Zealand Prime Minister: 'You have to be able to bring people with you respecting their intelligence … John Key has been able to achieve very significant economic reforms in New Zealand by doing just that: by explaining complex issues and then making a case for them' (Mulgan 2015).

In Chapter 11, Rodney Scott and Ross Boyd map the process by which the New Zealand Government set bold cross-portfolio outcome targets for state sector agencies. They contend that the current focus on collaborating across portfolio boundaries to achieve specified social impacts is the latest in a series of decadal transformations, beginning with the 1980s emphasis on managing inputs, followed by the 1990s focus on managing for outputs and, in the 2000s, by managing for outcomes. They provide a detailed account of the 10 crosscutting targets set by the New Zealand Government, which specify the 'result' to be obtained (specifying what social issue will be addressed), a 'target' (for example, specifying the degree of change) and a 'measure' (for example, specifying how progress towards the target will be calculated).

Further, they argue that the use of these social impact measures has been particularly important in generating focus, commitment, urgency and momentum. And, while they concede that their examples come from the public sector, their conclusions are likely to have relevance for collaboration involving other sectors. The authors also acknowledge important differences in the behaviour of performance-driven organisations (public sector) and mission-driven organisations (NFP sector), and point out that both are increasingly looking for evidence of impact. They also caution that public sector commissioners of public services will bring assumptions of behaviour from their own performance-driven backgrounds to any cross-sector collaborations; NFP organisations will, therefore, need to be able to navigate the same challenges of accountability and transparency as the public sector.

From 'fail-safe' commissioning to 'safe-to-fail' collaboration

Problems associated with the existence and persistence of 'gaps' and 'disconnects' are recurring themes in each of the foregoing chapters. An important 'take-home message' from the workshop and this book is that there is far too little recognition of important differences in the authorising environments in the public sector, the NFP sector and the business sector. For example, the authorising environment in the public sector is often characterised as being preoccupied with process (for understandable reasons of public accountability). The authorising environment in the NFP sector, on the other hand, is dominated by a concern for fidelity to 'mission' and values. And the authorising environment in business is dominated by the need to demonstrate a return on investment: 'if it pays, it plays.'

Contemporary governments accept their obligation to demonstrate the realisation of 'outcomes' and 'impact' as a consequence of the implementation of public policy. They also accept that a preoccupation with process can contribute to rigid and unresponsive organisational behaviour and business systems. The qualities of nimbleness, innovation and responsiveness are frequently cited as the necessary precursors for successful policy interventions—qualities commonly attributed to non-state sector actors (and routinely claimed not to exist in the state sector). Paradoxically, these very qualities can be compromised and constrained as a result of the persistence of rules-based systems for accountability and oversight in regimes for the outsourcing of public services.

Policy communities in government, academia, think tanks, the NFP sector and those parts of the business sector wishing to participate in social impact investment and/or markets for social policy implementation need to articulate an authorising framework that reconciles the need for public accountability and transparency with the need for experimentation and risk. Public sector commissioning and procurement frameworks need to transition from a fixation with fail-safe approaches to an acceptance of 'safe-to-fail' approaches. In a 1975 working paper investigating alternative approaches to dealing with uncertainty arising from the management of disastrous environmental events, Jones et al. contrast these two notions thusly:

> Two poles on the spectrum of strategies are fail-safe and safe-fail. The goal of a fail-safe policy strives to assure that nothing will go wrong. Systems are designed to be foolproof and strong enough to withstand any eventuality. Efforts are made to radically reduce the probability of failure. Often the managers of such systems operate as if that probability were zero.

> A safe-fail policy acknowledges that failure is inevitable and seeks systems that can easily survive failure when it comes. Rather than rely on reducing the occurrence of failure, this policy aims at reducing the cost of that failure. (Jones et al. 1975: 2)

Drawing on the ecological sciences, the authors hypothesise that periodic failures introduce 'step changes, natural or cultural selection forces' that can act to maintain flexibility and introduce resilience (Jones et al. 1975: 5). By contrast, eliminating the possibility of periodic 'disasters' could contribute to reduced flexibility (Jones et al. 1975).

'The real question', say the authors:

> [I]s whether the occasional experience of those shifts is a necessary condition in order to maintain the system's capacity to absorb the unexpected. If that is the case, then there might well be a place in environmental, institutional or societal management for disaster design—periodic 'mini-disasters' that prevent the evolution of inflexibility. That, combined with traditional fail-safe design for those parts that are more surely known, monitored and controlled could lead away from the hypotheticality trap to systems with rich options for experimentation, mistakes and hence learning. (Jones et al. 1975: 6)

The 'safe-fail' or 'safe-to-fail' concept has since influenced other policy domains such as urban design (see Ahern 2011). Social policy scholars and practitioners should be prepared to drop their disciplinary blinkers to consider the relevance of safe-to-fail approaches in the social policy space. This might involve what Sir Humphrey Appleby (the character so memorably played by British actor Nigel Hawthorne in the television series *Yes, Minister*) would characterise as a 'courageous' (that is, career-limiting) decision. But we must not consider such 'courage' to lie outside the realm of possibility for a minister or a public official, for to do so would be to capitulate to the perceived inevitability that our institutions, frameworks and systems for the creation of public benefit will never bridge the gap between the rhetoric and the reality.

Concluding remarks

While it remains for a considerable amount of water to pass under the bridge before categorical advancement can be discerned across the complex boundaries between the public and NFP sectors, there is at least a continuing interest and clear movement. Many of the questions raised by the contributors to this volume will, no doubt, be answered in subsequent research and subsequent practice. However, a clear message from this collection of work is that there remains a genuine drive towards improvement for better outcomes for the Australian community as a whole.

The contributions have focused on differing aspects, reported differing experience and identified differing examples of practice that can be duplicated and evaluated in different environments. Effective community change—which is really what we are talking about—has to start somewhere and the willingness to make these contributions bodes well for the incremental improvement in our understanding and practice in future years.

References

Ahern, J. 2011. 'From fail-safe to safe-to-fail: Sustainability and resilience in the new urban world.' *Landscape and Urban Planning* 100(4): 341–43.

Alford, J. L. and J. O'Flynn. 2012. *Rethinking Public Service Delivery: Managing with external providers*. Basingstoke, UK: Palgrave Macmillan.

Australasian Council of Auditors-General (ACAG). 1997. *Commercial Confidentiality and the Public Interest*. Canberra: Australasian Council of Auditors-General. Available from: acag.org.au/ccpi.htm (accessed 4 April 2016).

Barrett, P. 1999. Commercial confidentiality: A matter of public interest. Presentation to ACPAC Biennial Conference, Commercial Confidentiality: Striking the balance. Australian National Audit Office, Canberra, 21 February. Available from: anao.gov.au/~/media/Uploads/Documents/commercial_confidentiality.pdf (accessed 4 April 2016).

Bell, S. and A. Hindmoor. 2009. 'The governance of public affairs.' *Journal of Public Affairs* 9: 149–59.

Bell, S., A. Hindmoor and F. Mols. 2010. 'Persuasion as governance: A state-centric relational perspective.' *Public Administration* 88: 851–70.

Butcher, J. 2012. 'The national compact: Civilising the relationship between government and the not-for-profit sector in Australia.' In *Government–Nonprofit Relations in Times of Recession*, ed. R. Laforest, 165–88. Toronto: McGill–Queen's University Press.

Butcher, J. 2015a. 'Australian sub-national compacts with the not-for-profit sector: Pathways to cross-sector cooperation.' In *New Accountabilities, New Challenges*, ed. J. Wanna, 297–341. Canberra: ANU Press, with ANZSOG.

Butcher, J. 2015b. 'The third sector and government in Australia: Not-for-profit reform under Labor, 2007–13.' *Australian Journal of Political Science* 50(1): 148–63.

Butcher, J. and B. Dalton. 2014. 'Cross-sector partnership and human services in Australian states and territories: Reflections on a mutable relationship.' *Policy and Society* 33(2): 141–53.

Butcher, J. and D. J. Gilchrist. 2015. 'Prerequisites for cross-sector working.' *Pro Bono News: Analysis*, 25 August. Available from: probonoaustralia.com.au/news/2015/08/prerequisites-cross-sector-working#sthash.wRh6GumP.dpuf (accessed 4 April 2016).

Considine, M., S. O'Sullivan and P. Nguyen. 2014. 'Mission drift? The third sector and the pressure to be businesslike: Evidence from Job Services Australia.' *Third Sector Review* 20: 87–107.

Dalton, B. M. and J. Butcher. 2014. The rise of big charity in Australia. Presentation to the Association for Research on Nonprofit Organizations and Voluntary Action (ARNOVA) Conference. Denver, Colo., 19–22 November.

Davidson, B. 2011. 'Contestability in human services markets.' *The Journal of Australian Political Economy* 68: 213–39.

Department of Family and Community Services. 2012. *Red Tape Reduction Plan for NGOs*. Sydney: NSW Government. Available from: adhc.nsw.gov.au/__data/assets/file/0009/255690/Red_Tape_Reduction_Plan.pdf (accessed 1 August 2012).

Froelich, K. A. 1999. 'Diversification of revenue strategies: Evolving resource dependence in nonprofit organizations.' *Nonprofit and Voluntary Sector Quarterly* 28(3)(September): 246–68.

Furneaux, C. and N. Ryan. 2014. 'Modelling NPO–government relations: Australian case studies.' *Public Management Review* 16(8): 1113–40.

Jacks, T. 2015. 'Scott Morrison puts bill to abolish charity regulator on backburner.' *Sydney Morning Herald*, 7 February. Available from: smh.com.au/national/scott-morrison-puts-bill-to-abolish-charity-regulator-on-backburner-20150205-1378o9.html#ixzz3nkgrsPUf (accessed 6 October 2015).

Jones, D. D., C. S. Holling and R. Peterman. 1975. *Fail-safe vs. safe-fail catastrophes*. IIASA Working Paper, WP-75-93, August. International Institute for Applied Systems Analysis, Vienna. Available from: pure.iiasa.ac.at/335/ (accessed 4 April 2016).

Knight, P. and D. J. Gilchrist. 2014. *Australian Charities 2013: The first report on charities registered with the Australian Charities and Not-for-profits Commission*. Perth: Australian Charities and Not-for-profits Commission. Available: www.acnc.gov.au/curtincharitiesreport2013 (accessed 1 July 2014).

KPMG. 2014. *Evaluation of the Joint Development Phase of the NSW Social Benefit Bonds Trial*. Sydney: KPMG Government Advisory Services. Available from: dpc.nsw.gov.au/__data/assets/pdf_file/0006/168333/Evaluation_of_the_Joint_Development_Phase.pdf (accessed 4 April 2016).

Lyons, M. 2003. 'The legal and regulatory environment of the third sector.' *The Asian Journal of Public Administration* 25(1): 87–106.

McGregor-Lowndes, M. and C. Ryan. 2009. 'Reducing the compliance burden of non-profit organisations: Cutting red tape.' *Australian Journal of Public Administration* 68(1): 21–38.

Milward, H. B. 2014. 'The increasingly hollow state: Challenges and dilemmas for public administration.' *Asia Pacific Journal of Public Administration* 36(1): 70–79. DOI: 10.1080/23276665.2014.892275.

Mulgan, R. 2015. 'What can the Kiwis teach our new PM?' *Public Sector Informant*, October: 6–7.

Murray, I. 2014. 'Not-for-profit reform: Back to the future?' *Third Sector Review* 20(1): 109–39.

O'Flynn, J. 2014. 'Manus Island takes Australia to the edge of outsourcing.' *The Conversation*, 6 March. Available from: theconversation.com/manus-island-takes-australia-to-the-edge-of-outsourcing-23647 (accessed 4 April 2016).

Office of the Auditor-General, Western Australia (OAG WA). 2000. *A Means to an End: Contracting not-for-profit organisations for the delivery of community services*. Perth: Office of the Auditor-General, Western Australia. Available from: audit.wa.gov.au/wp-content/uploads/2013/05/report2000_03.pdf (accessed 7 July 2016).

Porter, C. and K. O'Dwyer. 2016. Retention of the Australian Charities and Not-for-profits Commission. Media release, 4 March. Commonwealth of Australia, Canberra. Available: christianporter.dss.gov.au/media-releases/retention-of-the-australian-charities-and-not-for-profits-commission (accessed 23 June 2016).

Productivity Commission. 2010. *Contribution of the Not-for-Profit Sector*. Canberra: Productivity Commission. Available from: pc.gov.au/projects/study/not-for-profit/report (accessed 24 February 2012).

Public Accounts and Estimates Committee (PAEC). 2002. *Report on the Department of Human Services: Service agreements for community, health and welfare services*. Melbourne: Public Accounts and Estimates Committee, Parliament of Victoria. Available from: parliament.vic.gov.au/images/stories/committees/paec/reports/47th_report_-_DHSServiceAgreements_2002.pdf (accessed 3 August 2012).

Queensland Audit Office (QAO). 2007. *Results of Performance Management Systems Audit of Management of Funding to Non-Government Organisations*. Brisbane: Queensland Audit Office. Available from: www.parliament.qld.gov.au/documents/tableOffice/TabledPapers/2007/TP1374-2007.PDF (accessed 7 July 2016).

Salamon, L. M. 2015. 'Introduction: The nonprofitization of the welfare state.' *Voluntas* 26: 2147–54. DOI: 10.1007/s11266-015-9638-3.

Saunders, P. 2009. 'Supping with the devil: Government contracts and the non-profit sector.' In *Supping with the Devil: Government contracts and the non-profit sector*, eds S. P. and M. Stewart-Weeks, 1–15. Sydney: Centre for Independent Studies.

Shergold, P. 2008. Contracting out government: Collaboration or control? Neil Walker Memorial Lecture. Centre for Social Impact, University of New South Wales, Sydney. Available from: www.

uws.edu.au/__data/assets/pdf_file/0009/1098207/contracting_out_government_collaboration_or_control.pdf (accessed 29 June 2016).

Shergold, P. 2013. *Service Sector Reform: A roadmap for community and human services reform. Final report*. Department of Human Services, Melbourne. Available from: vcoss.org.au/documents/2013/07/FINAL-Report-Service-Sector-Reform.pdf (accessed 7 July 2016).

Taylor, D. 2015. 'Strategies to stop NFPs being "hollowed out" by government: Part 2.' *Pro Bono News*, 18 June. Available from: probonoaustralia.com.au/news/2015/06/blog-strategies-stop-nfps-being-%E2%80%98hollowed-out%E2%80%99-government-part-2#sthash.32q61fcB.dpuf (accessed 4 April 2016).

Turnbull, M. 2015. Transcript of the Prime Minister, The Hon. Malcolm Turnbull MP. Doorstop Interview, 20 September. Parliament House, Canberra. Available from: malcolmturnbull.com.au/media/Ministry (accessed 4 April 2016).

Victorian Auditor-General's Office (VAGO). 2010. *Partnering with the Community Sector in Human Services and Health*. Melbourne: Victorian Auditor-General's Office. Available from: audit.vic.gov.au/reports__publications/reports_by_year/2009-10/20102605_comm_sector_partner.aspx (accessed 3 August 2012).

Wolch, J. R. 1990. *The Shadow State: Government and voluntary sector in transition*. New York: Foundation Center.